FAMILY TREE

ornelius Vanderbilt II
843-99)
m Alice Claypoole Gwynne

Margaret Louisa
m. Elliott F. Shepard

llen Vanderbilt
846-58)

illiam Kissam Vanderbilt I
849-1920)
m. Alva Murray Smith
m. Anne Harriman Sands
Rutherford

mily Thorn
m. William D. Sloane
m. Henry White

ederick William Vanderbilt
856-1938)
m. Louise Anthony Torrance

orence Adele
m. Hamilton McK. Twombly

iza Osgood
m. William S. Webb

eorge Washington Vanderbilt II
862-1914)
m. Edith Stuyvesant Dresser

Alice Gwynne

William Henry Vanderbilt II
(1872-92)

Cornelius Vanderbilt III
(1873-1942)
m. Grace Wilson

Gertrude
m. Harry Payne Whitney

Alfred Gwynne Vanderbilt
(1877-1915)
m. Elsie French
m. Margaret McKim

Reginald Claypoole Vanderbilt
(1880-1925)
m. Cathleen Neilson
m. Gloria Morgan

Gladys Moore
m. Count Laszlo Széchényi

Consuelo
m. Duke of Marlborough
m. Louis Jacques Balsan

William Kissam Vanderbilt II
(1878-1944)
m. Virginia Graham Fair
m. Rosamond Lancaster
Warburton

Harold Stirling Vanderbilt
(1884-   )
m. Gertrude L. Conaway

Cornelia Stuyvesant

Cornelius Vanderbilt IV
(1898-   )

Grace

William Henry Vanderbilt III
(1901-   )

Alfred Gwynne Vanderbilt II
(1912-   )

George Washington Vanderbilt III
(1914-   )

Cathleen

Gloria

Muriel

Consuelo

William Kissam Vanderbilt III
(1907-33)

THE VANDERBILTS
AND THEIR FORTUNES

By Edwin P. Hoyt

THE VANDERBILTS AND THEIR FORTUNES
JUMBOS AND JACKASSES

The Vanderbilts
and Their Fortunes

BY EDWIN P. HOYT

DOUBLEDAY & COMPANY, INC.
GARDEN CITY, NEW YORK
1962

CONTENTS

I
Beginnings

II
The Fortune

III
The Vanderbilt Goal

IV
The Consolidation and the Weakening

V
The Fragmentation

NOTES AND ACKNOWLEDGMENTS

Much of the research for this book was done in the New York Public Library and the library of the New York Historical Society. I am particularly grateful to so many of the large staff of the New York Public Library that I cannot name them, and to Miss Rachel Minick of the New York Historical Society, and to James J. Heslin, associate director of the Society (now director) and librarian, who allowed me to use the diaries of Frank Vanderbilt.

Loring McMillan, director of the Staten Island Historical Society was extremely helpful, as were a number of people connected with that voluntary organization.

Woodhull Young, curator of the Vanderbilt Museum at Centerport, Long Island, gave a great deal of his time, and went out of his way on countless occasions to be helpful. I am indebted also to Walter Fasbender, director of the museum for the use of books and other research material pertaining to William Kissam Vanderbilt II.

The Preservation Society of Newport County, Rhode Island, assisted, giving details on the Breakers, and the historians of the National Park Service at the Frederick William Vanderbilt house at Hyde Park, New York, now a historic site, gave information that was invaluable.

I am also grateful to Wayne Andrews, author of *The Vanderbilt Legend*, for personal information and the use of notes he has placed in the New York Public Library.

Also, my thanks are due to the courteous and helpful librarians at the Huntington, Long Island, public library, and to those at the Northport Public Library, particularly to Mrs. Dorothy Walker. And, of course, for many other kinds of help, I must mention Dr. O. M. Gruhzit, Steve Hubbard, Albert Zillian, and Olga Margaret, and for invaluable advice, my editor, Lee Barker.

I

BEGINNINGS

1

THE VAN DER BILTS

One day in 1947 Major Cornelius Vanderbilt, late of the Army of the United States, drove the length of Manhattan Island to pay a duty call on his mother. The sixth Cornelius Vanderbilt of the family line was coming to see the dowager empress of American society.

The course of the trip took Cornelius Vanderbilt up New York City's Fifth Avenue, naturally enough, and most fittingly. Fifth Avenue was Mrs. Vanderbilt's special domain. For nearly half a century this patrician matriarch had ruled American society from her mansion on the avenue. She ruled more strictly, if less officially, than her friends the kings and queens of Europe's royalty. Their domains, after all, were geographical and fixed. Hers was the kingdom of Family in a republic that both denied and bowed to Mrs. Vanderbilt's absolute rule.

As Cornelius Vanderbilt passed the northwest corner of Fifty-first Street and Fifth Avenue in his car, he saw the wrecking crew at work, tearing down the family house in which he had spent his boyhood. Already his own fifth-floor bedroom was gone. So was his father's walnut-paneled study and soundproof engineering laboratory. The work of destruction had proceeded downward from the roof as far as the second floor. There, from the lonely skeleton, the vacant windows of his mother's pink boudoir blinked at him, until the light changed, the flow of traffic moved on, and the major drove up the avenue—without a backward look.

House wreckers work fast. It took this wrecking crew only a few weeks to destroy the fifty-eight-room Vanderbilt mansion which had employed more than six hundred men for a year and a half in the building, almost seventy years earlier. The physical tearing-down was the last of it. Before the wrecking crew had gone to work, the unwanted contents of the house had been sold or given to museums: much of the family art collection went to the Metropolitan Museum of Art. Paramount Studios bought the carved panels, mirrors, and fixtures of the huge ballroom where the Prince of Wales and King Albert of the Belgians had danced. The fixtures were works of art; a Vanderbilt had paid perhaps $100,000 for their installation; but now they were sold as parts for movie sets for $3500. Paramount also bought the walls and trappings of the spacious formal dining room, which had seated thousands of leading figures in the world, over the years. The price was $975. The panels and walls of the study, where one Vanderbilt had died and another had retired night after night to drink in solitude—these brought $1250.

The valuables were carted away, the great brown stones were broken into rubble, and the Vanderbilt hold on Fifth Avenue slipped away, into the shadows of memory.

Old Mrs. Vanderbilt continued to live on Fifth Avenue after she left the big house. She could live nowhere else. Until her death she would dominate a Society which knew Park Avenue only as the street of the *nouveaux riches*. But in Mrs. Vanderbilt's declining years, her world of Society melted slowly away, and she could control it now from a twenty-eight room town house at the corner of Eighty-sixth Street and Fifth Avenue. It was not only possible for her to maintain her position and still live so simply— by Grace Vanderbilt's standards—it was also necessary. Less than three quarters of a century after the death of Commodore Vanderbilt, then the richest man in America, the widow of the fifth Cornelius Vanderbilt was too poor to maintain the chateau at 640 Fifth Avenue and the entertainments she had always lavished on her guests.

In one generation a Vanderbilt had created the great fortune. In two generations the family had become the richest in the world. In three generations the Vanderbilts became the first family of America. But at the end of four generations, power had slipped from their hands—and while the Vanderbilts did not suffer poverty, the family had lost its place of leadership in the affairs of America.

What had happened? What makes a fortune—and what destroys one?

Strange qualities, found in only a few men, produce the kind of power our society honors with riches instead of statues. At the pinnacle, these men are sometimes respected for their accomplishments, often hated for their methods, and always envied for their wealth.

Yet almost without exception the giants of business have found small comfort in riches alone. Fame and power, not money, are the spurs. Riches, like sweetmeats, pall all too soon. A man can live in only so much space; he can occupy himself with only so many pleasures at a given time. Once his physical wants are met, and even his vices are satisfied, a man develops more refined ambitions. Sometimes his desire swerves into the channels of history; he wants to be remembered by yet unborn generations and dreads the thought that the name he has made may pass into dust with his bones. Sometimes the great man yearns to create a dynasty in which power may be handed down from generation to generation in the manner of the Pharaohs.

The dynastic urge was strong among the men who established the largest American fortunes. Indeed, lacking that drive, the fortunes and even the names disappeared.

Alexander Turney Stewart created a fortune, but he died without heirs and both his fortune and his department store empire died just after him. John Jacob Astor created a fortune, and a dynasty, but his descendants transferred both to England, leaving only a straggling remainder on these shores to bear the name. John D. Rockefeller created a dynasty and a tradition as well as a fortune, all of them jealously guarded by close-mouthed descendants; and the fortune and the power remained marvelously intact.

There was yet another course. Cornelius Vanderbilt, the Commodore, created a tremendous fortune and a dynasty without a tradition. Later Vanderbilts had to pick their own ways. Each son's character decided the disposition of his share of the wealth.

Great wealth sets men apart from other men. The rich are always encased in cocoons of their own spinning. These men and women are insulated from the mass by the thick walls of mansions and exclusive clubs, by the high fences of estates and private bathing beaches. The rich of America conform to a tradition of wealth that has been handed down in Western society since medieval days. If a millionaire chooses to ride the trolley car or the subway, he is called "eccentric." But when a millionaire maintains five expensive foreign cars, a private yacht, several dwelling places, and all the trappings of conspicuous waste, he is considered normal. If a millionaire squanders wealth on Babylonian excesses, most Americans will cheer. In millionaires, the humbler of us find our alter egos.

It takes strength of character for a man to acquire great wealth and power. It takes character of a very different kind for the rich man's sons to live usefully and gracefully with the inherited millions. In the rise, conservation, and dissipation of every fortune there is a story. Luck and tragedy play their parts, but in the end the answer lies in character—the character of the men and women of the family determine when the fortune shall rise, and when it shall fall. So it was with the Vanderbilts.

The Vanderbilts are an old American family. In 1640 the great-great-great-grandfather of Commodore Vanderbilt left Holland to sail to the New World. Jan Aertson was his name, a poor farmer of the village called Bilt, in the province of Utrecht. Like many men of the Lowlands, Jan Aertson had heard tales of the new land across the ocean from seafarers, but unlike most he decided to leave home and family, friends and safety, to journey to the unknown land of promise where the strong might gain a fortune through strength alone. Here the accident of humble birth would no longer dog a man, and here the spicy breath of freedom blew fresh and clear.

Henry Hudson, the Englishman, had seen the promise and the savage beauty of this New World as he sailed his tiny *Half Moon* through the land-tamed harbor and up the broad North River that was to be named for him. Hudson had come searching for the Northwest Passage to India, but when he reported failure to the Dutch merchants who had backed him, the story he told of the land he had found sparked a flame that brought hundreds of sturdy burghers and farmers to America.

Daring these Dutchmen were, and touched with streaks of brilliance, although these qualities have paled in history beneath the legend of stolid Dutch strength and stubborn clinging to the land.

The Dutch were traders, not colonizers, the English sneered. Not colonizers? Dutch men gave the lie to that charge, farmers like Jan Aertson. They sailed in little ships of the Dutch West India Company, braving the two-month voyage across the vast ocean to the land of promise, and upon arriving inside the stockade at Fort Amsterdam at the lower tip of Manhattan Island, signed away freedom for three long years before they could seek their goal. Jan Aertson, the first Vanderbilt to arrive in the New World, spent his early years in America as an indentured servant, like many others.

Peter Wolpherson, to whom Jan was indentured, belonged to a wealthy patroon family; he was a landholder who derived his power from the parent Dutch West India Company. The company staked out large farms in the new colony and gave them to patroons who would guarantee to bring fifty colonists to New Netherlands within five years, but it was understood that the land still belonged to the company. In defiance of the West India Company charter, the Wolphersons began their own trade with the Indians, and acquired lands of their own on Long Island. They also encouraged their colonists to do the same. So when his three years of service ended, Jan Aertson van der Bilt, as he was known in the new world, traded for land of his own in the area now called Flatbush in Brooklyn. There Jan Aertson built his rush hut and cleared the granite boulders from the soil he would farm. New Netherlands soil was rich beyond the dreams of Hollanders who were used to fighting the sea for salty earth. Plums, pears, juicy apples—all the fruits they had known at home and more—grew quickly and well, and the vegetable patches bloomed in the warm sun of summer. The skins of beaver, mink, and deer, of otter, lynx, elk, and fox were prized by the company, and would buy a fine cow to fatten on the rich grass of the marshlands. Both the Indians and the early settlers traded with wampum, and the Indian tribal leaders were quick to parcel out the communal lands for strings of shells.

But not all the Indians were happy about the chieftains' prodigal disposal of tribal lands. The Indian hunter, chasing a handsome buck along an old trail might run afoul of a sweating farmer who objected to Indians hunting in his carefully planted crop of corn. The weary traveler, stopping to drink at a favorite spring, might find a stolid, angry burgher who claimed the water was his personal property.

As a man of the Wolphersons, Jan Aertson could not escape their part in the Indian troubles that began in 1643 when the Indians rose in anger against such wrongs. Most of the colonists sent their families to the stockade at Fort Amsterdam, safe from burning and scalping by tribes that were fighting for their rights and fighting with the vengeance of men set to redress ancient wrongs. Every able-bodied man in the colony was drafted into the company's military service for two months, until peace was restored, and Jan Aertson and his fellows could go back to their homes.

Though surrounded by wilderness and harassed by disturbed and often unfriendly Indians, Jan Aertson prospered. He husbanded the precious cattle and swine and chickens brought from the old country. Long before he died, Jan Aertson had raised a son, Aris, to manhood, a manhood that would be spent in a colony that flew a new flag and spoke the foreign tongue of the rapacious English. Jan Aertson lived to see the Dutch flag rise again, briefly, over New Amsterdam, and then fall forever. The future lay with the English, who had begun encroaching on Long Island early in the seventeenth century.

But the Dutch were stubborn. Late in the eighteenth century, long after the British triumphed, one found masons in Long Island's cemeteries carving inscriptions on the headstones of the dead—in Dutch. The Vanderbilt family records were kept in Dutch for a long time, though Jan Aertson kept no records at all. He could neither read nor write.

Before the English came, the Dutch had acquired title to Staten Island for ten shirts, thirty pairs of stockings, ten guns, thirty bars of lead, thirty pounds of powder, twelve coats, two pieces of duffel, thirty kettles, thirty hatchets, twenty hoes, and a case of nails and awls. It was a good bargain, and because Jan Aertson was a good bargainer among such men, he left fine lands when he died, a piece of Staten Island among them. His son, Aris van der Bilt, prospered in Brooklyn, and increased the family holdings there, for the colony was growing. Where there had been only a handful of settlers, seventeen hundred people (who owned nearly three hundred slaves) farmed and traded with the commercial town of New York.

Aris had no reason to use the land on Staten Island, since he had more than enough property to keep him busy in Brooklyn, and the piece of land on Staten Island was real wilderness, known in Brooklyn then as frontier country. Oaks and elms towered above the dense scrub and underbrush that covered much of the island, an almost impenetrable jungle in summer, an unfriendly prickly maze in winter. But part of the land was clear meadow, where the soil was fresh and black. It would yield well if a man was an able farmer, was willing to do the work, and did not mind the loneliness of island life. Jacob van der Bilt, son of Aris, who did not mind these things, bought the hundred acres on Staten Island from his father. Later, when he married, Jacob took his bride to live there.

Jacob and his wife ferried their belongings across from Brooklyn. They brought all they would need to keep a house and farm, for there was no store on Staten Island, no trading post, or even a neighbor close enough to hear a cry. The entire population of the island was some two hundred whites and a handful of tamed Indians who roamed the forest hunting deer and rabbit, and stayed out of the way of the settlers.

Jacob, a sailor as well as a farmer, like the rest, used his boat to ferry livestock to the farm and supplies for the house he built on the land, a good house, sitting on the edge of the sloping hill. He cut some of the timber and laid out his farm on the best bottom land, leaving the upland raw for game and his woodpile. Then he began to farm.

It was a life of unbelievable activity in which there was no time for loneliness. In the long summer days Jacob and his wife cleared the land and weeded the crops and milked the animals and fed and tended them. In the fall they harvested corn and oats and garden crops. The Van der Bilt family dried and smoked and preserved what it needed for the winter months. Winter was a time for hunting game for meat and furs and for cutting timber, and occasionally for visiting neighbors—a few miles away—when the weather permitted. And spring was the season of planting for another harvest.

Jacob came to the frontier land in 1718. In his second year on the island he bought a hundred acres more; then having all he could work, he settled down to consolidate his farm. For twenty years Jacob built upon this land, tended it and made it bloom for him. He became a fine farmer, well known on the island and respected as one of the most successful farmers in the district called New Dorp.

In the middle of the eighteenth century his New Dorp became the haven of the Moravian followers of John Huss, a protesting martyr who helped prepare the way for the Reformation. These Middle European refugees followed the Huguenots and the Waldenses in flight from an unfriendly Europe to the New World, where they called themselves Moravians. They built their mother church at Bethlehem, Pennsylvania, but Staten Island became the home of a smaller group. The Staten Island community of the sect was big enough and important enough that the founder, Count Zinzendorf, made his way across the Indian trails just after 1741 to visit the tiny community at New Dorp.

By 1742 the Moravians had attracted native American converts to the faith, the Dutch-speaking Jacob van der Bilt among them. Five years later, Jacob had become a lay brother in the church, and a leader in the movement to help the persecuted ones still stranded in Europe. Jacob donated heavily to the group which would build a little ship and sail it twelve times across the Atlantic in the next nine years to bring refugees to America.

Jacob was a more loyal churchman than many of his fellows. Long after the original Moravians had moved on west from Staten Island, Jacob clung to the faith. He signed a petition to the mother church for a chapel in New Dorp, and when the permission was granted, Jacob led in pledges to pay for building the church. At one time, when the fortunes of the Moravians ebbed in the late 1750s, Jacob was numbered among only three elders of the church on Staten Island.

When the old man died in 1761, his island had grown; there were nearly two thousand people on Staten Island instead of a handful of rough farmers who lived on the edge of wilderness, and New Dorp had become a community. There was no store yet in New Dorp but the church provided a gathering place; several houses were built nearby, and there was entertainment for the entire family in the visiting back and forth between neighbors, now sometimes within hailing distance of each other.

Old Jacob's farm had grown—it was called a plantation now. Two hundred acres of rolling upland on the south side of the island adjoined another thirty acres of salt meadow, where his cattle and horses grazed peacefully in the off-shore breeze. The wilderness was wild no longer. An attractive, sturdy house, whitewashed, a good barn, and a large apple orchard graced Jacob's lands. Behind the house the woods remained thick, since the old farmer had planned his wood cutting to be sure he had enough timber to supply the tall-chimneyed fireplaces for years. In his estate Jacob van der Bilt had left a number of Negro slaves, two wagons, plows, several sleds—all the equipment needed to operate an eighteenth-century farm. Besides all this, old Jacob owned an impressive number of sleek horses, fine milk cattle, and hogs and sheep, for the Van der Bilt farm had been run with a stolid precision that brought prosperity from land where Indians had chased deer and planted only handfuls of corn just a generation earlier.

Now this harvest of a life's planting was to be sold at auction, for that seemed the best way to serve the widow and the eleven children of old Jacob's marriage. Sold it was, and the next generation was the worse for it. Young Jacob, the old man's son, was a good farmer, too, but when he fell dead from his horse on the Courthouse Road just six years after the old man had died, the son's farm was only a quarter of the size his father's had been. That he held even so much was a tribute to young Jacob's industry, for one eleventh of his father's capital was little enough to begin on. After his untimely death, young Jacob's livestock and minor

assets were sold to provide for his widow and seven children, but
to preserve the slender heritage of land, the young widow offered
the farm itself for rent, not for sale.

It was 1767, just eight years before the drums were to roll and
the musket volleys to crackle in the air of Lexington and Concord.
The children of Mary and Jacob van der Bilt were shared out
among the family. Mary could not support them and they were too
young to support themselves. Cornelius, son of Jacob, great-great-
grandson of Jan Aertson, a boy who was to ferry British goods
across the bay during the Revolution, was a small child then.
He went to live with an uncle on the island, where he was treated
well enough but where he had to earn his keep.

There were no common schools on Staten Island in those pre-
Revolutionary days. The rudiments—and only the rudiments—of
reading, writing, and arithmetic were taught in classes supported
by the churches or by a handful of farmers. At school Cornelius
again modified the family name, making it more fittingly American—van Derbilt. He spent little time in school, for every man and
boy was needed on the farm to plant the corn and carry the feed
and harvest the vegetables and fruits. In the frosty days of winter
Cornelius milked the cows and tended the fires, but as he grew,
so did his world. Later, as a lanky stripling in homespun and oxhide
boots, Cornelius stacked the hay and drove the wagonloads of
grain to be milled. But his choice was work with the horses,
the quick-eyed snorting stallions; and with the boats, the broad-
beamed heavy scows the Dutch of the island called periaugers,
the name itself a hangover from the days when Philip and Alba
ruled the Lowlands with gauntlets of steel.

The ancestors of the periaugers Cornelius sailed were the old
Dutch canal scows. The new boats did the same work in the same
way in the New World that the flat-bottomed craft had done in
Holland since the Middle Ages. The scow, with its high freeboard
and shallow draft, was ideal for the waters of the Upper Bay and
the Kill Van Kull and for the marsh flats of New Jersey. The
periauger was easy to build from the rough lumber that could
be hewn and shaped with primitive farm tools; a shed full of
produce could be stacked in the deep, undecked cockpit; cattle

and swine could be driven directly into the scow, protected from their own rearing and jostling by the high sides. Or a load of hay could be pitched directly from wagon into cockpit, shipped across the bay, and pitched out again with no loss of effort. Every inch of the periauger was built for work, from her stout, flat keel to the sturdy, short mast.

A four-sided lugsail climbed the mast on wooden hoops and sprawled to catch the wind, supported aloft by a gaff spar. The periauger was steered by a rudder attached to a long tiller, which the boatman could handle even as he worked the sail, so one man could be both captain and crew if he was strong and agile enough.

The periauger handled as she looked: like a fat drudge. It took a mighty wind to raise her speed to half a dozen knots; her single sail was not designed to respond quickly to the shifting breezes; and she tended to yaw when tacked, making leeway discouragingly in the hands of any but the most able boatman.

But Cornelius was able and he delighted in taking the tiller to work the crude craft across deep water as the scow carried onions and cabbages and turnips to the markets of New York or freighted a load from Manhattan across to Brooklyn or even through The Narrows and down the Lower Bay.

Workbound as they were, the older boys of the island raced one another in these periaugers, and the boys and men were proud enough of their craft to paint them—white mast, perhaps, with red hull from waterline to gunwale, or blue trimmed in green or purple—gaily splashing color on the harbor as they went about their ferrying.

Before Cornelius was old enough to make the harbor trip alone, the war had enveloped the American colonies, and Staten Island fell into British military hands. The change did not bother the islanders much. The Van Derbilts and the other Dutch Huguenots and Waldenses and Walloons had all lived under many flags. They had suffered uprooting enough and change enough already, and their institutions were simple. Neither patriarchal home nor church gave rise to revolutionary ideas. Thus the Van Derbilt family of Staten Island was not stirred by talk of revolution;

the family worried about its own troubles and was further insulated by the lonely independence of island life.

The Van Derbilt cousins who had remained on Long Island in the stream of colonial life had a different attitude. They took active parts in the revolution. Another branch of the family, that of Jeremias Vanderbilt of Brooklyn, (who had changed the name further), signed a statement in public support of the colonies' Declaration of Independence, and thus made himself fair game for every Englishman and Tory. His son, John Vanderbilt, served as second major in a force of militia he helped raise in Flatbush to fight for the American cause.

But even had members of the Staten Island branch of the family been of a mind to join the revolutionaries, the pressure on Staten Island was all the other way. In the first year of the Revolution the island's wealthier Loyalists raised five hundred pounds to support the English war effort. In later years, when a tardy American Congress finally voted pensions for the soldiers of the Revolution, the entire list from Staten Island consisted of three names. A twelve-year-old boy—which Cornelius was then—would scarcely feel the call to arms in such an atmosphere.

When the war ended in 1783, Cornelius was a young man, but a young man with few material prospects. His inheritance, small as it was, had vanished in the destruction of the island's legal records by fire. Cornelius believed he had been cheated of his father's farm, but he did not know what to do to regain his property, so he did nothing.

If Cornelius Van Derbilt had inherited a farm, he might have ended his life as a prosperous burgher, but he had no land; he had not the temperament to save, penny by penny, and there was no way for him to buy a farm. Money was scarce on Staten Island in the days just after the Revolutionary War.

The island and the New Jersey side of New York harbor, like New York and the rest of the new nation, had lost much in the war. In the slump, some men left the island to seek their fortunes in the West, but such a drastic move had no appeal for Cornelius. He continued to work on the farms and periaugers of his uncles and cousins and, forced by circumstance, became a hard worker,

even if he was not gifted with strong imagination. Four years
after the end of the war he had saved enough money to buy a
periauger of his own. He was working a farm, too, on the edge
of Port Richmond, when the event occurred which would change
his life. He met a girl named Phebe Hand.

2

PHEBE HAND

Phebe Hand was born April 15, 1767, in the rambling colonial farmhouse of Grandfather Hand near Rahway, New Jersey. It was a quiet, placid place in the most peaceful of all the thirteen American colonies. Because it was slightly inland, the farm had little contact with the rude towns of New York harbor where the sea cast forth boisterous men from many lands.

New Jersey had lately felt the echoes of excitement in the enforcement, then tardy repeal, of the hated Stamp Act. But it was the merchants of New York, not New Jersey, who wrote their suppliers in England and told them to ship no more goods until the act was repealed. It was the men of Pennsylvania who determined not to pay an English debt, or plead an English cause until the stamps were gone. Peaceful New Jersey, remote from the Canadian border and the French and Indian troubles, protected and overshadowed by New York, played little part in the events that led up to the grumblings of dissent and the final, exasperated declaration of independence.

Phebe Hand's early years were spent happily in the big house on the Hand farm. Grandfather Hand was stern and uncompromising, a pillar in his church, but nonetheless, kind and gentle to Phebe. He was seldom too busy for a walk in the green woods or a trot on his knee before the blazing logs of the fireplace. Grandfather Hand told stories then, tales of ancestors who had come to Long Island more than a century before and had fished and hunted and grown their crops along the fertile lands of the island's north shore. From Southold, the early settlement, the Hands had moved west, toward the Dutch settlements at New Amsterdam and Breuckelen. The Dutch resisted the encroachment at first, but finally, midway in the seventeenth century, the English and the Netherlanders had split Long Island between them at a point near Oyster Bay. Even this division did not long satisfy the English. More and more Englishmen were coming to America, and it was not many years before they dominated all of Long Island. In 1664 King Charles II granted his brother James, Duke of York, all lands between the Connecticut River and the eastern side of Delaware Bay and all islands between Cape Cod and the Hudson River. So Long Island and New York and the green countryside of New Jersey were all of a piece. It was easy enough for one branch of the Hand family to take lands on the western shore of the bay.

The growth in population and the feeling that their interests differed from those of the colonists of New York caused the Hands and others of New Jersey to seek a governor of their own. In 1738 George II granted the petitions of the New Jerseymen and New Jersey became a separate colony. By the time Phebe was born forty thousand people lived in New Jersey, most of them in a broad circle around the west shore of New York harbor. There was plenty of good farmland, and, unlike New York, little trouble with Indians.

Grandfather Hand told Phebe about the trouble the Hands had had with Indians in the old days, the independent and troublesome Indians of Long Island. These were bloodcurdling tales of warfare, exciting to a child, but Phebe's favorite story concerned her great-great-grandmother, who had ruined her life for want of character. This girl had had two suitors; one of them was her own choice, but her father and mother pleaded the suit of the other who had more land and money. Caught in constant bickering, the girl finally agreed that she would accept the first suitor who showed his face at the door. Her parents secretly sent for their choice and he appeared first; Phebe's great-great-grandmother had weakly accepted him then and there, and was unhappy for the rest of her life.

Grandfather Hand told this story over and over to Phebe. It was the same as many of his tales, ending with a moral, designed to teach the girl that character was the most important attribute. Phebe, even as a little girl, curled her lip as Grandfather finished this story. She knew *she* would never have given in to marry a man she did not love, no matter how much or how long the bullying.

In these years before the war an impression of Grandfather Hand was stamped on Phebe's mind that overshadowed both her father and her mother. Yet Grandfather Hand did more; he not only provided for little Phebe in her girlhood, but before he died the old man set aside enough money to let her make choices in life, confident that at least Phebe would be her own woman.

But the Revolution swept across New Jersey. Indeed, New Jersey, the quietest, least quarrelsome of the colonies, became the camp-ground of the ragged army that embattled King George's noble generals and eventually wore them to defeat.

Grandfather Hand would not have countenanced investment of Phebe's money in the risky notes the Revolutionary government issued to support its declaration of independence. But Phebe's great-grandmother, who became her guardian in these days of 1776, converted Phebe's inheritance to cash, the Continental notes of the new government. Almost immediately this cash was worthless.

Even more serious, and confusing to a nine-year-old, the Hand family began to split up. Obadiah Hand, Phebe's father, chose the side of George III. Her Uncle Edward chose the side of the colonies, and she heard later that he had fought bravely, had even been promoted to major general in the American army. Phebe's brother sided with Uncle Edward, and also fought in the army of the Revolution. With this division the Hand household was broken up, and the big house was home no more. Phebe was sent to stay with a family pastor, the Reverend Mr. Elmer, in a house not far from Rahway. Here she saw the soldiers of the Revolution as they gathered, hungry, badly armed, and ragged in their bits of uniform and tattered civilian coats and breeches.

She heard of the disastrous battle of Long Island, where Washington lost half his force and more than half his arms. She heard of the British capture of Forts Washington and Lee, and of the march of the British toward Rahway.

Phebe was warned against the terrible Hessians, the thirty thousand German soldiers sent by the Duke of Hesse into virtual slavery as mercenaries, whose death and dismemberment brought profit to England's King George III and their own pitiless duke, not to themselves.

The reputation of the Hessians spread before them like flowing water across the flatlands of New Jersey. They spoke little English and, frustrated, they began to grab those things they wanted. Badly disciplined by their English officers, the Hessians roamed the countryside, robbing and despoiling. The wife of an American army chaplain was murdered in her own house near Rahway, as the Hessians followed the retreating Americans.

Little Phebe was unwise enough to be outside the Reverend Elmer's house the day blue-coated mercenaries passed, on their way to Princeton and Trenton, and one grinning Hessian seized her, but Phebe clawed and fought her way free. She was careful thereafter to stay clear of the soldiers.

Still, it was hardly safe for a little girl in these front lines of war. A sister, a Mrs. Johnson, had married and was living on Staten Island, in the middle of New York harbor, and although the British had occupied Staten Island, Phebe was sent to live with her married sister. It seems odd that she would be sent to stay out the war in the very stronghold of the enemy—and the Hessians'—but she was.

Phebe found the island a lonely place, fourteen miles long and seven miles wide, only three thousand people lived on it, and there was not even a cluster of buildings large enough to be called a village. It was farmland, but in the war it was more important than just rural land to feed the troops. From the heights that faced across to Brooklyn a little girl could look down on all the ships that entered New York harbor. So could a cannon. He who controlled The Narrows between Staten Island and Brooklyn had New York at his mercy, and he who controlled the Kill Van Kull that ran between the island and New Jersey could dominate the New Jersey ports as well. General William Howe, commander of the British, had seen this early in the war and in July 1776 had occupied Staten Island just at the time the Americans issued their Declaration of Independence.

By the time Phebe arrived on Staten Island, the British had landed twenty thousand troops there. Howe had taken over the Rose and Crown, a handsome white frame farmhouse that was reported to belong to one of the Van Derbilt family. But the accuracy of that report could hardly be verified, for in the burnings and pillaging by the Hessians and by the American rebels, most of the island's official records had been lost.

Staten Island was safer for a little girl than Rahway before the Battle of Trenton, but life was dangerous anywhere in the colonies in the war years and Staten Island was no exception. British officers dueled in the clearing that broke the wooded hills back of New Dorp, and British and Hessian troops roamed the island, eager to steal a farmer's horse or commandeer his winter's supply of feed. Women and girls were not safe out at night although the British officers did try to keep their redcoats and the Hessians under control here in friendly territory. But in the house of her sister Phebe was as safe as anyone on the island.

Anchored off the island shore Phebe could see the infamous prison ship *Jersey*, and when the wind was right she could smell its terrible odors of death and decay. The *Jersey* was fit for the work, a rotting hulk that had once been a proud ship of the line, but now was a prison where American captives could starve and stink in their chains.

British picket boats patrolled the shadows of the harbor during the hours of the night, hours in which Phebe and the others in the cottage by the shore feared to burn a light lest they be accused of signaling the rebels. Cutthroats skulked among the shadows of the harbor at night, too, and the Americans came to raid and burn, not caring what havoc they wreaked among the damned British and the double-damned Tories who freighted the enemy's goods across the bay.

Phebe Hand's sister, Mrs. Johnson, was a Loyalist—a Tory—and a very special friend of a young midshipman aboard one of the English ships of the line that lay anchored off Port Richmond. This young man told Mrs. Johnson she reminded him of his mother, and he was *so* fond of her little boy that he wanted to take the child to England with him when he finally sailed for home, but Mrs. Johnson would not let the child go. Thus, as Phebe recalled it, the Hand family lost a chance for alliance with English royalty, for the midshipman was the sailor duke, Duke of Clarence, who in 1830 became William IV, King of England.

Phebe was a revolutionary at heart, but she was in the minority. She was not afraid, but she knew that the islanders feared the rebel Americans as much or more than they feared the Hessians. If Staten Islanders traveled to New Jersey, they were suspected of spying for the British. And even Phebe had heard of General Washington's reference to the "treachery" of the Staten Islanders. Washington made no nice distinction between the Tory sympathizers and the Loyalist soldiers—the Royal Fencible Americans, the King's American Dragoons—twenty-nine Loyalist units in all— that were stationed on Staten Island during the war. But generally the Staten Islanders lived an ingrown island life, and minded their own business. Phebe's life was confined for the most part to the white, sand-scrubbed kitchen of the Port Richmond cottage, where she learned to cook and spin and weave and tend the needs of babies. She had learned to read, but she had no formal education, since the war disrupted life, and, besides, girls in those days learned their lessons in the kitchen and the parlor, not on the hard benches of the tiny schoolrooms provided by church or local community. Phebe was not expected to concern herself with political affairs or anything outside the home and family, so she kept to herself any thoughts she might have had about the war.

Finally, in the middle of November 1783, the war ended. Ships' boats and harbor boats were pressed into service day and night to move cannon, tents, kitchens, and kegs of powder to the transports and men-of-war that lay so restlessly at anchor offshore. Then, as Phebe could see from the cottage, boats were filled with bluecoats and redcoats—the army was embarking. Last, twelve thousand Loyalists were taken aboard the ships that flew the Union

Jack. Phebe did not know it then, but among them, bound for the cold and wild shore of Nova Scotia, was her father, Obadiah Hand.

On December 4, the fleet raised sail without a word for those on shore. The island air seemed still as death, although a breeze was blowing as His Majesty's fleet hoisted anchor and began to beat its way out through The Narrows, past the solemn fort where British guns had commanded the harbor entrance for so long.

Two groups of Americans stood on the heights above The Narrows. One group looked down happily on the burnished decks of the ships that passed in formation. Men and women shouted and laughed and clapped their hands; some jumped up and down in their joy at the departure of the despised British; others directed obscene gestures at the sailors and troops and Tories who passed below; still others fired their muskets in gestures of bravado.

The British fleet sailed on, glum and silent.

Perhaps it was the familiar, hated sound of musketry that broke the spell. The crowd howled on, until from a ship below a roar and a blaze and a puff of smoke burst forth, and a shot from one of the crushing 74s struck the bank beneath the feet of the roisterers. The air was silent then, and the fleet sailed on in dignity.

Phebe rightly belonged to the rowdy group, her sister to the second, a sad cluster of men and women who watched and waved tearfully as the British fleet stood out from land. Here were the friends, the wives, the sweethearts and the lovers of the occupation force.

The last sail gone, the two groups melted away and the men and women—Americans—went home to begin a new life under the republic the leaders of the Revolution had established by Articles of Confederation. Phebe was sixteen years old, a highly marriageable age. She was a big woman, with a slightly mannish face, plain hair that was drawn back severely and tied, her head covered usually, indoors and out, by a bonnet. She was strong and healthy and thoughtful in the face she showed the world. It was time for her to think about marriage, but she had seen no youth who attracted her. She knew what she wanted, and Phebe Hand minded her maiden's business for four years more, recalling the cowardly fate of her great-great-grandmother. But that was before she saw Cornelius Van Derbilt, and told herself as she first set eyes on his handsome laughing face that this man would become her husband.

3

NEW YORK, 1787

Four years after the successful American Revolution, Cornelius Van Derbilt's world was truly turned upside down, as the rueful English had seen in the hour of their defeat at Yorktown. Europe's kings and ruling classes slept uneasily at night, fearing the changes that haunted them. Yet their restlessness did not lessen the oppression or the debauchery of the European courts. Louis XVI's France was bankrupt but he spent no less because of this, nor did Louis's counselors cease to search for new ways to wring money from the overburdened people. The French Revolution, just two years off, fermented visibly in the filthy gutters of the cities and the hovels of the peasants.

Germany's princelings plotted against one another. George III tried vainly to hold power and prevent reform in the teeth of a determined Parliament. In Italy, in the Balkans, throughout the whole of the Western World, the American Revolution had sparked flames of rebellion.

Along the western shore of the Atlantic Ocean the revolutionaries who had started this chain struggled desperately for a national existence. The price of independence came high, the Americans were discovering. The American Revolutionary War had brought political freedom to the colonies but with political freedom came a responsibility some of the former colonial governments were unwilling to accept. Revolution had also severed the old economic ties with Mother England; the tiny American nation was unsure, disunited, and—equally dismaying—sunk deep in a well of economic depression.

Even Van Derbilt's market, New York City, the capital of the new confederation, had not yet recovered financially from the withdrawal of the combined English and Hessian garrison in 1783. In the fall of that year Obadiah Hand and twenty thousand other Americans sailed away with the British to Canada and Bermuda and the Bahamas—men, women, and children who feared less a re-rooting in a foreign land than the reprisals they fully expected from their revolutionary American brethren. The fears of the Loyalists were justified in fact: George Washington once said in anger that when war was won all that was left for the Tories was suicide.

Take twenty thousand from a population of thirty thousand and the bustle of a city is killed. The same exodus had occurred in 1776 when Washington retreated, and seven eighths of New York's population followed the rebels inland, fleeing almost overnight after General Howe's victory in the Battle of Long Island sealed the doom of New York. Old father Hand and other Loyalists flocked to New York that year, when they found the city safely in British hands. Then, at the end of the fighting, the quiescent period between Yorktown and the final peace brought hundreds more Tories trooping from the rebel lands to the New York island fortress.

But when the Loyalists and the British tars and soldiers and the blue-clad Hessians left in 1783, many of the rebels had settled elsewhere and did not return, so New York was a strange and desolate place; the change was noticeable in the filthy shanties of the poor behind City Hall and in the mansions of the rich that stood complacently along Broad Way.

The city was a cluster of houses and shops and taverns, then nestled starkly behind its protective battery of guns and guarded from flank attack by Fort Washington and Fort Lee. But even these handsome forts were poor bastions. The tiny Yankee garrisons were small match in spending power for the British who had manned the guns for seven years.

There were few enough rich men in New York now that the

Tories had fled; a scant three hundred families dabbled in the pretenses of fashion that had marked colonial high society.

The most important man in the city was not Mayor James Duane, as one might have suspected, but John Jay, the Secretary of Foreign Affairs of the new government. There was no national President under the loose, strong legislative form the jealous states had reached in their compromise. Jay was the most important executive officer in the government. With all the matters the states could not agree upon, at least they could agree that a single face must be turned abroad.

Jay and his fashionable, bright-eyed wife Sarah had arrived home just before the end of July 1784, after nearly five years of absence, in Spain and France. Jay had been the minister of the revolutionary government to the Spanish court, and there in Spain he and Sarah Jay had acquired the habits of the Continentals and the tastes of the very rich.

In New York the Jays moved into a stately town house at 133 Broad Way, far below the Bouwerie, that country lane which led to the cornfields and the sprawling old Dutch farms of the upper island. Nearly all the better sections of the town were located east of Broad Way. A house like the Jays' rented for more than a hundred pounds a year, ten times the amount a workman earned; and the cheapest single family dwelling was reserved by price for no lesser citizen than a merchant of the town.

The poor fed on fish and pork and rum, but the rich of New York were members of as gaudy a society as existed on the face of the earth. Mrs. Jay soon established herself as the foremost hostess of all New York. Her guest list included the tragic Aaron Burr and Alexander Hamilton, Gouverneur Morris, Dr. Benjamin Kissam (one of New York's finest physicians), James Madison, the Van Rensselaers, the Beekmans, the Verplancks, and the George Washingtons, when they were in the city.

Sarah Jay's dinners *à la française* were the talk of the town. Brissot de Warville, a French noble resident in New York, noted the fashions of Paris and London in her *salons*: ladies in billowing gowns of brilliant silk and satin, glittering jewels, and borrowed hair. If there was a town on the American continent where the English love of luxury displayed its folly, it was certainly New York.

The gentlemen who frequented Mrs. Jay's dinners and balls wore long fitted blue riding coats with shiny steel buttons, scarlet waistcoats, and yellow knee breeches. The shoes of the gentlemen, in daytime, were topped by leather gaiters that reached almost to their knees, gaiters that were shined and buffed by the gentlemen's personal slaves until the leather gleamed. At night these same gentlemen wore Paris stockings, stuffed if necessary, to achieve a well-turned calf. The men of post-Revolutionary days no longer wore wigs, or powdered their hair, or tied it in queues at the back as they had only a few years before. The fashion in the 1780s was the more sanitary, more comfortable short cut.

Each New York hostess strove to outdo her peers in presenting resplendent entertainment and unusual refreshments. For a ball the lower rooms of the house were cleared and arranged in the French style as *salons*; french doors were thrown open to achieve the effect of a single, continuous long room. Footmen in livery stood beside the doors and at the refreshment tables helping guests with a stately indifference that was unmatched outside London. Entertainment was supplied by the guests themselves, who danced in quadrilles—many of them noted for the glitter of their dress and the precision of their dancing. At one dinner and ball, given by the French ambassador, a company of eight couples gathered in a small room off the grand *salon*; then at a signal footmen threw open the doors to the ballroom, and the couples made their entrance two by two. Four of the men were dressed in French regimental uniform, four in American uniform. Four of the ladies wore blue ribbons around their heads and American flowers at their bosoms; four wore red ribbons and the lilies of France. For this party three of the rooms on the first floor of the ambassador's house had been set off for dancing, and in the fourth, the refreshment *salon*, the whole back wall was occupied by low shelves filled with cakes, oranges, apples, wines of every kind, and ice creams. The guest of honor, all in black save a pearl waistcoat and silver buckles at his knee and ankle, stood in the center of a changing group in the refreshment room, talking, sipping wine, glancing occasionally at the dancers who swept past the door, bowing gracefully and with a yellow glove fingering the long, shining sword at his side.

That was New York society.

But there was more to New York than society. There were merchants like John Vanderbilt, the cousin of Cornelius, and ship-builders and manufacturers of handmade goods who had no preten-sions but lived quietly, keeping to the common rooms of the taverns and to the plays and musical entertainments that delighted the townsmen and brought worried frowns to the growing number of ministers of the Gospel. These merchant citizens worked late over guttering candles at the high benches of their counting houses —worked and worried about the future of their city. They banded together in the New York State Chamber of Commerce, which met weekly, in the upper rooms of Fraunces Tavern, or even more often when they thought it necessary, to plan the commercial improvement of their common lot.

And the poor? The poor infested the town like the rats which overran their tumbledown shacks. The poor haunted the churches and the almshouses and the public jails. They were ill-clothed and worse fed, subsisting—not living as we know it—on rotten vegetables and consoled and anesthetized by cheap gin or plain spirits that was enough to take the skin off a strong man's palate. Rich or poor, New Yorkers had no common system of garbage disposal or refuse collection. The slaves and indentured servants of the rich carted the household's offal to the common dump every day in wooden barrels. The poor flipped their waste through the nearest window, to the woe of the unlucky passerby. The excreta, the mud, and the garbage piled in the roads, where it was squashed by human feet and horses' hoofs and the hoofs of cattle and swine. Soon the mess was beaten and festering and swollen. Then it disappeared in dust or was mashed into the roadway itself.

The poor lived in lean-tos and rickety huts near the tannery of Jacob Roosevelt on the west side of the city, an area bounded by swamp and river, an area the sniffing physicians called the "court-yard of the pillar of death." Every disease was endemic in the filth—the French disease, brought and perpetuated by the whores who crowded the streets and pushed their way to the cribs;

typhoid and typhus and malaria and more mysterious fevers, the dreaded yellow jack, and the vomiting disease that is called cholera. The poor sweated and suffered with their dirt and itching in the summer. In the winter they ached and froze and died in the humid cold—those who were not dying in debtors' prison. For in the poverty of the town and its port, free men slipped slowly, inexorably, into debt. Fully one seventh of the grown males of New York sat in debtors' prison, unable to work to pay their debts, unable to regain their freedom until the debts were paid. It was too bad for Cornelius Van Derbilt that he had not been born to luxury, for he had the attributes, if not the background, of a man who would have graced an eighteenth-century drawing room, if he had ever been allowed to enter one. But at least, living on Staten Island and farming, he paid his own way and did not fall into debt. He was even able to build a tiny house, depression or not.

There was little building in New York during this depression. By and large the depression continued, year in and year out, and the port of New York starved along with the city's poor. There was not a private hotel room in the city. The last guest climbed into the last empty bed in the common room of the public house, or if no beds were empty, he found the one least occupied and shoved his way among the sleepers.

This custom was no more medieval than others in the city's life. The roads were medieval, cobbled streets without sidewalks (where they were streets at all and not cowpaths), and so narrow that a man could scarcely walk down them without being turned out of the way by a lady in an enormous hoop skirt.

The common men of the town frequented the cheap taverns, and stood outside on windy days, hopefully watching the ladies in their billowy skirts and praying for a breeze. If wind came, and a lady's skirt was blown above her head, the view was extreme, for pantaloons had not yet been invented to cover ladies' limbs.

Undergarments were scanty, but not so the voluminous petticoats and dresses themselves. Leonard Kip's shop featured shallons, durances, tammies, antaloons, moreens, dorsetsheens, Persians, and taffeties. New York, then as now, was a blend of wealth and poverty, luxury and squalor, purity and bawdiness, honesty and criminality.

It had all the vices and virtues of a port, where seamen, adventurers, and ideas come and go; New York in those days had the importance of the capital city of a proud, if poor, young government; that was the city on February 5, 1787. The cold winds of February chilled the duck hunters on Beekman's swamp and the visitors to City Hall who came to congratulate the Honorable Arthur St. Clair on his election in 1787 as president of the Continental Congress, which was holding its meetings on the second floor. This Congress had much of importance to discuss; Daniel Shays had led a force of nearly fifteen hundred men in rebellion against the government of Massachusetts; his rebellion had frightened the officials of all the new states before the rebels were put down by General William Shepard and the Massachusetts militia. Just this day, the dispatches were to read in the *New-York Packet*, Shays had escaped into Vermont after a skirmish and had sadly told the two hundred men still with him it was now every man for himself.

Most of the erstwhile rebels shouldered their muskets and made for home and plow, but Shays, with a price of 150 pounds on his head, set off for the Canadian border, accompanied by a handful of lieutenants.

In Congress some blamed Shays' Rebellion on Governor Bowdoin of Massachusetts; some blamed the Massachusetts legislature; some simply termed Shays a malcontent. But Congress was not blind to the facts. Shays' support had come from poor, debt-burdened farmers, who had first appealed to the Massachusetts government for help to stop farm foreclosures. The post-Revolutionary depression was everywhere—and it was the sorest threat to the new nation.

The Chamber of Commerce of the State of New York called John Vanderbilt and others to a meeting that week of Shays' flight to Canada to discuss extraordinary business. The important concern of the Chamber was the promotion of the port's shipping, so badly in decline since the end of the war. It was winter and winter was a cold, desolate season for an Atlantic crossing, but that could hardly excuse the poor showing in the bay this February. Only one ship, the British packet *Lord Hyde,* entered the harbor on February 5. She had made the trip from Falmouth in forty-six days. But the *Lord Hyde* stood nearly alone off Whitehall, and anchored there, stark and alone; she was a reminder of the problems that worried Chamber men like Isaac Roosevelt and James Beekman.

New York's harbor was cold and green and *empty*; even the hundreds of sloops and scows of the region stood at anchor or bobbed at dockside, empty. At Whitehall slip each day there gathered a few of the ferrying scows from Staten Island, while the idle boatmen gossiped and smoked and waited patiently for commissions that would take them across the bay to Brooklyn or perhaps home to the island.

It seemed a desolate prospect for the future on that bleak day, February 5, 1787, but that was the wedding day of Cornelius Van Derbilt and Phebe Hand, son of the Dutch colonists and daughter of the English, who together would produce one of the most amazing men ever to rise to power in America.

4

CORNEEL

Phebe Hand Van Derbilt lay on her bed of labor for the fourth time at the end of May 1794 in a cottage on the Kill Van Kull. Phebe and Cornelius had lived there during the seven years since their marriage, and there two daughters and a son had already been born. On May 27, Phebe Hand's second son was born, and because he had his father's blue eyes, Phebe gave him his father's name. To differentiate the boy from his father, they called the boy Corneel.

This Corneel was a lusty, noisy baby, and big. He bawled and screamed for months, angry when Phebe left him to attend to her work in the fields and the gardens and sometimes even helped on the periauger. She was a good mother, but she also was a good farm wife who helped move the onions and cabbages to New York, where the more favored of the new republic's citizens disported themselves in gauze and lace and silver buckles, and where the poor starved in their rags.

The Van Derbilts were poor enough, but compared to life in the hovels of the city poor, their farm life on Staten Island was clean and healthful, and with Phebe's help the family prospered. After Corneel was born the house on the Kill Van Kull seemed too small, so soon the family moved to a newer, bigger house in Stapleton, a few miles to the northeast, where they would stay as long as Phebe lived.

The white shingled cottage at Stapleton had five rooms downstairs, and a steep stairway led to a narrow loft above—lighted by dormer windows. A huge fireplace stood at each end of the house, and a large porch looked out on the blue harbor fifty yards below.

Besides the house, the property included a farm of some forty acres where the elder Cornelius planted his crops and where Corneel began to help farm as soon as he was old enough to pull a weed.

Corneel's father had a good reputation as a worker. Otherwise he would never have been able to secure the mortgage they needed to buy the cottage in Stapleton. On the farm everybody worked; there was little else to do but work, for Staten Island was still lonely and isolated. Between Duxbury's Point at the tip of the island and The Narrows there were only a dozen houses, all of them belonging to farm families like the Van Derbilts. There was not yet a shop of any kind on the island, and no doctor hung his shingle within access of the Van Derbilts. From time to time a peddler with a pack on his back came to the Van Derbilt farm; such peddlers were the only sources of ready-made goods, but once or twice a year the whole family went to New York to buy the necessities that could not be made at home.

In this atmosphere the boy Corneel grew, like one of the weeds he pulled, tough and self-reliant. When he was only six years old, Corneel argued with an eight-year-old Negro boy about the merits of their respective farm nags, and when the boys decided to put the question of equine speed to a test, Corneel nearly foundered his father's plow horse, but won his point and the race. It was his earliest recollection of the willful pride that haunted him all his life.

Some of Corneel's willfulness and his stubborn spirit came from Phebe Hand. Her Tory father, Obadiah, was dead as far as Phebe was concerned; in fact news of the burial had been brought to Phebe's mother long before by someone who claimed to have witnessed the sad event. After the war, Mother Hand married again, a clergyman this time, but she seemed destined to be unlucky in the choice of husbands, for the clergyman died in less than four years.

Following the custom of the time, Phebe's mother began making the rounds of the family, staying with each child in turn and since travel was hard and dangerous, a turn might occupy several months.

Before one of these maternal visits, a stranger appeared on Staten Island and asked for Phebe's sister and her mother. It was a matter of some surprise when a stranger asked for anyone by name, and tongues began to wag. The stranger was directed to Phebe and when he arrived at the house he said he had come from Nova Scotia, where the American Loyalists had settled after the Revolution, and he brought a message from Obadiah Hand. Obadiah was not only alive, he was established now in the newer colony. He wanted Phebe's mother and the children to come with the messenger to Nova Scotia and begin life anew.

Phebe curled her lip and rose bristling in indignation. She would listen to no more such talk, she said brusquely, drawing her plain woolen shawl tight about her neck. Neither would she pass the story on to her mother.

The traveler left but promised to call on his return to the area before he went back to Canada. If Phebe changed her mind, he said, they could talk again.

Phebe always meant what she said, and when her mother came to visit, Phebe said absolutely nothing about the stranger's mission. The visit ended, Mother Hand mounted a horse behind a rider and set off to Phebe's sister's house for another maternal "visit," but she was stopped by a neighbor woman who asked if Mother Hand had heard the gossip, and the whole story came out.

The old lady returned to confront her daughter. Even in her last years Phebe Hand did not forget the look her mother gave her when she accused Phebe of concealing her father's message.

Phebe's arguments that the years and desertion had changed all their lives made no impression on Mother Hand. In the end, she remained with Phebe to wait for the messenger, determined to return with him to Canada and find her lost husband. The daughter could do nothing more, so she shrugged and accepted the inevitable. Phebe's mother did meet the messenger at the Van Derbilt house, and she did go to Nova Scotia with him. There, as the sailing ship pulled in to shore, stood Obadiah Hand, waiting. The old

couple married again and Mother Hand entered Obadiah's house
to stay.

The news of Mother Hand's final decision caused no stir in the
little cottage in Stapleton. Phebe was pitiless in her scorn for weaklings, especially moral weaklings, and this trait Corneel took from
her. He was even quicker than his mother to curl his lip in contempt, and Corneel's contempt, even as a boy, was turned against
his father because the old man would knuckle down neither to
farming nor to ferrying. Corneel made his own decisions and stuck
with them. He thought others ought to do the same.

One youthful decision was Corneel's flat determination to quit
school, even before he had mastered the simple spelling book or
had learned to read properly. The common schools of Staten Island
were not breeding grounds for scholarship, but there was a good
deal more to be learned in school than Corneel chose to learn. The
truth was, of course, that he was not very good at book learning,
and forever, because of it, his spelling, especially, was atrocious.

The family did not object when in 1805 Corneel refused to attend school longer because the boy's labor could be used on the
farm and ferry. Jacob, the Van Derbilt eldest son, had died that
year at the age of sixteen, and the father needed help more than
ever. Corneel, at eleven, began to do work far beyond the normal for
his age.

One day Corneel was sent to the Lower Bay to transfer a cargo
from a ship which had run aground on Sandy Hook, on the New
Jersey coast. The job took three teams of horses, three wagons, and
three crews. Corneel was in charge. His father had to be somewhere else that day, or at least he said he did, so the boy was to
lead the teams across the island, over the ferry to South Amboy
on the Jersey coast, and down to the sand bar where the packet had
run aground.

The boy directed his teams across the bar to the ship, and the
men set to work to get the cargo out of the hold in the few hours
the tide would permit and then cart it across the bar to the shallow-
draft lighters that waited to bring the goods to port.

Corneel drove his crews furiously to beat the unrelenting schedule of the tides. The job was done in good time, before nightfall,

but the weary men wanted to stop, eat, and rest before taking the ferry and the long ride home. Corneel had only enough money to pay for the ferry crossing. Nothing had been said to him about dinner. But as he looked at the tired men and the plodding, lathered horses, the boy knew he would never get them to work for the Van Derbilts again unless he did stop to let them eat.

Accordingly, he bought feed for the horses and the best meal he could afford for the men. When they came to the ferry, after dark, Corneel did not have enough money to pay for the crossing, but he offered the boatman a proposition: Corneel would leave one of the horses at the ferry. If he did not return in three days to claim the horse and pay the toll, the ferryman could sell the horse and keep the difference.

This arrangement was acceptable enough to the ferryman, but when Corneel's father heard of it, much later that night, the old man lost his temper. He could not understand how Corneel could be so concerned about his belly as to leave a horse behind. Corneel bridled and stood his ground. In the end, Phebe Hand mediated the dispute, but she did not bridge the growing chasm between father and son.

There was little time for a farm boy to enjoy himself on Staten Island, especially in the busy summer season when the crops were ripening and the demands on the ferry were greatest. But one night Cornelius promised his son he could have the boat the next day so that Corneel and a friend could go to New York.

In the morning the boys went down to the Van Derbilt wharf, only to find the old man stolidly pitching hay into the half-filled boat. The elder Van Derbilt paid no attention to their aggrieved surprise, but said the boys were to deliver the load of hay and *then* they could have the boat for their own use.

And to add to the injury, Cornelius peered at them for a moment, wiped the sweat off his forehead, and tossed the hay fork to Corneel. He said he guessed they could fill the boat the rest of the way while they were about it.

Corneel hated that just as he hated everything about farming, and the idea of consigning his future to the depths of an onion patch made him feel sick. He loved the water and the work aboard the periauger, and he saw in the sea, as on that ill-fated excursion to New York, a way to escape the humdrum life ashore.

When the weather was fair old Van Derbilt ran a regular ferry to New York from the landing at the foot of the property, below the white cottage. Every morning just after dawn a conch shell sounded from the wharf to speed the laggards with the produce they wanted hauled to the city's Whitehall slip. Old Cornelius ran the boat himself when he felt like it, and his children worked as crew. Corneel was there to run the boat when the old man had other things on his mind.

Van Derbilt's only serious competitor in the ferry business was his neighbor Van Duzer. It was a matter of pride, but of business acumen too, to be the first to New York each day. Most of the marketers were selling the same vegetables, and the first in port would command the highest prices. The ferry that got there first most often was likely to have more business than his competitor, so a brush with Van Duzer's periauger was all part of the game. If the two scows came close enough together, one captain would swipe at the other with an oar, hoping to break a halyard and knock down the lugsail, or even to push a rival overboard.

The trip took an hour and a half when the wind was favorable, and the wind usually ran fair from the wharf to New York. Coming home was often a different story. It could take hours to bring the tired passengers and crew home after dark, hours of tacking and rowing and poling to get the heavy periauger home.

Ferrying was hard work but Corneel saw something in the ferry business that escaped his father and the other boatmen. The boy knew no reason to sit in the slip at Whitehall gossiping with the others when he could be out on the harbor hauling produce or running errands for businessmen, not necessarily from New York to the island, but perhaps from Brooklyn to New Jersey. He suggested such a course, but the old man would not listen.

Corneel's impatience grew. He was nearly seventeen years old, and he threatened to run away to sea. His mother knew the boy meant what he said, so she talked of patience and family responsibility. Corneel *was* needed to help work farm and ferry, and he knew it. He had a brother now, Jacob Hand Van Derbilt, who had been born in 1807 and given the same first name as the dead son. But Corneel and Jacob Hand were the only two boys of the seven Van Derbilt children who lived, and Jake was thirteen years younger than his brother. It would be a long time before he could help out.

Just before his seventeenth birthday, Corneel went to his mother with a proposal for a business venture of his own. The family was not rich, but Phebe Hand had managed to save a good deal of money—every penny she could put away. How much? No one knew, for Phebe was close-mouthed, and she kept the money in an old grandfather clock that stood in the main room of the cottage. Phebe scrimped and saved and took the money from her husband before he could put it into foolish schemes. She had her own small savings when she came to marry Cornelius, but she had added to that amount many times over since thrift and closefistedness were her favorite virtues.

Phebe's saving ways had rescued the family more than once from serious trouble; on one occasion Cornelius came home to announce that he did not have the money to meet a mortgage payment that was due on the farm. They would lose the farm, Cornelius said, and would have to parcel out the children to relatives until they could get a fresh start. That night Phebe Hand went into her mysterious clock and found $3000 to pay off the mortgage.

Corneel did not want anything like so large a sum. He asked his mother to lend him $100 so he could buy a periauger of his own. Then, instead of relying on the local farmers and the produce haulage for his livelihood, Corneel would seek business all around the bay.

Phebe Hand sympathized with her son's itch to get away from his father and into business on his own, but she had not accumulated the money in her clock by softheartedness in money matters. She stated her conditions:

If Corneel would plow and plant corn in the eight-acre plot behind the house by his birthday, she would let him have the money.

It was the first of May, 1810. Corneel's birthday was the twenty-seventh, which meant he had fewer than twenty-seven days to do the entire job. He could not have done it alone, but promising fishing trips and pleasure cruises to his cronies, he persuaded them to help him. Already he showed the makings of an entrepreneur.

The job was done in time, and on his birthday Corneel claimed the money and went off to the harbor. He was as proud as the captain of the latest schooner as he sailed along the shore in his fat-bellied scow, until he piled it up, that very first day, on a rock that stood hidden near the shore.

II

THE FORTUNE

5

PERIAUGER DAYS

In this year 1810, when Corneel Van Derbilt went into business for himself, New York was a city of 80,000 people, the largest metropolis in the United States, and far ahead of both Boston and Philadelphia in population and in trade.

Staten Island was the city's market garden—separated from the city by seven miles of salt water, seven miles of protected harbor that was dotted with ships. Through the anchored ships the Staten Islanders steered their periaugers to trade in the market that was the life of New York. Everyone, it seemed, talked and thought and ate and slept little else but trade. Foreign visitors expressed amazement at the Continental atmosphere of New York and the drive of the city's people, but these same visitors expressed dismay at the dedication of the New Yorkers, even the ladies, to sordid affairs of trade.

A young British officer, dressed in the fine colors of his royal regiment, was paying court and compliment to one of the fashionable young women of New York, when one day she expressed herself most interested in those "who did well in commissions." The officer swelled with manly pride. He was glad, he said, that she appreciated officers and gentlemen.

"Officers and gentlemen?" the young lady asked in puzzled surprise. Why, what could he mean—she was talking about the commission merchants of Wall Street.

It was this trade, not gentlemanliness, that made New York

grow and rolled the cow pastures back beyond Fourteenth Street by 1810. Canal Street was still a stinking brook, full of sinkholes, that ran all the way across prickly huckleberry fields to the Hudson. What is now Center Street was part of a ten-acre lake sprawling over the marsh that would be filled by the gray approaches to the Brooklyn Bridge. The northern half of Manhattan Island, not yet part of the town, was still full of country houses and great estates, a hangover from the Dutch *bouweries* that had dominated the island culture in past decades. Cattle and horses grazed placidly along the East and Hudson rivers and in the tall green grass of the upper island. Across the Harlem River lay old Jonas Bronck's original farm, now whittled by the progress of the city below, although the Bronx was still largely pasture land.

On the tip of Manhattan Island, New York's port burgeoned. A long European war had settled down to a death struggle between Britain and Napoleon, but it was cheered in America, for it made the American market important to both sides. The British, starved for manpower, stopped American ships, recaptured escaped seamen, and by mistake impressed a few indignant Yankees. It *was* a mistake, for the British lion had its hands quite full enough with Napoleon, and Britain had no naval forces to spare for conducting a war with a tiny insufficiency halfway around the world. But British highhandedness led to American resentment and stirred the self-conscious little nation to a display of half-grown strength, like a bantam rooster attacking a bull, and so it was not to be long before John Jacob Astor's successful trading post on the southern bank of the mighty Columbia River would be overrun by the British, a show of avarice that outraged Americans (although it did not lessen trade with England up to the moment of the War of 1812).

New York traded everywhere. She traded with the mother countries of Europe, with their colonies in the sunny islands of the south, and with the Tories, now respectable on the storm-swept shores of Canada. New York drew more trade than Boston or Baltimore or Charleston—her tentacles reached across to the Bahamas, and up and down the Atlantic seacoast, wriggling in and out of the narrow river mouths to the fall line, where the growing cities nestled in protection from the sea.

As New York grew, so did the harbor towns of New Jersey and Long Island. For a time Elizabeth Town and New Brunswick had hopes of competing for trade with New York itself; they were fairly located on the Raritan River that served as a waterway for so much of the Atlantic coast, and they had become the most important grain centers in the Middle Atlantic states. Brooklyn, too, had awakened and begun to compete. Even the river towns of the Hudson felt the backwash of the activity in New York.

In his late teens Corneel Van Derbilt saw and felt this change far more than his father. In the swirling waters of New York harbor, Corneel sensed the opportunity for himself. He was willing to work and now had the tool of his chosen trade—his newly acquired periauger, which he had salvaged after the embarrassing accident and made as good as new. Corneel's arrangement with his family called for him to give up all his daytime earnings and part of the money he earned at night, but Corneel did not feel badly treated. Growing though it was, the little United States had a perennial labor shortage, a shortage that forced the continuation of the slave system. But slaves were not enough, so it was common practice for the labor of the immature to belong to every family. Only when a boy became a man could he gain such independence as Corneel enjoyed, and Corneel's unusual relationship with his family indicated the great confidence they put in his abilities. There were not many boys of seventeen who could be trusted to work as hard on their own as under their father's eye.

Young Van Derbilt proved that he merited the trust. In his first year as a boatman, while John Jacob Astor traded in furs and brought the fineries of Europe to bedeck the great ladies of New York, Corneel Van Derbilt worked every day and every night trading in whatever he could lay his hands on. There was traffic in pleasure seekers as well as in farmers. At night, when the day's jobs were done, the young men and women of Staten Island who could afford it went trouping across the harbor to Fraunces Tavern or one of the other spots of candlelight and ale, or perhaps journeyed to New York to see the latest performance of one of the traveling theater troups.

Corneel did not dawdle in taverns nor had he time to see theatrical performances but he could and did ferry those who wanted to waste their time and money. This seventeen-year-old Corneel's workday began at dawn and ended long after the stars were bright above the bay, a hard workday which gave Corneel a physique that would for all his life be admired by both men and women. He had grown to a height of more than six feet; his shoulders were browned and broadened by the poling and rowing of the periauger; his sandy hair gleamed golden in the sunshine and salt air, and his eyes, gimlet-like even then, could be either chilly as a wave or warm with laughter.

Corneel was agile for all his size. A man had to be agile to man a periauger alone, and Corneel was known as the best among a crew of fine boatmen on the island. He had earned the reputation, not because of his gimlet eye, wasp waist, or heavy shoulder, but because he matched co-ordination with quick thinking. It was good business to be best, so Corneel became best. Had it served his purpose to be second best, he would have contented himself with second best. For Corneel was interested in only two things: Corneel and money.

Jake van Duzer, son of the old Van Derbilt neighbor, was Corneel's great rival on the water just as old Van Duzer was the rival of Corneel's father in the staider ferry business. One day, when the wind blew foul, as it often did on the homeward trip from Manhattan, Van Duzer came up on Corneel and shouted that he was a better boatman than Corneel.

Corneel was minding his own business and at that moment he was poling a boatload of passengers through Buttermilk Channel, a treacherous strip of water that runs between Governors Island and Brooklyn port. The poling knotted the great biceps of Corneel's arms and displayed back muscles that strained beneath his heavy workshirt; it was a steady routine that depended on the sense of timing and grace of the boatman as much as on his strength. Corneel bent and pulled rhythmically, thoughts far away. Suddenly he heard the shout and looked up to see Van Duzer's periauger coming upon him out of nowhere, bound for the same shore. A look at the grinning Van Duzer, even though he was puffing and perspiring, showed that it really was to be a race.

Corneel frowned, and jammed the pole against his breastbone and heaved until the veins stood like pencils in his brown neck. Faster and faster went the beat, the long poles angling and flashing drops of water against the green surface. Faster, ever faster, it continued, until Corneel's eyeballs hurt with the strain and his lungs felt packed with sand. Then they struck the shore with a bump. Corneel had won, by half a scow-length.

But though he did win the race that day, the pole he manned had torn the flesh of his chest to the bone and left a wound whose jagged scar he carried to the grave. Yet it was all part of the game— and the racing and the shouting back and forth made even this hard work seem pleasant to Corneel, pleasant and profitable, too, but only for a time. The passage between Staten Island and White-hall slip was set at 18 cents. There was no fixed price, but that 18-cent fare was more or less established. Occasionally, in devilment or a foolish attempt to monopolize the trade, one of the boatmen would start a price war. But there was small money to be made at any rate in the ferry business in a periauger that might carry only twenty passengers. The trip took the best part of two hours, if the boatman did not run into severe winds. It was hard to make enough trips in a day to earn really large sums of money.

Corneel learned this lesson quickly and then he began to roam all of New York harbor looking for work for himself and his boat. He moved outside The Narrows to the south shore of New Jersey and far up the tidewater of the wide Hudson River, searching for hauling commissions and such business as might come his way.

By the end of that first summer as his own man, Corneel proved that his family had done well to trust him. He repaid the $100 loan to Phebe Hand, and contributed $1000 to the family income.

In the next two years John Jacob Astor was forced out of Astoria and came home to New York to find new uses for his fortune, the greatest in all America. In that same period Corneel laid the basis for his fortune, too—$500—and proudly continued to contribute $1000 each year to the family exchequer. He worked all the time to do it. In the off seasons, when the harbor was blocked by ice and even the trans-Atlantic packets lay at anchor, Corneel worked on the farm, repairing equipment and helping to make ready for the following spring. But there was unspoken agreement in the family that Corneel was for the sea, not for the land, and that he was to keep his independence in return for his contribution to family support.

Corneel's periauger excursions into the Lower Bay were brought to sudden, sharp end when in 1812 the petulant United States Government declared war on a flabbergasted Great Britain. However, the war did not interfere seriously with Corneel's fortunes, as it did with shipping magnates and traders, such as the Roosevelts and the Beekmans, or John Vanderbilt, Jr., scion of the Brooklyn branch of the family and now a New York alderman, whose vessels were seized by a British squadron lying in wait outside The Narrows.

Corneel now owned the largest periauger on the island, a craft he had called the *Dread*, in a youth's swashbuckling turn of mind. The *Dread* sported two masts and two lugsails. She was 62 feet long and almost half as wide. Brightly painted, the *Dread* was the pride of the island periauger fleet. She was Corneel's own boat and he sailed in her, but he also owned major shares in two other white-sailed periaugers. Corneel at nineteen was a leading entrepreneur in the Staten Island hauling trade.

When the war began on June 18, 1812, the season of New York's port was half ended for the year. British ships blockaded the harbor, but there were none too many of them. Initially a squadron stood outside The Narrows but it was not long before the major force was called to strengthen the thin British naval line elsewhere, leaving a frigate or sometimes a heavier capital ship to pick off the merchantmen that might try to sneak through the slim passage and lose themselves in the open Atlantic. Another British force stood in close along the shore of Long Island Sound to prevent the blockade runners from squeezing through the treacherous currents of the Hell Gate that connects the East River to the protected waters of Long Island Sound.

Small as was the blockading force, it terrified New Yorkers. De Witt Clinton, wartime mayor of New York, was called on to do something—anything—to end the port's starvation but there was little Clinton—or anyone—could do. However, later, at the end of the year 1812, when the *United States* won an historic victory over the British frigate *Macedonian,* Clinton could and did organize a victory dinner for the captain and crew of the *United States.* The dinner was held at the banquet room of the City Hotel on the corner of Cedar Street and Broadway.

Corneel, of course, did not attend this banquet, but he heard about it, and how the mayor called the navy men heroes and prophesied that the victory would mean the end of the blockade of their city, and Corneel's workshop—the port.

But the victory meant no such thing.

The British blockade was very effective, and although runners did squeeze through in foul weather or under the protection of darkness, the very presence of the British men-of-war so close off the harbor chilled the hearts of the captains of defenseless packets and slowed the flow of goods into New York to a thin trickle. New Yorkers lived in continual fear of British attack on their city, so they strengthened fortifications, enlarged the harbor forts, and citizens even threw up redoubts on the shores of Manhattan Island, along both the Hudson and the East rivers to repel potential invaders from the sea.

Such was the nervousness of the inhabitants that they kept a constant lookout for an attempt to run the gauntlet of Fort Richmond's guns high above The Narrows. Even the sound of cannon from beyond Sandy Hook or at Navesink on the Jersey coast sent spasms of fear through the city, fear that the British would again land troops on Long Island and threaten the Manhattan fortress from above, as in 1776. In the fall of 1813 a British fleet did come near the twenty-seven guns of Fort Richmond; the fires of the fort were stoked, the men were called to duty, and the cannon balls of the fortress were placed in position for quick heating so they would not only tear apart the bones and flesh of men but sear their way through the very timbers of the wooden ships. The fort's gunnery officer, Captain Bamford, began sighting his guns.

A southeasterly gale was blowing that fall day, just the kind of weather a canny seaman would choose were he to try to run through the thin strip of The Narrows. The wind astern would move the ships at their best and the crews, not then needed to tack and man the yards, could dispose themselves most strategically for the business of fighting.

The British did not come through The Narrows that day, but when the threat had actually passed, the commander of Fort Richmond knew the fidgety and frightened city would not be satisfied until facts dispelled the rumors in the streets. A look at the frothing green water and the spray scudding across the gulches of the waves convinced the garrison commander that he must have the services of the best boatman on Staten Island if his emissaries were to arrive in New York at all. He sought out Corneel Van Derbilt. Corneel said he would accept the job if the officers could stand the rigors of the trip. "I shall have to carry them under water part of the way," he said.

It was dangerous and foolhardy to make the trip in his boat that day, but Corneel did make it, safely, and delivered his human cargo, sallow and soaking, at the foot of Whitehall.

As an important man in the shipping affairs of Staten Island, Corneel felt no urge to seek the adventure that lured other youths to sea in ships in these days of war. There was fortune beckoning in the sea war, for since the tiny American navy could be of no decisive force in ending the war against a power such as Britain, the American government commissioned private ships to make war against the enemy. The ships were fast, armed merchantmen. They relied on speed to outrun any British ships of war they might sight. Privateers, they called themselves, although the enemy called them pirates, and perhaps rightly so, because the lures of wealth as well as patriotism stirred the breasts of the officers and men who shipped on the privateers.

The talk of wealth to be gained in the seaman's share of a privateering adventure did not arouse Corneel because, as he knew, the voyage of a privateer depended more on Providence than brains. *If* the privateer found an enemy merchant ship, and *if* the merchant cargo was valuable, *if* she was captured safe and sound, and *if* the privateer was not run down by a British man-of-war, she stood to make a handsome stake. But if she lost, a man was liable to find himself imprisoned or, equally disastrous, impressed into the crew of a British warship.

This caution was Corneel's inheritance from Phebe Hand. He would never stake his future on the whim of chance. Corneel, the best boatman on the island, captain of the biggest harbor freighter, and shareholder in the efforts of other men, knew exactly the results of his day-to-day work within the bay. Why go outside when there was money to be made at home?

Corneel wanted to get married at this time, too. He had chosen the girl, her name was Sophia Johnson, and she was his first cousin, daughter of Phebe Hand's sister. Sophia possessed a remarkable likeness to Phebe Hand; she had the same sturdy figure, she was quiet and resourceful, and within the home she demanded little, put on no airs, and was satisfactorily free from girlish sillinesses.

Both elder Van Derbilts objected to the marriage: they said Corneel was too young at nineteen to take on the responsibilities of family, and it was unseemly, even dangerous, to marry a first cousin —all the children might turn out to be idiots.

Corneel scoffed and dismissed parental objections. He was going to get married. He was going to marry Sophia. He was going to marry her this year. He did, and the young couple moved in with Cornelius and Phebe Hand.

Marriage had little outward effect on Corneel Van Derbilt. He had always been dignified and reserved, qualities he inherited from a father who sent children off to bed from the dinner table many a night, even after they had reached their teens, when they indulged in what seemed to him to be unseemly activity.

Like his father, Corneel smiled little and said less. He dressed roughly, as fitted a sailor. Yet unlike most of his contemporaries, Corneel did not indulge in youthful brawls, tavern sessions, or fighting. He had small taste for strong drink, although he loved good cigars. He had no compunctions about drink or drunkenness, he simply had no effort to waste on nonessentials. He believed the daylight hours and many of the night were made for work.

With scant education and neither desire nor time to improve himself by reading, Corneel developed into an uncouth and marvelously profane man. Before he reached his majority he could scarcely frame a sentence without interjecting a handful of oaths from an imaginative and heaping store. His size and strength alone saved him many a battle, for he had a ready tongue when angered (as well as a profane one), and visible disrespect for those he considered sluggard or in the wrong. Yet Corneel did not fight, except when provoked beyond reason, such as the day he ran afoul of a haughty army officer.

Corneel was transporting a detachment of soldiers from the shallow landing at Fort Richmond on The Narrows to the city when an officer pulled up in a boat from the Quarantine Station and hailed Van Derbilt's periauger.

Puffing with self-importance, cockaded hat clutched to hold it atop his head in the breeze, the landlubber officer draggled his scabbard and boots across the freeboard of the low vessel and peremptorily ordered the soldiers to transfer to the other boat and return to the Quarantine Station for inspection.

Why quarantine?

New York's Harbor Quarantine Station had been established just before the turn of the century, when plague and cholera and yellow fever had begun to torment the growing town. The authorities knew disease came from the ships, and they were determined to keep it aboard the ships, so they built the station at the end of Staten Island. No ship thereafter docked or unloaded passengers, crew, or cargo in New York port without first having been passed by inspectors from the Quarantine Station.

During the war of 1812 quarantine became a responsibility of the military and that was why the officer talked about "inspection." Still, these soldiers were coming to New York's Whitehall from Fort Richmond; and the officer knew it full well. "Inspection," as Corneel was sure, was simply a device to get the men off his boat. He took a look into the other periauger. It was manned by one of his principal competitors, a man no more above such a trick than Corneel would have been himself in other circumstances.

Indignant, Corneel protested to the pompous officer. He would not let the soldiers move a step, he said.

In rage, the officer turned on Van Derbilt, but his military boots slipped on the unfamiliar footing of the deck as he tried to draw his sword, and he was not quick enough. Corneel stepped forward, swung a heavy fist, knocked the officer down, dumped him into his rival's boat, and shoved off, heading straight for Manhattan with his fares. Nothing more was heard from *that* officer, nor did anyone try to pull such a trick on Corneel again.

But not all of Corneel's encounters with army officialdom were so brusque or so unsatisfactory. In the spring of 1814 Governor Daniel Tompkins called up the state militia to protect the city during one of the governor's periodic frets over the danger of imminent invasion by the British. The call came for three months of service, it meant the able-bodied men of the militia—and this meant every man who was not excused—would have to trade their normal incomes during the whole three months for the paltry pay of common soldiers. At Coffeehouse Slip, where the Staten Island boatmen gathered, this gubernatorial call was greeted with dismay, a prodigious amount of moaning, and a hundred schemes to escape military service.

The only sure way out of military duty was to obtain some kind of service contract with an arm of the state or federal government. In this the boatmen were limited, but a contract that would achieve this end was coming up, a contract to supply the six forts of New York harbor with provisions for the coming three months. The Staten Island boatmen rushed to place their bids for the job, each trying to undercut his rivals without ruining himself.

One boatman did not yield a penny below what he termed a fair price. In his atrocious spelling (for Corneel now spelled by the "rules of common sense") the young boatman offered to do the job at a rate that would offer him a good profit. The Commissary General of the American army, Matthew L. Davis, knew how the wind blew with the Staten Island boatmen. He gave the contract to Van Derbilt, the highest bidder of all. Questioned, the general snorted his contempt of boatmen who would cut their rates with the obvious end of escaping military service. He wanted the work done properly, the general said, not half done.

Corneel did not let the military contract interfere seriously with his daytime activities; he supplied the forts at night, using his big periauger. He asked that provisions be made ready at the wharf each night at six o'clock, and every evening, after a full day of work in the harbor, Corneel sailed off to one of the six forts, bearing beeves and swine and chickens for the stewing pots, guns and bullets and powder, and hay and greens. Corneel sailed to Harlem, far up the river, to the whirlpools and treacherous rocks of Hell Gate, to Ward's Island, to Fort Washington, Fort Lee, Governors Island, and to the fortifications at The Narrows.

The young boatman made great profits during the War of 1812, quite outside his military contract, because New York was hungry in this time of blockade. For a time the British Navy's ship *Plantaganet* stood off Sandy Hook, intercepting the barks and coastal schooners as they headed for port. From one coaster the *Plantaganet* captured a pipe organ destined for St. John's Episcopal Church in Manhattan, an organ which had been ordered from Philadelphia months before the war began. St. John's finally got its organ, but not before it was ransomed for $2000.

A half-dozen vessels slipped through Hell Gate every day, but in the harbor more than a hundred ships stood idle. The inactivity was felt in the pockets of rich and poor alike. What they wanted, and what Corneel supplied—running between farms and city—was food and firewood, the prices of which rose steadily during the war. Firewood sold for $3.00 a load in the winter of 1813–14, but luckily it was a mild winter, so pleasant in fact that boats ran to Albany two days before Christmas, and sloops plied the Hudson below West Point much later in the year.

Corneel made great profits on his meat and produce, but he could not supply everything. The price of brown sugar shot to $25 a hundredweight, Hyston tea sold for 17 shillings a pound. By the end of the war ordinary citizens were living on beans steeped in hot molasses, and an unsavory concoction of black butter pears, apples, and quinces stewed together was the major sustenance of the poor.

Not only was Corneel's New York hungry, but the young American government was hungry too. Rich citizens such as John Jacob Astor came to the government's rescue—for a price. Astor subscribed $2,000,000 for government loans (at 88 cents on the dollar).

And if Corneel seemed to be cleaning up in the harbor trade, the half-million dollars Astor made on *that* deal made Corneel's high prices seem tame.

Astor had taken possession of the house of the disgraced Aaron Burr, and he offered the brick villa for rent with grounds and grass suitable for a cow and a pair of horses. That villa was one of Astor's minor holdings; in 1814 he was the largest owner of real estate in New York City. He owned scores of blocks of three-story wooden houses, brick houses with slate roofs, and miles of undeveloped land north of Fourteenth Street.

When the war ended in 1815, Astor's fortunes soared again in the renewed activity of New York. That same year Corneel Van Derbilt bought a battered schooner from the American government and sailed south to Virginia, oystering. It was a profitable trade, though looked upon askance by deep-water sailors, since a boat once used for oystering never seemed thereafter to be able to shake the ripe odor of the shellfish. But Corneel was not one to cavil at a stink, or to allow himself to be swayed by such niceties when money was at stake.

Corneel loaded his schooner to the gunwales with oysters before he left the Virginia beds. Although she was lying dangerously low in the water, he started homeward in the face of predictions by his competitors that his ship would founder in passage. Luckily the weather held and Corneel did not lose ship or cargo. He was willing to take the risk, since the chance for profit was high and he was sure the weather would hold for *him*, or that if it did not, his seamanship would bring him through.

In the summer of 1815 Corneel joined forces with his brother-in-law, John DeForest, to build a coasting schooner. The schooner had two masts, fore and aft; sails hung from a gaff on each mast and were steadied by booms at the bottom. Each mast carried a jib forward, too, to catch the shifting breezes. The little ship was one of that species found so peculiarly adapted to New World navigation, with its many rivers and estuaries, where the wind draws up and down channel, as a rule, and occasions much beating to windward on short tacks. The square-rigged ship, whose sails are hung athwartships, is always at a disadvantage in seeking the wind in such waters. The schooner, with her fore and aft rig, responded like a reed to the wind; she took fewer hands than the square-riggers, and her low, rakish lines gave her speed in the coastal waters. The schooner, here, made the bigger ships look clumsy and outlandish.

They called this first new ship the *Charlotte*, in honor of De-Forest's wife, who was Corneel's older sister. The two young men put the *Charlotte* in the coasting trade after the war ended that year. They carried whale oil for the lamps of America, cheese, oil cake, wine and spirits, woolens, gunny cloth, and spices; and they sailed these goods up and down the length of the American coast. They sailed far south to pick up live oak, then put into the Carolinas for pitch pine and into the ragged Chesapeake Bay for locust wood for New York's shipbuilders.

Corneel sailed in the *Charlotte* in the winter months when the periaugers were confined by the ice in New York harbor. But in the summer months Corneel kept to the harbor and river trade, where he felt at home, and let his brother-in-law manage the coaster.

Sometimes Corneel traveled as far up the North River as Albany, hawking tons of melons he had bought on the Delaware shore. He stopped at every landing on the way up the broad river, sold wholesale or retail—it did not matter which—and he picked up local goods to sell elsewhere on his travels.

In the spring, when the shimmering, toothsome shad began their annual spawning run up the Hudson, Corneel visited the gill netters. He loaded thousands of frantic silver fish into his periauger, stacked them to the gunwales, and while they were yet flopping and alive, he headed south for the New Jersey shore to sell his cargo.

Every spring the farmers in the Middle Atlantic states put up shad for good winter eating. They pickled the three- and four-pound fish by the barrelful, gutting them and dousing them in brine—as many barrels full as they could afford. But the people of central and southern New Jersey were accustomed to buying their shad from fishermen along the Delaware, not from the north. When Corneel came down from the Hudson, he at first met sales resistance from his potential customers who did not know him or how fresh his fish might be; furthermore, they did not like change.

Corneel sailed into New Brunswick one day with a load of thirty thousand shad. He ignored the regular dealers after he found he was met with distrust. Instead, he hired half-a-dozen men to ride up all the roads toward Princeton, Flemington, and Freehold, shouting that there were fresh shad down at New Brunswick. When the farmers had come and he had sold out his cargo, Corneel picked up what freight he could find, some commissions and a handful of passengers at the wharf on the Raritan, and sailed back to the Upper Bay for another load.

They remembered Corneel Van Derbilt in New Brunswick, where he was later to settle for a while.

Although he was still in his early twenties, Corneel was doing very well as a sailor-businessman, and he was saving money for his future. When he had married and begun to raise his own family, Corneel secured his release from the old financial commitment to the elder Van Derbilts. His brother Jake, now approaching his teens, could help out with the farm and ferry.

Corneel needed all his money for his own family because a year after the marriage, Corneel's first child was born, a daughter; Corneel and Sophia called her Phoebe Jane. Were it not for the coming of a child, it would have been hard to know that Corneel was married at all. Sophia, though she bore a remarkable physical resemblance to her mother-in-law, had little family resemblance to Phebe Hand in character. Sophia was quiet and mousy; she cooked Corneel's meals when he was home, she kept her share of her mother-in-law's house; she bore the overbearing direction of Phebe Hand without complaint. By now, Corneel would have preferred a more spirited wife, but he did not complain. He just stopped coming home nights.

Unlike his father, Corneel kept the money and did the buying and made the decisions in his family and in these he was as thrifty and tightfisted as Phebe Hand. Sophia showed no objection to Corneel's ways; she showed so little emotion of any kind that Phebe Hand came to believe that Sophia had no spunk, for she did not even complain at Corneel's long hours or the frequent nights on which he did not appear.

As Corneel's profits from hauling grew, he again invested the money in other boats to make money from the labor of others. More profits came and Corneel invested them again. By his twenty-fourth birthday, on May 27, 1818, Corneel Van Derbilt had saved

$9000, a respectable sum for a man twice his age. With so much capital, he began to look around for an investment, and a future that offered him a chance to make his fortune. Corneel did not drift into wealth; he made his way by work, but work was not enough; it took planning, and Corneel had begun planning his future on the day he persuaded his mother to stake him to $100 to buy his periauger. And even a serious error in judgment did not hold him back long.

6

BELLONA

Even before the beginning of the War of 1812 the steamboat
had come to America to stay. Many men, a Roosevelt among them,
claimed first honors in bringing steam to the American waterways,
but Robert Fulton designed and built the most practical vessel of
all. One day in 1807 on New York's East River, Fulton's steamer,
the *Clermont*, puffed upstream at two miles an hour against a one-
mile tide, and the steamboat was adjudged a success.

That same year, Fulton allied himself with the wealthy Livingston family of New Jersey. Fulton and Chancellor Robert Livingston secured an exclusive franchise from the New York legislature
to operate steamboats in the waters of the Empire State. It was a
strange franchise, all the more potent because the holders were
granted power of seizure of any steam vessel caught poaching in
their territory. Anyone who wanted to run steam on the Hudson
or on the waters of the bay or Long Island Sound had to apply
to Messrs. Fulton and Livingston for a license. That license gave
the applicant the privilege of building a steamboat along the lines
of Fulton's design and the right to run his boat between points
designated by the monopolists.

The adjoining states of Connecticut and New Jersey did not
take kindly the New York government's arrogance in prescribing
conditions for shipping in coastal waters, and some Connecticut
ports refused to let the Fulton Monopoly boats dock at all. Both

Connecticut and New Jersey quietly encouraged independent operators to flout the New York law.

Before the coming of steam inland travel in America had been
a frightful adventure for the traveler, and one of the worst trips of
all was the one between New York and Philadelphia. First the
traveler had to ferry from Manhattan to Paulus Hook, then
ride by coach across the tidal flats of the Jersey Meadows. In the
wintertime passengers could expect to get out and push their coach
through the slippery clay or drifted snow. In the summer, even
inside the stifling coach with curtains drawn, they could not escape the hordes of stinging mosquitos or the stink of the tide
flats. On the other side of the Jersey peninsula, another ferry trip
took them to New Brunswick; then they suffered more miles of
jouncing coach ride to Trenton and—finally—took a river boat for
the only pleasant part of the trip, down the majestic Delaware
to Philadelphia. But on the return trip, even that Delaware River
trip was at the mercy of tide and wind.

With the coming of steam, Livingston built a boat called the
Raritan at the high cost—for the times—of $26,000 and set out to
revolutionize the travel route, hoping to get back their money in
the safety of monopoly. The *Raritan*, which ran from New York
to New Brunswick, lost money for two years, but then began to
show a profit as the obvious merits of the new route and method
of travel became known. The *Raritan* made the run to New Brunswick in nine hours, passengers avoided the terrible trip over the
Jersey Meadows, even though when they arrived at New Brunswick, they had to take coaches for the trip to Trenton.

By 1811 the Monopoly had licensed steamboats to operate between Philadelphia and Bordentown, Amboy and New York, New
York and Albany, and on Lake Champlain and the St. Lawrence
River between Montreal and Quebec. Fulton and Livingston were
venturing to control international as well as national commerce, but
at that moment Canadians paid little attention to their maneuvers.
His Majesty's forces were more interested in stirring up the Indians
of the Great Lakes region against the upstart United States than
with the pretensions of a tiny steamboat monopoly.

Corneel Van Derbilt examined the Monopoly boats, and then

predicted with the absolute certainty of youth that steam would never amount to anything.

This first quarter of the nineteenth century was the heyday of sail. Fast clippers and packet boats sped goods and passengers to the four corners of the earth, around the Horn, to Australia, and to the opium markets of China. Some fifteen hundred sloops and sailing craft still plied the Hudson and the harbor of New York, and framed against these graceful craft the new steamboats seemed ugly and crude. Corneel saw boilers and paddle wheels in the steamers hogging valuable cargo space. The expense of wood and crews was so great that he could not see how the boats could operate profitably. So Corneel stuck to his sailboats, while others fought the early battles of steam—and thus Corneel delayed his opportunity for fortune by a full seven years.

For while Corneel continued in the periauger and coastal sailing trades, others were snapping up the steamer runs. After the Monopoly was created, and began to sell its franchises, competitors sprang up to grasp a share of the freight and passenger business. Robert Fulton complained unhappily about the "pirates" who tried to capitalize on his invention, and the state of New York stepped in to help him. State agents waited on the busy docks of New York City for any steamboat captain foolhardy enough to risk seizure of his vessel by operating without a license. But they were only delaying the inevitable; neither Fulton nor state authority could halt or control the transportation revolution created by the harnessing of steam.

One of the "pirates" Fulton hated so much was Thomas Gibbons, a Savannah planter who had come to New Jersey to make his home. Gibbons was a substantial citizen who lived on an extensive estate called Bottle Hill, where he enjoyed a gracious life very much like the one he had left on the plantation in the South. Gibbons became interested in steamboating when he was a director of the New Brunswick bank, and as a bank director had an eye out for opportunities to increase his fortune as well as the support of his bank to provide him with capital and information. New Brunswick was the halfway point between Philadelphia and New York, and both the coaches, which traveled southwest to Trenton, and the boats, which traveled northeast to New York by way of Elizabeth, centered in New Brunswick.

The Fulton-Livingston Monopoly had by this time licensed Aaron Ogden, the son of a well-to-do New Jersey family, to run between New Jersey and New York, but Gibbons refused to let the dubious legality of that franchise stop him. He was wealthy enough to send his son William to Princeton College to study the law and he was wealthy enough, and stubborn enough, to set himself against the Monopoly.

Gibbons began his opposition venture in a small way by putting a rival ferry service on the free water of New York harbor, running between Elizabeth and New Brunswick, a service that could not be challenged by the Monopoly since no state but New York accepted the Fulton-Livingston licenses. Yet it was not long before Gibbons saw a way to move in on the lucrative New York-Philadelphia traffic without butting openly against the Monopoly. He connected his small steamer on the route from Elizabeth Town to New Brunswick with a sailing ferry that ran between Elizabeth and New York. The Gibbons line, then, was almost the sister of the Monopoly line, except that Gibbons had to transport his passengers and freight from Elizabeth Town to New York by sail, a slower trip that drew few passengers and far lower fares than those of his opposition. If he dared run his steamboat to Manhattan Island, New York authorities would seize it for the Monopoly.

By 1818 Corneel Van Derbilt saw that steamboating had come to stay and although he was prospering with his $9000 and several ships of his own, Corneel decided to learn the new ways of steamboating. As it happened, he made this decision at a time when Thomas Gibbons was looking for a young and aggressive captain.

Young Van Derbilt was already acquainted in New Brunswick, through his dealings there as a sharp and imaginative businessman. His reputation as a fearless captain had also spread to New Jersey, and in 1818, in his eagerness to compete with the Monopoly, a fearless captain, was just what Thomas Gibbons wanted. Gibbons made an offer and Corneel accepted: he would operate a new steamboat, the *Bellona*, for the Gibbons line. Gibbons would pay him $60 per month. The pay was little enough for a rising capitalist, but the new captain was unfamiliar with steam, and this tour of duty was to be an education for him as well as a job. Besides, Corneel knew Gibbons could find others to work for the same amount.

Salary was not the only inducement offered Corneel. Sophia and the two baby girls would move to New Brunswick, the center of operations of the Gibbons line, and Corneel could live in an inn Gibbons owned if his wife would operate it as a stopping point for Gibbons line passengers. More, Corneel was to receive half the proceeds of the bar aboard his steamboat. Gibbons would supply the bar furnishings, but at the end of the season Van Derbilt was to pay off his employer for the expense incurred. Monetarily, the bar and the inn were worth far more than the captaincy on which they depended. Altogether, they made the offer very attractive.

Corneel did not consult Sophia in making these arrangements. He signed a contract with Gibbons on June 24, 1818, a month after his twenty-fourth birthday, and told Sophia to get ready to move. They would call the inn Bellona Hall, he said, after the steamboat he was to run. Sophia would tend the inn and prepare meals for the passengers who wanted to rest before completing the trying journey between New York and Philadelphia.

Sophia was dismayed at her first sight of Bellona Hall, her new home. The inn, formerly called Halfway House, was a three-story unpainted clapboard building, standing on the lower steamboat landing of New Brunswick, just at the edge of the main section of the town. The dining and bar and parlor rooms were downstairs on the first floor. The other two floors were divided into sleeping rooms. But all rooms were in a uniform state of filth. The previous managers had no talent or interest in hotel keeping, and when the Van Derbilts took over the inn it had a reputation for slovenliness that was unsurpassed in New Brunswick.

They moved in, nonetheless, and Sophia began to scrub and clean while Corneel went about his captain's business. Gibbons was ready to beard the Monopoly. That much was apparent even in the design of the little open-decked *Bellona*, whose side-wheel paddles were a straight steal from the Fulton patents. Gibbons's earlier boat, *Stoughdenger*, laughingly referred to by competitors as *The*

Mouse of the Mountain, had been powered by strange fans called palmipedes, developed to avoid infringement on the Fulton patents. But the palmipedes were ineffectual paddling devices compared to the simple sensible paddle wheel, so now Gibbons was ready to stake all on open conflict with the Fulton-Livingston group. Corneel, in his new boat, would steam directly to New York, and thus eliminate the awkward transfer of passengers from steamboat to sailboat at Elizabeth Town.

The first step was to cut the rate for steamer passage below that of Aaron Ogden's rival line. The one-way passage had cost $4.00, but Corneel and Gibbons began a rate war in which the price fell to a dollar, sometimes dipped even lower in the fight to secure the trade.

Ogden sent a frantic warning to the Monopoly on the first day that Corneel steamed for New York, and then began a long game of cat-and-mouse, in which the New York authorities tried to catch Captain Van Derbilt—object: to haul Van Derbilt to Albany, secure a judgment against him and the Gibbons line, and seize the offending *Bellona* as booty, thus punishing the offenders and offering an example to all who flouted the Monopoly franchise. Gibbons and Van Derbilt were chosen because they were the most brazen in their disregard for the Monopoly and the laws of New York.

During one period an attempt was made everyday for sixty consecutive days to arrest Corneel—a job that proved more difficult than the officers expected. Corneel installed a secret closet in the hold of the *Bellona* where he could hide if the New Yorkers searched his ship. The police did just that, coming aboard time after time as the steamboat lay at dockside. One day, when he knew the police would be waiting for him in New York, Van Derbilt brought a young woman on the bridge of the steamboat before he left New Brunswick. On the trip he instructed her in the art of docking the *Bellona,* and warned his engineer to keep his wits about him in case of error. Then, as the steamboat neared New York, Van Derbilt went below and hid in the closet in the hold. When the steamboat pulled in to the New York wharf, the officers leaped aboard, and rushed to the bridge to arrest the captain, certain they had him cornered at last. On the bridge they found the girl, but no captain. Van Derbilt, grinning broadly to himself, was safely hidden in his secret closet.

When they did corner him one day, Van Derbilt ordered the officers off his steamboat, looked grimly at his watch, and told them that if they were not ashore within one minute he would cast off his lines and carry them to New Jersey, where he would have *them* arrested for trespassing. The New York officers, who knew how the citizens of New Jersey felt about the New York steamboat law, stayed on shore thereafter and tried to catch Corneel on the dock.

But one Sunday in 1819 the New Yorkers did arrest Van Derbilt and strangely enough, for all his remarkable command of profanity and his scowling ways in the past, Corneel offered neither resistance nor abuse as the officers took him to Albany on the next trip of the Monopoly line.

In Albany, Captain Van Derbilt, as Thomas Gibbons's employee, was sent for arraignment on charges of contempt of court for steaming in New York waters in direct violation of the law.

But when Captain Van Derbilt came to trial, the evidence showed conclusively that on the day in question the *Bellona* had been leased to Captain Tompkins, an officer who held a license under the Fulton-Livingston patents. Van Derbilt was released by red-faced officials, with the private advice that they would get him yet. But would they? It was doubtful, for he planned his every move carefully and he showed a great deal of ingenuity—in every way. The mature Corneel was an efficient and canny captain.

One icy day in January 1820 the sailing ship *Elizabeth* lay frozen in ice at the foot of Manhattan's Rector Street slip. Day after day Van Derbilt saw the crew chopping at the ice, but the *Elizabeth* could not get out of the cold ring that surrounded and pinned her. The only way to free the ship was to kedge her out— pull the anchor ahead of the ship, drop it, and haul the *Elizabeth* toward the anchor by her own chain. Even this solution seemed impossible to the crew, for the ice around the *Elizabeth* was not strong enough to bear the weight of even one man and they could not use a boat. Van Derbilt finally joined the idlers who were watching the men of the *Elizabeth* hack hopelessly at the ice, and remarked casually that he could get the ship free easily enough, and would do it for $100.

A hundred dollars was a lot of money in those days. A man could rent a house for a year for that amount. But the master of the *Elizabeth* was exasperated. He had a human cargo aboard; the *Elizabeth* was chartered by the well-meaning American Colonization Society that hoped to solve the problem of slavery in America by sending the Negroes back to Africa. Human cargo kept badly, and under the charter the *Elizabeth* was losing money every day she stayed in port. When he heard of Van Derbilt's boast, the captain agreed to pay if Corneel could really do the job.

That same evening Van Derbilt showed up at the Rector Street slip with five men, three pine boards, a long rope, and a small anchor. The ice was too thin to hold a man, but it was not too thin to hold a man whose weight was distributed over the strips of planking. Moving the boards, one in front of the other, and crawling forward slowly, Van Derbilt and his men managed to sink the anchor outside the circle of ice. The anchor rope was passed to the *Elizabeth*, and the ship kedged her way out. The next day at noon the ship was towed into the ice-free channel by a steamer, and was soon on her way to Africa, while Captain Van Derbilt, back on the bridge of the *Bellona*, was a hundred dollars richer for his few minutes of work.

The young captain spent most of each working day on the tiny bridge, located directly over the engine room. He had his midday meal there, perched on a stool. From there he controlled the *Bellona's* engine by tapping on the deck with his cane. One tap meant "Slow ahead." Two taps meant "Fast." Three taps meant "Stop." There was no need for verbal communication with the engineer, which was just as well because Corneel communicated very little with either crew or passengers. He took no backtalk from anyone, crew, passengers, or law officers, and the one who argued with him was apt to be ordered off the boat. But Corneel never shouted or blustered and he was so much the captain of his ship that he inspired absolute confidence among passengers, in a day when all too frequently steamboats burst their boilers, hurling scalded men, women, and children into the water. Corneel helped inspire that confidence by showing off occasionally: he would ride up to the dock, guiding the helmsman silently by hand movements and tapping the deck with his cane for the guidance of the engineer. Not one word did he speak, but the *Bellona* glided silently to a perfect landing. To the passengers it looked as though it were done by magic, and Corneel achieved a considered reputation.

The *Bellona* did a brisk trade, partly because of Corneel's reputation, partly because of the rate-cutting practices he was learning from Gibbons, and partly because the traffic to Philadelphia was always brisk. From New York, Corneel took the *Bellona* across to Elizabeth Town, then down the Arthur Kill that separates Staten Island from the New Jersey mainland, into the wide mouth of the Raritan River, and up the dozen miles to New Brunswick. That was the end of the line. The hardier passengers went on after the five-hour trip, but many stayed overnight, gathering strength for the next day's jostling trip.

Four hotels in New Brunswick catered to the travelers. Besides Sophia's hotel, there were the Bell Tavern, the White Hall Hotel, and Mann's Hotel. These were much more elegant houses, located in the middle of the town; Bellona Hall was in the rough district of New Brunswick, next door to the Raritan Hotel, a hostelry that catered to mule drivers and later to the bargemen who worked the Raritan Canal. Still, the Van Derbilt hotel had several advantages. Sophia kept clean rooms and a good table, with the help of her children who ran errands and carried the passengers' luggage. And since Bellona Hall stood at the foot of Burnet Street, directly on the Raritan, the passengers' luggage could be transferred from steamboat to room by hand. The stage stop was there, too. Thirty or forty of these four-horse stages would line up along Burnet Street four times a day, as the competing steamers came in to dock, and the drivers blistered the air with whips and cries, each touting the merits of his stage over all others. Half an hour after the boats arrived, when the passengers were all loaded, the drivers cracked their whips, clucked and smacked their lips at the horses, and, in clouds of dust or torrents of mud, depending on the weather, started their stages careening down the post road to Trenton. Halfway, the westbound stages passed their confreres from Trenton, which were bringing loads of passengers on their way to New York from Philadelphia and the South. So Bellona Hall prospered, although the competition for lodgings was nearly as fierce as the competition among the steamboats. Corneel had little time to mingle with the passengers at Bellona Hall, however, for each day but Sunday he rose early and set out on his round trip to New York at six in the morning, returning at four in the afternoon. He spent even less time at home now than in the days when he was scouring the harbor in his periauger, for as he showed his abilities to Gibbons, Corneel was given more and more responsibility in the operation of the line, and soon he was not confined to the New York–New Brunswick run but often went out of town on special business for Gibbons.

Three years after the move to New Brunswick, the twenty-seven-year old captain rented the upper half of a house fronting on Renwick Street in New York. With his new responsibilities Corneel often found it important, or at least he said it was important, to lay over in New York. The New York quarters were convenient too, for Corneel was growing away from Sophia, and he wanted female companionship when he sought the divertissements of the big city. Needless to say, there is no record of Sophia's ever even seeing the Renwick Street house.

If Corneel did not hesitate to spend money now in his pleasures, still he held tightly to the family tradition of waste not, want not. Even in such a small matter as rent of his hideaway, Corneel never lost a chance to make a good bargain better. In 1821, when he and one David Fenton rented the Renwick Street house, they shared the house and a total rent of $110. The following year Van Derbilt took the entire house for himself and he persuaded the owner to let him have it for $100 a year. In taking the entire house, Van Derbilt increased his expense in favor of pleasure, but he could afford to do so, for he was making an excellent income from his *Bellona* bar concession and from Bellona Hall.

Gibbons was prospering, too. His income from the steamboat and stage line was $40,000 a year. Van Derbilt's salary was raised to $2000, and then he was offered $5000 a year by the Monopoly to change allegiance, but he turned the Monopoly offer down scornfully. When Gibbons heard of the outside offer, he said he would match it, but Corneel refused more money, saying he believed that he should not get any more than the other captains of the line. The fact was that his captain's salary was a small part of the Van Derbilt income; he still had interests in other boats and ships, besides the hotel and bar concession.

Prosperity meant that Corneel could buy a home of his own in New Brunswick. One reason for the move reflected Corneel's astuteness in getting the most out of whatever he had. The children—a half dozen of them born in New Brunswick—occupied too much of the commercially profitable room at Bellona Hall, so the investment in a house further up Burnet Street made sense to Corneel. The family continued to operate the hotel, but now the Van Derbilts lived at a more fashionable address.

Even in New Brunswick, the Van Derbilt schism was apparent: Corneel and Sophia were seldom seen together outside the tavern. Corneel kept a team of horses for his own use, just as he kept a horse at his house in New York, and he began to indulge himself in the finest horseflesh he could find, often driving alone to visit friends in and around New Brunswick. Sometimes he went to take tea with the John Letsons at their boardinghouse. Letson was one of the oldest and most experienced stage drivers in the area, and he, like Van Derbilt, worked for Thomas Gibbons. While Van Derbilt called there frequently, he did not care much for Letson. On one occasion, when the evening steamboat failed to sail from New Brunswick to New York, Letson told the passengers they were being held over only so Captain Van Derbilt could be sure of a full house at Bellona Hall. But Van Derbilt was too shrewd ever to announce his antagonism. He complained about the driver to Gibbons, asked that the latter "stop Letson's mouth," but Letson's recommendation to passengers was important, so Corneel went to Letson's for tea all the same.

Van Derbilt began to spend some time among the young bloods of the town, few of whom suspected that he was married, let alone several times over a father. At Letson's he met John Terhune, a college man who kept a bookstore on Albany Street, and Terhune found Van Derbilt a fine-looking and likable fellow, even though

Corneel dressed roughly and abused the English language shamefully. (Van Derbilt never pronounced the name of the ship's tanks that produce steam as anything but "bilers.")

Despite his roughness, the handsome Corneel made a good impression on Terhune, the two spent a considerable amount of time together, and yet Terhune never discovered that Van Derbilt was married. When Terhune finally married, himself, that year, he asked Van Derbilt to attend his wedding at Princeton, and Corneel came alone. When Van Derbilt arrived at the church, Terhune could not believe it was the man he knew, for the captain was elegantly dressed in the finest broadcloth, a white shirt and the white high stock that was to become famous, and driving two horses before an expensive carriage on which the polished brass work gleamed. In a moment Corneel was encircled by a crowd of young ladies (most of whom he seemed to know), laughing and joking without a visible care in the world, or a family either.

In time Corneel and his horses became legendary in Middlesex County. In 1824, when the Marquis de Lafayette visited America on a homecoming trip of sorts, the New Brunswick city council, like scores of other municipal bodies, wanted to pay homage to the distinguished French hero of the American Revolution. Lafayette, second only to Washington himself, symbolized the successful struggle for freedom that was still fresh in the minds of the people of the nation, for America then was not yet fifty years old.

Lafayette accepted the New Brunswick invitation, as he accepted nearly all the invitations from his adopted country's town governments. On September 23 Lafayette took the ferry to the point of land where Jersey City is now located, then began to travel by coach across the state. He went by coach, instead of boat, because he had many stops to make: at Newark the town turned out to welcome him; at Rahway the citizens spread a banquet; and the next day New Jersey's First Squadron of Horse Artillery under Major VanDyke met the party and brought the distinguished visitor from Rahway to New Brunswick under escort. At the bridge over the Raritan, just before the procession entered town, the line stopped, Lafayette heard a military salute of sixty-nine cannon, marched through an arch of evergreens and flowers, and stepped into a new coach drawn by a double team of prancing horses, each horse groomed until its hide glistened. Those horses were borrowed for the special occasion from Corneel.

But while Corneel prospered by his doughty but illegal sailing to New York (and enjoyed the fruits of his labor), Gibbons still had to win the legal right to bring his steamboats into New York without license from the Monopoly. Ogden, who had used every other device to halt the competition on the Raritan, finally brought a case in federal court. Eventually the matter came before the United States Supreme Court, where the Gibbons case was presented by Daniel Webster and young William Gibbons. Webster made one of his greatest, most impassioned pleas. The court, led by Chief Justice John Marshall, ruled that no state had the right to grant such exclusive franchises for steamboat lines and Gibbons was free to compete now, legally.

After that court victory, Van Derbilt became the leading captain of the Gibbons line. He had brought his brother Jacob to pilot for him on the *Bellona*. When Jake learned steamboating, Corneel arranged for the younger Van Derbilt to have a boat of his own. He also brought Sophia's sister's husband, one of the Van Pelts, into the Gibbons line as a captain, and when he and Sophia later gave up Bellona Hall, the Van Pelts took over. Corneel always took care of his relatives.

In 1826, when Thomas Gibbons died, Corneel was virtually in charge of the steamboat line. Before long, he was offered part ownership or the chance to buy the whole line. But the price was too high, so Corneel began to look elsewhere, and to make even bigger plans.

From Gibbons, Van Derbilt had learned the secret of competition: give good service and cut rates when the fight is on, and make up the loss in other ways. During the fight with Ogden, when Corneel was charging only 12½ cents for the $4.00 trip to New York, the prices of meals and drinks in the *Bellona's* bar were raised more than enough to cover the losses on fare.

As he made ready to go into business for himself, Van Derbilt surrounded himself with friends and relatives whose loyalty he knew he could trust. He had a knack for inducing loyalty, he was a master of a hundred little tricks; he paid his men promptly on Saturday night, and they knew they would be paid on the dot, if the captain had to sell one of his horses to meet the payroll. Corneel's captains, then and later, ran their ships as they wished. As long as they conformed to his over-all policies, he did not interfere, and he did not look too closely into their personal affairs as long as his boats and ships made enough profit to suit him.

Even while Corneel continued to work for Gibbons, he put his own steamboat on the waters of New York harbor, a tiny chugging steamer called the *Caroline*. She ran as Corneel had run his periaugers in the beginning, wherever there was money to be made.

Corneel now worked for the Gibbons line in his own way, which meant he was not tied to a schedule. He ran many excursion trips, such as the "cotillion party" he carried on board the shiny, new *Bolivar* on July 10, 1827. They sailed at 7:30 P.M. to tour the bay, and returned to Manhattan's Whitehall slip at eleven. Or Corneel night-sailed any one of the half-dozen boats that were now in the Gibbons fleet, including the newest and best, the *Thistle*. When he did, let competitors beware!

Van Derbilt had built a remarkable record as a steamboat captain in a fast and risky trade. Gibbons, like the other owners, built his wooden boats less with an eye to the thickness of safety and more to the slimness of speed and economy. The boilers of all— the *Bellona*, the *Thistle*, and the rest—were primitive and tiny, usually overheated, and they showed an alarming tendency to explode without notice. This danger was not reduced by the habit of Van Derbilt and the other captains who tied down both the whistle and the safety valve when racing so no steam could escape, no matter how great the pressure in the boilers.

The wheels of Corneel's paddle-wheel steamers were located right amidships, at the level of the passenger decks, and the boilers were directly below deck, giving the shortest possible drive shaft and the greatest possible danger to life and limb. During the Marquis de Lafayette's triumphal tour, the good nobleman had nearly foundered when a similar steamboat carrying him down the Ohio River ran afoul of a snag. The snag tore the bottom out of the steamboat and sank the craft in a matter of minutes. Lafayette and his party escaped through the ladies' cabin. The Marquis accepted the narrow escape with his usual aplomb, but it took as brave a man to ride a steamboat in those days as to run one.

Smaller boats, such as the *Bellona* and the *Thistle*, were far more crude than the big river boats. The *Thistle* boasted both a ladies' cabin and a general cabin. The former was furnished with some regard to taste and comfort, including lace curtains, but the fittings of the latter consisted of wooden benches and a handy saloon bar. The *Bellona* had no private accommodations, and the passengers were herded together, without life preservers, to take their chances.

One time, when Van Derbilt was master of the *Thistle*, he raced the rival *Legislature* of the Monopoly line. The *Thistle's* overheated boiler burst during the race, scalding a handful of passengers and killing one man. An incident of this kind gave a steamboat commander a bad name, and no man could afford to have many such accidents. But Van Derbilt did not have many accidents. He was too careful for that and he was also lucky, even when he defied the laws of physics as well as those of New York.

After the Monopoly's grip on New York City had been broken, Van Derbilt could have avoided further trouble just by minding his own affairs. But with all else, he liked a joke, even if when it backfired he was apt to lose his temper. One day Corneel docked the *Thistle* in New York in the space allotted to the *Legislature*. Corneel was playing a joke on the captain of the rival steamer, but when that captain called in the harbor master, Corneel bridled and flatly refused to move. He did not move, either. The *Legislature* had to find another berth that day. Before the angry men could get a court order to arrest him, Corneel was gone.

The law? Van Derbilt grinned at the law. "What do I care for the law?" he said. "I got the power, h'ain't I?" Money, he was discovering, now that he had enough to please him, was important only because its wise use brought power.

In 1829, after Corneel refused to buy the line from William Gibbons, at Gibbons's price, the new owner began to look around for another buyer. Finally, when Van Derbilt made the definite decision to go into business for himself, Gibbons sold to the Ogden group. Corneel promptly put his own opposition boat on the New Brunswick route and cut the fare in half. The old line cut back to $1.25. Van Derbilt then retorted with an advertisement in the newspapers in behalf of his new company (which he called the Despatch Line):

"Travellers by the Despatch Line can be comfortably accommodated, avoiding the pressure of a crowd of ten-shilling passengers."

His *Caroline* was no more luxurious than the Ogden boats, but Van Derbilt made the passengers think she was, and he gave his competitors as much cause for worry with such tactics as he ever had when he worked for Gibbons. But after a few months of competition with Ogden, Corneel felt the yearning to move on into New York's greater potential market. To do so, he sold out to his competitors.

With the *Caroline* and $30,000—part of it saved in the years he worked for Gibbons and part of it a reward for his agreement to leave the area to Ogden—he packed a weeping Sophia and a handful of wide-eyed youngsters aboard his steamboat and said good-by to New Brunswick forever.

7

THE COMMODORE

In the fall of 1829 Abell and Dunscomb's foundry on Water Street in New York City exhibited a locomotive engine imported from England. This particular engine had been brought to the United States to draw freight over the new Delaware and Hudson canal, to connect two parts of the waterway that were separated by high ground. The canal and the locomotive were symbolic of the period and future in American transportation; this was the short period in which they complemented one another.

There were ten million whites and two million slaves in America; two hundred thousand people lived in New York City alone. Always a commercial town, New York had been forced to an about-face by the tariff of 1828, a triumph of the manufacturers over the commercial interests. The new high tariff on manufactures from abroad put a sharp crimp in the business of the mercantile houses that owned their own ships and traded briskly with the English market. The ocean-going sailing ships were too big and slow for the coastal trade, and while the merchants recovered their aplomb quickly enough to bring New York to the fore as a center for the distribution of American manufactures, the future of shipping lay with the fast, maneuverable steamboats, and the man who owned a steamboat had no difficulty finding goods to haul in it.

Passengers flocked to the steamboats as well. The old sailing sloops had changed little from the days of Alexander Hamilton, who had noted ruefully in a letter to his wife in New York that he had missed the coach from Philadelphia and would have to trust himself to the fortunes of the wind. The steamer *Chancellor Livingston* had steamed from New York to Providence in the remarkable time of seventeen and a half hours. Steamers made the trip from New York to Albany in nineteen hours; it had taken the old sailing vessels nine days to fight the tides and currents of the Hudson.

All this speed made the nation seem to grow much smaller. The remote spa of Saratoga Springs became truly accessible to the New York carriage trade in the summer. Philip Hone, retired mayor of New York, now spent the months of July and August at Saratoga, carrying his family and his own barouche and horses upriver by steamer to Albany, then driving the rest of the way.

The New York to which the Vanderbilts came in 1829 was much changed. The old Dutch architecture had almost completely given way to modernism, and modernism at this date meant buildings of warm, rich, brown Jersey freestone. Old John Jacob Astor had become the greatest and richest landlord in New York, a pioneer in the development of the nineteen-year lease, by which a tenant took land at a low rent but built his own building on it. At the end of the lease both land *and* building reverted to the owner. Astor was responsible for the changing face of New York in another way: he reasoned that the more tenants one could cram into an acre of land the better, so he broke his parcels into long, narrow lots with only twenty-five feet of street frontage, and faced with such cramming, New York began to rise in the air.

Vanderbilt was just thirty-five years old when he ferried his growing family and meager belongings to New York City and set out to beard the lions of transportation. As wife Sophia feared, everything about the new life was to be different. Even the name was undergoing its final change from the original Dutch van der Bilt to the modern American Vanderbilt. Few men would now know Vanderbilt as Corneel, and fewer would have the temerity to call him the familiar name to his face. For this Cornelius Vanderbilt was a modern man, an employer, a man who was changing with his times.

Poor Sophia! She would never be a great lady, and she knew it.

The family had long afforded a carriage, but Sophia never got quite used to such luxury. She was made for scrubbing and bearing and tending babies. She was painfully shy and constantly embarrassed by her dumpy figure and lack of schooling. Yet the carriage and the spirited horses were the only overt symbol of Vanderbilt's growing personal wealth. The family, now nearly a dozen strong, moved from one shabby house to another; from Stone Street to Madison Street, and then to East Broadway. The first two children, Phoebe Jane and Ethelinda, had secured most of their education in New Brunswick at the common school. Not so with the third child, William Henry (named for William Henry Harrison, a Vanderbilt hero), who was his father's apparent heir, although from the beginning Cornelius Vanderbilt did not waste affection on the chunky figure of his son. Nevertheless, William's education was to be several cuts above that of his father, reflecting the family's leap in social status. William was sent to the grammar school maintained by Columbia University, where he began to receive some infusion of culture and a better knowledge of higher arithmetic than his father had ever taken from books. The son turned into a bookkeeper, to his father's disgust. William Henry showed a fine head for figures—and absolutely no feeling for the shipping business.

The other children were even more disappointing to their virile father. Emily, Eliza, Sophia, Mary Alicia, Catherine Juliet, Marie Louise, and Frances grieved Vanderbilt because they were girls. Cornelius Jeremiah, born in 1825 at New Brunswick, was a true source of sorrow both to father and mother, for he was an epileptic, a grim reminder of the advice Phebe Hand had given against the marriage of cousins. Weak and sickly, from an early age Cornelius Jeremiah was given to epileptic fits. The growing distaste his father showed for him brought forth in Cornelius Jeremiah a dishonesty of spirit that angered Cornelius even more than his son's physical weakness. To top it off, like his older brother, Cornelius Jeremiah was to develop a fine head for figures, too, but figures of quite a different kind.

Even if Captain Vanderbilt had been more inclined to the pleasures of the home than those of the stable, he had little time in these years to devote to Sophia and the children. He had examined the competitive situation of steamboating on both the Hudson River and Long Island Sound. He decided to try both. First he selected the New York–Peekskill run, an easy day's round trip, and that was important because he had neither the big boats nor the resources necessary to go into expensive overnight cruising.

For such a young man, Vanderbilt had already established a fearsome reputation as a competitor. When he put the little 70-foot *Caroline* on the Peekskill run in 1829, the gentlemanly Robert Livingston Stevens, descendent of two of the nation's best families, withdrew from the route altogether since Vanderbilt's rate cutting was known so well along the Hudson. As noted, the Stevens-Ogden interests of New Jersey had already bought him off the New Brunswick–New York run.

The next year Vanderbilt bought his old *Bellona* and the much larger *General Jackson,* and began to expand his river runs.

One of Vanderbilt's regular passengers on the Peekskill service was Daniel Drew, a young man from Putnam County, New York, who had begun life in circumstances as humble as Vanderbilt's own. Now in his early thirties, three years younger than Vanderbilt, Drew had settled in New York at the Bull's Head Tavern on Third Avenue. The Bull's Head belonged to Henry Astor, John Jacob's brother, who had first been a camp follower of the Hessians in America and then a butcher. Drew and Astor became acquainted when Drew went into the drover's trade, buying cattle in the north and west and bringing them to market on New York's Bowery. Drew once outwitted Henry Astor completely when the younger man brought a scrawny, grass-fed herd to New York, stopped just outside the town, fed the herd all the salt the cattle would eat, and sent a message on to Henry to tell him to expect a fine herd of fat cattle to arrive that day. At noon, Drew stopped to water the thirsty cattle and a little later drove his beeves into the pens at the Bull's Head, bellies puffed out and looking as fat as cattle can be. Henry paid a top three cents a pound for a thousand gallons of water that day.

Astor exploded in his heavy German accent when he learned he had bought "watered stock"—and that is one story of the coining of the graphic term, which was later used in Wall Street to describe the technique by which Drew and Vanderbilt built their fortunes.

Even as a young man Drew had a prematurely wizened face with craggy features of the style of President Andrew Jackson: thin, mean lips and heavily lined cheeks that fit a melancholy temperament. He was given to praying piously in places of Methodist Episcopal worship, but also to solitary bouts of drunkenness. He would lock himself in an overheated hotel room, close all the blinds, and drink until unconscious.

Drew dressed most often in black: a high waistcoat that concealed most of his linen, somber coat and trousers. The tall, ascetic look he practiced belied Drew's rodent acquisitiveness. All this temperament was remarkable in a stringbean who looked the pillar of a church (which he became) and not the unscrupulous manipulator (which he was).

Riding the Vanderbilt boats up the river to Drewscliff, his home at Carmel, New York, Drew became intrigued by the possibilities for huge profits in the steamboat business. He had already built a sizable fortune, and had established the banking house of Drew, Robinson and Company on Wall Street. Here he could and did speculate in every conceivable commodity and business in the New York market.

Drew's opportunity in steamboating came in the summer of 1831, out of a disaster that befell Cornelius Vanderbilt and his brother Jake.

The Peekskill trade had become so lucrative that Vanderbilt had replaced a smaller boat with the *General Jackson*. She was 114 feet long and 22 feet wide, a respectable size for a day boat on the river. Jake had followed Cornelius into the river trade and was now his brother's most trusted captain and a junior partner.

Naturally he commanded the *General Jackson*, the pride of the tiny Vanderbilt fleet.

On June 7 Jake took the steamboat up the Hudson on his regular run. When his engineer reported that the boiler was overheating, across from Grassy Point, near Haverstraw, Captain Jake stopped the boat to blow off steam and thus relieve the pressure on the boiler.

The blowing was under way when suddenly the weakened boiler gave up altogether and exploded into the blue sky, carrying the engineer and eleven unfortunate passengers with it. The blast was so great it blew the bottom completely out of the *General Jackson*. Luckily the water was shallow and she held together well enough to be brought back to New York for repairs.

Ship repair was an expensive matter. Neither now nor at any other time did Vanderbilt ever carry insurance on his steamboats or ships. He preferred to carry the risk himself and keep the insurance premiums to pay for the infrequent accidents to his craft. But this repair job strained Vanderbilt's slender resources, and it was important that the *General Jackson* be put back into profitable service quickly. After the Haverstraw incident, Vanderbilt realized that the *General Jackson* might be less than popular on the Peekskill run, at least until the graves of the scalded were covered with grass, so he sent Jake south to try the waters of Virginia—and the wily Daniel Drew made preparations to go into competition on the Peekskill run.

On October 24, Jake appeared at Norfolk, Virginia, in the refurbished *General Jackson*, after a twenty-nine-and-a-half hour passage from New York. An advertisement in the Norfolk newspapers announced reassuringly that the steamboat was "copper fastened, coppered, with a low pressure engine and a first class new boiler." Jake set up at the wharf and began running from Norfolk to Richmond. He left Norfolk every Tuesday, Thursday, and Saturday at 7:00 A.M.; Richmond every other day but Monday at 7:30 A.M.

It was a good plan, but the reputation of the *General Jackson* had preceded her and the passengers stayed away by the hundreds; three weeks later Jake gave up. As a last-gasp try he began a series of excursion trips to the scenic shores of Old Point Comfort, at 25 cents a head.

A quarter of a dollar—that was just what Daniel Drew was charging for the whole trip from New York to Peekskill. When Vanderbilt's *General Jackson* left the Hudson, speeded by the acidulous comments of the press, Drew bought into a boat called the *Water Witch* to compete for the river traffic. Cornelius Vanderbilt put on his newest boat, the *Cinderella*, and started cutting rates. Drew retaliated with a publicity campaign among the upstate farmers. Newspapers, fliers, and rumormongers spread a prediction of Vanderbilt's evil intention of securing a monopoly and then wringing the sweat out of the farmers. That first season Drew's *Water Witch* lost $10,000 but Daniel Drew proclaimed that he was in the steamboat business to stay.

Vanderbilt finally bought Drew off for cash; then he took on the Hudson River Association, a cartel of steamboat operators who had banded together to preserve the river's peace and their rates. Dean Richmond, boss of the Albany branch of the Democratic party, and an old river man, as profane and tough as Vanderbilt himself, led the association, but the cartel, burdened with many different minds and many interests, was no match for the single-minded Vanderbilt. Within a few months the Association was glad to buy Vanderbilt off the river in turn and to pay him a monthly fee to keep his boats out of their Hudson territory.

The blackmail arrangement was quite satisfactory to Vanderbilt since there was plenty of water in Long Island Sound, and the economy of New York was better than ever. Foreign commerce, which had suffered under Andrew Jackson's tariff of '28, was thriving again by 1832. Sea-going ships were worth half again as much as they had been two years before, and, more important to Vanderbilt, freight loadings and rates were nearly doubled and manufacturers in the New England states along the Atlantic shore were fully employed and their business was growing despite the return of cheap imports.

Business, and the transportation business in particular, was booming in New York. Virginians just would not ride that Yankee boat with the blow-out boiler, and, at 25 cents a head, Captain Jake's business in Norfolk was terrible. He was losing money on every passenger, and not to competition either.

Captain Jake left the Norfolk run to the natives of Virginia and brought the *General Jackson* back to New York. This time, however, Cornelius sent them east on the Sound to Norwich, Connecticut, on a service that also stopped at Saybrook, New London, and later at Sag Harbor, Long Island. Vanderbilt also brought the other boats of his growing fleet to the waters of the Sound, leaving the Hudson and the Hudson River Association to the tender mercies of Daniel Drew.

For Drew, when he saw Vanderbilt going off the river, felt no further obligation to keep his promise to refrain from competition, and he put two boats on the river against the Association. Vanderbilt did not care. Eventually Drew forced the Association to take him in as a director. Then Drew installed a competing boat on the river in the name of a dummy company, and did so much harm to what was now his own business that his fellow directors voted to negotiate with the troublesome "stranger." Thereupon Drew wangled the job of negotiating with himself. He persuaded the other directors of the Association to buy off the outsider for $8000 more than they thought was necessary, pocketed the money and promptly abandoned the Association, using its own money to buy steamboats to compete. A few months later he founded the People's Line—which, despite its name, stood for everything *but* the people's interests.

The difference between Vanderbilt and Drew was that Drew was in the trade for everything he could get on a quick deal—and that only. It was a difference that was to separate them all their lives, for Vanderbilt was out to build a transportation empire and to do everything that effort implied. Their paths were to cross often in the years to come, but how different were to be their ends!

Vanderbilt's competition in the steamboat business on Long Island Sound was tough, but it was business competition, not chicanery. The coast line between Providence and New York City is ragged and dotted with ports that then were eminently suited to the shallow drafts of the steamboats, and in the new prosperity there was enough business from the many manufacturing towns to support all the relatively few steamboats that plied the coastal waters.

Yet New Englanders, and even the citizens of New York's Westchester County, did not look with total pleasure on the steamer traffic because it brought too many undesirable characters from New York to the country.

In the summer of 1832, as Sophia and the children sweltered in Manhattan, Cornelius Vanderbilt noted the growing revenues of his boats in the Sound trade with a satisfaction that helped him forget the heat. But early in July a Mrs. Fitzgerald and her two children were found dead in their apartment at 75 Cherry Street, and first police and then the doctors came to investigate.

Cholera!

The newspapers spread that fearful word up and down the city's streets. In a few days fear turned to panic, and the well to do began to leave the city. They bought passage by train and boat to every conceivable stopping place outside the ring of death that surrounded their island. They left their homes to rats and looters; doors unlocked, furniture askew, valuables strewn about in their escape from the dreadful sickness of the East. To New Jersey, to Westchester up the Hudson, to the eastern tip of Long Island, to the surf-driven shores of Far Rockaway they fled. The poor—more hardy, more phlegmatic, more used to death, and without the wealth to run away—stayed on for a fortnight.

July 14 brought 115 new cases of cholera and 66 deaths to New York.

July 15 brought 133 new cases and 74 deaths.

July 16, Monday, opened a new week of terror; 163 new cases and 94 deaths.

Then even the poor panicked. Men, women, and children scurried forth, jamming the roads, pushing their belongings before them in carts. The poor crowded into trains and the jitney services and steamboats, carrying children and food in their arms. Where were they going? Anywhere! Anywhere, just to get out of the sickening, death-dealing air of New York City.

Vanderbilt's steamers and others carried the crowds up the coast, into the cooler, more placid airs of New Rochelle, Rye, Larchmont, Greenwich, and beyond.

The steamboat business, it seemed, was better than ever, but only for a few trips. The latent antagonism of upstate and Connecticut citizens to city folk burst forth when the first cholera cases arrived with the New Yorkers. The citizens denied the steamboats the right to dock, and when the boats docked anyhow, the citizens with pitchforks and loaded rifles drove the boats from the docks. The steamers unloaded their passengers on deserted shores, far from the towns and villages, and there the hungry waifs of the plague wandered.

Vanderbilt did well in the panic. There was hardly a way to escape profit in the steamboat business if a captain knew his trade and did not tear the bottom out of his boat, for a hundred thousand people fled the city that summer and camped anxiously in the country until the end of August when the deaths stopped and life could once again begin.

To Vanderbilt, more profits meant more boats, so the Vanderbilt line grew quickly. New London was covered now by a Vanderbilt steamboat; his line ran to Providence and Stonington and to lesser ports of call along the Sound. But another development in transportation brought the threat of increased competition, more steamboats and more rate cutting: the new factor was the railroad. As railroads extended and speeded movement across the land, they usually ended at port towns, as did the Amboy and Camden road that opened on December 18, 1832. The Amboy and Camden connected with steamboats at both ends, and revolutionized, once again, the trip from New York to Philadelphia. A passenger who left New York on a steamboat for Amboy at six-thirty in the morning could be in Philadelphia by two o'clock in the afternoon— having traveled by boat, train, and boat—in seven and a half hours.

It was a fast trip, but also one that carried its own inconveniences and a new kind of danger. On one run a spark from a locomotive fell on the baggage car and set fire to a lady's bandbox. The high wind slashed through the slats of the baggage car, spread the fire to the rest of the baggage, and most of the train was destroyed before the locomotive could be stopped. Two gentlemen from Philadelphia lost all their clothes on that trip, and somehow a shipment of $60,000 in gold that was en route to a North Carolina bank was misplaced in the confusion and never again seen.

The next year that same Amboy and Camden Railroad nearly finished Cornelius Vanderbilt. He was traveling to Philadelphia one day when an axle broke as the engine was speeding at twenty-five miles an hour; the train jumped the track near Hightstown and crashed down a 30-foot embankment. Nearly everyone in Vanderbilt's compartment was killed. A man lay next to Vanderbilt with his breastbone turned up over his face, and Vanderbilt suffered several broken ribs and a punctured lung. The rescuers pulled him out of the shattered compartment and carried him to a cottage near the railroad. There he stayed for four weeks until he could be moved. His physician, Dr. Jared Linsly, arrived on the scene the day after the accident, bringing Sophia's sister, Mrs. Robbins, who nursed Vanderbilt until he was out of danger. Four weeks later, after Vanderbilt had been patched up, he was taken by horsecar and steamer to his house in New York, where he was sent to bed to finish recuperation.

They did not keep Vanderbilt in bed for long. The next year, 1834, he was back in business, stronger than ever. He was running the *Chancellor Livingston* on the New York–Providence route despite an occasional accident, such as that in which an inexperienced pilot ran down the rival *Washington* off Milford, Conn., killing one frightened passenger who fell between the hulls of the two ships. The number of accidents, as well as injuries to passengers (and mostly, the expense to the line), persuaded Vanderbilt to stop the usual practice of serving carafes of whisky and brandy on the dining tables of the *Chancellor Livingston*. The howl from passengers that accompanied this decision was only slightly muffled when the line offered carafes of red table wine instead.

Vanderbilt's narrow escape on the Amboy and Camden line did make him wary of railroads, but he could not avoid seeing the new development in transportation—the combined rail and sea voyage. The New York–Providence–Boston trip was an excellent example of this change. Providence, the capital of Rhode Island, became a stopping point on the route from New York to Boston when the Boston and Providence Railroad was completed. Passengers could travel by steamer to Providence, then board a train and avoid the rough and dangerous waters of Point Judith outside Cape Cod. But the railroad was not willing to turn all the revenue for the trip from Providence to New York over to an outsider, so the railroad promoters started their own line of steamers. In 1835, to meet the competition, Cornelius Vanderbilt built his most ambitious steamboat to date—the *Lexington*. She was the fastest craft afloat on Long Island Sound, and the most luxurious. The *General Jackson* had grown old and rickety by now, so Vanderbilt gave command of his new ship to Captain Jake, who in 1834 had married and settled down—as much as a Vanderbilt was likely to settle down.

Marriage certainly did not slow the fire-eating Jake. On her first trip on June 1, 1835, the *Lexington* steamed from New York to Providence in 12 hours 28 minutes, to set a new record. That was the opening of a Vanderbilt campaign to run the railroad line off the Sound.

The established fare was $5.00 for the passage from Providence to New York. Cornelius cut the fare in half, as usual. But this time he cut with a flair; the Vanderbilt line offered a round trip for the price of a one-way trip—the first steamboat excursion fare. Naturally Cornelius did not expect to lose money. As the fare went down, again the price of drinks and meals on the steamer went up, so the cost to the traveler was the same as it had been on full-fare trips—or at least the total income of the ship for the trip was the same. And most steamboat passengers drank, if only to keep their courage up.

The railroad met the competition, so the following year the *Lexington* ran at $3.00 per trip. Then another steamboat company came in to compete for the business, and Vanderbilt and the railroad ganged up on the outsider like a pair of squabbling brothers joining forces to fight a stranger. They cut the fare to $1.00 until the third company abandoned the route, and then returned to their own fight.

While Jake was running the *Lexington*, the competitive company advertised that its *Bunker Hill* would "leave five minutes after the *Lexington* to prevent the reckless destruction of property and to protect the passengers," for the reckless Jake would as soon ram another steamboat as look at it in those days.

It was in 1837 that the press honored Cornelius with the title "Commodore." At that time he was operating the greatest fleet on Long Island Sound, and was to become the greatest steamboat operator in America, so the title was well-enough deserved. It stuck, and forever after, Vanderbilt was so called. Yet the press was indiscriminate in handing out titles; other men with far less renown or ability were known by the same name. Vanderbilt became famous because he outlasted and outshone them all.

Vanderbilt moved the *Lexington* onto the Stonington route after the Providence and Stonington Railroad was completed in 1838, and Stonington, tucked behind Fishers Island in Long Island Sound, became one of the most important towns in all Connecticut. A company called the Transportation Company ran both ships and trains on the route. Then a third competitor entered the field—the Atlantic Steamship Company—which had built a 500-ton boat called the *John W. Richmond*. The Atlantic line boasted that the *Richmond* was even faster than Vanderbilt's *Lexington*, and the Transportation Company, which had nothing in the class of either steamboat, finally offered Vanderbilt $60,000 for the *Lexington* if she could beat the *Richmond*. She could and did, so Vanderbilt sold, after raising the price. The Transportation Company still had a good bargain until the *Lexington* caught fire one night off Eaton's Neck, Long Island, and sank with a loss of a hundred lives.

In 1838, when he was entering the Stonington route, Vanderbilt still did not neglect business closer to home. That year he bought a half interest in the Staten Island ferry and began to compete with his cousin Oliver Vanderbilt. Cornelius and his new partner, Oroondates Mauran, wasted no time in getting the upper hand. They ran the *Samson*, the *Hercules*, and the *Bolivar* to Tompkinsville, Stapleton, and the Vanderbilt landing at Clifton. Oliver Vanderbilt, who owned the *Wave*, found that blood was not one drop thicker than water when Cornelius's money was at stake. One day, bringing the *Wave* in to shore, Oliver saw that his cousin had fenced the landing and dumped gravel on the dock. Oliver found another landing. Cornelius cut the Staten Island ferry fare from 25 cents to 6¼ cents. Oliver met the competition and stayed in business, and then renamed his line the Citizen's Line, told the public about his cousin's conduct, and appealed for public support. He was showing Cornelius that not all the troublesome

Vanderbilts stemmed from the one branch. Oliver remained in business, a thorn in the side of Cornelius and his strangely named partner (Mauran's mother had selected the name Oroondates from a book about the romantic Orient).

In 1839 Vanderbilt went into business with his old enemy Daniel Drew in what they called the New Jersey Steam Navigation company—not that they planned to confine their efforts to New Jersey waters. Shortly afterward they bought the Boston and New York Transportation Company, with which Vanderbilt had competed at Providence. Here Vanderbilt and Drew established a stormy business relationship that was to continue in one way or another for the next thirty years. As a result of the bargain Cornelius sent his first son, William Henry, to work for Drew in the investment firm of Drew, Robinson and Company. Vanderbilt had become an important power in the transportation business to command such attention from Drew, whose star was then shining brightly in the financial world. Yet in New York, while Cornelius was respected as a smart Dutchman who had made more than a half-million dollars, the family was socially unknown. The Beekmans and the Roosevelts, the Verplancks, and even the newly rich William Backhouse Astors were happy enough to ride a Vanderbilt investment, if they had a chance, or to take his money in a transaction, but in social affairs Cornelius Vanderbilt was ignored. It hurt even the thick-skinned Cornelius so much that in 1839 he decided to move home again, to build on the tract of land on Stapleton's Bay Street known on the island as "Corneel's Lot." William Henry took a lonely room in a private rooming house in Manhattan to continue his labors in the Drew financial company. Sophia, the girls, the miserable Cornelius Jeremiah, and proud Cornelius himself moved to a handsome mansion on Staten Island, overlooking the water, that he had built for $27,000. Sophia was delighted because she had never been happy in New York, and in the village atmosphere of Staten Island she was "somebody," the wife of the island's wealthiest citizen.

The new Vanderbilt house fit a wealthy citizen; it was built in the Gothic style, modified by a Grecian touch, Corinthian columns, and enough other foreign notes to give it the impressive air that passed for "European culture" in that day. The marble was Egyptian, the glass was French, and English workmen were brought to New York to build the staircase. The front door boasted a painting-on-glass of Vanderbilt's steamer the *Cleopatra,* a symbol of the source of Vanderbilt's wealth.

Cornelius Vanderbilt was home again—now the head of the family. Old Cornelius, his father, had died in 1832, leaving the gabled Dutch cottage and all his other possessions to Phebe Hand.

Corneel—Cornelius—the Commodore—he had come a long way in his forty-five years; he had achieved more in twoscore years than all the other Vanderbilts together in 260 years. But now he was just reaching the height of his powers, and he was about to go on to a new career in which he would make such a reputation for himself that few would remember he was once known as the king of Long Island Sound.

8

RATE CUTTING AND RAMPAGE

The early years of the 1840s were Sophia Vanderbilt's happiest. She was at home among people she could understand; her children were growing up as ladies and gentlemen, attending the fashionable Episcopal day school conducted by the Reverend William G. French. No one on Staten Island snubbed Sophia as had the haughty ladies of New York; her house was the showplace of the county, and her daughters were marrying extremely well for the children of self-made parents. Phoebe Jane married a business-man named J. M. Cross and went to live in New York. Ethelinda married Daniel B. Allen, who was to become Vanderbilt's princi-pal assistant in the steamship business. Eliza married George Os-good, a broker in Wall Street. Emily was to marry W. K. Thorn, a millionaire in his own right; Sophia to marry Daniel Torrance of a wealthy Montreal family; Marie Louise to marry Horace F. Clark, a lawyer who handled many of Vanderbilt's affairs. Mary Alicia made a more romantic match with the well-to-do but foreign Nicholas LaBau. Catherine Juliet, after the death of her first love, was to marry Gustave LaFitte, and go with him to live in high style in his native France. Only sickly Frances was to remain un-married.

Sophia's dark, private tragedy was the loss of her husband's respect. Sophia had never really held Corneel's love except perhaps during those first few lusty years of marriage, but until this period Cornelius had let Sophia maintain her self-respect; until now he had always managed to maintain a fiction, at least, of connubial regularity. But living on the Staten Island that represented her victory and his defeat by the social lions of New York, Sophia found her victory empty, for Cornelius began to commute to New York on the Staten Island ferry he owned, and to come home only when conscience or his affection for the children spurred him. This was not every day.

Sophia was to give Cornelius one more satisfaction in their marriage. In 1842 she gave birth to their fourth son, whom they named George Washington—after the third boy who had died in infancy. George, alone among the Vanderbilt boys, was like his father; even as a baby he gave promise of the same strapping frame and strength of character, and as George grew, he became the pride of Vanderbilt's life, the one member of the family who could do no wrong.

William Henry, whose chubby figure and quiet ways had always offended his father, fell into complete disfavor. During the first year as a clerk in Drew's brokerage house William earned the princely sum of $150. The second year he was raised to twice that amount, the third to $1000 a year. Coming from stingy old Daniel Drew, this series of advances was success, of a sort, for the boy who had failed in his first job as a ship chandler's clerk, and had been discharged—by his father; but a bookkeeper's advancement in the financial community did not impress Cornelius, and he gave his son little encouragement or praise.

While the Vanderbilt family lorded it on Staten Island, William Henry sweated in his furnished room. Three years of clerking for Uncle Daniel Drew had left him little richer than before. He saved little—how could he? But when he was earning $19 a week, he decided to marry Maria Louisa Kissam, daughter of a Brooklyn minister. This marriage, however, was still a definite social lift for the Vanderbilts. The Kissams came from an old and respected New York family; a Kissam had been prominent in the social life of the town when it was the capital of the infant republic. The Brooklyn minister was poor now, to be sure, but his daughter brought a new, respectable tone to the Vanderbilt family.

Yet Vanderbilt would do nothing to help the young couple

and they bravely began married life in William Henry's furnished room. Sophia did what she could for William Henry and her new daughter-in-law but she had little control over the money that was spent in the house. Sophia's help consisted largely in smuggling goods and furnishings to Maria Louisa, and contributing the pocket money she was able to conceal from Cornelius's sharp eyes.

Finally, in the strain of the long hours of the countinghouse, William's health failed. His doctors were not specific about the illness, probably it was the nervousness of a son who was rejected by a highly successful but irritable father, but the doctors said William Henry must move to the open air if he wanted to live. William Henry reluctantly asked his father for help, but the help he received was scarcely magnanimous—just enough money to enable him to buy a farm on Staten Island, a farm of seventy acres on New Dorp Lane, between the old Moravian Church and the water, a house that was a sharp contrast to the mansion of Cornelius. William Henry and Louisa went to live in a shabby little farmer's shack with a lean-to kitchen. The Commodore felt this was perfectly proper, since as he grew older, he began to espouse self-help as ardently as he had always divorced himself from weakness. And being a self-made man, the Commodore had the usual feeling that his children were taking advantage of him, and should show some signs at least of being able to make their own way as he had his. He could not understand that William Henry's nervousness was something beyond the son's control, and certainly he had no inkling that he was probably the cause of all his son's worries.

Cornelius Jeremiah, now in late adolescence and a tireless delinquent, brought sorrow to his mother and endless shame and misery to Vanderbilt. The boy did badly at school, he lied and he cheated and he stole, and while some were inclined to be sympathetic because of his epilepsy, instinctively the Commodore knew that the disease had nothing to do with the weakness of character the boy exhibited. But he was not sure how much responsibility he, the Commodore, had for Cornelius Jeremiah's condition.

When the boy was twelve they had sent him to an insane asylum in Northampton, Massachusetts. Sharing the ignorance of the times, the Vanderbilts thought epilepsy was a form of insanity. Treatment consisted mostly of urging the boy to use his will power (of which he had none) to overcome the loathsome affliction.

The Northampton doctors gave young Vanderbilt the run of the Massachusetts village, although he returned daily to the institution for meals and care. But in the end they discharged him. There was nothing they could do, the doctors told the elder Vanderbilts, so Cornelius Jeremiah came home to worry his mother some more and to irritate Vanderbilt with his misdeeds. Yet Cornelius Vanderbilt sometimes exhibited a very different side of character. "I would give anything in the world if I could cure the boy," the Commodore once told an acquaintance.

Sophia knew that Cornelius's relations with his mother took the place of the normal confidence that exists between husband and wife. Sophia never knew what Cornelius planned to do and seldom dared to ask. Phebe Hand's interest was only maternal and casual, and perhaps that was why Cornelius went to her for advice and solace, as with the news that he was moving back to Staten Island. Shrewdly his mother had guessed then that Corneel had been defeated by the social leaders of New York, and he admitted it, but only to her. Only with Phebe Hand did Cornelius ever let down. Only she knew the importance he placed in money and the power it brought. Perhaps that was because alone among his family, Phebe Hand asked for nothing. Her wants were well met by the simple estate of her husband. Her very independence, unusual in Vanderbilt's family life, made her his confidante. Phebe felt sorry for Sophia, and interceded in behalf of her daughter-in-law when she could, but she felt that Corneel's family affairs were really none of her business, and Sophia's problem vis-à-vis her husband was that she never showed independence. Phebe Hand could do nothing about *that*.

Vanderbilt always respected independence where he found it. One day on his way to the one-room office in lower Manhattan, he drove from the Staten Island house to Vanderbilt Landing a little later than usual, to find one of his ferries just pulling out.

Captain Braisted, standing on the bridge of the ferry, saw his employer hurrying to the dock but did not give the order to reverse engines.

Crew members expected the captain to be looking for another berth the moment the ferry returned to Staten Island, but as the ferry churned its way slowly toward New York, Vanderbilt merely stood on his dock, leaning on his stick. And as the ship pulled away, the captain could see his employer, grim and silent, nodding his head slowly up and down in affirmation. Vanderbilt respected a man who had courage and stuck to his job. Captain Braisted knew he had nothing to fear.

Everything that had gone before was simply preparation for the decade of 1840, which marked the rise of Cornelius Vanderbilt's national power and reputation. Vanderbilt was in his forty-sixth year in 1840, still spare and youthful, still filled with the endless energy that had made him injure himself to pole his periauger across New York bay in time to win an impromptu race with young Van Duzer rather than to suffer defeat. From the Staten Island mansion Cornelius could look out across the waters to Manhattan, sure that a respectable number of the steamers docked there bore the Vanderbilt flag, that they worked daily to build the Vanderbilt empire, knowing that his fortune was growing every day. He would, in time, become the greatest shipping power of his day, and would build more than thirty ships and operate at least a hundred.

The steamboat *Cleopatra*, whose likeness graced the front door of the Vanderbilt mansion, was placed on the New York to Norwich route in 1840. That year Cornelius was operating again on the Hudson and in New Jersey. And at this period of his life, despite his scars from the Amboy and Camden wreck, Vanderbilt was beginning to take a lively interest in railroads, seeing them as adjuncts to his steamboat business. Railroads had begun to come of age—and, of them all, Vanderbilt was most interested in the New York and Harlem Railroad which dominated New York.

The railroad was one of the earliest chartered in 1831 to run from Prince Street north along the center line of Fourth Avenue as far as Harlem. Originally the operators had planned to run locomotives right through the center of Manhattan, but when two black fire-eaters blew up and another burned in the crowded area below Fourteenth Street, the city fathers intervened. Locomotives were banned within the built-up sections of the city for forty years thereafter, and the trains ran from the terminal at Center and Chambers streets to the edge of town under horse power.

New York's population had grown by 100,000 since Vanderbilt first came to live there in 1829. It was far too large a city to countenance in its center the threat to life and limb that railroad trains offered. There was danger enough to property and life in the new gas mains that ran beneath the city streets, without asking for locomotive explosions. Yet the ban on railroads in the crowded city created a new set of problems in mass transportation.

Two thirds of the island was covered by houses, but the transportation system had not kept pace, and the rush-hour traffic was so startling that it struck terror into the hearts of strangers, if not the natives (who were used to it). Morning and evening were bad enough, but midday was worst—from twelve to three, when the businessmen went home to dinner and returned to business. In addition to the horse-drawn cars of the railway, two- and four-horse stages charged up and down the streets, carrying twenty-five thousand patrons every day. The town was overcrowded, the traffic vile, and the cost of transportation outrageous: prices on the public buses were 37½ cents for a ride of a mile and 50 cents for two miles.

But Vanderbilt did not first turn to his own New York when his eyes rested on the business of land transportation. He followed the wakes of his steamboats instead. Vanderbilt and Daniel Drew became directors of the Stonington and Boston Railroad; it served their interests as proprietors of the steamboat line that met the railhead, and by 1847 they controlled that railroad. Vanderbilt developed a healthy interest in the Long Island Railroad as well, when he learned that the road planned to run trains as far east as Greenport, the fishing and shipbuilding center on the northern pincer of Long Island's eastern claw. In 1844 the Long Island's railhead was brought to Greenport, and that year Vanderbilt secured enough financial interest in the railroad to be elected to the board of directors. One term as a director was enough for him to establish Vanderbilt steamboats as the carriers for Long Island freight and passengers bound for Connecticut. The Long Island trains left Brooklyn at 8:00 A.M. and by early afternoon passengers could transfer at Greenport to the *Cleopatra,* the *Worcester,* or the *New Haven,* all Vanderbilt steamers, which crossed Long Island Sound to make train connections at Norwich for Worcester, and Stonington for Boston.

On the board of directors of the Long Island Railroad, Vanderbilt found himself in close contact with George Law, son of an Irish immigrant, who had made *his* first million running horsecars on the streets of New York. Law was a partner in Daniel Drew's People's Line that ran up the Hudson River. Wherever one turned in the transportation business, the figures of Vanderbilt, Drew, and Law seemed to emerge.

In his own right, George Law owned the *Oregon,* reckoned by most students of steamboats to be the fastest and most luxurious steamer afloat. She was 330 feet long, with a 35-foot beam, and she could steam at twenty-five miles an hour on the choppy waters of the Sound. The *Oregon* weighed a thousand tons and could carry six hundred passengers; the promenade deck alone ran forward from the cabin on the main deck for 200 feet to the bowsprit.

The main cabin of the *Oregon* held two hundred berths laid end to end. It might not be luxurious for the common passengers to be so crowded, but it was profitable for the operator of the line. Each berth was warmly covered with Mackinaw blankets, Marseilles quilts (with the name of the steamer stitched into each quilt), bolsters, pillows, and soft linen. The curtains that lined the windows were made of richly tinted *satin de laine.*

In the dining rooms the service was the finest of French china and star-cut glass, and the silver was Prince Albert plate. Off the main cabin were located a barbershop for the unshaven and a washroom which was equipped with washbowls cut from marble slabs.

The ladies' cabin extended 70 feet along the upper deck. Seven tiers of berths lined the walls, and there were three private staterooms on each side of the ship, painted in white enamel. Raised flowers of *boiserie* decorated the gilt pillars, and an intricate Swiss clock hung above the central door, set in stained glass.

Above, on the top deck, the *Oregon* boasted sixty private staterooms for those willing to pay for the last word in luxurious travel; three of these staterooms were double, and one, which held an oversized French bed, was fitted out as a bridal suite.

Throughout, the *Oregon* was furnished with superb rich drapes and carvings. Mirrors in gilt frames reflected from nearly every wall. George Law had spent $30,000 on the *Oregon's* furniture alone.

Law boasted that his steamboat could outrun anything on the Sound, and he once raced Vanderbilt's swift *Traveller* to prove it. The *Traveller* was the pride of the Commodore's fleet, not as luxurious as the *Oregon*, but not as heavy either. The two boats finished their twenty-mile race in 57 minutes, in a dead heat, so both Law and Vanderbilt claimed victory. Law then issued a general challenge—to steamboats on the Sound and on the Hudson. He would meet any comer who thought he might be able to beat the *Oregon* in a race.

The Commodore, who refused to play second fiddle to anyone, took up the challenge in 1847 in behalf of his newest and most expensive steamboat, the *Cornelius Vanderbilt*. He and Law each put up $1000 for a purse, but the prize money was the least of it. There was a million dollars' worth of publicity value in the race for the victor, for New Yorkers took a healthy interest in steamboating, and a continually full passenger list would be the real fruit of victory.

The race between the *Oregon* and the *Cornelius Vanderbilt* was to be run on the Hudson River, not on the Sound. Law took personal charge of his steamer, and the Commodore took command of his *Cornelius Vanderbilt* from the moment the two boats whistled and started off from the foot of Manhattan Island. The steamers churned along the muddy river, bow to bow, until they reached the turn at Croton Point, some forty miles up the Hudson. Here, the Commodore, in his excitement, began issuing orders and countermanding them so quickly that the engineer could not understand what was happening, and feared some disaster was

about to strike, so he stopped the engine altogether. A roaring
Vanderbilt had it started again in a moment, but the *Oregon*
had her advantage and the *Cornelius Vanderbilt* smoked home in
the *Oregon's* wake, Vanderbilt cursing and shaking his fist at the
laughing figure of Law on the other ship.

Just below Yonkers Law's smirk faded to a nervous grin when
his engineer reported that the *Oregon* was almost out of fuel, with
a quarter of the distance yet to go. Law ordered his crew to smash
the furniture, tear down the paneling—to find anything and everything that would burn and throw it in the firebox. Thus fueled
with a good portion of the $30,000 in furnishings, the *Oregon*
never lost her advantage, and she won the race handily.

It was like Napoleon's defeat in Russia, Vanderbilt told his
friend Charles Haswell: his first loss.

That statement was not strictly true. Cornelius had been torn
by an even greater conflict the year before, in a personal matter,
an affair in which the entire family except William Henry had
been allied against him.

After five years of commuting, by 1846, the Commodore had
become thoroughly sick of the Staten Island countryside. He was
worth several million dollars; he commanded the respect of Wall
Street; he had gained entrance to satisfactory clubs; and he felt no
need to apologize to anyone, so he decided he would live among his
peers.

Consequently Cornelius commissioned the building of a $55,000
mansion at 10 Washington Place, in what is now the fringe of
Greenwich Village. It was to be a four-story brick house, not
pretentious as New York mansions went, but quite large enough
and quite respectable for a man of Vanderbilt's means and tastes.
The important part, from Vanderbilt's point of view, was the commodious stable area in the rear of the mansion, where he would
keep his horses and carriages.

Calmly enough, Cornelius announced his decision to move the
family back to New York—and Sophia went into hysterics. His
wife's attitude was understandable enough to Vanderbilt, for she
was going through the change of life. He sympathized in a way
and reasoned with her, refraining from swearing as much as possi-

ble, but Sophia was inconsolable. She had been uprooted twice: once from Staten Island to go to New Brunswick; once again after she had made friends in New Brunswick, to live in the hell of New York. Whenever Cornelius brought up the matter of moving, Sophia burst into tears.

Cornelius had grown quite indifferent to Sophia's wishes, but for the sake of appearances he preferred to have her accept his judgment. When she dug in her heels and refused to move, Vanderbilt packed her off on a trip to the popular resort at Sharon Springs to think things over, and when she still refused to move, he sent her to Canada with daughter Ethelinda and her husband. The trip lasted several months, and as Sophia traveled, the Commodore's workmen installed the brown stone copings outside the Washington Place house, and he ordered new furnishings and carpets. The word came back that Sophia was still unreconciled, that she would never consent to move from the Staten Island house. The Commodore said, "All right then; come home."

So Mother and children came home to Staten Island, a disconsolate group. They were no sooner home than Cornelius clapped Sophia into Dr. McDonald's sanitarium at Flushing, then moved triumphantly into the house in New York.

The rumor, repeated even after Cornelius's death, was that he had taken more than a shine to his children's governess, a Miss Smith. Family members denied the rumor stoutly, but it persisted. The facts were elusive, and it was only known that when Sophia left the house, the governess fled, in the interest of her good name —which could mean anything. Nor would the governess return as long as Mrs. Vanderbilt was confined, although her return was demanded by Cornelius. The household must have a mistress, to supervise the cooking and the cleaning, so William Henry was called upon for help. He installed a niece of the Reverend Mr. Kissam, his father-in-law—a twenty-five-year-old girl—to be companion to Marie Louise, who was then just eighteen, not old enough to take the responsibility for the mansion in New York.

When other members of the family chided William on his choice of a young, unmarried girl, the Commodore's eldest son admitted he had taken the line of least resistance. His father was "bound to fall under the influence of some woman," William Henry said, and from his point of view it might better be someone he chose.

Miss Kissam remained in the house for several months, Sophia in the sanitarium. Ultimately Vanderbilt and Sophia compromised—Sophia agreed to live on Washington Place and Phebe Hand convinced her son of the unseemliness of the current arrangement. Sophia came home; Miss Kissam left.

After his wife's return to the family Vanderbilt spent less and less time at the house. If he had to keep up appearances, he still didn't have to put up with all that complaining. For recreation he drove a pair of fast trotters along the country roads outside the city limits. Perhaps his destination would be John Snediker's tavern on the Jamaica road, a house famous for its spring asparagus dinners; or he might go to Nick Vandyn's on the hill at Flatbush, to the Widow Bradshaw's place at 125th Street and Third Avenue, where the widow dispensed liquors, gossip, and her tasty chicken fricassee, or to Cato's roadhouse on the east side of New York City, where Vanderbilt met the most prominent horse fanciers of the day. Cato's place—an old mansion—was surrounded by tall trees and green lawns. Guests drove through the white fence and put up their rigs, then headed for the long bar or, on a pleasant afternoon for the veranda. There were races and bets any day at Cato's, and Cato himself sometimes drove a team in a race. Cato's was a place where the lords of the road met on equal terms, their millions forgotten for the moment in the heat of arguments over shape of fetlock and trotting pace.

Still, no one could accuse Vanderbilt of neglecting his chosen mission: the creation of a fortune that would put even John Jacob Astor's riches to shame. Old man Astor was doddering, he shook with ague and slobbered in his food. He was so feeble and so nearly blind that a manservant stood behind him at his meals to guide the quivering forkfuls into the old millionaire's mouth. Like Vanderbilt, Astor had tragedy in the family, but while William H. Vanderbilt had proved himself dull in his father's eyes, and Cornelius Jeremiah weak, Astor's heir and namesake had turned out to be actually feeble-minded, confined for nearly all his life in a house of his own, attended by servants and a physician. Yet where the failing Astor had been able to place most of his affairs in the hands of his second son, William Backhouse Astor, Vanderbilt was forced to turn to his sons-in-law. Daniel B. Allen, Ethelinda's husband, became a director of the Stonington rail line, as did William K. Thorn, Emily's husband. From his office in a high-gabled old house opposite the Bowling Green, Vanderbilt controlled an enormous shipping fleet, and he needed good men to manage his day-to-day affairs so that he could roam afield, searching for new ways to increase his fortune.

One way to make money was to watch the pennies. Not all the Vanderbilt steamers were as luxurious as the *Cornelius Vanderbilt*, nor did Vanderbilt worry about public complaint concerning the way he ran his steamers, as long as his competitors did not overwhelm him. Indeed, one of his boats, the *Bolivar*, was known as the slowest steamer on the Sound. The *Bolivar*, at a time when there was little steamer competition for New Haven traffic, was settled like a maiden aunt on that run. She was the same old Staten Island ferry, 120 feet long, but wheezy now. A resident of New Haven once wagered that he could drive a team of horses to New York faster than the *Bolivar* could steam there. He proved it, too, setting out at the same moment the old tub sailed, and casually waving her in at the New York dock at the end of the day.

But where it counted, Vanderbilt was ready to spend money, nor did he think always in terms of financial profit. On June 25, 1847, Vanderbilt footed the bill for a shipboard reception for President James K. Polk and some five hundred politicians, officials, and friends of the President. The Commodore placed his steamer the *Cornelius Vanderbilt* at the presidential disposal, took the bridge himself, and managed a five-hour excursion from Castle Gardens, on which all the drinks and food were on the house. There were other things in life besides money he had discovered; prestige was one of them.

The party for President Polk did not stem from any deep regard by Vanderbilt for the Democratic party. In all his life, Vanderbilt voted only twice, and one of those times was for Polk's Whig opponent, Henry Clay, in the election of 1844. Vanderbilt *had* been truly interested in the Clay campaign; at that time he was living in the Cleopatra mansion on Staten Island and he had arranged Clay meetings and processions on the island. When the Clay-Frelinghuysen forces staged a rally in New York, Vanderbilt brought a troop of horses and five hundred Staten Islanders to swell the parade, and he led the island contingent himself, astride one of his finest mounts.

Vanderbilt, in his finery, was always an imposing sight and as usual, on this day he drew the glances of the crowd, admiring for the most part. But there was no admiration in the black looks cast on the Whig procession by the Democrats. One self-appointed Democratic champion of that day was a gentleman by the name of Yankee Sullivan, a prizefighter of irascible kidney who kept a saloon on Chatham Street, just opposite City Hall Park on the line of march.

As the Whig procession passed by, Sullivan stepped into his doorway, surrounded by a gang of bibulous cronies who were too far gone in liquor to contemplate the odds, and outraged that the Whigs would dare march in the shadow of Tammany Hall.

Sullivan staggered out of his doorway, waving a hamlike fist and shouting that he could "whip any Whig on sight." Spying the meticulous Vanderbilt astride his prancing horse, Sullivan laughed and seized the reins. The frightened horse reared high, and Vanderbilt purpling, slashed Sullivan across the back with his whip and when the fighter continued to hang on, jumped off his horse and took after him.

Whether it was the drink, or the heat, or the surprise, the professional fighter seemed to be a tame rooster that day. Vanderbilt knocked Sullivan down and beat the fighter nearly senseless before he remembered who and where he was, mounted his horse, panting, and rode off.

Yankee Sullivan recovered from his beating but Henry Clay lost in November, in spite of the efforts of Vanderbilt and other loyal Whigs, but four years later, when Clay was ready to try again, Vanderbilt was again ready to support him.

On March 7, 1848, Vanderbilt gave a steamboat reception for Clay much like the one he had tendered President Polk: free transportation, free lunch, and free liquor, with the Commodore in personal charge, but Clay's second defeat, in the Whig convention of 1848, put an end to Vanderbilt's political interest.

"There's no future in politics," the Commodore told Chauncey Depew a few years later when Depew was trying to decide whether to accept a government appointment to be minister to Japan or a Vanderbilt appointment to become a railroad lawyer.

"Don't be a damned fool!" the Commodore said. "The railroads hold the future, not Japan."

Depew heeded those words, and never regretted it.

The Commodore disliked politics because, after 1848, he saw how great a part chance played in political success and how little hard work and ability counted. He was willing to take chances, but he was not willing to trust his fortunes to the slippery ground of public popularity.

Besides, after 1848 the Commodore had much else to occupy his mind; for one thing, in the summer of 1848 he developed a frightening heart condition that would have invalided a man with less courage. For no reason at all, his heart sometimes ran like a triphammer. Dr. Linsly treated him, gave him potions and packs to reduce the swelling in his legs that accompanied the heart trouble, and advised his patient to relax and take life easy.

The Commodore did nothing of the kind; he was not built to take life easy; he worked harder than ever and stayed up half the night playing whist at the Racket and Manhattan clubs. Privately estranged from Sophia now, it was rumored, but only rumored, that the Commodore had a succession of young mistresses, yet business occupied Vanderbilt's mind more than any of his vices. Intimates saw him often in frowning concentration in his office, poring over brightly colored maps that he shoved in the drawer before him when they entered the room. He kept the drawer locked, so no one knew what he was examining so carefully, or even what realm of affairs he had in mind.

The secret of his success, Vanderbilt once told a young reporter, was that he minded his own business, and never told anybody what he was going to do until he had done it. Every morning, Vanderbilt got up, ate his breakfast, which might be a lamb chop and a pair of egg yolks, drove down to the Bowling Green office, digested his newspaper reading and looked at his maps.

It was 1848 and gold had been discovered in California. The next year more than 750 ships cleared the Atlantic ports of the United States for San Francisco; 214 of these ships sailed from New York alone, and nearly a hundred thousand passengers arrived in San Francisco that year. There was no railroad across the continent and the wagon trails to the Pacific were spattered with fierce Indians, so in the interests of speed and safety the most sensible route west was the circuitous one by sea, around the southern tip of South America.

The early voyagers traveled around the Horn, past the cape where the clouds alternated between gray and black and where the wind always seemed to blow a frigid gale. It was a dangerous journey, but the stakes were great and then, as always, men would brave any danger for gold.

With the vast increase in California traffic, two new steamship companies were formed to handle the trade, not to sail around the Horn, as did the three- and four-mastered square-riggers, but to sail from New York to the narrow Isthmus of Panama. From the east side of the Isthmus passengers made their way overland to the Pacific side and boarded other ships which took them to San Francisco.

The twin Atlantic and Pacific steamship companies were formed so quickly that Vanderbilt had no chance to invest in them. George ("Liveoak") Law, his steamboat racing opponent, took over one of the companies—the United States Mail Steamship Company—and secured the U. S. Government's freight business and a mail subsidy as well. Since competitors had the jump on him and he had no subsidy, Vanderbilt saw no profit in setting up a line that would run through Panama. It would be more than a man-sized job to cut rates and scheme against an established company that had all the advantages. Those considerations would have slowed him down but might not have stopped the Commodore; what really changed his mind was a look at the map of the Americas.

As he stared at the colored maps in the privacy of his office, the Commodore's attention was drawn, again and again, to the little Republic of Nicaragua, a country of triangular shape that lies between Honduras and Costa Rica. Nicaragua was then famous for its coffee, bananas, scorpions, and palm trees, yet it had one outstanding geographical feature that intrigued Vanderbilt, Lake Nicaragua, which runs along the southern border of the nation, abutting Costa Rica.

The canny Commodore saw how he could turn that geographical feature into a transportation fortune. On the Atlantic side, the San Juan River connected Lake Nicaragua with the ocean at San Juan del Norte. True, the river was as crooked as a snake and shallow in spots, and sometimes the rains of the mountains churned the San Juan into mill-run speed. But the river was there, and torrent and rapids held no fears for an old steamboat captain who had braved Hell Gate in bad weather.

Lake Nicaragua sprawls to within twelve miles of the Pacific Coast at one point on its 3000 square miles of surface. Once he reached the lake, Vanderbilt could send ships from New York to San Juan del Norte, then up the river and into Lake Nicaragua, on their way to the Pacific Coast and San Francisco. In distance, the route would be five hundred miles shorter than the route through Panama, and in time it might save travelers five days to a week. The Nicaragua route would put Vanderbilt in an impressive competitive position against the U. S. Mail Steamship Company that ran to the south. There was only one problem—the twelve miles of jungle and mountains that separated Lake Nicaragua from the Pacific. Vanderbilt looked long and hard at his maps, and then he made up his mind. He would build a canal.

9

THE NORTH STAR

As the Commodore worried over his plan to connect the Atlantic and the Pacific oceans singlehandedly, some fifteen ships a week were still sailing for California around the Horn. Aboard one ship, a three-masted schooner, was a crewman named Cornelius Jeremiah Vanderbilt, the epileptic son of the Commodore, who set out in the fever of the 1849 gold rush for California.

Joining the rugged crew of a sailing ship was a foolhardy venture for a young man who suffered from fits, for young Vanderbilt knew, better than anyone else, the dangers he ran in scrambling aloft to set a yard or reef a sail. An epileptic seizure then would mean death in the sea or a crippling fall to the oak-hard deck.

The doctors knew little more about his disease than did Cornelius Jeremiah, but while they recommended sea voyages for epilepsy, they did not mean as member of the crew.

Cornelius Jeremiah had failed repeatedly in business, first as a clerk in the whirling world of finance, then as an apprentice in William T. Miller's tannery in the swamp area of Manhattan. Once he had been sent to clerk and study law in the office of his brother-in-law, Horace F. Clark. Here, too, Cornelius Jeremiah had failed. These failures were not caused by his epilepsy, but by his refusal to stick to business.

The disease, the disapproval of his strong father, and his excursions in high life had already left telltale scars on the young man. His fine wavy brown hair and heavy brows accentuated deep-set eyes, bony face, and the heavy, sensuous underlip that was the family mark. The face might have seemed handsome had it shown power, but there was no power in that face, only lines of weakness and suffering. Cornelius Jeremiah lived with the color of death; even the heavy lip was pale; the entire face seemed somehow sad and petulant.

For years Cornelius Jeremiah had been an easy mark for the creatures of the evening who roamed New York's streets. Gamblers, saloons, and pleasure houses need see only the name—Cornelius Vanderbilt, Jr., he signed it then—to roll out the best in the house and extend unlimited credit. Even when the Commodore had finally refused to honor the bills, Cornelius Jeremiah could buy what he wanted with the magic of his name and a promise to pay later. After all, the sharpers reasoned, the old man was bound to die sometime.

This kind of weakness had nothing to do with Cornelius Jeremiah's disease either, unless one were to hold that being weak, and despised, turned the young man into something weaker still. There was the indolence of his grandfather in Cornelius Jeremiah, and unlike old Cornelius, the farmer, the grandson was able to gratify his love of the easy life.

The young man took his mercurial pleasures where he found them, in gourmet food and heady drink, with the fancy ladies of the night and at the gaming tables. He was clapped in the foul common tank of Ludlow Street jail for drunkenness when one of his hosts mistook an epileptic fit for a more common seizure. Some distrustful creditors had already begun to file civil suits against him, as they were to do scores of times in the years ahead.

Nor did shipping out in the forecastle of a sailing ship solve Cornelius Jeremiah's problems. Before the schooner came in sight of the Strait of Magellan the would-be sailor had again become ill with his frightful disease (about which he had told no one before sailing) and he had been unable to help work the ship at all. On arrival in San Francisco he was paid off and abandoned by a disgusted captain. In a few days the money had disappeared in the saloons of the Barbary Coast. Destitute, Cornelius Jeremiah wrote a sight draft on his father. In those days a man's word was his bond; a draft on an individual was acceptable enough in most banking quarters, for if the addressee refused to pay, the drafter was ruined. When his son's draft arrived unannounced in the Commodore's office, at first the wrathful Vanderbilt refused to honor it. Reconsidering, Vanderbilt brought his son home, on Cornelius Jeremiah's promise to re-enter the Bloomingdale asylum. A few days later Cornelius Jeremiah had again pleaded his way to freedom, for Vanderbilt did not know what to do with him. Cornelius Jeremiah traveled to Washington, ran out of funds, signed another draft, and was jailed for fraud. This time the Commodore bailed his son out on the condition that he return to Bloomingdale for an extended stay.

The problem of his second son saddened the Commodore, and worried him, but did not slow for a moment his drive on Nicaragua. While extricating the boy from trouble, Vanderbilt had sent an agent to Nicaragua to explain his canal scheme to that nation's government. He promised to pay $10,000 to the Nicaraguan government on signing a contract for the building of the canal, then to give the government $200,000 in canal stock and 20 per cent of the profits for twenty years; 25 per cent thereafter. In exchange he wanted the exclusive right to move ships, passengers, and cargo across Nicaragua from ocean to ocean.

The Nicaraguan government accepted this windfall gratefully, the contract was signed, and Vanderbilt formed a stock company called the American Atlantic and Pacific Ship Canal Company. It was an immediate sensation in Wall Street.

Vanderbilt failed actually to build the canal half a century before Panama was finally crossed by water, but not because the Commodore became faint of heart. Vanderbilt ran afoul of diplomatic protocol and British banking interests. Although the Monroe Doctrine had been proclaimed in 1823, Great Britain had long ignored the American policy in Central America when it suited the purposes of the Crown to do so. British settlers in Honduras had persuaded the mother country to intervene in their behalf in 1835, and Great Britain had forced the Nicaraguan government to give Britain control of the area around the San Juan

River. Britain had gone even so far as to change the name of the town San Juan del Norte to Greytown.

Vanderbilt's canal proposal aroused a great deal of interest in Washington. He was not the first in America to talk about an isthmian canal, but what his idea lacked in historic precedence the Commodore made up in persuasion. President Zachary Taylor had no objection to the plan but he saw the canal question as only a part of the larger problem of British encroachment in what he regarded as American waters.

The result of the President's attitude was the Clayton-Bulwer Treaty of 1850 in which the British gave up most of their extra-territorial rights in the area. In exchange, however, the American government promised that the United States would not build or take control of an isthmian ship canal without the concurrence of Britain in the enterprise.

Vanderbilt felt that he had been betrayed, and many of his friends in Congress agreed. Yet even this disappointment did not stop the Commodore, for during the talks about the isthmian canal he discovered that some Englishmen had more than a flicker of interest in such a project. In the fall of 1850 the Commodore went to London. It was his first trip to Europe, but he took no time to play tourist, and after a great amount of jockeying back and forth, the British banking firm of Baring Brothers asked him to substantiate his rosy picture of profits with the facts. Vanderbilt went home and sent men back to Britain to show plans for a $31,000,000 canal, whereupon the British bankers threw up their hands. They could prove, on paper, that it would take nearly a million tons of merchant shipping a year to make the canal pay out, while there was only half that amount of shipping afloat on the Atlantic and Pacific oceans together. It did not seem to occur to Baring Brothers that Vanderbilt, alone, planned to send each of his own fleet of ocean-going ships through that canal at least a half-dozen times a year.

So the canal idea died, but Vanderbilt's contract with the Nica-raguans remained very much alive, and the Clayton-Bulwer Treaty, which stopped him from building a canal, was to help Vanderbilt push through his Nicaragua scheme without building a canal at all. In protecting themselves against the dangerous possibility that the Americans alone might build and control such an important international waterway, the British had agreed to recognize the sovereignty of all Latin-American governments. Greytown was no longer even quasi-legally the province of Her Majesty, Victoria Regina, daughter of the sailor-duke of Staten Island renown. San Juan del Norte was the official name of the town again, and the imperious British businessmen in Nicaragua lost their extralegal status.

Vanderbilt's contract with the government at Nicaragua stipulated that if the canal could not be built, he could build a rail line across the twelve-mile land barrier, or run stages across the isthmus if he chose. He chose to establish a stage line, and he formed a new company for the dual ocean venture—the Accessory Transit Company. A Vanderbilt steamer was to run from New York to San Juan del Norte. Passengers would then transfer to a river boat, which would brave the rapids for the trip to San Carlos, the town at the head of the river. Lake steamers would take travelers across Lake Nicaragua to Virgin Bay, and there the passengers were to descend into handsome blue and white carriages, for the twelve-mile run to the Pacific, where they would board another Vanderbilt steamer bound for San Francisco.

Before the line began operating, even before the canal scheme was finally killed, someone began to buy Ship Canal Company stock so heavily that the price jumped sharply, and the rumor went out along Wall Street that the British were hand in glove with Vanderbilt, which raised the price even higher.

No sooner had the price gone sky-high than another rumor swept through Wall Street to the effect that the whole scheme was dead, and Vanderbilt was giving up his plan of establishing a Nicaragua route.

Immediately the stock began to drop in price.

Since there was to be no canal this maneuver was Vanderbilt's way of buying up his canal company stock at rock-bottom prices, and keeping the capital invested at par value, plus the profits he made from those who bought high and sold at the low price.

Vanderbilt's second gesture was to run the 150-foot steamer

Central America to the San Juan River, along with the shallow-draft river boat *Director*. The natives of Nicaragua knew it was impossible to take a steamboat up the San Juan, because when the river was in flood its murky currents were much too swift for any boat. When the river was shrunk in the dry season the dreadful Castillo Rapids were exposed, ready to rip the bottom out of anything larger than a dugout canoe.

The Commodore's answer was to pull a cigar from the case he carried in his inside breast pocket (he never carried cigars outside, lest someone ask him for one), clip the end of the cigar, light up, blow a blast of blue smoke, and take the wheel of the *Director* himself. Up the river they went, 119 miles, Vanderbilt and a frightened crew, with full steam in the boiler and the safety valve tied down tight. It was New Year's Day, 1851. What a way to celebrate!

At the end of this wild ride Vanderbilt returned to New York and launched Accessory Transit with a splash heard across the continent. It took a healthy fortune to set up competition to the subsidized United States and Pacific Mail lines that met in Panama, but Vanderbilt now had such a fortune. His coastal steamboats ran from Boston to the Virginia shore, he was navigating the Hudson again, to the great pain of his rivals, and his boats had never left New Jersey waters. After holding a half interest in the Staten Island ferry for years, he bought out the genial Oroondates Mauran and controlled the entire system. He owned large pieces of real estate on Staten Island, at Perth Amboy, and at Coney Island, where he also operated the Oceanic Hotel. The Commodore seldom revealed the true extent of his wealth, but at this time he must have been worth nearly $7,000,000 in ready assets, not counting the value of his various monopolies in the steamboat trade. He was earning $100,000 a month from the steamboats alone.

The Vanderbilt fortune backed the building of a macadam road across the twelve-mile isthmus land route in Nicaragua, and Vanderbilt money paid for the blue carriages that would be drawn overland by multiple teams of mules. Vanderbilt sent his new *Independence* around to San Francisco just after her launching, along with the *North America*. They would start the service from San Francisco to San Juan del Sur. The *Prometheus* and the *Daniel Webster* were separated from the coastal trade to make the Atlantic passage from San Juan del Norte to New York.

The Commodore then began advertising his new New York–California service. The normal fare from New York to San Francisco was $600. Vanderbilt cut the price by a third, and promised a trip that was two days shorter than that over the Panama route. Business boomed from the beginning. On August 12, 1851, the *Prometheus* arrived in New York bearing the line's first passengers and a cargo of gold from San Francisco.

On her third trip, in October, the *Prometheus* ran afoul of British policy, which had been slow to follow the spirit of the treaty with America. Vanderbilt's Captain Churchill was weighing anchor in San Juan del Norte when a boatload of Greytown officials rowed out to demand $123 in port dues, a figure these dusky "officers" may have picked out of an arithmetic book. Captain Churchill reminded them of the Clayton–Bulwer Treaty. They had never heard of it. He shrugged his shoulders, said he was not going to pay, and pointed gently but unmistakably to their boat. He planned to leave the harbor within the next few minutes, he said. If they did not care to go to New York, perhaps they would like to disembark.

The native officers rowed wrathfully away, and Captain Churchill ordered his ship's anchor weighed. As he was heading out to sea, Her Britannic Majesty's brig *Express* sidled alongside, and fired a round shot over the forecastle, not clearing the deckhouse by ten feet. Immediately another shot crossed *Prometheus's* stern. Captain Churchill sent a boat over to the Britisher, demanding an explanation. This was British water, came the insolent reply, and if the captain did not want to anchor and settle with the Greytown officials, the *Express* would clear her decks with a round of grapeshot. Captain Churchill thought of his five hundred passengers, and paid, under protest.

Such harassment was frequent enough to give the Commodore high blood pressure. Incidents of this nature continued until finally the President ordered the U. S. Navy to send ships to protect American interests in Nicaragua. The U.S.S. *Cyane* bombarded

Greytown one day. Thereafter the town was definitely known as San Juan del Norte, and Vanderbilt's ships were no longer bothered by the British.

When Vanderbilt cut the fare to San Francisco, the opposition lines cut their fares even lower, and the old Vanderbilt game of rate war was on again. Eventually the cost of a first-class passage from New York to California dropped to $50, but as prices decreased, so did the service, but when the prices came back up again, the service did not, and in less than a year Vanderbilt's passengers were beginning to air their feelings about the new line in the San Francisco newspapers. They complained of filthy conditions, spoiled food, insolence of the crews and even ignorance of basic seamanship by Vanderbilt's captains. The experience of one ship captain, a correspondent charged, had been confined to running a Staten Island ferry before he was assigned to a ship on the San Juan del Norte-to-San Francisco run.

Vanderbilt avoided direct responsibility for the poor service by a shell game that would have put a carnival gambler to shame. He owned some of the line's ships in his own name and others in the names of subsidiary companies. He and Uncle Daniel Drew, together, owned the *North America*. When that ship ran aground and the crew plundered the passengers, who was responsible under the law? Accessory Transit Company said it had no responsibility, for the *North America* was a Vanderbilt ship. Not at all! The ship was chartered to the company, said Vanderbilt.

But eventually Vanderbilt shifted part of the responsibility for the ships in this hazardous trade by selling the company seven of his own ships for nearly $1,500,000. They were, of course, his older ships, which had served his purposes already, and some of them were at retirement age. Vanderbilt had used most of them in the coastal runs for years; some of them were worn-out hulks; and if further evidence of his personal acumen was needed—by devious means he controlled Accessory Transit Company anyhow.

The adventurers who went to California to seek gold faced cheerfully the prospects of murder, treachery, and fraud, for all the human emotions were honed sharp in the gold fields. Many a grizzled miner burst into San Francisco from the pine-clad mountains, bent on a hell-raising spending spree, his pockets full of dust or nuggets and his mouth watering for whisky, to stop in a Barbary Coast saloon and then, hours later, to find himself lying sourly in an alley with empty pockets and a lump on his head, or even worse, trussed to a bunk in a filthy four-master that was outward bound. Those dangers were ever-present, and constantly called to mind in song and story. But the reaching of California and the homeward journey were as dangerous to life and pocketbook, particularly, it seemed, if one traveled aboard a Vanderbilt ship.

In the summer of 1852 one of the ships the Commodore had unloaded on his company, the *Lewis*, set out from San Juan for San Francisco with 653 passengers aboard. There were 670 passengers on the manifest, but seventeen had died of cholera before the *Lewis* ever left Nicaragua and another nineteen men died on the trip north.

There were no provisions, in those days, for careful medical inspection on shipboard and if there was a doctor aboard a ship, it was only because he happened to be a passenger. Some of Vanderbilt's captains, too, seemed to lack judgment and experience, as charged. On the clear, calm morning of February 16, 1853, Vanderbilt's *Independence* was steaming south along the coast of Santa Margarita Island, about three hundred yards off shore. The dawn came early in these southern latitudes, and by five o'clock in the morning some of the passengers, perhaps awakened by six-legged visitors in their triple-tiered bunks, had come on deck for a walk and a smoke. The captain was on deck, too, standing the morning watch.

Suddenly one of the passengers called the captain's attention to breakers, dead ahead, but not so close as to cause any alarm. The captain smiled, and consulted his chart. "Breakers?" he asked. "Nonsense!" It must be a school of whales, he told the landlubber good-naturedly. Sometimes, he explained, if whales were packed tightly in an area, they gave the impression of breakers. He had seen them so, a hundred times.

The *Independence* sailed on in the clear, cool morning, not altering course one degree, and while the early-bird passengers watched with mouths agape, she struck the captain's whales, which turned out to be a reef with teeth like spikes. The ship struck hard and buried the reef in her wooden insides. Then the captain, true to form, ordered full steam astern, and she backed off, to fill her torn belly more rapidly. Cold water rushed into the engine room, the main boiler burst and started a fire in the hold, which was soon ablaze and out of control.

The captain ordered passengers and crew to abandon ship, for she was sinking fast, even as she burned. The crew launched the lifeboats, loaded them and headed for the nearby shore. But Vanderbilt ships did not carry enough lifeboats to hold all the crew and passengers. The captain ordered the boats back to pick up more men, now clustered in the stern of the smoking, listing vessel—and some of the crew refused to return. A hundred and fifty lives were lost that day, most of them passengers who jumped off the burning hull to drown in the sea, in sight of land and their fellows on shore.

Two months later the aged *Lewis* ran aground in a heavy fog four miles from Bolinas Bay, and while all hands were saved, the ship was a total wreck and the passengers lost their belongings.

Dozens of such tales were told of ships in the California trade, not just Vanderbilt ships, but those of his competitors as well. The steamship operators were not in business to bottle-feed passengers; they promised to carry men to California for a price, and they did so, subject to acts of God and normal (or so they said) human error.

The *Lewis* was lost in April 1853, but Accessory Transit was operating so successfully that Vanderbilt felt it would be possible for him to take his first long vacation. Even the news that George Law had gone into competition in the Staten Island ferry service did not upset the Commodore.

Vanderbilt planned a trip to Europe. He held a fortune of $11,000,000, he said (in another of his rare revelations of his personal affairs) and he had the money invested so that it returned him 25 per cent a year. With an annual income of $2,750,000, he felt it safe to be gone from his business affairs for four or five months.

The Commodore chose two of his associates to operate Accessory Transit in his absence. The New York end of the business would be managed by Charles Morgan, an old steamboat operator who had made his own fortune on the Charleston line before he joined with Vanderbilt. The San Francisco office would be in the hands of Cornelius Garrison, a shrewd banker, who not only knew the West but had also lived and worked in Panama, and so was familiar with the strange didos of Latin-American politics.

Both men enjoyed Vanderbilt's confidence—as much as any man ever did. The Commodore never took anyone completely into his confidence, but at least he trusted Garrison and Morgan enough to take a grand tour of Europe and leave them in charge.

The trip was to be made in a Vanderbilt steamer—a new one called the *North Star*. For this one trip the *North Star* would be used as a yacht, but she was easily convertible for the freight and passenger trades. Vanderbilt never missed a trick. He invited his entire immediate family except Phebe Hand, who was too feeble at eighty-six to make the trip, daughter Frances, who was invalided, and the impossible Cornelius Jeremiah, who was left with his sister Frances. But William Henry and his wife were to go, and young George Washington, all the eight other daughters, the husbands of the seven who were married, one grandchild, and Sophia.

Such a large entourage demanded special care not lavished on ordinary steamer passengers. Dr. Linsly, now the Vanderbilt physician of more than twenty years, was commandeered from his practice to watch over the Commodore's heart and the ills of the others, and the Reverend J. O. Choules, a Baptist minister, went along to lead the party's prayers.

The *North Star* was finally completed in May 1854. She was an impressive ship: 270 feet long, 38 feet of beam, driven by four coal-fed boilers, and was furnished throughout with all the attention to detail that an unlimited purse can command. The owner's saloon, where the passengers would gather for amusements, was designed in the style of Louis XV, with rosewood furniture. The room held two sofas, four smaller couches, and six armchairs. One of the new Van Horn steam heaters was installed to keep the saloon and the ten adjoining staterooms comfortably warm under any conditions. The stove itself was a masterpiece; ugly working parts were carefully concealed behind gilded bronze trellis work, topped by a solid marble slab.

Each of the adjoining staterooms was decorated in a different color. One room was fitted with red lace curtains, red lambrequins, red spreads over the berths, and a dominating red motif in the upholstered furniture. Another stateroom was decorated in blue, one all in orange, one in red and gold.

Forward of the main saloon was the *pièce de resistance:* the dining saloon. The walls of this room were made of brightly polished igneous marble; panels of Naples granite were laid against a surface of yellow Pyrenean marble. The ceiling was white, lined with scrollwork of purple, light green, and gold, around medallion portraits of famous American statesmen. The china was decorated in ruby and gold. Over the stairway to the passenger quarters hung a painting of Vanderbilt's Greek revival mansion on Staten Island, a house he now called his summer villa.

The master of this impressive vessel was to be Captain Asa Eldridge, a bearded seaman of vast experience in India, Liverpool, and the California trade. The purser was John Keefe, restaurant man extraordinary, borrowed for the trip from the Racket Club, where Vanderbilt spent much of his free time. The crew included young bloods from some of the best families in America, who shipped as ordinary hands to bask in the reflected glory of the Commodore.

Vanderbilt was in a hurry to get away. His normal caution deserted him, and the *North Star* was treated only to a single tryout voyage to Sandy Hook before sailing day. Captain Eldridge pronounced her shipshape, so on the morning of May 19 passengers and crew assembled at the Alliance Wharf at the foot of Corlears Street in New York. About five hundred business associates and well-wishers were on hand. They had invitations to travel on the yacht as far as Sandy Hook, then return on the *Francis Skiddy*. At ten-thirty that morning the propeller was turning over, and the ship was in motion.

At ten thirty-three she was stopped, stuck dead on a reef in the harbor, to the embarrassment of Commodore, captain, and pilot.

Signals went off in all directions; one to the Secretary of the

Navy, who broke precedence to authorize use of the Brooklyn Navy Yard's drydock for repairs. The *North Star* was warped off her perch and across the harbor into the yard. The five hundred once-gay spirits disembarked gloomily and went home, and Navy men set about inspection of the ship's bottom.

The yacht was not seriously damaged. By the next afternoon she was ready to sail. Then, an hour before sailing time, the firemen struck for higher wages, believing that they had the Commodore over a barrel. They should have known their man better; Vanderbilt rose in a towering rage and threw them all off the ship; within an hour his people had collected the requisite number of live bodies to stoke the furnaces, and the *North Star* was truly off.

As the party passed Phebe Hand's simple cottage on Staten Island, the harbor was treated to a display of pyrotechnics and gunfire in honor of the old woman. At Sandy Hook, Pilot John Martineau was put over the side into a boat with a purse of gold in his hand, just to show the world the Commodore had a heart of the same and no ill feeling.

The next morning normal shipboard routine began. The Commodore did the swearing and the Reverend Mr. Choules did the praying. The swearing was inadvertent, but the praying was well planned. Grace was said at all meals, Mr. Choules held evening prayers and counted the assemblage nightly at nine, and at eleven o'clock on Sunday morning all who were physically able were expected to be in the saloon for regular ministration to their souls.

The green firemen stoked their furnaces well, too. By noon of the twenty-first, the *North Star* was nearly two hundred miles at sea. The weather was balmy, although three of the ladies belied this and took to their beds, not to arise even for church on Sunday. The crew snapped into the routine quickly enough. One of the young amateur seamen, ordered to strike two bells, reported seriously that he could only find one bell, and Captain Eldridge's prominent nose quivered. But there was no real problem of any kind.

In the daytime the passengers sat in the sun and watched the sea or played cards or read. In the evenings, after dinner, they assembled in the saloon to hear music contributed by the ladies. Several of them possessed remarkable voices, Mr. Choules reported later. Mr. LaBau, Mary Alicia's husband, frequently treated the assemblage to arias from Italian opera, and once or twice the crew was invited to entertain with a minstrel show.

On the first of June the *North Star* arrived at Southampton, and the triumphal party set out for London. It was Queen's Drawing Room day, which meant all London was in turmoil with lords jostling ladies for the privilege of seeing and being seen by Her Majesty, Victoria, in the very exclusive reception at Buckingham Palace.

The Vanderbilt party had difficulty even in staying together, for London's hotels were jammed. Finally St. James's Hotel in Jermyn Street agreed to house all the Americans and they went there to stay in a group. After lunch, that first day, some of the group repaired to Hyde Park, where Vanderbilt sniffed audibly at the quality of horseflesh which drew the noble carriages, but the tourists *were* impressed with the lush liveries and white wigs of the coachmen and footmen who brought the nobility to see Her Majesty at Buckingham Palace.

The Vanderbilt party was not invited to the palace, Queen's Drawing Room, or any other doings. No lords or ladies fell over themselves to mingle with the rich Americans, no cabinet ministers came to call.

Not just the Queen, but all Britain's nobility treated Vanderbilt shabbily because of the American millionaire's humble beginnings. The closest he came to royalty was at the opera in Covent Garden. Her Majesty, like the Vanderbilts, came to see Meyerbeer's *Les Huguenots*, but Vanderbilt was not much impressed with the dumpy Queen, or with her consort, Prince Albert, just a tall man with a paunch and a bald head.

There were some parties given for the Vanderbilts in London, however. George Peabody, the rich expatriate, who had lent his opera boxes to Vanderbilt to see the Queen, had the Vanderbilts to dinner at his home at Richmond, where they encountered Stephen A. Douglas, the fiery little Senator from Illinois, who was on a tour of inspection of Western Europe. American Minister Joseph R. Ingersoll invited the Vanderbilts to one of his official parties, and the Rt. Hon. Thomas Challis, Lord Mayor of London, invited them to another, but he was the only important Englishman to show the Vanderbilt party any courtesy.

Yet, in spite of the snubs, they enjoyed themselves. They went to Ascot to watch the thoroughbreds, and to Mme. Tussaud's wax museum to see the Queen, almost lifelike. The young among the crowd braved Madame's Chamber of Horrors, where they saw Bluebeard and Jack the Ripper.

Son-in-Law Daniel Allen left the party for a few days to run over to Leipsig and visit his son, who was enjoying a classical education in that city since the Vanderbilt children, not to be outdone by the Astors, who had studied abroad, were determined to give their sons and daughters every one of the advantages that would turn them into cultured men and women who could enter the gilded world of society.

Not long afterward the party left unfriendly England and went on to Russia, where Vanderbilt was treated with far more dignity. The Grand Duke Constantin, son of the Czar, lent the Commodore his carriage, and the royal family extended the party many privileges. The group toured the Czar's collection of classic art at the Hermitage. They stayed at Denmouth's Hotel off the Nevsky Perspectif, beside the Moika Canal. They saw the Emperor's dacha on Neva Yellagin island, and later, on the trip to Copenhagen, gazed across the green lawns and orchards of Ven island, where the famous astronomer Tycho Brahe had lived.

They spent a few weeks in Italy, but did not visit Rome because an epidemic was scouring the city. Then the *North Star* carried them to Constantinople for a few days, and after that last stop, the party started home.

On his return to New York, Vanderbilt learned that he had been betrayed by Messrs. Morgan and Garrison, the two gentlemen he had entrusted with the affairs of Accessory Transit. In the five months of his absence the pair had set out to ruin the company and lose the franchise for travel across Nicaragua. No sooner had Vanderbilt sailed outside Sandy Hook than they went in league with a small, sandy-haired, frail filibuster named William Walker. His object was control of Nicaragua. Their object was to place control of the Nicaraguan steamer route in their own hands. To achieve this end, they promised to lend Walker $20,000 of Accessory Transit money to ship guns and supplies to his force of bandits and to give free passage on Accessory ships to the men he recruited to fight the existing government in Nicaragua. When he was in control he was to revoke Accessory Transit's charter and give the franchise to a new company they would form.

When the Commodore returned, Garrison and Morgan were already carrying out this plan and a raging Vanderbilt set out to punish them properly, but not in the courts, for the courts were too slow for Vanderbilt. "You have undertaken to cheat me," the Commodore wrote his onetime friends. "I'll ruin you."

For the first time, Vanderbilt involved himself in a public argument over a business problem. Within a few days both Vanderbilt and the Morgan-Garrison group were sending copies of their acrid correspondence to the newspapers as well as to each other, and New York, now a city of more than 600,000 scandal-hungry souls, loved every moment of this battle between the colossi. The issue was money, for only the smell of good green cash ever aroused the Commodore to such heights of fury as he now achieved.

Accessory Transit had flatly refused to pay Vanderbilt the 20 per cent of the gross receipts he demanded as agent on both ends of the route. The company blithely declared that Vanderbilt owed money to Accessory Transit, and demanded a look at *his* books.

Vanderbilt sputtered, called for arbitration, and sued, but that was *pro forma*—his real revenge was of a pattern with the old man's other business maneuvers, which had proved so eminently successful all through the years. He formed the People's Independent line, a new steamship company. The People's Independent line, the Commodore announced casually, would run to California over the Panama route (since Accessory Transit still held the Nicaragua route, and Morgan and Garrison for the moment held control of Accessory Transit).

Furthermore the Commodore's fare for steerage passage would be only $35, first-class passage would be about a quarter of the going rate.

Accessory Transit knew what was coming—the old Vanderbilt

game of rate cutting and rampage—and so did George Law, whose United States Mail company still ran from New York to Panama, and the Pacific Mail company, which ran from Panama to San Francisco.

Accessory Transit shuddered and settled Vanderbilt's tremendous claims in full, and gave him back control of the company in the settlement. Trying to buy him off, George Law bought the *North Star* for $400,000 and the Pacific Mail bought two other Vanderbilt ships at inflated prices. Since the Commodore's valuations ($500,000 for the *North Star*) were always exaggerated, the Commodore's out-of-pocket expense for the European trip could not have been very high. Actually, considering his counter-coup against Morgan, Garrison, Law, and all his other competitors, the five months' trip had proved quite profitable, for in his absence his old enemies, as well as his new ones, thought they had a clear field, and now he had got the better of them once again.

All these transactions had been accomplished by the end of 1854, but Vanderbilt did not stop there, for he was still after the scalps of Morgan and Garrison.

These worthies, of course, realized that if they did not stop the Commodore, he would ruin them as he had promised. They had already lost control of the Accessory Transit Company they had tried to steal, but when the Commodore said "ruin," he had meant pushing them down to a point where their widows would cry for mercy.

Morgan and Garrison still hoped that William Walker would seize control of the Nicaraguan government, and believed that move would put them on top once again, for if Walker did win, their arrangement with him was specific, and because Walker was a visionary who had become a fanatic, and not at all interested apparently in financial gain for himself, they were sure their position would be secure.

Walker was a man of his word. He had originally come from Tennessee, where he had pursued a gentle education, and had, remarkably, been successively a journalist, doctor, and lawyer before he turned soldier and professional revolutionary. Walker was intelligent, abstemious, and totally amoral in matters of war and politics, and he also commanded the complete loyalty of the men around him. If anyone could bring off the revolution they needed, Garrison and Morgan believed, Walker was their man.

In March 1855 Walker finally sailed for Nicaragua with about fifty soldiers of fortune, and $20,000 of Accessory Transit money that Morgan and Garrison had given him in Vanderbilt's absence, to lead an army he hoped to recruit on the spot, and throw out President Fruto Chamorro. Then Walker would make Federico Castillon president of Nicaragua, and as the power behind the presidency, he would tear up Vanderbilt's charter and turn the boodle over to Morgan and Garrison.

On October 11, 1855, the diminutive Walker hoisted his 130 pounds aboard the Vanderbilt lake steamer La Virgen as she was standing at the dock of the town of the same name. In a soft voice General Walker told Captain Hornsby his ship was commandeered "for the purposes of the revolution." This was at 10:00 P.M. At three o'clock the next morning La Virgen, now the pride of the revolutionary fleet, dropped anchor in the entrance to Granada, the capital of the Chamorro government. Walker sprang over the side into a launch, and led his men to attack and capture the sleeping town, scarcely raising a fight.

Federico Castillon became the new President of Nicaragua, and the new President revoked the charter of the Accessory Transit Company to cross Nicaragua, as promised. Furthermore, the Nicaraguan government seized Vanderbilt's river steamers and lake steamers, the mules and stagecoaches, and all the property of Accessory Transit within Nicaragua.

Vanderbilt's answer was to stop all his ships from sailing to Nicaragua. Walker had expected that action and delayed the seizure of Vanderbilt property until one last boatload of recruits had sailed on an Accessory Transit ship.

Walker had not expected Vanderbilt to be able to stop sailings from the San Francisco end of the line, where Garrison was still supposed to be in control, because it was taking Vanderbilt time to oust the man he had installed. But Vanderbilt's personal agents met ships that were to sail for Nicaragua and ordered them to Panama instead, and in a few days Walker was isolated, omnipotent in Nicaragua, but unable to ship men, medicines, guns, or money from the outside.

Morgan and Garrison, who were ready to establish their own independent line and take over the franchise, were delayed by Vanderbilt, who used every legal, financial, and physical means he knew. The struggle continued through the year 1856, providing vast amusement to New Yorkers, for the New York newspapers christened this war "the war of the Commodores," and reported with glee each skirmish on the home front (and there were far more skirmishes in New York than in Nicaragua in this war).

"Commodore" George Law, always eager to injure Vanderbilt's business and hopeful of a chunk of the Nicaragua franchise for himself, shipped ammunition to Walker in his own ships. "Commodore" Charles Morgan recruited a force of men in New Orleans, and hired ships to sail for San Juan del Norte, for though Vanderbilt controlled Accessory Transit and its ships, Walker controlled Nicaragua, and everything there. "Commodore" Garrison, however, was effectively immobilized in San Francisco.

Then, as the ships were making ready to sail, Vanderbilt personally persuaded the governments of Honduras, Guatemala, San Salvador, and Costa Rica to ally themselves with him, and throw out the Walker government of Nicaragua, and restore "normality."

Having made his junta with the neighboring governments of Central America, Vanderbilt sent Sylvanus Spencer and William Webster, a pair of desperate men who knew Nicaragua well, to undo Walker. They persuaded President Mora of Costa Rica to send a hundred Costa Ricans secretly down the San Carlos River to the junction with the San Juan, where they seized San Juan del Norte, and Vanderbilt's lake steamers, which had given Walker his armada. Vanderbilt's men cut the transit line with this move, so Walker could get no more help from the New York end of the line. The relief ships, when they arrived, found the terminal closed. Because there was no way to move recruits inland, finally the ships of "Commodore" Morgan and "Commodore" Law went back to the United States, without unloading.

Walker's men were short of medical supplies, food, and ammunition. Decimated by malaria and yellow fever, the tiny force grew tinier each day. Finally, in May 1857, Walker was persuaded to surrender to American Navy forces sent to Nicaragua to end the trouble. The U.S.S. *St. Mary's* took Walker off to Panama. The Nicaraguan revolt was ended.

Walker was released by the Navy in Panama and came to New York the following month. Much to the disgust of the Commodore, the thirty-year-old adventurer was lionized by New Yorkers. Walker was greeted at the Battery by a 100-gun salute and a crowd of eager well-wishers, and he conferred with Morgan and Garrison, who had come to New York, raised more funds, and later in the year tried once again to capture San Juan del Norte.

This time Commodore Vanderbilt was angered enough to demand immediate intervention by the United States Government. The President of the United States sent a detachment of United States marines to find Walker, disarm him, and throw him out of Nicaragua.

By the spring of '58, Accessory Transit was safely back in control of the Nicaragua franchise. But now that he had it, some thought Vanderbilt acted like a man who did not want this shipping prize, and that was a correct assessment. Having won his battle, and having destroyed Morgan and Garrison as important factors in American shipping, Vanderbilt let George Law and the Pacific Mail company know he planned to shift all his ships from Nicaragua to the Panama route. Quickly they bought him off, and at one point they were paying the Commodore at the rate of $670,000 a year, just to stay out of Panama. But that blackmail was too much for anyone to stand and by 1859 both companies had stopped paying entirely. Vanderbilt expected such a *volte-face*, and he did not complain.

There was a good reason for the Commodore's earlier reluctance to rebuild the Nicaragua route. Two or three years before his competitors, Vanderbilt sensed that the rush to California was slowing down, and he knew the decreased traffic would no longer support competing lines and yield the kind of profits he demanded from his investments. The California traffic was no longer a bonanza, so Vanderbilt let his enemies force him out of it—in his own way, and at his own price. He was no longer interested in Nicaragua anyway, for he had disposed of the men who had betrayed him, and as far as business was concerned, he had an idea now that offered far more room for maneuvering and profit.

10

RAILROAD EMPIRE

Back in 1855, when Commodore Cornelius Vanderbilt began fighting for control of Nicaraguan shipping, he was sixty-one years old and still as straight and lean as he had been at forty. That was the year Vanderbilt hit full stride as the nation's leading financial figure and fortune maker.

New York offered unlimited opportunity. Rail and steam and sailing ship connections with cities all over the globe made the city the hub of the nation. An unwavering flow of *émigrés* from the poverty and oppression of Europe kept the city alive to every material change or invention and to every new idea. In 1852 when Louis Kossuth, Hungary's refugee revolutionary, had come to New York to raise money for his Independent Hungarian Government, Kossuth issued special certificates which would be convertible into dollars or British pounds one year after he gained control of the Hungarian treasury, and raised enough money to support his futile campaign to overthrow the monarchy. New Yorkers, literally, had money to throw away.

The city had moved up above Forty-second Street. Along the east side, where the Dutch and early English settlers had kept their summer homes, the Astors were erecting row upon row of narrow-fronted tenements to house the jostling masses. Almost single-handedly, the Astors were creating the slums of Hell's Kitchen as they built and sold, multiplying the Astor fortune and the city's problems.

City government was tucked in the pocket of Tammany Hall, the local midwife of the Democratic organization. Tammany had begun as a secret society—a lodge of sorts, formed in the name of St. Tammany, after an Indian chieftain who had been sanctified by the clan. Within only a few years Tammany had bullied and wormed its way into City Hall. The slippery Fernando Wood was Tammany's mayor after 1855, and the corruption in city government was an evil on which the reformers dwelt in press and pulpit. Philip Hone, the gentleman auctioneer who had served as mayor in 1826–1827, refused to use the words he would need, he said, to describe Mayor Wood. Partially, of course, Hone's attitude stemmed from that old Federalist's aversion to Democrats. The Federalists, who became Whigs in the 1830s, had a tradition of putting up gentlemen for high office. Richard Varick, De Witt Clinton, Aaron Clark, James Harper of the publishing firm, these had been proper public servants. Wood, the conservatives felt, was nothing more than chief milkmaid for Tammany Hall.

The ladies of New York wore modified hoop skirts in this day, and pantaloons had finally been invented, so even if the breezes did hoist both dress and petticoat, the embarrassed female was exposed no higher than the ankle.

If a gentleman affected an overcoat, as the Commodore did, it was short and form-fitting, although it might be fur-trimmed, as Vanderbilt's always were, or heavily worked with hand embroidery.

At the Astor House, the city's finest hotel, ladies and gentlemen clustered in the magnificent chandeliered ballroom, waltzing to the music of a string orchestra in the balcony. The finest soirees were held at the Astor, and when they attended the parties, ladies wore low-cut, sleeved gowns of fine lace and silks. The gentlemen, top hats and pistols checked in the cloakroom, wore clothes that were even then strikingly similar to the full evening dress of the twentieth century; stiff white shirt, white tie, white waistcoat, black swallowtail coat and black trousers. The cut was different—a manly chest was more important than broad shoulders, and, a tapering at the waist was achieved by the stronger sex with corsets, just as by the girls.

Gentlemen did their drinking in saloons, where dogs might freely enter but ladies never. Men wore capes as well as coats, and still fought duels from time to time, although duelling had never recovered in the North from the blow dealt chivalry by the death of Alexander Hamilton at the hand of Aaron Burr.

The Vanderbilt girls, like other young ladies of the day, learned French and music and singing. They occupied themselves otherwise by making quilts for their hope chests and needlepoint samplers which expressed the hope that the Almighty keep an eye on the household. By 1855 almost all of the Vanderbilt girls were married and the Lord was keeping an eye on the household, as they requested. Vanderbilt was considered by his doctor to be a serious cardiac case, and it was a marvel to some how he stayed alive. In 1854 he had amazed Dr. Linsly with his vitality by standing up for eighteen consecutive days, when his legs swelled and his heart began palpitating wildly. Then, suddenly, the Commodore was well again, as cheerful and tough as ever.

Perhaps this heart condition began to soften the Commodore a bit toward his own family. With the exception of George Washington Vanderbilt, the youngest son, the Commodore had always expressed small use for his male offspring. The females, of course, he raised and provided for; that was all. They were nice girls, he said, but they married and then they were no longer Vanderbilts.

George Washington Vanderbilt showed no interest in either the shipping empire or the growing variety of Vanderbilt financial affairs. In 1856 George entered West Point, to train for a career in the army. The Commodore would have given an eyetooth had his son been commercially inclined, but such was his love for George that he accepted the boy's decision without the insult or derision he always heaped on others who disagreed with him.

William Henry Vanderbilt, the eldest son, was still in exile in Staten Island, an unwieldy lump of laziness and premature obesity, according to acquaintances. The Commodore concurred in this harsh judgment until a few examples of William Henry's native shrewdness changed the father's mind. On one occasion the young man asked the Commodore if he could have the manure from the commodious Vanderbilt stables for his farm. The Commodore asked his son how much he would pay.

"Four dollars a load," William Henry replied.

The old man knew he had been selling the sweepings locally for two dollars a wagonload, the going price of the day. He accepted the offer, certain that his freehanded son should be taught a lesson.

But one day, stepping out of his office off the Bowling Green, he saw William Henry making ready to sail a scow piled with manure across the bay to the Staten Island farm. There must have been twenty wagonloads of fertilizer in the boat.

"How many loads?" asked the Commodore, just to make conversation.

"One *scow* load," grinned the son.

The Commodore had been outfoxed. The boy's business sense, or innate dishonesty, appealed to the old man. Vanderbilt was further impressed when William Henry showed a spark of independence. The Commodore had bought the Staten Island farm for William Henry, but that gift was the end of it as far as the elder Vanderbilt was concerned. When William Henry wanted to buy another hundred acres of land, his father turned down the young man's request for a loan. So William Henry mortgaged his farm and bought the land.

A mortage, to Commodore Vanderbilt, was a sign of personal weakness and financial instability. When he learned that William Henry had mortgaged the property he had bought for him, the Commodore reached into his store of profanity and began exercising words he had not used for years.

What had William done with all the money he made on the farm? Vanderbilt asked.

He really did not want an answer but his son-in-law W. K. Thorn gave him one. Thorn reminded the Commodore that William Henry was raising a half-dozen children, and sending them to private school on Staten Island to be educated "as befitted the grandchildren of one of the nation's prime citizens."

Vanderbilt finally cooled down, and wrote a check to the mortgage holder when he realized that William Henry had not been wasting money.

William Henry proved himself to be a man of several parts when he lived on Staten Island. He was active in the affairs of South-field, the town in which the New Dorp farm was located, and in May 1856 he served on the Southfield grand jury, a task that interrupted his work in planting season. But he still did well with his crops of corn, potatoes, and oats, for he managed to get more work out of his men than any other farmer on the island. His technique was simple enough: he put the men on trial during the first few days. Being on trial they worked their hardest and William watched them. At the end of the first week of work he measured their output in rows of corn planted or in hay baled. Then William set standards, based on their eager efforts of the trial period, and thereafter the men either met the standards or they were docked.

As these facts became known to the Commodore, William Henry was called more and more frequently to the office on Battery Place, sometimes for three or four days at a time. Instead of receiving specific orders to perform certain jobs for his father, as in the past, William was given an increasing degree of suzerainty over the Commodore's extensive business holdings on Staten Island. Vanderbilt had a large real-estate development that began at Vanderbilt Landing; he sold a plot on Vanderbilt Avenue in 1856 to son-in-law Thorn for $8000 and sold to others for even higher prices. He owned a large share of the stock of the Staten Island Railway, a thirteen-mile line that ran along the long eastern shore of the island. In 1857, when the railroad went bankrupt, Vanderbilt put William Henry in charge, as receiver; the son took over the line as president, and within five years ran the stock up from nothing to a value of $175 a share.

Generally William Henry got along well enough with his neighbors, although they stood in awe of him, since he was the son of the richest man who had ever come from the island, and he was an uncommunicative man whose shyness was often misread as insolence. The tax collector, an Irishman, had little use for William Henry because young Vanderbilt was notoriously slow about paying his taxes. Since the collector's income depended on his collections (he got 10 per cent), William Henry got on his nerves.

One day the collector threatened to seize William Henry's finest carriage if Vanderbilt did not pay up immediately. William Henry, with a touch of the paternal spirit showing, said he would shoot the collector if he dared touch the Vanderbilt carriage.

But when William Henry was called to the Commodore's office at 9 Battery Place across the bay a few days later, the collector drove up to the Vanderbilt farm in a rickety buggy, dismounted, hitched his horse to William Henry's stylish coupé, tied the buggy to the back, lighted up his corncob pipe and drove up New Dorp Lane into Richmond Road.

Vanderbilt, on his return from the city, found the carriage gone and purpled in anger. He had been outwitted by a simple Irishman. The story got around, and William Henry had to bear the embarrassment, but he did, and eventually laughed about it himself. Thereafter he was better liked by his neighbors for having shown a bit of human failing, even though he showed little enough of the Commodore's spirit of adventure.

The other son, the epileptic Cornelius Jeremiah, as far as the Commodore could see, had absolutely none of the Vanderbilt characteristics.

This estimate was not quite correct: Cornelius Jeremiah had his father's love for the long chance. The Commodore belonged to the old Elm Park Pleasure Association, a group made up of several hundred business leaders who raced their trotters in the park above Ninetieth Street. His second son belonged to no such exalted group, but where the Commodore risked tens and hundreds on the nose of a horse, or the turn of a card at his whist table, Cornelius Jeremiah risked hundreds and thousands on the turn of a faro card at Danser's gaming rooms on Barclay Street or in roulette at George Beers' establishment at Thirteenth Street and University Place.

The young man's gambling could not be stopped. Vanderbilt put him in the Bloomingdale insane asylum again in 1854 to prevent prosecution on a bad check charge, but by '55 Cornelius Jeremiah was out, back to his wheedling, his good intentions, and his broken promises.

At thirty-one the black-haired young Vanderbilt married Miss Ellen Williams, the sweet, kindhearted daughter of the chief justice of the New York Supreme Court, a man of moderate means.

The Commodore prophesied before the wedding that if Ellen had jewelry, securities, or even expensive clothes—Cornelius Jeremiah would hock them all for money to lose at the gaming tables. Judge Williams was somewhat taken aback by this frank admission by the prospective bridegroom's father, but his daughter decided it was her particular mission in life to reform Cornelius Jeremiah and she married him anyway.

It was as the Commodore said; the jewels, the family plate, everything the young couple owned went to the pawnbroker's. Only through the kindness of Sophia, who wept with Ellen over Cornelius Jeremiah's infirmities, did the pair manage to live at all. Cornelius Jeremiah did not work, he lived a catch-as-catch-can existence, scrounging money where he could find it, borrowing from friends, and writing bad checks, which were ultimately covered by his father to keep a bearer of the family name from exchanging it for a prison number.

Finally the Commodore took pity, not on his son, for whom he had small pity left, but on his daughter-in-law, for whose virtue even the crusty old Vanderbilt had profound respect. The Commodore "lent" the pair $10,000 to build a house on land near Hartford, Connecticut, where Cornelius Jeremiah was to manage a farm. The couple traveled off to Connecticut, but in a few weeks Ellen was back again, requesting an interview with her father-in-law. Vanderbilt acceded grudgingly, wincing and wondering how much the girl wanted this time. But when she came into his office, she gratefully returned to him $1500 that they had not needed. The Commodore was thunderstruck, and then and there he increased Cornelius Jeremiah's allowance to $200 a month. With this money, plus the earnings from farming, the young Vanderbilts should have been able to live well, but they kept four servants, and Cornelius Jeremiah could not stay away from the gambling hells of New York. He came to the city, ostensibly on business, but almost always the young man returned to his bride empty-handed, or bearing record of another set of I.O.U.s given to some gambler or generous soul who knew the name but not the man.

Cornelius Jeremiah borrowed money from anyone and everyone. He owed the lottery policy king, Zachariah Simpson, $10,000. He borrowed, at various times, a total of $50,000 from softhearted Horace Greeley, the great editor of the New York *Tribune*. When the Commodore heard that Greeley was lending his son money, he took it upon himself to march down to the rooms of the *Tribune* to straighten Greeley out.

"I hear you're lendin' Corneel money," he charged the editor.

Greeley looked up from his desk, coldly, and admitted this was true.

Vanderbilt warned Greeley that he would not bail Corneel out.

"Who the devil asked you to?" Greeley snorted.

The Commodore strode out of the room, pink with rage. It was not that the old man was free of vices, himself, or that he expected his son to be an angel; for years the Commodore had maintained a succession of brief liaisons with young women, all discreet and all kept well hidden from press and public. But that was vice, not weakness. Corneel's constant borrowing, his wastefulness—that was weakness that the Commodore could not abide.

Yet he tried, time and again to understand. Disturbed as he was about Cornelius Jeremiah, he visited his son and Ellen at Hartford; he told Ellen he would give almost anything to have Cornelius Jeremiah a whole man, for he was well aware that the fault might be his—and not his son's.

As to others in the family, Vanderbilt usually felt kindly toward his own, although he had little day-to-day contact with any save his brother Jake, and that relationship was clouded for several years when Jake suspected the Commodore of cheating him in a business deal.

One day, after he had refused to speak or communicate with his elder brother for some months, Jake stepped out of his hilltop mansion on Staten Island to find a handsome team hitched to a new carriage, tied to the post before the house. Attached was a note in the Commodore's virtually undecipherable scrawl, inviting Jake to dinner that very night at 10 Washington Place. Even Jake could not resist that gesture: he went.

Jake was by no means as wealthy as the Commodore, nor did he wish to be as wealthy. He had made a respectable fortune in the shipping business and in the management of the ferry line and now his great pleasure was to play the country squire. Jake had none of the drive for empire that marked the Commodore's career.

Vanderbilt, even in his sixties, could no more bear to be defeated than when he was a boy poling a periauger through Buttermilk Channel. One day when Jake was driving one of his teams of trotters along a narrow road and approaching an even narrower bridge, he heard hoofbeats pounding up behind him. Jake paid small attention, except to snap the reins so the trotters would be sure to reach the one-way bridge before the carriage behind.

But the pounding grew louder and the beat faster. Jake knew he was challenged, he pushed his horses, even used the whip. He approached the bridge—in a moment he would be on it, and no one could pass him.

But at the very last split second another team flashed by, cut him off, and left Jake's carriage smashed into the side of the bridge, his horses rearing and neighing in fright. The reckless driver, Jake saw in that flashing instant, was the Commodore, cigar clenched in his teeth, his magnificent gray head faced straight ahead, the nobility of his face marred only by a broad grin of success.

"You didn't ought to try to beat your brother," he warned the discomfited Jake, after he had stopped, picked up his brother, and the two repaired to Jake's house to talk.

The famous Vanderbilt profile had become of real note in the nation; he was even proposed as a candidate for the presidency of the United States by members of the dying Whig party. But in 1856, the year of the talk, Vanderbilt had given up all political ambition.

While the Vanderbilt acumen impressed some senators and earned him the sobriquet of "Lion of Wall Street," the Commodore's reputation did not impress certain younger contemporaries on the New York scene. Vanderbilt for a time was bedeviled by cats which came around his mansion on Washington Place nightly to sing until the small hours of the morning. The Commodore's remedy was as direct as usual, he found the leader of one of New York's street gangs, a young man named Ikey Vesuvius, and offered this youth a dollar for every dead cat he could produce the next day. Night fell, and with it came silence; no cats disturbed the Vanderbilt sleep.

The next morning Vanderbilt was prepared to pay ten dollars or so and compliments to the youngsters who had restored his rest. He was not prepared when the young men came to the house bearing more than a hundred cat corpses for inspection and bounty.

The Commodore refused to pay.

Ikey and friends disappeared, hurling insults.

That night Ikey's street gang covered the whole of lower New York for felines. They found cats in cemeteries, cats in alleys, cats in areaways. They stole cats and kidnaped cats, and enticed cats away from their window boxes. Then they delivered the cats, tails tied together, over the garden wall at the Commodore's house.

There never was such commotion as that made by the dozens of cats, scores of cats, of all sizes and shapes, tails tied together so none could escape.

The Commodore slept little, even less than before he had met Ikey Vesuvius. The next day, knowing he was defeated, he paid. The joke, Vanderbilt realized, was on him for a change.

But in more serious matters the Commodore never learned to appreciate a joke, except the ones he played himself. His great venture of the late fifties was to enter the trans-Atlantic shipping trade. As usual, the Commodore stepped into the ocean trade with an unerring sense of timing, and a grim sense of competition.

The principal competitors on the Atlantic routes were the British Cunard line and the American Collins line, each subsidized by its respective government. Both Cunard and Collins had operated sailing ships before they went into steam. Edward Collins had made a fortune in the old Dramatic Line that ran sailing ships across the Atlantic in the remarkable time of fourteen days. But now, in the 1850s while the packets and four-masted sailing ships were still building, the day of sail was on the wane. Sailing ships would struggle fiercely for the Atlantic trade for a few more years. The sailing ship *Dreadnought* under Captain Samuel Samuels would actually beat the time of Cunard's steamer the *Canada* in 1856, arriving at Sandy Hook from Liverpool on the exact day that the *Canada* would reach Boston, the *Canada* having sailed from Liverpool a day earlier. And in 1859 the *Dreadnought* would set a record to Liverpool, sailing the Atlantic in 13 days 8 hours, but already the great white sails were smudged, finally to disappear in clouds of oily black smoke from the steamers that overtook them.

Collins and Cunard raced for passengers and cargo. In 1852 the Collins steamer *Pacific* made the Atlantic crossing in less than ten days. Collins's subsidy of $18,000 a trip was increased to $33,000, for while he had proved American ships could challenge Britannia on the ocean, his line was limping financially. The tragic sinking of the wooden steamer *Arctic* off Cape Race in 1854 nearly ruined the line. Collins lost his wife, son, and daughter, who were among the three hundred dead; in a business way, his line lost some of its new-found confidence and public respect.

It was just at this time that Vanderbilt made his bid for the Atlantic trade. He first proposed that he and Collins split the Atlantic mail subsidy given by the Post Office Department, but Collins refused indignantly. Vanderbilt then offered Congress to make the Atlantic run regularly in exchange for a government subsidy of $15,000 a voyage. Congress, quite aware of the Vanderbilt methods of competition, decided to stick with the Collins line.

Then Vanderbilt suddenly displayed himself—for the only time in his life—as a foe of monopoly, and so impressed President Franklin Pierce with his arguments that the President vetoed the Collins subsidy bill, leaving the Atlantic trade open for all comers —including Vanderbilt. When press and public began to accuse the Commodore of corrupting the President, Vanderbilt expressed mortification at this woeful misunderstanding of his motives.

An aroused Congress restored the Collins subsidy, but Vanderbilt took off his kid gloves and set out to rule or ruin the American merchant marine. He rescued the *North Star* from George Law and began steaming her across the ocean with a sister ship, the *Ariel*, built especially for this route. In 1855 the Collins line was better and faster and more regular than Vanderbilt's, but the unlucky Collins could not prosper. In 1856 Collins's queen liner, the *Pacific*, disappeared in a storm between Liverpool and New York, and in 1858 Vanderbilt was carrying the first cabin passengers across the Atlantic for $80, less than half the normal fare. In the ruinous rate war, the weaker Collins line collapsed.

Vanderbilt never did get the Collins subsidy, although he caused Congress to revoke Collins's subsidy, took Collins's business and eventually won the right to carry the U.S. mails for the price of the postage on the letters. The Commodore's consolidated line competed with Cunard's fast British ships, but press, public, and Congress expressed disgust at the quality of American (Vanderbilt) ocean transportation, for the Commodore was up to his old tricks again. He built magnificent steamers, such as the *Vanderbilt*, his greatest and most powerful one, and when pressed, he could lay a handsome table, provide kingly accommodations, and race the fastest Cunarders to defeat, but most of the time he did not do these things; he slashed service and raised prices to the occasional costs of cutting rates, pouring on coal, and pleasing palates. By 1860 the newspapers complained that Vanderbilt steamers everywhere were notorious for overcrowding, poor food, filth, and danger to the passengers. On one trip on the New York–Panama run, instead of twenty or thirty firemen, one Vanderbilt ship carried only ten firemen, two of whom died on the trip, and eight stewards to wait on three hundred and fifty passengers. In May 1860 the good ship *Northern Light* sailed from New York with an official passenger list of 890, but actually carrying more than a thousand persons. There were not enough benches for all aboard to lie down at the same time, let alone enough berths and table space in the dining rooms.

Not all this flummery was Vanderbilt's. He complained constantly that his captains cheated him and were cheated in turn by their suppliers. Passenger and even cargo manifests meant practically nothing, for the captain was usually ready to take money under the table, then put it in his pocket rather than the owner's. Daniel Torrance, daughter Sophia's husband, was the agent for the Vanderbilt Atlantic lines, but he could not control the dishonesty any more than could the Commodore from his more lofty seat, for that was the universal system. Nor was there a pressing need for control since costs were so low; Vanderbilt bought several of the Collins ships for as little as ten cents on the dollar. The *Moses Taylor*, for example, had cost Collins $250,000 but after Collins's line collapsed Vanderbilt picked the ship up in its prime for $25,000 cash. In such circumstances, Vanderbilt did not look too carefully at his captains' practices as long as they were loyal to him. He was rich enough; in 1860 he finally bought the Pacific Mail Steamship Company for $2,000,000, to become the most important man in American shipping, a virtual monopolist of the American seas. He had come a long way in his sixty-six years.

Shrewdness, drive, and not a little bit of luck had brought the Vanderbilt fortune so far, yet even Vanderbilt luck and strength could not control the currents that swirled around the Commodore's shipping in 1860—he still could not get the mail subsidy he wanted from Congress. Southern members of Congress were struggling for economic parity with the industrial North; the southerners bore Vanderbilt no ill will, but they saw no reason to spend southern money in subsidy of northern shipping when British bottoms were willing to carry American goods and mails more cheaply.

This southern attitude was merely a puff that warned of the storm in American politics. Vanderbilt was aware of the nature of the opposition to his request for subsidy in 1860, and as a businessman, he tried to meet it by trading: he would operate a line to Europe from the South as well as from the North, starting with a Norfolk–Le Havre service, and perhaps later extending the service to other southern ports.

It was a daring scheme, and had the political climate been such that it could have succeeded, Vanderbilt's plan would certainly have helped in the industrialization of the South, and would have decreased tensions between the two great sections of the nation. It was amazing how this man's mind worked; at sixty-six, a year past the age when Americans are generally considered ready only for the discard, Vanderbilt was planning and maneuvering, first in one field of transportation, then in another, thinking progressively in bigger terms, his holdings forever growing—and still his greatest years and his greatest feats were ahead of him. His contemporaries were growing feeble and were dying off, one by one, but Vanderbilt remained young in spirit, looking for new fields to dominate.

That was not to say that the Commodore believed himself immortal, for in 1857 the old man had considered the problems attendant to his death, and had ordered a vault built at the Moravian Cemetery on Staten Island, the burial place of his Dutch forefathers who had settled the land and built the church itself. The Commodore's vault was expensive but it was simple; the total cost was $6000 for a 30-foot by 40-foot building made of plain granite, fronted by two Corinthian columns. Atop the roof a shaft was raised 20 feet high. In front of the mausoleum, before the iron doors, stood a marble statue symbolizing Grief.

But with that exception Vanderbilt's thoughts dwelt very much on the here-and-now and he was more active than ever in almost every way. In September 1860 the distinguished Baron Renfrew visited New York and Vanderbilt was selected to join the reception committee for the important visitor, along with August Belmont; the Rothschild representative in America; William Backhouse Astor; Peter Cooper; Moses Taylor, the banker; James I. Roosevelt; William H. Aspinwall; W. C. Rhinelander; Lambert Suydam; Peter Marie; and John Jacob Astor II. A distinguished assemblage this, gathering for the moment representatives of the old Dutch elite, English colonial society, and in Vanderbilt and the Astors the first, second, and third generations of the new society of self-made men.

The Commodore was called to committee after committee. His favor and donations were sought for charities and good causes of the day. The teetotaling Anti-Slavery Society left him alone, knowing of his fondness for a glass of gin and his unfortunate failure to exhibit any real interest in religion. But other charity workers searched him out, only to be disappointed, generally, when they found him. He was uninterested in the plight of the heathen African or the misbegotten Chinee, and talk of local monuments and parks brought mumbled answers and begrudging small contributions.

The Commodore was always a firm believer in the old axiom

that charity begins at home, but with him at this stage of life, it also ended there. He intended to preserve his money for better use than charities, and in 1860, even as he argued with Congress about shipping subsidy, and unfolded the complete plan for a southern shipping line, Vanderbilt was using a great deal of his huge fortune to dabble in railroad stocks. That quiet, distrustful duality was one of the Commodore's least-known qualities, yet it was one of two qualities that, plus luck, assured him success in the business world. He was always ready to jump two ways: if one carefully planned scheme failed, he had one of an entirely different kind at his fingertips; and then he brought into play his second great quality, the ability to keep his business to himself, never telling anyone what he was doing until after he had done it.

Quietly, with no apparent aim in mind, the Commodore had begun to acquire large railroad interests some years before. In particular he had been watching the Harlem line—The New York and Harlem Railroad. In 1844 the Harlem had reached White Plains, the seat of Westchester County, although by 1846 the Harlem had competition upstate: the Poughkeepsie and Hudson River Rail Road was organized to run straight up the river and serve all the towns on the east bank of the Hudson, from New York City to Greenbush, across the river from Albany. Then, in 1848, the young New York, New Haven and Hartford Railroad bought a perpetual right to operate on the Harlem's right of way inside New York City, an exchange significant to a student of railroads since it showed the importance and solidity of the Harlem line. Finally, by 1852, the Harlem line had reached almost to Albany.

Vanderbilt, even as he fought the battle of the steamship lines, sensed the ebbing tide of federal government interest in the United States merchant marine. The Commodore argued once again before Congress the necessity of federal assistance to any steamship operator over the long run; if federal assistance, in the form of mail subsidy at least, was to be denied, then there was small future in the ocean-going steamship business for anyone.

But Congress, in that year, would not be budged. The Democratic party, of course, had split squarely across the seams, and in their hope to control the American presidency in 1860, the south-erners nominated John Breckinridge of Kentucky, the northern Democrats nominated Stephen A. Douglas, Vanderbilt's acquaint-ance from the London visit. The Constitutional Union party, an interdenominational, intersectional, and intersocial squadron of compromisers nominated the good-natured John Bell of Tennes-see—an effort as hollow as the bells they rang in their political processions.

From the West a silicon-faced Abraham Lincoln walked off with the Republican nomination and the presidency. This Lincoln had been studying law at night in Illinois while Vanderbilt was shooing sailing ships off Long Island Sound, and Lincoln, the politician, had learned his trade as well as Vanderbilt had learned to make his way in the business world. Lincoln had seen his op-portunities, and used them; he made his own chances where tai-lored ones did not seem to exist. Each of these men was ready now to rise to his full stature, but before they could rise, each had a few details to clear away.

The election over, Lincoln did his best to conciliate an irrec-oncilable South and Vanderbilt went ahead with his plans for the trans-Atlantic connection between Norfolk and Le Havre. As late as February 1861, long after most southern states had voted to secede, Vanderbilt was still trying to establish the service, and the subsidy.

That same month President-elect Lincoln left his Illinois home for Washington and an endless series of meetings with Senator Seward, who would be his Secretary of State, and Senator Douglas, his former opponent, who would be his strong hand in the early days of this national crisis.

As these two dissimilar men—the politician and the merchant sea lord—went their dissimilar ways, yet another man rose above others in the South to confound all plans of unity and business progress. On February 9, 1861, United States Senator Jefferson Davis threw off the mantle of the Union's legislature to become President of the new Confederate States of America.

Lincoln's union and Vanderbilt's American sea monopoly were shattered.

But the Union's loss was to be Vanderbilt's gain; for the second time in his life a war was to help build his fortune. The government had no merchant navy, nor any transport ships of its own. If the War Department wanted to move troops by sea, it must build, buy, or charter ships from citizen owners. In the first days of the struggle building them was out of the question, and since nearly everyone expected a short war, the War Department chose to charter ships.

Even before the firing on Fort Sumter the War Department chartered Vanderbilt's *Daniel Webster*. On February 14, 1861, the ship steamed to Port Jefferson in the Dry Tortugas to Fort Taylor at Key West, and to Port Isabel on the Brazos River in Texas. She took supplies to the troops on the islands, but removed the federal troops from the indefensible position on the Brazos. To Vanderbilt, that charter job meant a fee of $25,000.

When war came in April, other Vanderbilt ships went into the federal charter service. The *Illinois*, in October 1861, was chartered as part of the seventy-seven-ship fleet that was to carry the Dupont-Sherman expedition against Port Royal and Beaufort, South Carolina, and the *Northern Light* carried other troops. Rates ranged from $700 to $2500 per day, depending on the size of the ship. The Army took the *Ocean Queen* from October 5, 1861, to January 15, 1862, at $2500 per day; that same year Vanderbilt's *Daniel Webster* carried part of General McClellan's Army of the Potomac on the start of its Peninsula campaign; and still later that ship was taken over altogether by the U. S. Sanitary Commission and turned into a hospital ship.

The *Ariel*, the great modern *Vanderbilt*, and other ships of the line were available for charter, too, but when not on government service, they kept making the regular Atlantic and South Atlantic runs, dodging the South's fast if tiny navy.

Vanderbilt prospered in the early war years, that was unquestionable, but he provided a service the government needed desperately, at a time when price was no object. Only once was he involved in anything that seemed shoddy—the name that sprang up to describe the new class of merchants and manufacturers who enriched themselves at government expense, selling cheap and tawdry merchandise for the use of the struggling troops, and charging holdup prices to the government for the inferior goods.

Secretary of War Stanton tried to enlist Vanderbilt in government service during the war but without success. The Commodore refused a job, and refused any government compensation on a part-time or advisory basis. Dollar-a-year men were not yet within the federal ken, so there seemed no way Vanderbilt could be used if he would not take a job, but there was one way to use the Commodore's services—on an unofficial basis. In 1862 General Nathaniel Banks was ordered to proceed against New Orleans by sea. Vanderbilt agreed to help find ships and outfit them for the campaign, although he turned the actual job of ship chartering over to an agent, as was customary.

By December 4 the ships were found and loaded with supplies and men and on that day the Commodore and other dignitaries toasted in champagne the fleet's departure from the Brooklyn Navy Yard. A few months later Congress was asking who had paid for the champagne: the chartered ships were rotten and dangerous, and the captains and crews were incompetent. The soldiers aboard one logy transport forced the crew to put her in to shore a few hours after sailing and when the paint was chipped off the hull, pulpy, rotten timbers were exposed. This and several other ships did not even reach New Orleans.

Some Congressmen wanted to reprimand Vanderbilt by congressional resolution, but he had enough influence and enough friends to escape this indignity, although he did not escape uncomfortable hours of congressional testimony before the probing fingers of angry United States senators. Nor did he escape the harsh charges of the press. The civilian role in the Banks expedition was labeled "fraud," and the implication was very clear that Vanderbilt had been a principal party in defrauding the government and risking the lives of brave young Union soldiers.

In these dark hours the public forgot that Vanderbilt had given his own son to the Union Army. George Washington, Vanderbilt's favorite, served steadily in the Grand Army of the Republic. After graduation from West Point in the class of '60 Lieutenant Vanderbilt had been stationed in the Oregon Territory for a time.

but when war broke out, he was sent to Boston in charge of army recruiting, then, after a year, was appointed to the staff of Brigadier General Tyler. The new job was assistant adjutant general—and it meant promotion to the rank of captain. George went with General Halleck into the Corinth campaign, fell sick with what seems to have been tuberculosis, and by 1863 was so ill he sailed for France to try to recover his broken health on the sunny shore of the Riviera.

Vanderbilt ships also suffered losses on the high seas in these war years, losses and indignities at the hands of the Confederates. The *Ariel*, on Vanderbilt service, was hailed off the coast of Cuba by the fearsome Confederate raider *Alabama*. The *Ariel* tried to outrun the Confederate ship, but was brought up short by shots across her bow. For some reason the southerners decided not to sink her, although they disarmed the 120 U. S. Marines aboard and forced the captain to sign a bond of $250,000 which pledged Vanderbilt to pay the sum to the Confederate government thirty days after southern independence was recognized. The Commodore swore, and redoubled his efforts to help the Union win the war.

Vanderbilt offered the government his favorite steamer, the *Vanderbilt*, and the offer was gratefully accepted. With his steamers now tied up on government business, Vanderbilt quite naturally paid more attention to railroads than before, for railroads in the 1860s had suddenly achieved a prime importance in transporting supplies and soldiers quickly to the far reaches of the Union. In 1862 the Commodore began plowing his war profits into the stock of the Harlem road, then that of the Hudson River Railroad and even in the New York Central, a tiny line that connected Albany and Buffalo, a line that did not seem important until one realized that it was a vital link in the most direct rail route from New York to the Great Lakes, and thus to the West.

That same year, 1862, Vanderbilt was elected a director of the Erie Railroad, but the Harlem occupied most of his attention, for it represented the greatest opportunity. In '62 the financial condition of the Harlem was grim; the road had issued 110,000 shares of stock to help finance its stiff competition with the Hudson line, for the Harlem's route lay far east of the Hudson River towns, and the rival road seemed to be carrying all the traffic. The Harlem paid no dividends that year and the Commodore bought Harlem stock that had a $100 par value for $9 per share.

Railroads were still forbidden to operate in the downtown section of New York city; citizens remembered too well the fatal explosions that had rocked New York in the early days of the Harlem road. Yet now there was a rumor that the city fathers might extend the tracks of the Harlem down to the Battery, and were that true the road would become immensely more valuable, if only because of the extra income from intracity transportation.

When the rumor persisted, Harlem stock began to rise. The stock rose to 30, then to 40, and Vanderbilt continued to buy. When it reached 50, he used the Harlem shares he had bought at 9 and 30 and 40 as collateral to buy more.

By April 1863 Vanderbilt held more than 55,000 shares of Harlem stock—more than $2,750,000 of his cash was tied up in the line. While he declared an income that year of nearly $700,000, Vanderbilt's cash position was tenuous, for much of his money was held in solid investment, not in liquid assets.

Daniel Drew, the psalm-singing, secret-drinking old church deacon, had been at ins and outs with Vanderbilt for years—sometimes in with the Commodore on one deal while at the same time doing his best to skin him on another. Drew always had more than a casual eye turned on the Commodore's affairs, thus he must have been well aware that as Vanderbilt bought Harlem stock, the Commodore also was sidling up to the members of the New York Common Council and bribing them, one by one, to secure their votes in favor of granting the street-operating franchise to the Harlem line. It was common knowledge on Wall Street that the pay-off had been high enough to persuade the councilmen to stick by their word.

At this point, Uncle Daniel Drew came out from behind his Book of Common Prayer, and conferred with the higher authority, the gentlemen of the New York City Council. Daniel proposed that they all join him in selling the Harlem short.

It was a neat conspiracy against Vanderbilt—all the more refined because both Vanderbilt and Drew had joined the Harlem board, and just at this time Drew helped vote Vanderbilt into the presidency of the road, even as he worked to ruin the Vanderbilt venture.

The Commodore's plan for the Harlem had greatly increased confidence in the Harlem among the speculators of Wall Street, for Vanderbilt had long been known in New York financial circles as a powerful figure, who usually accomplished what he set out to do. So the bulls of Wall Street began to stir themselves.

Harlem stock had not stopped at 50, but was still rising. Drew's plan was to wait until the stock hit 75, then sell short, which meant the sellers would guarantee to deliver stock they did not yet own, at a price of $75 for each share.

The beauty of the plan was its simplicity: the council would deny the Harlem final authority for the street railway franchise. The price of Harlem would fall—perhaps even back down to 9 (they hoped). Then the councilmen would buy stock at $9.00 a share, and deliver it to their buyers who were already committed to pay $75.

It was an almost foolproof scheme, and the best part, as far as Uncle Daniel Drew was concerned, was that it did not cost him a penny in pay-off money. Vanderbilt, in effect, was going to make the payoff *and* Drew's profit.

But the plan did not work out quite as anticipated. In the first place, Harlem stock went crazy, and before the city councilmen could complete their short-sales, the stock went to 110. That was a higher figure than most of these men liked to use as a base, but they made their stock deals, selling short at 110—guaranteeing to deliver at that figure at a later date.

On June 25, when Vanderbilt's crews had already begun tearing up the streets, following preliminary approval of the plan, the council vetoed the franchise. Harlem dropped from 110 to 72 that very day like a stone. Uncle Daniel Drew grinned, and the councilmen rubbed their hands and counted their new carriages. Each councilman had already made $38 a share—on paper. They smirked and waited for the Harlem stock to fall further.

But none of the conspirators foresaw the single variable that could upset their careful plan: if someone bought Harlem heavily it would hold up the price of the stock.

Neither Drew nor the councilmen expected that Vanderbilt would do more than roar, shake his fist, and get out as quickly as possible, cutting his losses. They knew he was involved in railroads, but they also knew he was a steamboat man, and his excursions into rails on the stock market were regarded as simply those of another speculator, such as Daniel Drew, for in those days nearly everyone in business speculated in railroad stocks.

No one in Wall Street dreamed that Vanderbilt had a plan for the Harlem, or that he was so deeply committed in Harlem stock that he was prepared to stake his fortune on the issue at hand. So, after that first day, when Harlem had dropped so quickly, the councilmen and Daniel Drew were astounded to see Harlem stock level off, then begin, slowly, to rise. Vanderbilt was buying. Each hour he looked at the stock board grimly, and mentally calculated his margin of safety, the amount of cash he could risk without endangering his other holdings—but he continued to buy Harlem shares.

The Commodore's buying was supported by his brokers, by every liquid asset he owned, and some that must have been hardly there at all, buying and gathering up the stock certificates and putting them in his safe. With the Commodore's buying, the price of Harlem crept up to 80, to 95, to 108. Then it spurted to 125, and then to 150, to the dismay of the short sellers.

The councilmen, their friends, and Uncle Daniel Drew had been too greedy. They had guaranteed to deliver—at 110—more shares than now could be purchased on the market. Yet they had to deliver (and the Commodore was buying these options at $110 wherever he could find them).

The gray-faced short sellers had no recourse but to wait, and hope that something would drive the price of Harlem down. But Vanderbilt held the stock in his safe, and he held up the price. As the warrants came due, and the short sellers had to produce stock or go to jail, they had to buy at the Commodore's price: $180 per share. That meant they *lost*—some of them lost $70 on each share they had pledged, and the Commodore took the profit.

So Daniel Drew's scheme backfired. Commodore Vanderbilt made a fortune, Daniel Drew lost one, and the councilmen lost the shirts off their backs for their double-dealing, but more important, in acquiring control of the little New York and Harlem Railroad, Commodore Vanderbilt started a journey that would lead him to the greatest fortune in the nation.

III

THE VANDERBILT GOAL

11

NEW YORK CENTRAL

The wasteful, bloody years of war changed the entire art of money-making in the United States. The ability to find and use capital became more important than the capital itself. Men with a flair for handling money and new resources became the new million-aires; those to whom money meant land and ships and trade prospered less spectacularly.

The new breed brought new blood and new names to the front pages of the newspapers. Andrew Carnegie, child of Scottish weavers, started in telegraphy, then ground out a foothold on the periphery of the railroads. His fortune gushed in the western Pennsylvania oil boom. John D. Rockefeller, the son of a traveling medicine man, was first a bookkeeper, then went into trade, then found his own fortune in oil with the artful use of slender credit.

Jay Gould, a farmer's son, started his fortune on borrowed money. Gould had a boy's job with a village storekeeper in his New York home town. One day he overheard his employer talking about a piece of property, and an offer of $2000. Gould borrowed $2500 from his father, bought the land, and in two weeks sold it to his employer for $4000. Jay Gould was fired from his job when the employer figured out what had happened, but his life pattern was set.

Jay Cooke, a descendent of Yankee stock, made his fortune in the early days of the Civil War after the Union realized that the Confederacy would carry on a real war. It was costing the North a million dollars a day to fight for preservation of a nation. Cooke established himself as a war-bond salesman. He raised money for the government and kept a share of it for himself.

Jim Fisk, son of a Vermont peddler, learned the secrets of the financial world from no less a teacher than Daniel Drew, went on to become Drew's peer and to outfox the old man in speculation.

All these and others whose names became household words in America struggled for fame and fortune during the Civil War years. Few of the new crop of fortune makers risked life or limb in the front lines. They sent substitutes, then struggled manfully in the pits of the exchanges, showing their patriotism in arranging loans, making commission sales, and in procuring supplies for the boys in blue. If these stay-at-homes made handsome profits from their "war work," it was no more than was expected.

These men, several of them almost Vanderbilt's equals in brass, understood the Commodore far better than the archdeacons of the society in which he had matured, even though Vanderbilt was a child of Washington's time, and these new figures were yet unborn when he was rampaging along the Raritan and the shores of Long Island Sound.

The Commodore understood this new breed, too. With rare acumen, Vanderbilt *knew* the society in which he lived. In the war years, while close to the span of threescore years and ten, Vanderbilt still displayed a phenomenal grasp of the forces at work in his country and used them to his advantage. The good that accrued to the public was certainly not the spur that drove the Commodore, but that did not mean he had no patriotism or that he did no good. Vanderbilt firmly believed that what was good for Vanderbilt was good for the nation.

During the war when A. T. Stewart, the merchant king, gave $100,000 to the U. S. Sanitary Commission to treat the maimed and sick of the army, Vanderbilt also gave $100,000. Stewart had forced the figure; he had promised to give just as much as Vanderbilt, and every time Vanderbilt raised his pledge, Stewart met it. Vanderbilt was annoyed at the extent to which pride forced him to be charitable in this case, but he was not unpatriotic. In the spirit of his time, he saw no reason to make sacrifices in serving the government. But he *did* serve and several times he gave valuable service without personal compensation.

When the Confederate ironclad *Merrimac* was terrorizing Union shipping in the days before the fight with the *Monitor*, Vanderbilt went to Lincoln with an offer to stop her. He would steam out in his ship the *Vanderbilt* to meet the ironclad, protecting the ship's machinery from water-line shots with five hundred bales of cotton. Then, cool as a cucumber, he would ram the *Merrimac* and sink her. Lincoln asked Vanderbilt what kind of money he wanted to do this, for Lincoln did not believe the shipping king would risk his prize ship for nothing. Vanderbilt looked hurt, for he really did not want money for this job, and finally he convinced the President that he meant what he said. Had the *Merrimac* ever ventured forth again after her inconclusive battle with the *Monitor*, Vanderbilt might have gone down as a hero in the pages of naval history.

Except in such heroic enterprises Vanderbilt was far too old to take active part in the war, but he was not too old to sponsor rallies and help stir up the lukewarm sentiment of his city. In 1861 the Commodore served as vice-president of a Grand Rally that urged the selection of George Opdyke for mayor, to run against the incumbent Fernando Wood. Wood had been so unwise in 1861 as to suggest that New York secede from the Union, since much of the city's business was conducted with the southern states. Moreover Wood was a Democrat, in a year when no Democrats were wanted. Vanderbilt helped dump him.

The next year, in fawn coat, top hat, and carrying the eternal walking stick and smoking his infernal cigar, Vanderbilt lent his presence to mass meetings, fund-raising meetings, morale meetings, and recruiting meetings.

In 1863, when he had increased his prestige by victory in the Harlem River Railroad fight, he met with others at the Cooper Institute to ratify the Union ticket and pass a motion of censure against Democratic Governor Horatio Seymour, a censure prompted by the suspicion of Vanderbilt and many others that the Democrats did not want to win the war, but just to end it.

In June 1863 when General Robert E. Lee moved North to

Gettysburg for his desperate attempt to crush the Union forces, Commodore Vanderbilt was engaged in an equally grim struggle on the stock market, for he had been buying heavily in the stock of the Hudson River Railroad that ran parallel to his Harlem line. The bears of Wall Street, led by singed old grizzly Uncle Daniel Drew, decided to make a killing by forcing down the price of Hudson River stock, much in the way that they had tried to force down the price of Harlem. Vanderbilt was out of the city when he learned the news, but he gave orders to buy. He bought, steadily, and the price rose again. When accounts were settled, the bears had bloody snouts, and Vanderbilt had made more than $3,000,000, plus gaining control of the Hudson line.

William Henry Vanderbilt, the placid farmer-son, had proved in his operation of the Staten Island Railroad that he could help his father in railroad management, so the Commodore brought William into mainland railroading as operating vice-president of the Harlem line. There, as in the tiny Staten Island Railroad, William showed he knew how to follow orders and the Commodore began to treat him with some friendliness. Even Cornelius Jeremiah appeared to be tending to business on his Hartford farm, under the loving eyes and care of his wife Ellen.

By 1863 it seemed that the family had returned to a degree of harmony the Vanderbilts had not known for a quarter of a century. This atmosphere was heightened by a celebration held on December 19, 1863, the fiftieth anniversary of the marriage of Cornelius and Sophia.

Although the Commodore and Sophia had barely been on speaking terms for ten years, a hundred and fifty of the family and friends came to the house on Washington Place to honor them. Nearly half those assembled were children and grandchildren; the rest included brothers and sisters and husbands and wives, a parson or two and assorted cousins and nieces. The one important absentee was son George Washington Vanderbilt, who lay gravely ill on the French Riviera.

The house was spotless and brightly lighted, albeit a little shabby, since the Commodore really preferred friendly old drapes and rugs to new ones.

The guests arrived by carriage, coupé, phaeton, and ordinary hack, to be handed down by a liveried footman and directed to the front door of the house. Inside in the front parlor a Christmas tree of sorts had been erected—six feet of framework and ivy. But this was a family tree, not a Christmas tree—and its flowered decorations spelled out the names of the thirteen Vanderbilt children.

The arty N. B. LaBau (Mary Alicia's husband) took the floor to talk of the marvels of steam and to quote copiously from the Bible. William Henry delivered a short but dull address. Cornelius Jeremiah offered pious hopes that no one of the children would leave a blot on the escutcheon, an implied promise that he was still traveling the road toward reform. The grandchildren lined up and sang. LaBau sang, too, accompanied by the Seventh Regiment band which had been laid on for the occasion. Finally supper was announced at 10 P.M., and the group marched into the dining room behind the band.

After supper LaBau sang again, a composition of his own called "Resin in the Bow":

> "In Wall Street he is a tornado;
> He blows stock about as the dust;
> When speculators have made their pie, Sir,
> The Commodore breaks in the crust."

It was sheer flattery, but the Commodore loved every minute of it.

Daughter Ethelinda's son, the boy who had studied à la Astor in Germany, made a little set speech to the Commodore, expressing the delicate sentiments of the grandchildren:

"The habits of an active business life have, naturally, disinclined you for participation in social pleasures, but, I think, no one will contradict me in the assertion that we have uniformly experienced from you gentle treatment."

It was the Commodore's anniversary, that was obvious enough, although Sophia came out well in a material way. The Commodore gave her a solid-gold model of his *Roanoke* with music boxes inside. In turn, she gave him a solid-gold model of a house, for which he cared as little as she cared for the ship model.

William gave a present to his father that was as uninspired and simple as himself: a dressing case. Cornelius Jeremiah, pressed as usual for funds, managed to pawn something to buy a handsome bracelet for his mother, and a pill box covered with Scotch plaid for his father. George, from his far-off sickbed, sent his mother a fancy change purse and his father a gold-headed cane that had been made in China. There were chessmen, Bibles, brooches, bracelets, sticks by the dozen, card cases, gold chains, and every conceivable gewgaw in the display of gifts that emblazoned the table.

In the drawing room guests admired a marble bust of the Commodore, a memento of his *North Star* trip to Europe, when he had sat for a sculptor in Italy. Another bust, of Wilhelm Tell's son, was stationed on a marble table opposite. The room was ringed with fragrant flowers, and the central floral piece was a mass of heliotrope surrounding a huge white star of japonicas.

The band played and N. B. LaBau sang until twelve o'clock. Then, since the Commodore did not stay up past midnight, the fiftieth anniversary party was over.

Just a few weeks later, Vanderbilt suffered the worst personal tragedy of his life. Sophia sailed for France to visit and comfort young George, but, in January, George died from his illness, and Sophia sadly brought the body home for the funeral and the burial in the Vanderbilt mausoleum on Staten Island.

Cornelius Jeremiah disappointed his father again that year. The restless young man sought an appointment as a treasury agent in the newly occupied territories of the Confederacy. The papers said Vanderbilt was trying to get the job for his son, but the Commodore quickly disabused the public of that notion. He gave the press a full statement denying that he wanted anything from the government for himself or anyone in his family. Cornelius Jeremiah did not get the job.

Cornelius Jeremiah went South, and, using the family name carelessly (for years he signed himself Cornelius Vanderbilt, Jr.), the Vanderbilt black sheep talked his way through the Union lines. Ellen, his long-suffering wife, waited patiently in Hartford while her husband went off on this carpetbag expedition to make their fortune.

Cornelius Jeremiah's destination was New Orleans. His traveling companion, George Cook, paid all the traveling expenses; furthermore, Cornelius Jeremiah borrowed $4000 from Cook and gave him I.O.U.s. When the treasury agent plan fell through, young Vanderbilt tried to recoup in a cotton speculation, expecting to make thousands of dollars in profit in a quick sale of cotton, bought with local currency in a market where local currency was nearly worthless and sold for good money in the North.

General Banks—the same who had drunk champagne with the Commodore at the Brooklyn Navy Yard—was in command of the Union garrison. He appeared ready to open every door for a scion of the Vanderbilts. But the trouble was that Cornelius Jeremiah had opened too many doors already, some of them in the Vieux Carré, where the ladies and gamblers, as usual, had fleeced him of the $4000 borrowed from his friend Cook.

Cornelius Jeremiah continued to borrow money from everyone, including, in his own words—"a bore: to get rid of him." It was a sure-fire way of getting rid of people. Within a matter of weeks there was no one left to borrow from. Then Cornelius Jeremiah drew a draft on Horace Greeley for $1700—and wrote a letter imploring Greeley to honor it; otherwise, he warned Greeley, he would be dishonored and ruined. The implication was clear that the kindly Greeley would then be responsible for a suicide. Greeley did pay the draft, but soon even that money ran out, and finally Cornelius Jeremiah wrote a series of bad checks on the Hartford County Bank. When they began to bounce, the Commodore had his son brought North again, and bailed him out—on the promise that Cornelius Jeremiah would go into an insane asylum at Litchfield, Connecticut, for further treatment that both knew would be totally useless.

In his railroad affairs the Commodore fared more happily than in family matters. Having secured control of the Hudson River and Harlem lines, he made plans to put these together and end the ruinous competition. Vanderbilt went to the New York legislature and began to buy votes in favor of the scheme. The eager legislators took his money, introduced a consolidation bill, and gave Vanderbilt every indication that the bill would pass. Since Wall Street knew consolidation would cut expenses but not revenues, the stock of the Harlem line began to rise and soon it went to 150. To buy and be sure to keep control, at this high figure, Vanderbilt had to sell some of his other holdings, which he did not need for control, in exchange for ready cash, which he did need at the moment.

Hearing that the Commodore was short of cash, Daniel Drew and the bears decided the time was now ripe to make the killing of which they had been cheated twice before. Drew stuffed his valise with greenbacks and traveled to Albany. His money, he found, was just as good as the Commodore's; and the legislators already had the Commodore's money. The double cross was on.

It was the same old squeeze play. The legislators, sure that Vanderbilt was in no position to fight back, sold short, risking as much as each dared. Then they voted down the consolidation bill. Harlem dropped that day from 150 to 90. The legislators wanted to force the price down to 50, make their fortunes, and give Vanderbilt a lesson once and for all.

But a cornered Commodore was an even tougher customer than an ascendant one. The Commodore bought. He mortgaged his other holdings, he sold other properties, he endangered the very foundation of his fortune. But he bought. His brokers bought. His friends bought.

In the end, Vanderbilt had purchased 137,000 shares of Harlem stock—27,000 more than existed: he owned every share available in Wall Street. To deliver on their promises, again the short sellers would have to come to Vanderbilt for stock, for there was no other source in the open market. Vanderbilt alone controlled the price and the short sellers had to have stock.

How much would he take per share?

One thousand dollars per share, said the Commodore.

Wall Street gasped. Half the houses on the Street had bet against Vanderbilt and sold short. Those houses would be forced into bankruptcy. Wall Street, in brief, would be ruined as a financial center.

In this hour of triumph there was only one man who could influence Vanderbilt—his ally and sometime adviser, Leonard Jerome, grandfather of Winston Churchill.

The brokers descended on Jerome with the tale of their plight. Jerome took pity on them, and went to the Commodore. Vanderbilt was enjoying every minute of his triumph, but even in victory he could see that ruin of the brokerage houses would hurt the entire business world and thus hurt him. In the end he yielded to Jerome's entreaty, and let the speculators buy stock from him to fulfill their commitments—at $285 per share.

It was a nice figure. When the brokers and legislators heard it, their eyes bugged and their tongues lolled. For at $285 the offending brokerage houses would survive. But the legislators—those who had gone deepest into the scheme—would be ruined, which was exactly Vanderbilt's idea. He regarded the enemy brokers as fair game, but enemies who fought with his own weapons. He regarded the bought legislators who would not stay bought as predators ripe for extermination.

From the second Harlem crisis Vanderbilt made $25,000,000, on paper. Actually his profit turned out to be somewhat less because many of the legislators went bankrupt. But what he missed in dollars he made up in satisfaction and there were dollars enough. As for the satisfaction, he had the pleasure of breaking up one of the most dishonest legislative bodies that ever graced the halls of Albany's Capitol. Even those who questioned his methods and his aims had to admit that.

The Harlem crisis shook all New York. Vanderbilt still wanted to consolidate his lines, but neither he nor anyone else could approach the legislature on a railroad matter until the scandal of 1864 had died out, so the Commodore put his holdings together privately, began to work them as if they were in law the single railroad they were now in fact, and began to improve the roads.

William Henry Vanderbilt, the plodding but now trusted son, moved up to become chief operating executive of the Hudson, the more important of the two roads. Without daily responsibility, the

Commodore sat in his small plain office downtown and made his plans for the future. His personal staff consisted of a secretary, who occupied a stool in a corner of the office, and whose function was to write letters, take instructions, and write an occasional draft for the Commodore's uneven, spidery signature. The Commodore seldom used ordinary checks to draw on his bank accounts. On one occasion an ordinary check he had signed was refused, and the money was not paid by the bank until the order came in on a cheap scrap of paper made out in the Commodore's usual style. He did business at an unpretentious table with a single drawer, which held nothing but a handful of cigars. The Commodore's head held the details of his business life.

As Vanderbilt sat at his plain table in these later war years, he was planning the consolidation of the roads he owned with the New York Central, which in its own area had effected the consolidation of nine tiny roads in the Great Lakes and Albany regions of New York State. The Central, of course, provided rail communication for an important region of the country and the line ended at Albany, where Vanderbilt's began. In the course of a year the Commodore transferred much westbound freight to the Central, but he did not receive an equal amount of the Central's New York-bound traffic on his rail lines—a sore point. Daniel Drew, who still operated the People's Line on the Hudson, had an arrangement with the Central management to take shipments of freight and passengers at Albany and bring them to New York.

In 1865 Vanderbilt began quietly to buy Central stock. A year later he owned $2,500,000 in Central shares but was not even a director of the road. He was biding his time.

It was in 1866 that the Commodore persuaded the rising young Republican lawyer and politician Chauncey Depew to forsake the foreign service appointment to Japan and go to work for the Vanderbilt railroads. Depew became Vanderbilt's chief lobbyist in Albany. The Commodore was laying the groundwork more carefully this time for his consolidation plan; he also secured the election of Horace F. Clark (Marie Louise's husband) as a director of the Central.

That year the Central railroad agreed to ship its goods by the

Hudson rail route the year round instead of just during those months when the Hudson River was frozen over. The Central granted the Hudson a prorated share of all long-distance hauling charges. Further, the Central board agreed to pay the Hudson a $100,000 bonus each year.

Bonus for what?

When the controlling stockholders of the Central heard about the management's concessions to Vanderbilt, they became outraged, forced an election, pushed Vanderbilt's man off the board, and elected a new president of the line who outlawed the bonus to Vanderbilt's Hudson line.

Vanderbilt sat in his tiny office and said nothing.

At the end of each busy day, after a session with his trotters, the Commodore adjourned to the house or to one of his clubs for a session of whist. He was genial and seemed self-satisfied. He would talk about anything under the sun—but he would not talk railroads.

The year wore on to a close, and as the Christmas season approached, the Hudson River froze over as usual. On the seventeenth of January, when the river was completely closed to Daniel Drew's steamboats, the Commodore made his move.

In a two-paragraph advertisement in the New York newspapers, the Commodore announced that the Hudson River Railroad had canceled its transshipment arrangements with the Central as of that day. The Hudson would accept no more Central baggage. It would accept no more Central passengers. If passengers or baggage from the Central were to move on the Hudson line, they would pay full Hudson fares. They would also get themselves across the river from Albany to Greenbush, the end of the Hudson road.

The Central, whose business with New York City had been booming, was suddenly left without any means of shipping goods to New York. Drew's frozen steamboat line was no help.

There was absolutely nothing the Central's managers could do. Vanderbilt held their railroad's future in his hand. Two days later, the Central gave in. By the end of the year John Jacob Astor III and the rest of the owners had asked Vanderbilt to become president of the railway, and the Commodore had agreed to accept, with the air of a lord conferring a great favor on his subjects.

Commodore Vanderbilt was now in control of railroads which extended from the nation's largest city to Albany and Buffalo on the Great Lakes. He had access to the Hudson River at every desirable point. Although he had sold most of his steamboats, he kept enough of them to apply gentle pressure wherever they could help the rail lines. He had acquired a great transportation empire. His control was not yet permanent, but he had the three roads in his hands, his men managed them, and he could do what he liked with them for the time being, at least.

The Commodore was seventy-three years old, not as spry as he had been at sixty but spry enough, still able to astound his friends and frighten his enemies; he suffered from a hernia and wore a truss. His heart bothered him less, but his kidneys more. He worked a short day, never ate the whites of eggs, and pampered himself at other meals. In 1867, the same year that he grabbed the Central, the Commodore joined Horace Greeley and Gerrit Smith to put up a bond and extricate Jefferson Davis from his fortress prison, an action which cost Horace Greeley his political career, but cost Vanderbilt nothing for Vanderbilt's position was in no way dependent on public popularity.

Vanderbilt ran his combined railroads according to a formula of his own:

1. Buy the railroad.

2. Stop the stealing that went on under the other man.

3. Improve the railroad in every practical way, within reasonable expense.

4. Consolidate the railroad with any other road that can be run with it economically.

5. Water its stock.

6. Make it pay a large dividend.

The Commodore followed this advice to the letter. Shortly after he took over as president of the Central, he combined the Central and the Hudson as operating lines and changed the name of the new line to the New York Central and Hudson River Railroad. Then he proposed an 80 per cent dividend to be paid in scrip, and finally he declared that the combined railroad company was worth $45,000,000 more than the railroads had been worth singly. So he issued $45,000,000 more in stock for himself.

Even blasé Wall Street was aghast. It was, said Vanderbilt's enemies, the greatest job of "stock watering" ever accomplished in the United States. But that was a matter of opinion. The fact was that the old railroads had paid 6 per cent dividends—sometimes. Vanderbilt's consolidated line was to pay 8 and 10 per cent, even with the new $45,000,000 in shares to drain off earnings. That alone was proof that the Commodore was right in his evaluation of his own efforts, and if that was stock watering, well so be it. The Commodore had made it stick.

12

FAST HORSES AND FAST WOMEN

Each year after 1840 the Commodore traveled to Saratoga to take the water and avoid the heat of New York's dripping summer. The spa itself had grown steadily since the days when Philip Hone and his friends made the long trip up the Hudson by sailing sloop and carriage.

Saratoga now boasted a dozen hotels, the most famous of them, the United States and the Congress, were as large and luxurious as anything in Europe.

For years Vanderbilt stayed at the United States Hotel, where he had a special suite—the same one every year. As he grew older, Vanderbilt lengthened his visits to Saratoga, until finally he remained there during the entire months of July and August, conducting his business in person on the porch of the hotel, or in hastily scrawled messages to his subordinates in New York.

Sophia usually joined the Commodore on these vacations, their troubles buried in the mutual desire to escape New York's heat. But as the years rolled along, there had been less at Saratoga that interested Sophia, while the Commodore constantly found new avenues of pleasure there.

In 1845 the proprietor of the United States Hotel had built a clubhouse at the rear of the property, so the most wealthy of his guests could drink and play cards in peace when they were not escorting the ladies to the trotting races.

Now that William Henry had proved himself able to handle a railroad or two, the Commodore decided that his son should become a member of this club. That meant, usually, that the two Vanderbilts were at the table, along with Chester W. Chapin, president of the Boston & Albany; Joseph Harper, a New York Central director; Azariah Boody of the Baltimore & Ohio, and a Mr. Peabody, a wealthy gentleman from Philadelphia.

The Commodore had foresworn his glass of gin in later years and switched to less potent beer. He liked to sip champagne sometimes, but his regular afternoon refreshment was a glass of beer and the ever-present black cigar.

Whist, of which he had been uncommonly fond for forty years, had given way to the more exciting game of five-point euchre. The ante in the Vanderbilt card club was always $1.00, and often $60 or more made its way into the pot before a hand was played out. In the course of a two-month season, a considerable amount of money changed hands, usually, it seemed, traveling from the others to Vanderbilt.

An early morning breakfast, a cigar on the long-railed porch of the United States Hotel, a few hours of cards, a trip to the race course, either to race his own trotters or to watch, dinner, a few more hours of cards, and to bed by twelve. That was the Commodore's schedule at Saratoga. Sophia, who had little place in the scheme, had tired of it long ago. In 1865, when the United States Hotel burned to the ground, she found herself thrust into the unfamiliar surroundings of the Congress, which she liked even less, so in 1868, sick at heart after the death of George, Sophia decided to remain in New York, at the home of son-in-law Horace Clark.

The Commodore went to Saratoga without her. He was carrying out his usual daily schedule on August 17 when the word came that Sophia was dead. The Commodore had his private car, *Duchess*, attached to a special train and sped back to the city to pay his homage. He and Sophia had grown apart in recent years, to be sure, but she was the mother of his children; nor could a man live with a woman for more than half a century without feeling the loss once she was gone.

Sophia was buried in the old Moravian Cemetery, in the Vanderbilt mausoleum, near her beloved George and Phebe Hand, and Cornelius the father. The cemetery had a well-kept look to it now, largely thanks to Vanderbilt's gifts. He had given the church fifty-four acres of land to enlarge the cemetery, and cash to improve the land.

Alexander Turney Stewart and Horace Greeley were both pall-bearers at Sophia's funeral, walking behind the carriage hearse as it wound its way down Manhattan Island to the Staten Island ferry, and across, up the green, wooded lanes of New Dorp to the cemetery, past the familiar landmarks, the family cottage where they had begun married life, the mansion where Sophia had been so happy, William Henry's well-tended farm, Jake's house on top of the hill.

Then, when Sophia had been buried, Vanderbilt put all the past behind him, to begin a new kind of bachelor existence.

Business affairs in the morning, trotters in one of the parks or along the avenues in the afternoon, dinner and whist at one of his clubs—it was a lonely life for the seventy-four-year-old millionaire, but he kept himself busy.

And the ease with which he managed his affairs belied the Commodore's still eagle eye and fooled most of his enemies into thinking he was growing old and soft. Nothing could have been further from the truth.

For some time the Commodore had been looking around for a spot on the lower west side of New York—but not too far down—to build a new freight terminal. His eyes settled on St. John's Park, an airy spot in the middle of a well-to-do residential neighborhood —a park very similar to Gramercy Park on the other side of the city.

The Commodore began a quiet investigation and it was not long before he learned that the park itself was owned principally by Trinity Church. The property owners around the park had a share of it, too, but Trinity was the principal proprietor. Vanderbilt offered the vestrymen $1,000,000 for the property, and much to the disgust of the other property owners, they sold.

There was a storm of protest in the city. St. John's Park was merely an old landmark, but it suddenly became the "garden spot of downtown," and "one of the few breathing places for the city poor," in the pages of the daily newspapers. The property owners, when they learned that Vanderbilt intended to bring his damned railroad in there, went up in smoke.

But the Commodore paid no attention, for it was more important to him to make the Central into a better railroad than any of its three component lines could have been, and if he could accomplish that, save money and increase profits, he didn't care what anyone thought. Two million dollars had already gone into repair and replacement of equipment, but it was not a perfect road yet by far. Travelers could not go from New York to Buffalo, Boston, or Albany without danger of being killed; one night as the Commodore sat in his library in Washington Place playing cards, one of his trains was derailed, and the carnage was dreadful.

In the legislative investigation that followed, Vanderbilt was asked what he had done and where he had been when he heard of the accident. He had been at home, he said. He had done nothing. He had been playing cards, and he made it an inviolable rule never to be disturbed by business matters when he was playing cards.

Nevertheless, Vanderbilt took care of the operating side of the line in his own way. He inaugurated the practice of selling tickets on the platform rather than on the trains. Before Vanderbilt's time, tickets had been sold almost entirely by the conductors who ranged the cars. Conductors, thus, were very important men until Vanderbilt cut them down to size, a job he undertook first on the Hudson River Railroad.

On the Hudson line there was one rosy-cheeked, well-fed conductor, a favorite of all, who had been on the line for twenty years. His name was Jerry Phipps.

One day, after Vanderbilt had consolidated his three hundred miles of railroad, the Commodore called Conductor Phipps into the little office. Fortified by several bracers of brandy, the chubby conductor made his way into the presence of the great man.

Vanderbilt fixed conductor Phipps with a steely eye, and then glanced down to a piece of paper before him on the table. The

Commodore had done a little checking on the conductor's finances, he said. He had learned that conductor Phipps owned twenty-five houses in Rochester, fifteen in Syracuse, and five in New York City.

Jerry Phipps modestly admitted that was true. He had amassed, he said, deprecatingly, a small fortune, nothing like the Commodore's, of course—perhaps it totaled $300,000.

"On a thousand dollars a year?" Vanderbilt asked, for that was the pay of a conductor on the road.

The conductor indicated admiringly that what little he had stolen was nothing compared to the Commodore's own stock watering.

Vanderbilt brushed off the comparison. What kind of reparation did Phipps propose to make? Or would he rather go to jail for stealing from the road?

"How about three hundred dollars to call it square?" Phipps asked in moonfaced innocence.

Vanderbilt roared, and when his blood pressure had subsided only a little, he scribbled something on a piece of paper, thrust it across the table, and told Phipps to take it to the treasurer, pick up his pay, and never appear in a Central uniform again.

Phipps left. Vanderbilt then got to work cleaning house in the conductor department. Before he was through, he had installed the modern form of ticket sales, and set up the complicated system of checks and balances on on-train purchases that most American railroads use even today. That was not, however, completely the end of the Phipps story, and the sequel was enough to drive an executive into the nearest saloon. A year later, as Vanderbilt was walking through the train from his private car, a practice he followed when he traveled just to keep a check on operations, he saw ex-conductor Phipps sitting with three companions enjoying a bottle of champagne.

The Commodore remembered Phipps only too well. Calling the present conductor over, he asked if a fare had been collected from Phipps, or if he had a ticket.

Why no, said the conductor. Everybody knew Jerry Phipps was a friend of the Commodore's. Phipps had been traveling on the line regularly for a year, but all he ever did was show the pass the Commodore had given him.

Vanderbilt demanded the pass, and the conductor retrieved it. The Commodore saw in his hand the order of discharge he had given Jerry Phipps the year before.

But whatever ailed the old man's penmanship did not affect his business sense in running the railroads. The Vanderbilt fortune continued to grow. The best part, now, was that under the tax laws there were no income taxes collected on dividends from rail shares, so while Vanderbilt's millionaire friends paid taxes on hundreds of thousands and millions of dollars this year, Vanderbilt paid taxes on an income of $46,000—as gross a misrepresentation of annual growth as existed in the nation. That income represented his earnings from interest and miscellaneous commercial stocks. That same year, his railroad earnings alone must have been $1,000,000 on untaxed railroad stock.

This tax advantage in railroad stock had attracted a number of shrewd manipulators to the railroad industry—men who were interested only in fast profits. In the sixties, Daniel Drew, Jim Fisk, and Jay Gould mastered the art of stealing railroads, and all of them had proved most successful in this trade. Uncle Daniel was Fisk's principal mentor, and he used Fisk's undeniable talents as a confidence man to bamboozle his partners in various enterprises. The pair had peddled off Connecticut's Stonington line to a handful of Boston speculators for a handsome profit, and then had turned their attentions to the Erie Railroad which ran from New Jersey, across from New York City, west to the great lakes, on the west side of the Hudson and inland, while Vanderbilt's lines ran on the east side of the river. By 1868 Drew was a major holder of Erie stock, and had already made one fortune by using confidential information on the Erie to sell his own road's stock short.

The Commodore's interest in the Erie was obvious. He had tried to combine forces with both the Erie and the Pennsylvania, for he always avoided ruinous competition—or tried to—when he could make money without competing. But the Erie had rebuffed his advances, much to his disgust. For a little while he let the matter rest, then he began to make his move.

The Commodore already controlled a large chunk of Erie stock, so he decided, quietly, as he had before, to begin buying and take over the road, cut competition and increase his profits.

But Daniel Drew and the others had invested heavily in Erie bonds—convertible bonds. Now they used their power on the Erie board to authorize conversion of the bonds to stock, and Vanderbilt took the matter to the courts, where each side had bought its own judge. Drew, Fisk, and Gould fled from New York before they could be arrested on an order from Vanderbilt's judge and conducted operations from the west bank of the Hudson where Vanderbilt's bought judge had no jurisdiction.

Vanderbilt had mortgaged his Erie stock and other stocks to buy control of the Erie line. But each time he thought he had enough stock to assume control, newly printed Erie stock came on the market and he had to buy more shares to try to keep the price up. The money for these shares went directly into the pockets of Fisk and Gould, much to Vanderbilt's annoyance, but there was nothing he could do about it for once. He was well hooked by his own scheme, and had to keep on buying as long as the presses kept on printing, just to keep his investment covered.

Fisk, Drew, and Gould dumped 100,000 shares of wet-inked Erie stock on the market that year. Vanderbilt lost an initial $7,000,000 when this wily den of bears sold short and then panicked the Street with the stock certificates they printed on order to meet their commitments.

Although the triumvirate had fled New York, they had not gone empty-handed. From their short-selling operation and flotation of new stock, they had netted some $6,000,000. They stuffed it in suitcases and took it to Taylor's Hotel in Jersey City. Fisk brought his paramour, Josie Mansfield, along, and business and pleasure went on as before.

The Erie war, as it was known around the country, began at the first of the year, and battles were fought all spring and summer, both in the stock market and along the railroad lines, for Vanderbilt, at first trying to keep the price of Erie up, was still determined to push Gould, Fisk, and company out of the railroad management. The Erie cut its rates from $7.00 to $5.00 for the trip from Buffalo to Jersey City. Vanderbilt cut the freight rates on the New

York Central and growled. Fisk, he predicted, would not bedevil the poor much longer. Someone was going to shoot him one of these days, the Commodore said.

Jay Gould, another for whom the Commodore predicted an untimely end, packed his valise with greenbacks and started for Albany, hopeful that he could make the legislators see some reason to legalize the fraudulent stock the conspirators had issued. After dispensing a million dollars, Gould persuaded the lawmakers that the printing press was mightier than Vanderbilt's bought injunction against using it—and the legislature legalized the steal.

Vanderbilt would not give up. He kept harrying the three all year and he had Gould arrested in Albany. Meanwhile, to bolster his own position, he watered the stock of his carefully tended New York Central, as he had the Harlem and the Hudson; he declared a stock dividend, and issued himself another $26,000,000 in Central stock. In putting together his three railroads, he *created* $71,000,000 in stock value, simply by saying this was so.

In the final analysis, Vanderbilt settled with Fisk and Gould on the Erie fight. Those two had eased a failing old Uncle Daniel Drew out of the picture altogether; then they bought back Erie stock at prices that returned Vanderbilt all but a million dollars of the money he had spent in trying to control the Erie.

"Never kick a skunk," the Commodore remarked thereafter, when reminded of his dealings with Drew, Fisk, and Gould, but the sting of the Erie failure was salved by the Central's success.

Having recouped amazingly, considering what he had lost in his war with the Erie, Vanderbilt continued to improve the New York Central line. He had retained a handful of steamboats, and put the *Connecticut* and the *C. Vanderbilt* on the Troy route to force his steamboat competitors to abandon landings that fed other railroads and transfer their passengers and freight to his Central system.

He opened negotiations with John D. Rockefeller, now an important oil magnate, to ship 100,000 barrels of oil over the New York Central lines, and when Rockefeller refused to come to him, the crusty old Commodore dropped his pride and went to Rockefeller. He got the business, just as he usually got what he wanted

—even when it involved such odd desires as the Commodore's to speak with the dead. A new occult science, called spiritualism, had seized the gullible of the nation within the past few years. Mediums—those who claimed to be go-betweens who could summon loved ones back from the spirit world—did a thriving business in the America of the sixties and seventies. The Commodore, in these later years, yearned for contact with his mother, Phebe Hand, and had even softened toward the father he had liked so little during the other's lifetime. He would give a hundred thousand dollars, Vanderbilt told a friend, if he could have a painted likeness of his father to match that of Phebe Hand that hung in the house on Washington Place.

He could not do that, but he thought he could keep in contact with the "other world" through spiritualism. After a few tentative sessions in darkened rooms when the Commodore was convinced that the mediums actually brought him in touch with his mother and father, he became a firm believer, and began to visit professional spiritualists regularly.

One of his favorites was a female medium who lived on Staten Island. He went across on brother Jake's ferries regularly to engage in rapping ceremonies, magic circles, and other strange rites of communication with the dead.

A gentleman named Van Kleeck, one of the early mediums, had been converted back to paths of righteousness, and had then gone on a lecture tour to expose the tricks of his trade and earn an honest dollar. He lectured often in New York, where his speeches were disrupted (by spiritualists and anti-spiritualists) with hoots and catcalls and often ended in something near riots, so strong were the views on both sides. Van Kleeck's confessions caused some other spiritualists to renounce their calling, but they did not shake Vanderbilt's faith in the universality of spirits. Anyone with the cheek to go and see him was likely to get a hearing, and any medium who had something new in the spook world would find the Commodore an interested listener.

At this time, into the lonely old man's life stepped a pair of young women—mediums—who had more than one commodity that Vanderbilt wanted. They were Victoria Woodhull and her sister Tennie Celeste Claflin, later to shorten her name to Tennie C. Claflin and finally to the more euphonious Tennessee Claflin.

Victoria Woodhull was the strong one of the pair, a girl with a wide, open face, heavy eyebrows, and a broad mouth. She was buxom, but that was the way men liked them in those days of brocade and bustle, and what Victoria lacked in the qualities of Venus, she made up in the qualities of Hera. Victoria wanted to be a wife to every man she met. Her sister, Tennessee, ran her a close second.

The pair had been raised in squalor in the town of Homer, Ohio, where their father was a surveyor and a postmaster. Their mother, Roxanna, claimed to be the illegitimate daughter of a former governor of Pennsylvania; she was a female martinet who did her best to keep order in a tumble-down house which was spilling over with children and relatives.

When Victoria was eleven, the whole family was run out of town when her father, Buck, was caught burning down his gristmill for the insurance money. The Claflins formed a medicine company and sold a complexion cure made from vegetable juice. It didn't help anyone, but it didn't hurt them much either. These were the days when Victoria and Tennessee learned the performing arts they were to use so well later.

In 1853, when Victoria was sixteen, she married a respectable physician, Dr. Canning Woodhull, and bore two children, a boy named Byron and a girl named Zulu Maud. Not long afterwards, however, Victoria carted the family off to California to become an actress because she had been offered a job in a San Francisco theater. After a brief career on the stage, she realized that there was much more gold for her to dig in the occult, for Victoria had the histrionic ability, convincing appearance, and sex appeal to be a first-class medium. Having made that decision, she deserted Dr. Woodhull, who would have been nothing but a drag in her new life.

Victoria went back to the Middle West, dispensing more than rappings, and brought Tennessee into the trade. They practiced fortunetelling, magnetic healing, and other more interesting trades.

Business boomed: one of their customers in Cincinnati, where they first put out the shingle, was Jesse Grant, father of the President; they had a male clientele envied by every other spiritualist in the Middle West.

But Tennessee displayed more greed than good sense. She tried to blackmail one of her regular companions in clairvoyance; he didn't pay—but he did file a criminal charge against her. The firm of Claflin and Woodhull, Clairvoyants, closed its doors and the girls left town in a hurry.

In a further tour of the Midwest, Victoria picked up a bosom companion—Colonel James Harvey Blood—and then the entire crew, including old Buck Claflin, made its way to New York. Blood was the brains; Victoria and Tennessee were the attractions. It was apparently his idea to move in on the Commodore when he learned that the old man was one of the three million Americans who believed in ghosts. Move in they did, first to a house at 17 Great Jones Street, near Broadway. Victoria was thirty, and the leggy Tennessee was a luscious, slightly bucktoothed twenty-two.

In his loneliness the Commodore was creating problems at the mansion on Washington Place, where he could not keep his hands off the help. His daughters, who kept maternal eyes on the running of the house, complained that housemaids refused to stay on —for the old man demanded far too much extracurricular activity. Then Woodhull and Claflin solved his problem.

The girls came into the Commodore's life as healers. Suffering now from kidney stones, heart trouble, hernia, a liver disorder, and old age, the Commodore needed a great deal of healing. He had been getting it from a wizard who used mild electric shock treatment to brace the old boy up. But Tennessee and Victoria promised magnetic healing by the laying on of hands, after they had been brought around by their father Buck and introduced to the Commodore with a great show of gentility.

Vanderbilt immediately took to Tennessee as the younger and prettier of the two. Within a few days he had her installed as his official healer and constant companion. The housemaids were safe, and Claflin and Woodhull had their feet fairly planted on the ladder leading to fame and fortune.

The Commodore wanted to marry Tennessee. She was more than willing, but here William Henry and the girls stepped in with both fear and anguish. It was all right for their father to keep the girl around the house and call her "little sparrow." It was all right for her to practice healing him and call him "old boy." But they drew the line at marriage. Instead, knowing his need and glandular determination, they encouraged another candidate.

In the fall of 1868 the Vanderbilts were honored by a visit from Miss Frank Crawford of Mobile, Alabama, and her mother. Mrs. Crawford was the granddaughter of Phebe Hand's long-lost brother. Miss Frank, who was twenty-nine years old, was a distant cousin of the Commodore, and thus she represented a tie of sorts with Phebe Hand. Equally important, she was young, unmarried, and willing, and, from the children's point of view, eminently respectable.

Tennessee Claflin continued to care for the Commodore's spiritual needs, but he began an awkward courtship of Frank, totally ignoring the widowed mother.

The Crawfords had come North to escape the summer heat of Mobile and to cure Frank of some malaise attributed to Alabama's humid climate. She arrived pale, thin, and ailing. After a tour of the spas and the visit to New York City, the Commodore cautioned her in a note not to try to gain *too much* weight. After all, he wrote gaily, one hundred twenty-five pounds would be quite enough for her beautiful figure.

Frank responded to these compliments with a request for a signed photograph of the Commodore, no small trophy to show around the parlors of Mobile, for the Commodore was generally acknowledged now to be the biggest man in American business, and undoubtedly the richest.

Late in October, with a promise to return the next year, Frank and her mother went back to Mobile and Vanderbilt resumed his interest in business.

For several years now he had operated his railroads as a single system, although he had no legal right to combine them under the franchises granted by the New York state legislature. At this point there were material advantages to legalizing the combination, and the stench of the legislative sell-out of 1864 had been lost in the greater corruption that swept the state and city machines in the late sixties.

Vanderbilt combined forces with Jay Gould and Jim Fisk, who wanted more concessions for the Erie. Together, the railroaders were able to buy legislative approval of the laws they wanted, early in 1869, and then having co-operated for a few days, the competitors promptly began a rate war.

The Commodore used exactly the same tactics in railroading that he had used in steamboating: force competitors to the wall and eventually buy them out. In this fight he cut the freight rates on the New York Central by 75 per cent. Where it had previously cost $160 to ship a carload of cattle from Buffalo to New York City, Vanderbilt charged only $40. The Erie cut back. Finally Vanderbilt dropped his price to a dollar a carload. Thereupon Fisk, who had learned his trade well under that old drover Daniel Drew, bought more than five thousand head of cattle and shipped them to New York—all on Vanderbilt's railroad.

When the story hit Wall Street, and the brokers began to wag their heads and grin over Fisk's coup, the Commodore exploded.

But when he cooled down, he decided it was best to let Fisk and Gould strut on their dunghill, while he kept to his own, and he pulled out of the Erie fight. "From now on," he said, "I'll leave them blowers alone."

At this stage of his life, the Commodore began to spend more time with his trotters and less in business affairs. He still made the important decisions, but William Henry had become manager of the Vanderbilt railroads, ably assisted by Chauncey Depew in Albany, who dealt with the legislators and handled the railroad's legal business.

The way to Vanderbilt's heart, all New York knew, was through the stable door. The Commodore maintained a stable full of rigs and tack in the coachhouse that backed on his city mansion, and a standing offer of $10,000 for a really fast trotter. He spent as much time petting and looking at his prides as he did in showing and racing them.

William Henry kept his own trotters and although his interest in the sport seemed much milder, he drove to upper Manhattan whenever he could to race in a maroon rig with horses that were almost—but not quite—as fast as his father's. Side whiskers flying, ruddy face aglow, his heavy body smacked squarely in the center of the seat, William Henry drove as he ran railroads: stolidly and well, with great attention to detail, and with never a risky or radical idea. The operating head of a great railroad empire now, William Henry still looked the humorless bank clerk and bookkeeper he had been in his youth.

William Henry was always careful, so great was the Commodore's power, to keep his own bread well buttered, never to offend the old man. He was running the roads, but he never made a policy move without asking the Commodore's permission. When employees gave William Henry a welcome-home celebration after a trip, he sat down before a day had passed to assure his father in writing that all the success of the railroad was really due to the Commodore; William Henry did not want Vanderbilt to begin to believe he was getting too big for his britches. Although in this year he was forty-eight years old, had nine children of his own and lived graciously in a mansion on Fifth Avenue, the Commodore still treated him like a boy.

In financial matters William Henry was shrewd enough. He had made a fortune for himself on Wall Street, using capital lent him by the Commodore. One time—during the second Hudson fight with Drew—the Commodore advised William Henry to sell Hudson stock short when it was at 110. A few days later, when the stock hit 137, the old man came around to see how his son had fared. He asked how far William Henry had gone in the market.

William Henry, with the contemplation of a cow chewing her cud, replied that he had gone in at 110 on 10,000 shares, hoping to make $260,000 in profit.

Pulling a long face, the Commodore offered his condolences. If William Henry had sold short at 110, and the price of the stock was now 137, the younger man stood to lose $27 a share, or $270,000.

"Too bad," the Commodore sympathized.

"Not at all," William Henry replied impassively. The Commodore had advised him to sell short, but before he did anything, he snooped around to find out what the Commodore was doing. When he learned that his father was buying, William bought too. Therefore he had made $270,000.

Such incidents sent William Henry's stock rising with Vanderbilt, who began to show signs of paternal pride in the son he had formerly regarded as a clod. As William Henry rose in his father's esteem, Cornelius Jeremiah, now forty-four, continued to fall. At one point the father exclaimed that he would give a million dollars if the epileptic were not named Vanderbilt, for in 1867 the younger man had even been forced into personal bankruptcy, and had taken a gold cup from brother-in-law Horace Clark's house and pawned it.

From the Connecticut farm, Cornelius Jeremiah continued to try to make his way in the worlds of business and government, unfortunately relying on influence and money rather than on his abilities. In March 1869 Alexander Turney Stewart was named Secretary of the Treasury by President Grant. The ink was not dry on the appointment when Cornelius Jeremiah applied for a job as tax assessor for the Ninth District in the state of New York. The application was endorsed by Cornelius Jeremiah's unflinching friend, Horace Greeley.

Young Vanderbilt did not get the job, because Stewart did not get his. The Stewart appointment was not confirmed by the Senate because Senator Sumner of Massachusetts found a conflict of interest between Stewart's government contracts and the secretaryship.

Such luck plagued Cornelius Jeremiah. He would not stop his gambling, despite the entreaties of his wife and the castigation of his father. That same year he drew another sight draft on Horace Greeley, this time for less than $125. He dared not ask for more, and he could not ask his father for anything at all. The Commodore, whose patience with his exasperating second son had been greater than anyone could have expected, was growing tired.

13

THE LAST DAYS OF A MOGUL

The United States Government fell into the hands of plunderers at the outset of the first Grant administration in 1868, but such corruption was an old story to New York City and New York State, whose governments had been systematically milked by a Democratic Tammany Hall for twenty years.

During Fernando Wood's administrations in New York City, in the fifties, Tammany had organized the cheating on city contracts, the bribery, and the collections from criminals for protection. When Boss Tweed hoisted his huge bulk onto the throne of the Grand Sachem of Tammany he removed the ceiling on corruption, and from then on, the sky was the limit.

Tammany sent its repeaters and fixers and bully boys to the polls in election after election. Tammany's stock in trade was control of more polling places than the Republicans. In 1868 Boss Tweed elected John T. Hoffman as governor, and then the stealing doubled.

For his trouble in putting Hoffman in the governor's chair, Tweed wanted control of both the state and the New York city government. He drew a new charter for the city, then persuaded a number of leading citizens to back the charter move, including Peter Cooper, innocent old president of the Citizens' Association, a group dedicated to stamping out corruption.

Tweed's next step was to bribe the state legislature. He did a better job than even Vanderbilt had done in the past: all but two

members of the state senate were on the Tweed gift list that
year. The total cost was $600,000.

Wholesale theft had now been legalized, approval of all city
expenditures was placed in the hands of Tweed, City Comptroller
Richard B. Connolly, and "Elegant" Oakey Hall, the mayor. On
May 5, 1869, the triumvirate approved padded bills that totaled
almost $6,500,000, keeping most of it for themselves. In eighteen
months New York paid $2,703,308.48 to various newspapers for
"advertising." Eighty-seven newspapers were given outright bribes.
Some strange bills were rendered by businessmen, too. Andrew J.
Garvey, a plasterer, received $138,187 for two days' work on the
new courthouse in City Hall Park, and $2,870,464.06 for other
work. Tweed, born the son of a Scottish chairmaker, became New
York's third largest real-estate owner. Comptroller Connolly and
Mayor Hall did almost as well.

When the outraged citizens began to complain and tried to pull
themselves together to oust the criminals, the names of the Vanderbilts were singularly absent from the list of the public-spirited.
The Vanderbilts, like Gould and Fisk, were too deeply involved
with the Tweed Ring to cry out, even had they been reformers—
and certainly no one in New York ever said the Vanderbilts were
reformers.

In 1867 Boss Tweed served as a special representative of the
Vanderbilt interests in Albany as well as a state senator from New
York City. But that year Jim Fisk and Jay Gould made Tweed a
better offer: if Tweed would come over to their side, they would
make him a director of the Erie Railroad, give him a block of stock,
and keep him well supplied with money to feed the hungry mouths
of his loyal state legislators.

The Fisk and Gould offer was too good to turn down, and between 1868 and 1871 Boss Tweed collected $1,504,912.71 for legal
expenses alone—legal expenses being part of the bribery of public
officials in this case. Jay Gould paid $586,000 of that amount, Fisk
almost $200,000, while the Vanderbilts paid only $18,950 to the
ring's fund.

Anyway, between business and the ministrations of Tennessee
Claflin and his long-distance pursuit of the more elegant Miss

Frank Crawford, the Commodore had no time or inclination for local politics.

The Crawfords came North again in the summer of 1869 to take the waters at Saratoga and see their rich city cousins. In mid-August the Commodore asked Frank to marry him, and she accepted without hesitation, but she wanted to be married by her own Episcopal minister, the Rev. Dr. Charles F. Deems. The good Dr. Deems could not be readily located, so an eager Vanderbilt persuaded her to elope to Canada. On August 20 the Commodore had a prenuptial property agreement prepared, which gave Frank $500,000 in first mortgage bonds of the New York and Harlem (at par). Both signed the document, then they departed by special train for New London, Ontario.

Vanderbilt suggested that they get married in Canada because he did not want to raise a fuss in the United States, but it was difficult for Vanderbilt to order up a special train and board it with a young lady without arousing suspicions. Before they left Saratoga the news was out.

Whenever the train stopped, crowds gathered to demonstrate with rockets and torpedoes, even though it was Sunday. As they sped through one little town, Frank laughed aloud when she saw a man climb atop the depot scantlings to get a good look at her.

It was a cloudy, cool day, unmarred by dust or rain, quite comfortable for traveling. At two o'clock in the afternoon waiters set the dining table, and they ate a nourishing dinner of broiled chickens and lamb chops, as the train chugged north to Canada.

The marriage was performed by a minister in Wellington. After the ceremony, the train was turned around and the happy couple went back to Syracuse, where a great crowd of people gathered to see the seventy-five-year-old railroad magnate and his thirty-year-old bride. They pushed their way through the streets to the Vanderbilt Hotel, then went up to rooms filled with flowers; there were eight bouquets to decorate the parlor alone, including a pyramid of flowers that stood three feet tall.

The next day they returned to Saratoga and the Congress Hotel, where they were greeted by William Henry and his wife, and later by assorted other relatives. Frank was embarrassed when they went to dinner in the huge dining room because the fashionable ladies kept raising and lowering their lorgnettes, intrigued by the woman who had walked off with the business world's aging first citizen.

After the midday meal, Vanderbilt and his bride retired to their rooms for a short nap. A bit later the Commodore stole downstairs to enjoy a cigar, while Frank stayed in the room, luxuriating in bed. Her single complaint at this point was that she nearly stifled from the perfume of the baskets of tuberoses and heliotrope that filled the room. One bouquet, she marveled, had come all the way from Rochester in a *tin box*.

The next day more people began to call, including N. B. LaBau, Mary Alicia's musical husband. Frank thought him a nice little fellow, although a trifle strange. Mrs. Baldwin, the wife of the locomotive king called; so did General Granger and Alexander Turney Stewart. Frank started an argument with old Stewart when he praised General Grant. As a loyal Mobile girl who had lived through the war in the heart of the southland, Frank could not stomach Stewart's praise of his hero—who was anathema to her.

That afternoon "Com," as she called him, drove her out in a buggy to try his new horse, Myron Perry. Frank enjoyed the speedy drive around the mile-long track in a double top buggy. They made the circuit in 2:36. Quite a breeze, she said.

At the grandstand they took a box to watch Mountain Boy race Lady Thorne. During the excitement, Uncle Jake Vanderbilt came up and insisted on kissing the bride. Frank, in her new black silk gown, was scrutinized by thousands of people—and loved every minute of it.

In New York as at Saratoga, the winter-summer marriage was the talk of polite society, and many noses were elevated and many sniffs sniffed at the idea of *that old man* marrying *that shameless woman*. No matter where the senior Vanderbilts went, to Delmonico's for supper or to a public meeting, Frank was an object of attention and envy. Her notoriety had not evaporated on November 10, when the new freight yard and terminal at St. John's Park were dedicated, and an $800,000 bronze memorial was unveiled in honor of the Commodore. Frank and several of her friends watched the ceremonies from Mrs. Rice's house at 145 Hudson Street, and were watched themselves in turn.

President Grant had been invited to make the address, but had sent his regrets, so "Elegant" Oakey Hall, the college-educated, crooked mayor, was the speaker of the day. Mayor Hall told Jim Fisk, Jay Gould, August Belmont, broker Henry Clews, and a thousand others how great a man the Commodore had become; twenty-four sailors from the U.S.S. *Tallahassee* stood at attention while the band played "America" and "He's a Jolly Good Fellow"; then the crowd came to the business at hand: the unveiling of Vanderbilt's memorial.

The monument was a bronze, made by the sculptor Albert de Groot, son of one of Vanderbilt's fellow captains on the old New Brunswick steamer line. It was 150 feet long and 31 feet high, it covered 3125 square feet and weighed 50 tons; it included replicas of steamers and locomotives, primeval forests, cogwheels, anchors, periaugers, wild ducks, and houses, statues of Neptune and Liberty, and a colossal figure of Commodore Vanderbilt himself, in a fur-trimmed overcoat, looking down from on high.

As a monument it was startling. As a piece of art, it was monstrous.

In the Long Room of the Stock Exchange, the Burlesque and Glee Club held its own ceremony that day. The chairman of the affair delivered a serious address—well, a seriocomic address—in sepulchral tones, lauding the virtues of an unknown shrouded figure. At the climax, the shroud was dropped from the figure, revealing a lolling tongue, protruding eyes, and contracted features. In one hand the statue held a watering can, on which was painted the figure at which New York Central stock stood when Vanderbilt legalized the consolidation of his three railroads.

The other hand of the figure was encased in a boxing glove.

Altogether it was a heartfelt tribute by the financial men to one of the slickest operators Wall Street had ever seen. The Wall Streeters didn't hate Vanderbilt, they admired him right down to his shoelaces for what he had been able to do, and they acknowledged the Commodore as the smartest man in American business, because he did just about what he wanted to do, and made it pay.

These Wall Streeters had little influence on Vanderbilt now, as he had retired from speculation in the stock market. The one person who could influence the Commodore was his wife Frank. When she first set foot in her new home at 10 Washington Place, Frank had insisted on redecorating. The Commodore balked, and swore a bit when she also demanded new furniture and rugs, but eventually she had her own way, even to the point of bringing her mother to live with them, for beneath a pious and somewhat vacant expression beat the brain of a true businesswoman—who, like her husband, usually got what she wanted.

But even Frank had to feel her way with the Commodore in money matters. One time Frank asked Vanderbilt to do something for Dr. Deems, her friend and pastor. The Commodore first presented the man of God with a one-way ticket to the West Indies. But when Frank continued to pester Vanderbilt to help her Dr. Deems, the Commodore really did help. He bought a church on Mercer Street (worth $50,000), refurbished it, and gave it to the minister. It was rededicated as an Episcopal church and called the Church of the Strangers, and thereafter, it became *the* official church of the Commodore Vanderbilts.

Then the new Mrs. Vanderbilt began to persuade the Commodore to do something for her relatives, and before much time passed, her brother had become eastern freight agent of the New York Central. Frank's cousin, Bishop H. N. McTyeire, who headed a little Methodist Episcopal school in the South, was most anxious to establish a great university. He could think of no better source of money than his cousin's husband, who seemed to be the richest man in the country. Besides, Vanderbilt had joined with Horace Greeley to bail Jefferson Davis out of prison in 1867, hadn't he? The Commodore obviously had a tender spot in his heart for the South.

Bishop McTyeire enlisted Dr. Deems and Cousin Frank to help pry money away from Vanderbilt, and, although not immediately successful, they did not stop trying.

Before taking care of his wife's relatives, however, Vanderbilt felt a responsibility to do something for his old playmates, Victoria Claflin Woodhull and Tennessee Claflin, so he did one thing he knew how to do well: he set them up in the brokerage business on Wall Street. Immediately the ladies began to earn money, because Vanderbilt made their fortunes with a few well-timed tips on the movement of the market, and not long after, he supplied the capital which established *Woodhull and Claflin's Weekly,* a newspaper that advocated free love and the election of Victoria to the presidency.

At this, some critics charged that the Commodore was in his dotage, and he was pleased to have them think so. In the fall of 1872, when he was seventy-eight years old, and the far younger Jim Fisk had met the untimely end Vanderbilt predicted, Vanderbilt was still active as president of the New York Central. He extended the railroad empire to include the Michigan Central Railroad, and the Lake Shore line in Illinois. That gave him lines running to Chicago, both north and south of Lake Erie. He reached an accommodation with canny John D. Rockefeller to carry most of Standard Oil's business. Rockefeller established a company with the innocent name of the South Development Company, which handled the shipping of petroleum products. Vanderbilt and other agreeable railroad operators charged Rockefeller as low a rate as anyone else, and then slipped a handsome rebate under the table to the South Development Company. It was an excellent arrangement for all concerned, except the Rockefeller and Vanderbilt competitors.

William Henry handled most of the details of such arrangements, for he was a detail man. The Commodore had finally grudgingly accepted this eldest son as his principal heir, the person who would eventually *control* his fortune. He had misgivings, but Vanderbilt wanted to make sure his enterprises were kept intact when he died, and he was certain that the only way to keep the fortune together was to leave it in the hands of one person. Having chosen William Henry, with all those misgivings, Vanderbilt now prepared his son to assume the reins of power.

In his youth Vanderbilt had lusted for money for its own sake, but in his last years he learned that money itself was meaningless, beyond the amount that would provide necessities and luxuries for the family.

"A million or two is as much as anyone ought to have," he had told an acquaintance at Saratoga.

The acquaintance suggested that he would be glad to take a few surplus millions off Vanderbilt's hands, so the Commodore concluded his thought:

"But what you have is not worth anything unless you have the power. And if you give away the surplus, you give away the control."

That was Vanderbilt's mature philosophy.

In the seventies others in the New York Central family wanted to push on past Chicago, but the Commodore had no desire to extend himself, for he was too old to change the character of his holdings and to start an entirely new system, and neither William, nor any of his sons-in-law had shown the drive and imagination it would take to forge ahead in new times. Cornelius Jeremiah, of course, was not even under consideration. Vanderbilt's greatest disappointment, even now, was that son's weakness. No longer a young man, the second son had failed again in his promises of reform. In the spring of 1872 Ellen died, and to forget his grief, Cornelius Jeremiah started on a tour of the nation. By mid-summer he was roaming around the Colorado country. He had kept in close touch with Horace Greeley all this time, and Cornelius Jeremiah wrote his friend in June that he had received a letter from the Commodore in which the old man had been quite affectionate. It must have been too much for the epileptic, for within a few months the Commodore was writing correspondents outside New York that there was some wild man traveling around the country writing drafts on the Commodore, and posing as his son—an imposter, Vanderbilt said.

But if the Commodore vacillated in his attitude toward his second son, he became ever more pliant—to a point—in the hands of his new wife, who sometimes referred to herself as "my old man's darling." Bishop McTyeire's prayers—and Frank's pleas—were granted when the Commodore gave nearly a half-million dollars in Vanderbilt railroad bonds for the enlargement of the bishop's college. In gratitude the trustees changed the name of the institution to Vanderbilt University in the spring of 1873. He also gave a plot of land on Staten Island for the establishment of a female seminary, and was prepared to give an additional half-million dollars in bonds if the plan for that institution had not fallen through.

It was bonds he gave—always railway bonds—for the principal could be guarded, the interest paid, and with care, control need never be lost to the family.

The Commodore worried endlessly about control, no mistaking that. He lectured William Henry on the subject, he wondered aloud to minor officials of the railroad line about whether the family would have the gumption to retain the railroad after he was dead, or if they would lose it by squabbling. He was under no illusions about the attitudes of his daughters and their husbands toward William Henry or the hopes of each daughter for a major share of the fortune. If his daughters held a balance of control, he knew, they would combine to oust William Henry and put in one of his sons-in-law. In six months, he said, the girls would be squabbling over the management of the railroads; it would not be long before they lost control of the roads, and then the Vanderbilt empire would vanish. The Commodore had slaved to build the fortune and the family name, and he wanted both retained intact. Had he died as early as 1854 (when he was only a shipping king) he would have been forgotten quickly, Vanderbilt knew. The railroads had made the name, and the name had come to mean more to him than the money.

He was so mindful of the importance of control by 1873 that after he gave up playing the stock market, he quarreled with his brokers over their speculations and took his business to the new Wall Street firm of Barton and Allen, a house where he hoped his words would have more weight, since Barton was his nephew and Allen was a grandson, the child of daughter Ethelinda.

Vanderbilt did not speculate again, nor was he willing to borrow, if any other method would accomplish the same ends. When he took over the Lake Shore Railroad the line was threatened with bankruptcy. With his unlimited credit, Vanderbilt could have gone to a banker, on his title as president of the Lake Shore, and borrowed the money he needed to straighten out the railroad's problems of indebtedness and keep it out of the hands of receivers.

But Vanderbilt chose, instead, to lend the Lake Shore several thousand shares of his own securities, to be used as collateral by the railroad to secure loans. That way he was lending, not borrowing.

He had become thoroughly conservative since he had a great deal to protect and much to lose, and he blamed much of the nation's trouble—as the panic of 1873—on overextension of credit.

"I'll tell you what's the matter," he said one day; "people undertake to do about four times as much business as they can legitimately undertake." (Just as he had in earlier days.) What he advocated, in these times, was "pay as we go," and he practiced what he preached.

Vanderbilt established the New York Central Station at its present location on Forty-second Street and Park Avenue, a valuable piece of land even then, at minimum cost, paying as he went. When he decided he needed a new station, he first examined the terminals of his roads. The Hudson River line entered New York on the west side of the city and terminated at Thirtieth Street and Tenth Avenue, with a horsecar extension to Chambers Street. The Harlem tracks came down the east side of the city—along Park Avenue (which was the northern extension of Fourth Avenue) to the Harlem station at Twenty-sixth Street. The Commodore decided the Harlem entrance was much better than that of the Hudson, but that neither terminal was large enough, and he estimated that Forty-second Street and Park Avenue would be just the place for a terminal—neither too far downtown, with its crowded streets, nor too far from the center of population.

Vanderbilt approached Peter Goelet, the son of the old Dutch family, with an offer to buy the block between Forty-sixth and Forty-seventh streets, and between Madison and Park avenues. Goelet offered the property on a lease for ninety-nine years, but the Commodore said he never leased, he always bought, and Goelet said he never sold, he always leased. It was an impasse, but only for a few days, for Goelet came to view his property not long afterward and found the Commodore's men digging in the ground. The Commodore had taken possession by exercising the Harlem's right, as a railroad, of eminent domain. All Goelet could do was fight for the highest possible value for the property to be fixed in court.

The Commodore then set out to build Grand Central Terminal and to connect the Harlem and Hudson lines north of the city.

He built the tiny Spuyten Duyvil and Port Morris railroad, which is the connecting link of the Harlem and Hudson divisions of the New York Central even today, and he spent $3,000,000 erecting the largest railroad station in the world on the site of the present Grand Central Terminal, still paying as he went.

So, in 1873, when the stock market appeared to be especially shaky in the early months of spring, the Commodore cocked a blue eye at the figures on the boards, and again warned his relatives.

Barton and Allen, who had promised not to speculate in rails, broke their promise. In one terrible half-hour on April 16, stock values dropped $25,000,000, and Barton and Allen learned they had overextended their commitments and were bankrupt.

Vanderbilt could have saved his young relatives, but they had broken their promise to him, so he refused to interfere.

Young Allen, the grandson who had eulogized the Commodore's fairness a decade before at the golden wedding party, now had a taste of it that he would never forget. Fairness worked both ways, the Commodore figured.

Allen was only one of hundreds of men ruined in Wall Street that year, as the momentary panic of spring developed into a more serious crisis—the panic of 1873, which came in September, caused by crop failures and, again, by speculation in railroad stocks. The panic did not stem from or affect the Commodore's major holdings; not eastern railroads but western lines were the direct cause of the disaster.

Year after year these railroads had been spreading their fingers west, the Union Pacific, the Great Northern, and smaller roads had absorbed nearly all the loose capital in the country. Great banking firms—even some abroad—were deeply committed in their construction, to an extent where failure of a single railroad might mean failure of a major bank.

On September 18 the banker Jay Cooke learned that one railroad could not pay a million-dollar note. That day Jay Cooke and Company failed, and the landslide began. Within an hour the price of stocks began to fall, thousands lost their entire fortunes in less than twenty-four hours, and by the end of September the Stock Exchange closed its doors, beginning a depression that would last for five years.

Like nearly everything in the nation, Vanderbilt's railroad empire decreased in paper value, but Vanderbilt control was still solid, he knew it, and on September 18 was so confident of his own position that he did not even rush to inform himself of the news of Wall Street.

The Commodore had been out driving that afternoon. When, at seven o'clock, he returned to the stables behind 10 Washington Place, a reporter was waiting for him.

What did the Commodore think? asked the reporter.

The Commodore did not think anything, he said, nor would he worry about the matter until after he had eaten his supper. Then he would see what the afternoon newspapers reported.

When he had consulted the newspapers and his associates the Commodore realized that the problem was indeed serious. The following day the firm of Robinson and Suydam failed. So did Richard Schell, one of the bastions of the street.

Vanderbilt's Lake Shore Railroad owed the failing Union Trust Company $1,750,000 on a call loan, but Vanderbilt did not pay, for he could not—and maintain enough cash to meet his payrolls.

Nor would that amount have saved the bank. The immediate trouble was that there was little cash in any of the banks when the panic struck and small depositors began to mob the tellers with withdrawals, and when the depositors lost their confidence, nothing less than the U. S. Treasury's resources could have stopped the slide.

A few days later Vanderbilt met President Grant and his Secretary of the Treasury at the Fifth Avenue Hotel with a proposal for Treasury intervention. Vanderbilt offered to put up $10,000,000 in the securities of his railroads if the Treasury would unfreeze $30,-000,000 in gold—but Grant, no financier, did not look kindly on such a plan.

During the panic Vanderbilt showed the public a face of icy calm when, actually, his position was scarcely better than that of anyone else in the financial community—save that he had withheld enough cash to meet current obligations. It was not until nearly two months afterward that the Commodore could pay off the $1,750,000 note due the Union Trust, and then he made the payment to the bank's receivers. He became, in a way, a goat, charged with more responsibility for the panic than he deserved, because he had not saved the day. In 1869, when Jay Gould and Jim Fisk had tried to corner the gold market with the connivance of Grant's brother-in-law, Vanderbilt's commitments had kept Black Friday from setting off a major depression, and an image grew of the Commodore as a benign financial genius. But in '73 the financial men felt that Vanderbilt had failed them. There were ugly rumors that he could have stopped the panic if he had wanted to, but that he had refrained from sheer cold-bloodedness. The press, which had long been critical of Vanderbilt steamers and railroads, now declared war on him.

He was caricatured and lampooned by press and magazines as a vulture who grew fat, feasting on the bodies of the poor.

In all probability, the newspapers misunderstood the old man. He was a builder, where he had once been a speculator; an organizational genius, who had given up manipulation. His primary interest was in salvation of the transportation system he had built up. If he had done what the newspapers wanted, it is doubtful whether he would have affected the course of the panic very much, but he would most surely have lost his own fortune.

Had it been possible for the Commodore to save the nation, or even Wall Street, without throwing his own fortune down the drain, he would have done so, if only because of his own view of the Vanderbilt image. He wanted the name Vanderbilt honored and remembered in history. He was proud of his accomplishments and could not bear even to contemplate erosion of his transportation empire, let alone its end through failure.

But the Commodore's problem was that, as powerful as he might be, and as tough and resourceful a figure as he had always been, the public believed him to be even richer, even more powerful, and even more resourceful than he was. He was a legend before he died.

14

DEATH OF THE COMMODORE

Particularly after the panic of 1873, the newspapers delighted in embroidering the few facts they could unearth about Commodore Vanderbilt's personal life, especially when those facts indicated family trouble. A tragic Horace Greeley had died in 1872 after his unsuccessful bid for the American presidency, and with Greeley gone, the only friend of any Vanderbilt among the newspapermen was Thurlow Weed, the former Albany editor who came to New York to operate the *Commercial Advertiser*. Weed was an admirer of the Commodore.

Cornelius Jeremiah lost his ablest and almost his only supporter when Greeley died, but when he had returned from his western tour, penniless, the Commodore increased this son's allowance by $50 a month, a sign that raised the second son's hopes for a real reconciliation with his father, and a place in the Commodore's scheme of things.

In the summer of 1874 the Commodore received a flattering letter from Cornelius Jeremiah, proposing that the old man give him a job in the railroad business, and three years in which to prove his ability. Since Cornelius Jeremiah expected his father to live ten more years (he said), that would give them seven years to come to some kind of emotional and financial accommodation.

In the fall of 1874 Cornelius Jeremiah came down from his home in Hartford to New York City to pursue this suggestion in person. The Commodore seemed taken enough with the idea to do something about it, and William Henry offered his father a plan conceived to find out whether Cornelius Jeremiah was really ready to reform or whether he was up to his old tricks again.

William Henry hired a detective to follow Cornelius Jeremiah, after the latter arrived and put up at the Fifth Avenue Hotel. The detective picked up his quarry at 11:00 A.M. on October 22 at the hotel, and followed him on what he later reported as an orgy of drunkenness, gambling, and consort with wild women.

This report cooked Cornelius Jeremiah's goose and while from time to time, in his last days, the old man breathed a sigh for what might have been, that was all. Cornelius Jeremiah was given no job with the railroad, nor any last chance to prove himself to his father, who was now in his eightieth year.

For a man so old, the Commodore was still remarkably active. From nine in the morning until eleven he worked in his uptown office at the New York Central Station; then at one he stopped in at the old downtown office he still retained. After that, he called it a business day, and went to the stables. He had given up most of his town clubs, for he did not play cards nearly so often as he used to, since Frank did not approve of cards and he had begun to acquire a semblance of religious piety to please her. He did his best to stop swearing in public. He also learned some prayers and hymns and began to contemplate the morals related in *Pilgrim's Progress*, the only book in which he had ever shown much interest.

By 1874 the Commodore had revised his will several times. In 1873, when Marie Louise's Horace F. Clark died, the funeral emphasized the separation of the daughters from the family line. A special train drew a special funeral car and other Vanderbilt private cars to Woodlawn Cemetery in the Bronx. When her time came, Marie Louise would be expected to join her husband at Woodlawn, not in the family vault on Staten Island, for the girls were no longer Vanderbilts, as the Commodore had said.

But Vanderbilt's preoccupation with those who bore the name did not mean he was unkind to lesser relatives. His relatives by marriage, the Simonsons, had been put to work building his ships.

The De Groots, De Forests and Van Pelts, to whom he was also related by marriage, had sailed his ships, and he had made some of them rich. Brother Jake, who had sailed for him and worked with him, was worth more than a quarter of a million dollars—and could have been wealthier had Jake been more ambitious. But Jake was an easygoing type; he was happy to control the Staten Island ferry, the Staten Island Railroad, and to spend his time racing his trotters along the island's country roads.

This year, 1874, marked Commodore Vanderbilt's last visit to Staten Island. He went to Saratoga as usual that year; he drove out around the city, but not as often as before, spending more time in the stables, just looking at his horses, fingering their manes, admiring their strength and youth.

In the two years 1874–76 the Commodore slowed down visibly, then in the spring of 1876 he fell ill with an intestinal inflammation, and when he was flat on his back he developed a bladder infection. He could not pass water, and lived in almost constant pain.

During that illness the newspapers reported that he was dead. Few people believed them, because the papers had been reporting Vanderbilt's death regularly since 1870; the Associated Press had once been flummoxed into sending out the rail king's obituary by telegraph.

When the death report was denied, and reporters came to see for themselves, the Commodore heard them at the door.

"It's a damned lie," he shouted downstairs.

Hearing that voice, the reporters retreated, satisfied. The old curmudgeon was still alive, after all.

But as his illness persisted, the newspapermen set up a death watch in a house across the street, to listen to the rumors and watch the traffic to the house.

Sometimes the traffic was high. Dr. Linsly, the family physician for nearly half a century, called in the best of specialists since the Commodore had unlimited funds but only one life. At one time or another a half-dozen doctors were in attendance at 10 Washington Place.

After the middle of May Dr. Linsly spent nearly all his time at the house. Considering the diseases he had and his extreme age, the Commodore should have been dead. Yet he would not let go.

He was moved into a room on the second floor of the four-story house so the rest of the family could get a little sleep. But he insisted that someone be with him all the time he was awake, and since he was in pain most of the time, he slept very little. Frank and her mother, Mrs. Crawford, were often hailed from their beds at three o'clock in the morning and ordered to sing hymns for the Commodore. "Show pity, Lord; O Lord, forgive!" began one of his favorites. After his women had crept downstairs to play the small organ and sing, a beatific smile would cross his face and he would rest.

But usually his temper was terrible and he shouted at everyone around him. He had provided for total gifts of a million dollars to Vanderbilt University; he had endowed Dr. Deems and the minister's Church of the Strangers on Mercer Street; he was more pious and more charitable than ever before, but he still cursed like a sailor.

"Can't I keep some of you sluts here?" he roared at Mrs. Crawford one day when she did not appear at the first sound of his voice.

He carried on a running battle with one of his six professional nurses, Lizzie, and kept her in tears most of the time with his abuse. Almost daily she threatened to quit, only to be solaced by Dr. Linsly and the two women of the house, and Vanderbilt, when the pain was gone, would apologize. One day coming upon him quietly after an outburst, they found Vanderbilt in tears. "I've been swearing again, and I'm sorry," he said. He was doing his best to behave—but the wasting of his body gave him no peace.

Whenever possible Vanderbilt was encouraged to move into a wheel chair and go into the library to get some sun—both to keep him from getting bed sores and to give him the slight exercise this required. In late May, however, he was almost always too ill to be moved. He lay in pain and contemplated the hereafter. He said he hoped God would give religion to all his family (particularly since Vanderbilt knew *he* had not brought them much in the first eighty-one years of his life). He wanted his mausoleum enlarged, and gave instructions to William to spare no expense in this project.

He improved a little in early June—at least enough so that when Dr. Deems called and began telling him what Paul had said when that sinner was in pain, Vanderbilt cut him off. He did not give a damn what Paul said.

The ladies were present, and Vanderbilt realized these were most unseemly words for a man who was supposed to be making a separate peace with God. The Commodore apologized awkwardly. He had been in great pain at the moment Dr. Deems referred to Paul, he said.

The pain continued for months, and months. His abdomen became so sensitive that when one of his expensive specialists wanted to touch him, the Commodore first insisted on examining the doctor's fingernails.

He was visited by strange dreams in this illness. At one time he dreamed he was at the bottom of the sea. It took all the power of the steamer *Vanderbilt* to pull him out, but in the end she did, and he was saved.

He tore up his will again, and brought the lawyers in to draw a new one. When it was finished, he called for William Henry and made him sit down beside the bed.

"After I'm dead there will be a great responsibility resting on you," he told his eldest son. "You will find a piece of paper left to direct you—you will find my will—and there are several pieces of paper attached to it, which I charge you to carry out faithfully, as I have directed in the will."

Still his daughters continued to press him to divide the fortune equally. Sometimes the sisters came singly, sometimes they came in groups, but each of them, at one time or another, made her plea for a large share of the fortune for *her* children.

William Henry stood over the Commodore when he could, to keep the harpies off, but he could not protect his father all the time. The poor Commodore could not even die like other men; he had to remain constantly on his guard against the vultures in his own family.

By the end of June it did not seem as if there was any way to save him, or any more that could be done. They tried to feed him brandy to quiet him, but he would take nothing that would affect his mind, fearful that he might say something to prejudice his will.

Vanderbilt argued hotly with Mary Alicia, who was the most outspoken in her demands. Finally he told Mary Alicia he had left all the girls enough to live like ladies, that was the end of it, and he would not discuss it further. He would not even see Cornelius Jeremiah when he came to call.

"I don't want to see Corneel whether I'm dead or alive," he shouted.

Finally he gave in and saw Cornelius Jeremiah, but only in the presence of others.

The pain grew worse as the summer wore on. One day Dr. Linsly went across the street to buy off an organ grinder who was playing in the neighborhood, for the Commodore hated that particular noise. A few years before, Vanderbilt had kept organ grinders away simply by opening the window, pointing a gun, and shouting at them. It was the measure of the old man's weakness that he acceded in the bribe.

Vanderbilt passed no water for days. Finally when he did get some relief an evil green slime was ejected; the doctors were afraid to operate, and afraid not to.

Eventually they went at him with a cystoscope and removed a number of stones from his bladder, a terrible ordeal. Afterwards, Dr. Linsly thought Vanderbilt was going to die, and when Dr. Deems came to give him the last rites of the Episcopal church, he lay, waxen, on the bed, hardly breathing.

Yet the next day he was better, far better than before.

One of his expensive doctors died, but Vanderbilt hung on.

Mary Alicia—Mrs. LaBau—came again and again, trying to persuade her father to change his will. She came with Emily, Eliza, and Sophia. Phoebe and Ethelinda came, but Vanderbilt was unmoved. He did, however, use their supplications as an excuse to redress some old wrongs. Earlier, Sophia had opened her catlike mouth about Frank and the fortune. Vanderbilt forced his daughter to apologize in his presence.

By fall there was no hope left that Vanderbilt would ever leave his house again, alive. Time was fighting his determination. Time would win, but when?

"The old man must die! I can't stand this hell any longer," Frank said in one unguarded moment.

Frank had missed the Saratoga season that year, although Vanderbilt had told her to go without him. William Henry went, and sat on the front porch of the Congress Hotel and made bets on the races. But Frank went nowhere except to the Philadelphia Exposition, and there only over a week end.

They fed him beefsteak and tea, which he liked, and beef tea, which he spat out all over the bed. When the heat was worst they stood at his side, one at the head, one at the feet, and one in the middle, waving handkerchiefs soaked in bay rum to cool him, and at the same time they applied cracked ice to his swollen belly.

When the pain was intolerable, they gave him laudanum. For his general welfare, he had "magnetizing rubs"—more of the mild electrical shock he had so long enjoyed. The doctors squirmed in the presence of this folk medicine, but they had no choice. Vanderbilt insisted on having his way.

Frank scraped the dandruff from his head, sang hymns, said prayers, and read to him. Thurlow Weed brought him a bottle of Santa Cruz rum.

He threw things and swore some more, and kept salt cellars under the posts of his bed to ward off evil spirits. By October he was so much better he was more trouble than ever, but as winter closed in, he failed.

Finally, on January 4, 1877, he felt that his end was just a few hours away, and he called for a gathering of the family.

James Gordon Bennett, the editor of the New York *Herald*, had just been horsewhipped on the steps of the Union League Club by Frederick May, the brother of a girl in whom Bennett was interested. Bennett had challenged his assailant to a duel and now the affair was the talk of the town. Vanderbilt even roused himself enough from the business of dying to demand that the articles in the papers be read to him, and delivered a homily on the evils of fighting.

At ten o'clock some thirty relatives gathered in the sick room. Dr. Linsly and Dr. Eliott helped Vanderbilt clear his throat and raised his head with pillows. Two of the consulting physicians, Dr.

Austin Flint and Dr. W. H. Van Buren, stood at the foot of the bed, looked wise and said there was nothing to be done.

One by one, William Henry and his sisters stepped forward to speak a last word to their father. He was so weak he could hardly move his head, but he heard, and understood them.

Someone suggested a song, and Mrs. Crawford began to sing.

"Show pity, Lord; O Lord, forgive!
Let a repenting sinner live . . ."

When it was over, the Commodore brightened for a moment. "Nearer, my God, to Thee," Mrs. Crawford sang. "Come Ye Sinners, Poor and Needy . . ."

The Commodore tried to join in, but his throat produced only an awful croak.

Dr. Deems prayed, kneeling by the Commodore's bedside. The Commodore followed the prayer, and tried to repeat the last line, but his voice failed.

He tried to speak, but he choked. The doctors cleared his throat again.

"That is a good prayer," the old man whispered. He grasped the pastor's hand.

He tried to speak again, but was too weak. At ten-thirty he stopped trying. A few minutes later he seemed to be unconscious. His eyes were fixed and glassy.

One physician said to the other that there was no sight in the eyes. Vanderbilt heard, raised his hand, and closed his own eyelids. Ten minutes later he drew a deep breath and died.

Dr. Linsly performed an autopsy while the family made ready to bury their patriarch. Death had been caused by ulceration and perforation of the colon and peritonitis. But the doctors discovered, too, that the Commodore had been living for months on sheer will power. His bladder, kidneys, liver, heart, and both lungs were almost destroyed. He had Bright's disease, cystitis, an enlarged prostate, and scrotal hernia.

They laid the Commodore out in his usual clothes; a black suit, white shirt, high standing collar and white cravat. They put him in a coffin lined with pearl satin and they packed him in ice.

They hung a large piece of mourning crepe outside the front door of the house, and burned lights beside the coffin all night long. When the press announced his death, flags all over New York were lowered to half mast. Beginning early the next morning, great numbers of people called at the house to pay their last respects. (One of the first to arrive discovered that the mourning crepe had been stolen from the door during the night.)

The coffin was moved to the hall and placed on a black catafalque two feet high so that the Commodore's feet pointed toward his front door. A simple laurel cross lay on the coffin and on a stand at the head was Frank's tribute, a large crown of camellias and roses attached to a small cross of violets.

At ten-fifteen on January 7, 1877, the body was carried from the house on a bier by six men while a hundred and fifty policemen formed two lines, and down a path cleared through the snow the night before the procession made its way from the house to the Church of the Strangers. Dr. Deems led, William Henry, Frank, and the other relatives followed the casket.

Every seat in the church was filled. Admission was by ticket alone. The family filed into the center pews, which were reserved for them. It was a large gathering: Vanderbilt left sixty-three children, grandchildren, and great-grandchildren, plus a brother and sisters. His sister Charlotte was not there. She lay dying herself in her house on Griffin Street in Tompkinsville, Staten Island.

Dr. Deems read the funeral service and gave a typical and highly laudatory funeral oration. The organ began a dirge, and the family filed out, to follow the casket on its hearse to the Staten Island ferry.

Three ferries carried sixty carriages and sleighs of the procession across the bay to Vanderbilt Landing. At two o'clock they landed, and began the long, winding procession across the four miles from the landing to the Moravian Cemetery at New Dorp.

The horses toiled through the hills; it was after three o'clock when the first carriage reached the entrance to the cemetery. As the coffin passed through the gate the big bell in the church steeple began to toll its dirge. A few minutes later the slow procession entered the white frame church where a crowd had been waiting silently since one o'clock to pay its last respects to a neighbor and most famous citizen.

After a simple service and another eulogy, the Commodore's wasted body was carried out of the church, along the winding paths in the cemetery to the solid but unpretentious mausoleum. The gates were swung back slowly, the pallbearers raised their burden and carefully laid the Commodore beside his mother and his beloved George. The family turned and went away, the gates were shut securely behind them, and their clang, like the noise of a locomotive bell, sounded the last note of the funeral procession. Vanderbilt was dead and buried, but his kingdom of the rails lived on. It was the end of the beginning.

IV

THE CONSOLIDATION
AND
THE WEAKENING

15

THE GREAT WILL FIGHT

Although the richest man in America was dead, his passing was but a matter of momentary concern in a nation worried about the disputed Hayes-Tilden election. Vanderbilt had been expected to die for many months and presumably the financial world was prepared for the news, while the election dispute had reopened the unhealed wounds of the Civil War.

The press honored the Commodore's memory in detailed obituary notices, recalling some of his personal characteristics and the rags-to-riches story of his life. Still, the drama was played out of the story in short order, and the nation's interest returned to Washington and the frantic search for an election decision, and, for relief, to the tale of the New York *Herald* editor, James Gordon Bennett, and Frederick May, who, after several delays, were going reluctantly to Maryland to fight the celebrated duel—the one that arose from the public quarrel the Commodore had lamented in his last moments.

Wall Street, which suffered a mild case of the fidgets on the day the Commodore died, snapped back to normal trading within a matter of hours. As Jay Gould put it complacently, there was "more stability on the Street" in 1877 than there had been a few years before, when the death of such an important man would have shaken the business world. If this was true (and it was), far more credit for the change went to the old lion who had just been escorted to his grave than to jackals like Gould and Daniel Drew.

Vanderbilt had created his fortune by hard work and clear vision; he had amalgamated a solid system of railroads, and had taken every step he knew to be sure his holdings were retained, intact.

One day, two years before, a Philadelphia lawyer named Phillips had encountered Vanderbilt at Saratoga. The lawyer asked what would happen to the stock market when the Commodore died.

Nothing! Vanderbilt thundered, because no Vanderbilt stock would be sold.

Yet Vanderbilt must have recalled that casual conversation later, because he changed his will to make *sure* that no stock would be sold.

The Commodore's aim, even on his deathbed, never changed; that was why he had resisted the demands of the girls, knowing that his children were quite likely to contest the will if they did not like it, and certain that most of them would not.

From the moment of the Commodore's death, New York's drawing rooms, club lounges, and barrooms buzzed with speculation. How much had Vanderbilt been worth, and who was going to get it?

The newspapers made wild guesses as to the total and put the figure around $60,000,000. As to who would receive the lion's share, or whether there would be a major share, the curious had to wait, along with the family, for the opening of the will.

Many outside the family believed the daughters would share equally—or almost equally—with the sons. Even the daughters expected to become millionaires. It was true that William Henry Vanderbilt was now operating head of the Vanderbilt railroads, but Ethelinda's Daniel B. Allen and Mary Louise's Horace Clark had worked with the Commodore in the days before Vanderbilt became the richest man in the country. Allen and Clark had old Vanderbilt's confidence while William Henry was plowing his Staten Island farm. That was worth something, wasn't it?

Just how much it was worth the family learned on January 8, the day after the Commodore's funeral, when the Vanderbilt clan gathered at the home of daughter Emily (Mrs. Thorn) at 12 West Sixteenth Street in New York City. The future of a great railroad system was at stake.

The Commodore had unconsciously drawn his will with dramatic flair. First came the bequest to his wife Frank. This clause was changed slightly but significantly from the prenuptial agreement. Instead of railroad bonds, which might one day conceivably have a stock control value, Frank was to receive her half-million dollars in government bonds. She was to have the house at 10 Washington Place for the rest of her life, plus two carriages and any pair of her husband's expensive trotters she might want. On her death the house was to revert to William Henry, the statuary to William Henry's thirty-four-year-old son, Cornelius Vanderbilt II.

There was nothing unexpected in the bequest to Frank Vanderbilt. All the family had known of the prenuptial settlement and had approved, more or less.

Next came clauses dealing with the lives of the Vanderbilt girls. Phoebe Jane, Emily, Marie Louise, Sophia, and Mary Alicia were each to have $250,000 in railroad bonds. Ethelinda was to have the income from a $400,000 trust fund. Eliza was to have a trust fund of $300,000 and Catherine a trust fund of $500,000.

Cornelius Jeremiah was to have a trust fund of $200,000, administered by William Henry.

There were a few minor bequests to friends and the faithful in Vanderbilt's service. Brother Jake was willed $50,000; faithful Dr. Linsly received $10,000; Captain James Braisted, the skipper who had once left Vanderbilt on the pier at Staten Island, was to have $4000.

There was a small annuity for the Commodore's sister Phebe, and there were even smaller ones for nieces and cousins. Dr. Deems inherited $20,000 and Lambert Wardell, Vanderbilt's private secretary for thirty years, received an equal sum.

As an afterthought, wife Frank was to have two thousand shares of New York Central stock. But all the rest—the control, the entire Vanderbilt empire—was to go to William Henry and his sons. Grandson Cornelius Vanderbilt II received some $5,500,000 worth of New York Central stock in his own right and the family portraits of Phebe Hand and Sophia that hung at 10 Washington Place. William Henry's three other sons, William Kissam Vanderbilt, twenty-eight, Frederick William Vanderbilt, twenty-one, and George Washington Vanderbilt, fifteen, were each to have $2,000,-000 worth of stock. William Henry was named the residuary legatee—and all Vanderbilt's holdings not excepted were given to him.

The girls and Cornelius Jeremiah were stunned. Before they could recover, the reading of the will was over, and William Henry and the lawyers were on their way to the surrogate's office to file the document for probate.

That very day James Gordon Bennett and Frederick May met in mortal combat in a field on the Maryland-Delaware border, exchanged shots three times without hitting each other, and then shook hands, honor satisfied. But in New York the duel of the Vanderbilts was just beginning. At least three of the children believed they had been wronged. Mary Alicia, the widow of N. B. LaBau, Ethelinda, the wife of Daniel B. Allen, and Cornelius Jeremiah left their sister's house to consult their lawyers.

There was no way of knowing at that moment how much the Commodore had left to William Henry. When the press asked Chauncey Depew for a figure, he told them it was $105,000,000—almost the exact amount that the federal government had on hand at the moment. Vanderbilt, without a doubt, had been the richest man in the United States, wealthier by far than anyone had believed.

Mary Alicia, Ethelinda, and Cornelius Jeremiah convinced themselves that their elder brother had schemed against them to obtain control of the estate. They remembered only that Vanderbilt had talked earlier about sharing the riches equally among his children. What they did not remember was that those words had been spoken thirty years before, at a time when Vanderbilt's wealth rested in his ability to operate ships. The later years had brought a complete change in the Commodore's fortune, the ephemeral shipping empire had been transmuted into a solid railroad network, and when the Commodore saw what he had—the immensity of it—the desire for immortality became an overriding passion. Preservation of this empire could be assured only if the railroads could be kept in one set of hands—a man's hands.

At the end of February, Mary Alicia, Ethelinda, and Cornelius

Jeremiah went before the surrogate judge to protest the will. After the preliminaries, Ethelinda dropped her complaint, but Mary Alicia and Cornelius Jeremiah brought suit to have the will thrown out, and Cornelius Jeremiah brought a civil suit against his brother for $7,000,000.

The Vanderbilt will case went to trial in Surrogate's Court on November 12, 1877. Mary Alicia and Cornelius Jeremiah wanted to prove that Vanderbilt had been senile when he drew his last will. Their lawyers claimed that the Commodore's bladder and kidney disorders had impaired his mind, and that he had been influenced improperly by William Henry. Mary Alicia and Cornelius Jeremiah also proposed to prove in Surrogate's Court that Vanderbilt had been addicted to spiritualism for the last ten years of his life and that he had been mentally unbalanced for nearly all that decade.

The Surrogate's Court was a small room, holding only five rows of chairs and usually, at best, the room was half deserted, but during the Vanderbilt case, every chair was filled, and reporters and spectators overflowed into the hallway of the courthouse. The will had been admitted to probate in the summer, but the suit was to go on, nonetheless.

In the second row, on one side of the room, sat the heavy William Henry, now head of the Vanderbilt family. He was a big man in every sense of the word, six feet tall, weighing two hundred pounds. His heavy, florid face was made to look heavier still by the curling side whiskers that sprayed out past his ears in twists of brown and gray and by his clothing, for William Henry was severely dressed in the black he always favored. Over his linen he wore a heavy beaver frock coat, and he carried a black silk hat heavily wrapped in the crepe of mourning. As William Henry waited for the proceedings to begin he leaned forward and chewed pensively on the head of his heavy cane.

At William Henry's side sat his son Frederick William, and just behind them sat William Kissam Vanderbilt and Cornelius Vanderbilt II, whose handsome tall figure and short side whiskers reminded others in the room of the old Commodore in his prime.

Daniel B. Allen, Ethelinda's husband, came into the courtroom and walked carefully across the aisle to sit down. Neither William Henry nor any of his three sons looked at Allen, although at one time Daniel and William Henry had been the best of friends. But friendship had been left back in the Staten Island days, when William Henry was a poor, neglected dirt farmer and Daniel Allen was the Commodore's right-hand man.

On this day, the men were worlds apart. Allen was the husband and sympathizer of one of the complaining sisters and thus he was a threat to William Henry. If the distinguished, elderly Allen had once lent William Henry $5000 without a tremor—that was all forgotten today. William Henry's mouth was a thin, white line in the red face, and his hazel eyes were focused straight ahead.

To overthrow the Commodore's will, Mary Alicia and Cornelius Jeremiah began to wash a great deal of dirty Vanderbilt linen. Their lawyers exhibited every detail of the Commodore's last illness; they delved into the dim past to note the commitment of Sophia to the insane asylum some thirty years before. They went as far as the court would allow to show that Vanderbilt's lust had caused him to take up with Tennessee Claflin and Victoria Woodhull, and had brought about the July and December marriage with Frank Crawford. They hailed forth a handful of witnesses to testify about the Commodore's prostate troubles, which were supposed to have forced him into these excesses. They also brought witnesses to discuss the Commodore's recourse to spiritualism.

Victoria Woodhull hinted in *Woodhull and Claflin's Weekly* that she could tell the world a great deal about the Commodore's affairs, except that her lips were sealed. Cynical critics guessed that her lips had been sealed with gold, and they were not surprised when Claflin and Woodhull suddenly disappeared during the trial, to turn up in London with stockings full of cash and heads full of forgetfulness about the Commodore.

Daniel Drew was called to testify, but he was nearly eighty years old, feeble, and could not remember anything that might be helpful to the court.

As the case proceeded, Daniel Allen took the stand to portray William as a whining weakling who never once stood up to his father. Allen's inference was clear: William Henry had plotted from the beginning to gain control of the fortune.

In making these charges, the other children tarred the memory of the tough old Commodore, and oddly, this distressed the New York newspapers.

After years of lambasting the Commodore, the newspaper editors suddenly realized that they had grown quite fond of the old lion and that they missed the familiar sound of his roar. It seemed improper, somehow, to hear his character assaulted without the usual profane response from Vanderbilt himself.

In smearing the Commodore's name, however, the unhappy heirs did not come off scot free. The constant nagging of the girls, even when their father was on his deathbed, was fully exposed by witnesses and William Henry's lawyers, who also lacerated Cornelius Jeremiah's threadbare reputation when this second son was called to the witness stand. Cornelius Jeremiah's physical weakness, his gambling, his debts, and jailings were all brutally detailed.

Then, Cornelius Jeremiah played his trump card. As previously noted, Cornelius Jeremiah had come to New York in 1874, seeking a reconciliation with his father. Supposedly he had been followed by a detective on an orgy, and the old man had finally lost his patience.

But Cornelius Jeremiah now charged that William Henry had arranged for the secret investigation. William Henry had hired the detective. William Henry had identified the man that the detective was to follow. William Henry had received the report and transmitted it to the Commodore.

The detective (his lawyers claimed) had failed to identify Cornelius Jeremiah as the man he had shadowed on that fateful trip into the underworld. The detective said, in fact, that Cornelius Jeremiah was *not* the man. Cornelius Jeremiah's lawyer charged that William Henry had hired a man to impersonate his client, a man named Peter Perego Bombalier. William Henry had sent Bombalier on a day of carousing, the lawyer said, and had then identified the immoral one to the detective as his younger brother. The claim was made that William Henry had staged this affair to disgrace Cornelius Jeremiah and turn the Commodore finally against the younger man. Bombalier, unfortunately, had recently moved to Havana and could not be reached to confirm or deny this tale, and it *was* known that Cornelius Jeremiah could write a good letter, and that he had impressed the Commodore with his claims of reform during the last months. Cornelius Jeremiah charged that publicly (in any act the Commodore might notice) William Henry had always treated him in a manner that was above reproach. Privately, he said, his elder brother had treated him with hatred and contempt.

The newspapers scoffed at this unlikely story, but apparently it was a telling blow to William Henry, who was thoroughly sick of laundering family linen in the courtroom. Suddenly the case against the estate and the suit against William Henry were both dropped. It was rumored that William Henry had made a handsome settlement on Cornelius Jeremiah, and had given each of the sisters a half-million dollars more than the amount stipulated in the will. In his last days the Commodore had often enjoined William Henry to carry out the terms of the will faithfully, but the son could not stand more opening of the family's closets and so sealed them once and for all time with gold. Someone also paid the daughters of Horace Greeley the $61,000 Cornelius Jeremiah had borrowed from the late editor over the years. At first it was made known that William Henry had made the payment. Later, Cornelius Jeremiah claimed he had paid the debt himself, but the action was characteristic of William Henry and out of character for Cornelius Jeremiah, who often took but seldom gave.

All this unpleasantness had occupied a great deal of William Henry's time, and he was glad to end it and turn his full attention to business. With the able assistance of Chauncey Depew he had been handling the details of operating the Vanderbilt lines for nearly ten years, as chief executive officer, if not as final authority, but now, in the summer of 1877, came William Henry's first great test as an executive, a direct result of the depression that had begun in the panic of 1873.

After the stock market tumbled and industries began to shut down, rail shipments began to decline. It was not an immediate or sharp decline. The New York Central was still paying dividends of 8 and 10 per cent after the depression began. But a year after the panic, in August 1874, the Commodore had realized that the railroads could not long remain unaffected, so he had invited the heads of the most important eastern railroads to a conference at Saratoga. His object was, as before, formation of a trust to eliminate wasteful competition, a combine in which he hoped to include the Pennsylvania, the Erie, and the Baltimore & Ohio. Colonel Thomas A. Scott of the Pennsylvania showed up at Saratoga, and the business heirs of the unfortunate Jim Fisk came to represent the Erie, but John W. Garrett of the Baltimore & Ohio scoffed at the idea of a combination. It was just a Vanderbilt ruse to take them into camp, Garrett said, and he was going to run his own show.

Commodore Vanderbilt was not above using such a ruse in a business matter, but the colonel was wrong in this instance. The Commodore had long been a believer in the combination of railroads, quite confident of his own ability to keep from being swallowed up by others and to come out on top in any disagreement among partners. In 1874, when the momentum of his freight business showed signs of faltering, Vanderbilt had traveled personally to Baltimore to face Garrett and outline the case for common action and, immediately, for a united front against the common foe, the railroad union organizers who were trying to do their share of building American union labor upward from a base of 300,000 members. Vanderbilt found Garrett to be a stubborn, cantankerous, opinionated man, who again charged the Commodore with selfishness. If Garrett had known Vanderbilt's history, he would not have made such a mistake, or would have at least known the direct and immediate results of butting heads with Vanderbilt on an issue the Commodore considered vital.

The Commodore had clamped his jaw and stamped out of Garrett's office, to declare a railroad war on the Baltimore & Ohio, pledging all the weapons at his disposal: his financial influence, his power over transshipment of goods from Baltimore to points on the Central lines, and his ability to divert traffic from Garrett's railroad to those of Garrett's direct competitors.

Within a few months Garrett saw the error of waging war with the Commodore, even if the B.&O. owner remained unconvinced that the railroad association would bring him any benefits. He capitulated, and the association of eastern railroads was organized, with jurisdiction over every important road east of Chicago. The association set rates, fixed territories, and adjudicated disputes; it was in fact, a plain, old-fashioned trust that existed until the Sherman Antitrust Act caught up with the membership sixteen years later.

Thus in 1877, when the depression hit the railroads hard, the dead hand of the Commodore was still on the wheel, steering expertly. At his insistence, the eastern railroads were prepared to meet the emergency with a united front.

The first road to take action to meet the fall in revenue was the Pennsylvania. At the beginning of June Colonel Scott announced a pay cut for all employees who earned more than a dollar a day. The B.&O. and the others followed suit.

As summer came on, the railroad workers responded to these cuts in pay by striking. When their strikes were broken by private detectives and professional thugs, the strikers turned to riot and pillage.

William Henry Vanderbilt declared a 10 per cent wage cut in June. There was no immediate reaction from his New York Central employees, although the Lake Shore men went out on strike, an action Vanderbilt attributed to the unfamiliarity of the Lake Shore employees with Vanderbilt paternalism. He showed no undue concern and did not leave Saratoga, where he and the family were summering.

The strike spread to railroads all over the North and Middle West—and beyond the railroads, as thousands of men who had lost their jobs in four years of depression joined the railroad workers in mob action. The city of Baltimore fell into the hands of rioters; in Reading, Pennsylvania, strikers and militia fought a running battle in the streets; soldiers fired on strikers at Cumberland, Maryland.

On July 21 strikers captured the railroad yards at Pittsburgh, and when a sheriff's posse moved to disperse a milling crowd of railroad men and unemployed that seemed bent on tearing the railroad installations apart, the crowd became a mob and the deputies and militiamen who had been called from Philadelphia fired into the ranks, killing more than twenty persons and injuring many others. Then the mob began to break into stores, stealing guns and ammunition. And thus armed, the mob began to fight back. Three soldiers were killed as they ran for refuge in the yard roundhouse, where a score of their companions were besieged. Sheriff Fife was killed, and Major General Pearson was badly wounded before police and military reinforcements came into the yards and routed the mob.

On July 23 Chicago fell into the hands of the rioters; the same day at Albany the New York Central's employees struck and called a mass meeting in Capitol Park to set a course of action. The Central employees voted to demand an immediate 25 per cent wage increase and formed a grievance committee to call on William Henry at Saratoga two days later and present the demand. It was an impassioned but thoroughly unrealistic maneuver, and in saner times the strikers would have realized that no railroad president would—or could—give in to it. But the men were angry and afraid, they were spurred on by their leaders, and as a railroad president, William Henry was still an unknown quantity.

The Commodore, his men knew, would have reacted with characteristic vigor. But what would his son do?

After he had heard the news, William Henry told questioning reporters he knew nothing whatsoever about the strike meeting in Albany, but, privately, that same night he wired Governor Robinson to order twelve hundred troops to Albany to stop the strike. The Central, he said, would meet the expense. When the Central's employees' committee waited on him at Saratoga, William Henry swore at John Smiley, one of the committeemen, and flatly refused to discuss their demands until the men went back to work.

The committeemen so reported to the employees at Albany. Some men wanted to continue the strike, but the engineers— highest paid men of all the railroad's employees—refused to cooperate; they said they were going to take the trains out no matter what the others did.

The strike on the Central collapsed, the militiamen were dispersed, and William Henry came off without any real trouble or any great expense. The 10 per cent wage cut he had made was not rescinded, and William Henry never would discuss the demands, but he did make one gesture: he bestowed $100,000 on the employees of the New York Central, to divide as they saw fit. Despite the continuing hard times, or perhaps because of them, the men did not try to strike again.

William Henry never had the feeling for his men that the Commodore had acquired by working shoulder to shoulder with them on his steamboats, so he understood them and used them as an industrialist used raw material. The Commodore could be highhanded when he wanted to, but he also was both tougher and more generous in business matters than William Henry, a difference that was readily apparent in small ways. J. T. Lloyd of Boston, who published *Lloyd's Railway Guides*, had been riding free on the New York Central trains for many years. All Lloyd had to do was drop a note to the Commodore, and indicate how many annual passes he wanted from year to year. But the first year after William Henry took over, Lloyd's application was turned down.

At that time, Lloyd was preparing to print an eight-foot-long railroad, express, and telegraphic map of the United States. It would be circulated to business concerns all over the country and also would be sold to the public.

When he learned in 1878 that William Henry was not going to grant the usual courtesies, Publisher Lloyd immediately went to his Boston printers with a plan. There was a large, blank space on the map above the title. On naval charts this space, an empty stretch of the Atlantic Ocean, is decorated with mermaids, spouting whales, and perhaps an intricate compass rose. But Lloyd had a better use for it.

The publisher directed his artist to draw a picture of a railroad disaster to fill this space. When finished, the picture showed railroad cars wrecked and on fire. Headless torsos, heads, arms, legs, and baggage were strewn in all directions. Blood ran in streams from the bodies. The legend beneath the picture read: "Killed and wounded on the New York Central Railroad." And under the legend was placed a row of coffins, listing chronologically all the

New York Central's accidents in previous years. Below the coffins was a large picture of William Henry Vanderbilt, sideburns flaring, identified as the "Owner of the Road."

Lloyd went even further. He had the New York Central route omitted completely from the map. Conversely he built up Vanderbilt's principal competitor by having his artist draw the lines of the Erie three times as large as the lines of the other railroads in the country. Then Lloyd had fifty copies of this map printed and sent to New York Central agents—without comment. A few days later, when he was sure the agents had received the proofs, Lloyd sent copies to Vanderbilt and all the members of the New York Central board of directors.

First Vanderbilt threatened to sue.

Lloyd told him to go ahead and sue.

Then Vanderbilt must have realized it was smarter and less expensive to give in. Lloyd got his passes from that time on without argument.

Altogether William Henry's attitude toward the Vanderbilt empire was far different from that of the Commodore. The Commodore had made the fortune, and he had known how large a part chance had played in his success. William Henry stepped into an established business, not as the entrepreneur who took the risks, but as the manager.

William Henry was more interested in a man's material possessions than in his brain power—for, unlike his father, he felt that brains and money could be equated almost exactly.

One time the president of one of the New York Central's subsidiaries came into Vanderbilt's office to offer his resignation. Vanderbilt was inclined to accept it, for he did not think much of the man's appearance. But before he let the man go, he was careful to confirm his own opinion by talking to Chauncey Depew, who had known the man well for many years. He called Depew in, mentioned the man's name, and asked the all-important question.

"Has he got anything?" William Henry asked.

"Two million dollars," said Depew.

"Valuable man," said William Henry.

Yet that was only William Henry Vanderbilt's business face.

Within the family, William Henry was a comfortable, homey man who loved his wife and children, about whom there was never a single breath of scandal, and who was inclined to family get-togethers and informal manners. In all his life William Henry never referred to the Commodore in any way but as "the old man." Even when William Henry was fifty years old the Commodore still called him Billy, and William Henry's sons went by family nicknames, too. The eldest, named for his grandfather, was Corneel; the second, named for William and his maternal grandfather, was known within the family as Willie K.

But in spite of this informality, the Vanderbilts did yearn to mingle with those they considered their equals. Perhaps the Vanderbilt vulgarity annoyed the moguls of New York society, although William Henry would have found that hard to believe, for in his dotage, John Jacob Astor, the Commodore's contemporary, was a sloppy old man who spoke broken English and had no manners at all, and Henry Astor, his brother, was a butcher.

Commodore Vanderbilt was admittedly a little too boisterous and racy for the thin blood of the socialites, but so had been John Jacob Astor until he became the nation's richest man.

How, then, did the Astors enter polite society when the Vanderbilts were barred? Why were the Astors acceptable after they became rich, but not the Vanderbilts? How had a Mrs. Astor become the acknowledged leader of Society scarcely a score of years after the death of old John Jacob in 1848?

The answer was that Astor money was a little older than Vanderbilt money, that John Jacob had taken the Astor money out of horrid trade and put it into respectable land, and that it was a question of timing.

Commodore Vanderbilt was a self-made man—so was John Jacob Astor. William Henry Vanderbilt had a fair education—so did William Backhouse Astor. William Henry's children were given the best of educations in America and in Europe. So were William Backhouse Astor's children, and they were a generation older.

In the 1840s, when William Astor, Jr., was growing up, the rich and cultured people of New York were glad to welcome other persons of wealth and culture. When young Astor came home from school in Europe, having met and mingled with many people on the Continent who were accepted in New York's social whirl, it was embarrassing to snub him.

Slowly the bars were lowered, and then he married Caroline Schermerhorn, the daughter of one of New York's finest families —and the greenbacks and blue blood were linked.

Caroline Schermerhorn Astor came from an impeccable family line, and with her new wealth she had the means and the entree to dominate Society, which was her aim. But she also had the problem of her husband's lowly antecedents.

From across the water the ancient families of Europe looked on this upstart Society with varying emotions, ranging from open amusement to sharp rejection. Where family crests could be traced in England to the First Crusade the lords and ladies had little incentive to take seriously the pretensions of a noisy claque whose leader's coat of arms could well have sported a skinning knife couchant and meat cleaver rampant.

But Caroline Schermerhorn Astor was determined to change all that. When she learned that the pretensions of the new Society were not taken seriously abroad, Mrs. Astor hardened the lines, raised the fiscal requirements, and set out to create a caste in which snobbery and money would make up for lineal shortages. The second and third generations of Vanderbilts were still in trade, still actually *working* in the railroad lines. So even when the Vanderbilts married and moved into houses on Fifth Avenue, they found the doors of high society closed to them. They were a generation too soon for Mrs. Astor.

Despite all his material success, William Henry Vanderbilt was snubbed time and again, but his background of public grammar school, his years of hand-gnarling toil in the fields of Staten Island, and his long apprenticeship in the Commodore's railroads had left him at heart a farmer and a bookkeeper, and so the snubbing did not disturb him unduly. William Henry's sons had entirely different points of view. When they married, all the children married above the middle-class station into which they had been born, and some of them married into fine, old families. These

Vanderbilts felt the full force of the injustice of Mrs. Astor and her friends, and Willie K., the second son, felt the sting most of all, for he had rubbed shoulders with royalty in school in Geneva and he had married a girl who dreamed of one day being queen of New York's social world.

Willie K. was a medium-sized, curly-haired young man who combined the well-chiseled features of his grandfather and the open countenance of his dainty mother. When his European education was ended he returned to New York to enter the service of the railroad—at the age of nineteen. He joined the railroad in 1868, the year of his grandmother Sophia's death—when the Commodore had effectively consolidated his railroad properties into the great New York Central Railroad System. Willie began to work his way through the ranks, as his grandfather demanded, and seven years later, on April 20, 1875, he married Miss Alva Smith, the daughter of a southern cotton merchant who had been ruined by the Civil War.

Alva was a comely girl of middle size with clear skin, a wealth of curly brown hair she pinned behind her ears to hang loosely down her back, halfway to her tapered waist. Her figure might be adjudged a trifle plump by modern tastes, but she was well shaped and dainty of foot. Her face was gay and mobile, a broad forehead and dark brows accented her eyes and small, straight nose, and her chin and cheeks were round and feminine; a slight reverse bow at the corners of her mouth was the only indication that she might have a temper, too.

Alva had been born into high society. Her family was prominent in Mobile in the days when the ultimate in American luxury was to be found in the mansions of the South. But if the Smith family fortune was lost in the war, Alva's mother still had plenty of spunk. She bundled up her four daughters and brought them to New York where they had at least a chance of making proper marriages. Mrs. Smith even ran a boardinghouse in New York to make both ends meet.

Such were the ways of Society that Alva and her family were considered outsiders in New York—for they had never been properly introduced. Alva's mother had no money to keep up the expensive pretenses that would have been necessary, but Alva's dear friend, Consuelo Yznaga, daughter of a rich Cuban, *was* in the social whirl. She had married the Duke of Manchester, and in New York there was no easier key to social success than a title. One of Alva's sisters had married Consuelo's brother Ferdinand Yznaga, so Alva's tie was secured.

Two years after his marriage to Alva, in the year the Commodore died, Willie K. was made second vice-president of the New York Central. With that post went a large income. Since Willie K. had inherited $2,000,000 from his grandfather, he and Alva were in a position to extend themselves. In 1878 they decided to build a $3,000,000 palace on Fifth Avenue. They employed Richard Morris Hunt, one of the finest architects in New York, to design for them a house for the northwest corner of Fifth Avenue and Fifty-second Street. When completed, Willie K.'s house included a two-story dining room and banquet hall, stained-glass windows, ornate carving, rich tapestries, and a double fireplace with an oak mantel.

The exterior was Caen stone, a soft but durable French stone that was particularly useful for ornate carvings. The house itself was largely decorated in the Regency style. The tub in the master bathroom was cut from a solid piece of marble. On the third floor, over the dining hall, Willie K. had built a gymnasium that was two stories high. The construction of the house was Alva Vanderbilt's first step in her campaign to overpower Mrs. Astor.

However, it was not seemly for the head of the Vanderbilts to be outdone by his son, so in 1879 William Henry went to Christian Herter and his brother, the architect-decorators, to commission the most stately house they could design. He purchased the land lying on the west side of Fifth Avenue, between Fifty-first and Fifty-second streets, and gave his architects and builders a free hand, except to specifiy that the exterior be brownstone rather than the red and black marble they first suggested. William Henry had nothing against the marble, it was far more elegant, but it would add at least a year to the construction time to have the house so faced, and William Henry wanted to live in his house, not just die in it.

The style of architecture was rococo, then in fashion. The stern simplicity of Dutch brick and even modified colonial was no longer popular.

The terrible depression that began in 1833 was just ending, and William Henry helped it end—by putting $3,000,000 into circulation in the construction of this palace.

Between six hundred and seven hundred men worked for a year and a half on the mansion. William Henry imported sixty foreign sculptors and carvers at artists' wages to decorate the interior. Two hundred and fifty workmen were employed on the wood carving alone, working from Christian Herter's designs.

The architects told William Henry the house was built to last a thousand years. It was really to be three houses in one. Half the mansion—58 rooms—between Fifty-first and Fifty-second streets, was to be occupied by William Henry and his household. The other half was split into two dwellings—one for his daughter Margaret Louisa, who had married Elliott F. Shepard, the other for daughter Emily Thorn, who was now Mrs. William D. Sloane.

Even as the house was building, William Henry began amassing the beginnings of a vast and heterogeneous art collection that was to make the mansion a great showplace. Earlier, he had purchased a few paintings by American artists. He continued to patronize American art, but few American painters had such réclame in the eyes of the rich as the currently popular French painters and the recognized old masters.

As his world expanded, William Henry's concern for his personal fortune increased, and his interest in the railroad empire decreased. It was 1879, the Commodore had been dead for two years, and times had changed. Daniel Drew died that year, the old Daniel Drew who had given the Commodore such a merry chase on the Hudson in the early days, had gone into business with the Commodore for a while, and then had tried to whip him in market speculations on the Harlem, the Hudson, and the Erie. William Henry remembered Drew well as an old skinflint who had worked him in the banking house until his health broke; nevertheless he was discomfited to learn that when Drew died, the old speculator's estate was reduced to a Bible, his watch and chain, the clothes he wore, his sealskin coat, and a handful of personal effects—total value: $500.

William Henry looked around him. Drew had once owned steamboat lines, railroads, and a banking house, and what was left of it? William Henry owned 87 per cent of the shares of the New York Central and its subsidiary railroads. What would be left of that in twenty years?

He decided that far too much of his personal fortune was tied up in a single business. His fortune was too exposed to the growing demand for government regulation of the railroads. Chauncey Depew advised him to sell some stock, because New York's legislators were in an ugly mood and there were rumors in Albany about new high taxes and new restrictions. William Henry felt he had put up with enough.

"We get kicked and cuffed by congressional committees, legislatures and the public, and I feel inclined to have others take some of it, instead of taking it all myself," he said.

So William Henry called in J. Pierpont Morgan, the young banker, and told him what he intended to do.

On November 26, 1879, Drexel, Morgan and Company took over stock and options on 250,000 shares of Vanderbilt's New York Central holdings at $120 a share. William Henry took $32,000,000 in United States government bonds that paid 4 per cent interest, but within a matter of hours Central stock was selling at $130 a share, which meant that Morgan and company cleared $2,500,000 for simply handling the transaction—buying and selling a stock that everybody seemed to want.

Morgan sold the stock, in the United States and in London, spreading the ownership in such a way that it would be almost impossible for anyone to corner enough stock to assume control. William Henry still had $30,000,000 invested in railroads, he told reporters, and it was nonsense to talk about his getting out of the railroad business—he still controlled 500,000 of the 900,000 outstanding shares of the New York Central.

But he did not actually own nearly so much stock as that (which he did not tell the reporters), and something new had been added to the railroad: three new directors. J. Pierpont Morgan was one of the new directors, Cyrus Field was another, and the third was Solon Humphreys. Morgan was a Vanderbilt banker, but who were Humphreys and Field? Both were representatives of Jay Gould, the old enemy of the Commodore!

Fighting Gould and his allies every step of the way, the Commodore had created the New York Central from three tiny railroads, roads with a combined trackage scarcely exceeding five hundred miles. When he died, the Central was twenty times as large, and more than twenty times as prosperous, and the Commodore had made his eldest son the caretaker to be sure the fruit of his life's work, the living railroad he had built, remained intact. Three years later, for the first time, outside interests—and not only outside interests but enemy interests—were represented on the railroad's board. The one person the Commodore had finally trusted had sold him down the river. It was the beginning of the end.

16

THE PUBLIC BE DAMNED

The House of Morgan brought more than prestige to the board of the New York Central Railroad. Just before William Henry's wholesale transfer of stock, Central was selling at $119 per share; a month later the price held at $135. J. Pierpont Morgan, who had arranged the sale, was the unprepossessing, quiet scion of the great London and New York banking house. He had not only made a fortune in the purchase but had also increased the value of the remaining Vanderbilt holdings. More than that, Morgan was beginning a career in the management and manipulation of railroads that was to make his reputation as one of the greatest bankers of all time.

Morgan was closely associated with William Henry—he sat on the Vanderbilt's board, and he had been William Henry's neighbor for ten years. Morgan lived in a big high-stooped house at 6 East Fortieth Street, next to Vanderbilt's old house on the corner of Fifth Avenue and Fortieth Street. But aside from business and residence, the pair had little enough in common.

Morgan was young—forty-two years old. He had been educated in fine schools in Connecticut; Vevey, Switzerland; and at the University of Göttingen. He was a founder and patron of the Metropolitan Museum of Art, a board member of countless charities, an art collector of note, and a cultured gentleman who was accepted in many—but not all—drawing rooms. Vanderbilt, older than his fifty-eight years would indicate, had not yet arrived either socially or intellectually. William Henry did exhibit some interest in the arts after he returned from his eye-opening trip to Europe on the *North Star* in 1853. But his cultural awakening had been slow.

One attribute which led toward cultural and social acceptability in New York was an interest in classical music. William Henry was truly fond of opera. In 1879 the Academy of Music at Fourteenth Street and Irving Place was the operatic center of the city. But the Vanderbilts could not squeeze into the golden circle of the Academy of Music. All the boxes in the theater had long since been sold to families who were hearing grand opera when the Vanderbilts were grubbing in their Staten Island potato fields. That point was made quite clear by the governors of the academy, when they refused the $30,000 William Henry offered for a box for the 1880 opera season.

So William Henry and his friends decided to build their own opera house. Along with Jay Gould, his new if hated associate, the broker Henry Clews, and others of the new rich, Vanderbilt organized the Metropolitan Opera Company on April 28, 1880, and purchased a piece of land at Thirty-ninth and Broadway for $600,000.

The Vanderbilts acquired five boxes in what was to be known as the Diamond Circle. Young Cornelius II had his own box. So did Willie K. The Metropolitan Opera House was to be more lavish in every way than the shabby, although socially correct, Academy of Music. To begin, the new opera company gave an architect $430,000 with which to build a splendid auditorium.

Opera was one of Vanderbilt's very few interests other than business, but now he also began to display some charitable instincts. He gave $100,000 to Vanderbilt University that year, built a $6000 parsonage at the Moravian Church on Staten Island, bought Mrs. Fountain's four-and-a-half-acre farm next to the cemetery for another $5000 and gave it to the church for a superintendent's house. He also gave the Moravian Church $10,000 to improve the roads and lakes on the grounds. And he began planning a magnificent family mausoleum, as requested by the Commodore on his deathbed. The Commodore had decided that all male members of the Vanderbilt line and their wives would be buried in the mausoleum, but only the families of those who bore the Vanderbilt name would be buried there. Daughters, who ceased to be Vanderbilts on marriage, would continue to follow their husbands to their scattered graves.

The new mausoleum had to be large; William Henry's eldest son Cornelius already had four sons of his own. Willie K. had one boy, and young George was still unmarried.

William Henry also spent time and money on his city. Over a decade before he had become interested in financing the movement of an Egyptian obelisk from Alexandria, Egypt, to New York City. These were the days when the culture of ancient Egypt fascinated America. The Metropolitan Museum of Art sent a large force of archaeologists to Egypt to dig into ruins and ship mummies, statues, painting, jewelry, and even parts of tombs back to the museum.

William Henry Hurlbert, a correspondent of the New York World in Egypt, learned that several nations were taking obelisks and other important stone pieces out of the country. Hurlbert suggested that New York ought to have one, and the Khedive agreed, for the nineteenth-century Egyptians cared little for the relics of the past. A few years after Hurlbert suggested the idea, U. S. Navy Lt. Comdr. Henry Honeychurch Garringe worked out a practical plan to bring one of the obelisks to America. This particular monument was known as Cleopatra's Needle, although it had nothing to do with Cleopatra and had been erected in Heliopolis in 1500 B.C., about fourteen hundred years before Cleopatra graced the Egyptian scene. It cost $100,000 to move the obelisk, far more than expected, but Vanderbilt paid the bill. He and New York's commissioner of parks agreed that a site in Central Park near the Metropolitan Museum would best display the obelisk since at that time their site represented the highest point in New York City. There Cleopatra's Needle was erected in 1881.

William Henry's other monument, his brownstone palace, was completed in the fall of 1881. The house was even more splendid than had been expected. William Henry's side of the block-long building was numbered 640 Fifth Avenue, although a number scarcely did justice to the four-story mansion. The bronze entrance doors—called the Gates of Paradise—were originally cast by Barbedienne for the Italian Prince of San Donato. They contained ten panels drawn from descriptions in the Old Testament, showing the wonders of Heaven. Vanderbilt purchased the gates, plus a considerable amount of bric-a-brac, in the sale of the Prince's castle, paying $25,000 for the gates alone.

Inside the doors was the vestibule, a great hall in itself, planned to accomodate the most elaborate receptions. The floors were marble, the walls were covered with polished marble which had been drawn from the old Roman quarries in North Africa, and surmounted by a mosaic frieze, and the room was lighted through a roof of colored glass, which, on sunny days, gave a dazzling luster to the dominant piece in the room—a vase of green malachite. The vase was one of a pair but the other was not available to Vanderbilt at any price, for it stood in the Palace of the Czar in Petrograd. Even in this grand room, two such vases would have been too much, for on its pedestal the great piece stood 8 feet 4 inches in height. Above it, suspended from moldings, hung two almost life-sized flying figures of Fame, whose wings and feet touched the vase.

In the center of the building the atrium—the grand hall—rose to the roof of the house, four floors above, with balconies on the four sides, in the style of an Italian palace. The atrium resembled nothing so much as an ornate hotel lobby, all claw-footed chairs, horsehair couches, oriental rugs, marble and gilt. Carvings, bronzes, and statuary were placed in every conceivable spot, presenting such a confusing hodgepodge to the eye that pleasure could scarcely be gained from any of them, yet this technique of room stuffing was typical of the day; Mrs. A. T. Stewart's mansion (known as the Marble Palace) was equally jammed with objects of art. The very rich were bent on surpassing one another in sheer volume of antiquities, leaving the selection and quality to an army of decorators, whose taste in these matters seemed invariably to be overcome by their own cupidity.

One wall of the atrium displayed a huge tapestry from the

royal manufactory at Lille (where Louis XIV had commissioned many of the greatest works), showing Agamemnon preparing to sacrifice Iphigenia. Varicolored marble columns rose to the roof, overpowering all that stood below, the marble busts, the German bronze of a female falconer, the grotesque features of the statue of the Japanese god of the sea.

Other rooms opened off the central atrium. On one side, beyond a tall, gingerbread arch draped ornately in velvet, was the drawing room. On the opposite side, a pair of female busts guarded the entrance to the potted palms of the conservatory.

Even the staircase was impressive. At the foot of the stairs that led from the atrium, the newel post represented a life-sized female slave, cast in bronze and overlaid with gold. The figure was half turned to expose the right breast, but was otherwise heavily draped in Grecian style, the arm holding high an urn. At night, the statue lit up, illuminated by a tiara studded with electric bulbs.

The stairs were covered with heavy carpet, and the railing was made of bronze, cushioned in deep red plush. On the inside wall of the stairway, workmen installed paneling made to imitate courses of stone. The impression was that of the stairway of an old stone castle. Above, on the first landing, stood an eight-day clock with a stained-glass window, framed against one of six tapestries that lined the balcony walls.

Another balcony, directly above the drawing room, was surrounded by life-sized friezes, and the ceiling was given to a single painting of a medieval hunting scene. In the room below were Japanese bronzes, cloisonnés, lacquers, and china pieces, a drinking flagon that had belonged to Stephen, the sixteenth-century king of Poland, and a Dutch ship's model made of silver gilt. The drawing room held a number of bookcases, too, whose glass doors showed matched sets of volumes bound in vellum and leather, obviously purchased in sets to fill the cases, not for reading, and each of these bookcases was topped by a handful of smaller bronzes, Satsuma vases, Chinese bowls, and Meissen figurines—creating a housemaid's nightmare.

It was obviously impossible to live amid such tasteless splendor, and the family did not. The favorite household room was the library on the second floor, a room paneled in rosewood inlaid with mother-of-pearl and brass in designs drawn from ancient Greek myths. The library was gaudy enough, but at least it was comfortable, and the books in this room were sometimes read. Seven family portraits hung on the walls, including that of the Commodore, in the place of honor, above a large black Chinese cabinet inlaid with mother-of-pearl. The library even boasted a leopard rug.

Mrs. Vanderbilt's boudoir, 26 feet long and 18 feet wide, overlooked Fifth Avenue. From there, Louisa Kissam, daughter of an impecunious Brooklyn minister, controlled the destinies of a score of servants, conferring with her cook, her housekeeper, and the butler, in this room of dark-blue silk brocade.

The house had fireproof safes in the pantry to store the family silver. It had a complete internal telephone system and even boasted a refrigerator that was operated by electricity, with that wonders of wonders, a glass door.

The stable, behind the house, was a two-story building in which any middle-class citizen would be proud to live. It had polished hardwood floors and a glass-roofed courtyard where the horses could be walked without exposing them to the weather.

By the time the Vanderbilts moved into their house, most of William Henry's children were married—only nineteen-year-old George was still living at home. But the house was gay enough. William Henry liked to show off both the house and his art collection, so he gave frequent art receptions. He commissioned the private publication of a three-volume description of the house, with expensive color plates pasted individually into each volume, a set of books so heavy that it took a strong man to lift all three volumes.

This private book claimed there was nothing ostentatious about what was actually the most ostentatious house in all America. There was absolutely no showiness to the Vanderbilt house, claimed the author. There were no bowling alleys or menageries, "nothing but what a reasonable and practical family may live up to," he wrote. "It is as sincere a home as exists anywhere."

R. Marcel Lancelot, the artist who had been commissioned to

do the etching that decorated the introduction to the book, drew for that space a picture of a locomotive emerging from a tunnel, smoke belching from its tall smokestack. A score of cherubs flew around the locomotive bearing trays of sweets and fruits. A pair of nubian boys brought other trays of delicacies forward for the delectation of the passengers who would soon disembark. But a single cherub, in the middle of the picture, was clutching a bottle in his hand as he flew alongside the train. On the bottle, tiny, but clearly visible, were labeled the letters GIN.

That private joke expressed the attitude of much of the intellectual world toward the riches of the Vanderbilts. It was not a comment on William Henry's habits, for this Vanderbilt was the most abstemious of men: in fact, he had not touched a cigar since 1853. One night during the *North Star* trip to Europe, the Commodore had spied his son on deck, smoking a cigar and watching the movement of the waves. The Commodore leaned on the rail next to his son, looked at the glowing cigar in distaste, and asked William Henry to give up the vile tobacco habit.

"Billy," said the father, "I'll give you ten thousand dollars if you'll do it."

Even at thirty-two, William Henry was a respectful and obedient son. His father did not need to promise him money, he said, throwing the cigar into the sea.

And the Commodore, touched by this display of filial respect, beamed, reached into his inner pocket, withdrew a Havana of his own, and lighted up with pleasure.

William Henry never smoked again. Nor did he drink to excess —an occasional glass of champagne or a really rare vintage wine. He was a picky eater, and his favorite food was shellfish.

His habits were dictated partly by health. In his later years, William Henry found it difficult to control his weight. He suffered from high blood pressure, and the family doctor was quite certain that one day the head of the Vanderbilt family would die from some disease associated with hardening of the arteries. William Henry's health was deteriorating steadily, in spite of his careful habits.

Yet the years had been crueler to his younger brother, Cornelius

Jeremiah. In 1880, following the settlement of the claim against the Commodore's estate, Cornelius Jeremiah took a trip around the world, accompanied by his physician and companion, Dr. George N. Terry.

At the end of the tour the pair returned to this country. Cornelius Jeremiah was still suffering from his epileptic seizures, but he had the money now to gratify his every wish, and to travel in luxurious style.

In February 1882 Cornelius Jeremiah and Dr. Terry went to Hot Springs, Arkansas, for the baths and the rest cure offered by the resort. Later they went on to Florida, to wait until the cold weather ended in the North. Toward the end of March they traveled to New York where they took front rooms at the Glenham Hotel on Fifth Avenue. There had been no reconciliation of the brothers, so Cornelius Jeremiah neither called on William Henry nor informed his brother that he was in the city.

On April 1, a Saturday, Cornelius Jeremiah went to bed early, complaining that he was not feeling well. On Sunday at two o'clock in the afternoon Dr. Terry heard a loud noise and rushed into Cornelius's room. He saw Cornelius Jeremiah lying on the bed, bleeding from the temple. There was a .38-caliber Smith & Wesson revolver in his hand.

Dr. Terry telephoned to William Henry Vanderbilt, who came in a carriage to the hotel, accompanied by his son Willie K. Father and son sat by the side of Cornelius Jeremiah, but four hours later the epileptic died without regaining consciousness.

The funeral, William Henry decided, would be held at Dr. Deems's Church of the Strangers. A special train would take the casket from New York to Hartford, where Cornelius Jeremiah had just completed the building of a new house of his own. His remains were to be buried there beside his wife. The question of a Staten Island burial was never raised.

The funeral of the Commodore's second son was brief and simple. General John C. Frémont sent a letter of regret, a wreath, and a personal representative. Frémont was president of the Associated Pioneers of California, an organization Cornelius Jeremiah had joined after his ill-fated trip around the Horn to the gold fields. A handful of persons stood in the Church of the Strangers to hear Dr. Deems read the service. Uncle Jake came. So did William Henry and his wife Louisa. Mary Alicia, who was now Mrs. Francis Berger, came to pay last respects to the one member of the family who had joined with her in contesting the Commodore's will.

William Henry, the head of the Vanderbilt family, escorted his brother's body to Hartford and saw it decently buried.

As he had promised, Cornelius Jeremiah left nothing to anyone named Vanderbilt. He left $1000 to each of his sisters, and $50,000 to his friend Samuel P. Colt, the firearms manufacturer. Other bequests ate up a great deal of the remainder of his half-million-dollar fortune, but Dr. George Terry, his friend and companion, received $120,000.

The scandal of his brother's suicide brought disappointment, shock, and worry to the head of the Vanderbilt family. Less than a month after Cornelius Jeremiah's death, William Henry was the target of an assassin. On April 30, 1882, a mailman working in a branch post office noted that one of the leather mail pouches was smoking. He dumped out a load of singed letters and the remains of a small box. The box had been addressed to W. H. Vanderbilt. The bomb had not hurt anyone when it exploded, but it was not the kind of gift calculated to make a railroad president sleep soundly at night.

Family problems, high blood pressure, and business worries combined unfairly to give William Henry a reputation for bad temper. By disposition he was a placid man, but his worries had become a heavy burden by 1882. In recent years he had suffered some business reverses, which, although they were minor, were exasperating. He had been a major stockholder in the Western Union Telegraph Company until Jay Gould created a competitive company called American Union, with the single aim of unloading it on Western Union. Gould had done just that in 1881, and Vanderbilt, victim of a business trick that would have done his father proud, resigned from Western Union's board and sold out.

William Henry had once held 30,000 shares of Union Pacific stock, but had decided it was not a good investment. At one time he had nearly enough stock to control the Rock Island Railroad, but he did not take full advantage of his situation in that railroad either.

William Henry's most serious railroad problem in 1882 involved a road called the Nickel Plate, which had been built by a group of speculators to parallel the New York Central's lines between New York and Chicago. Officially the road was called the New York, Chicago and St. Louis Railroad. But whatever it was called, it meant trouble for Vanderbilt. There was some talk that the road had been built specifically to force the New York Central to buy it. This was not true, but the road was in the hands of speculators in 1882, and they were playing Vanderbilt off against Jay Gould. If Gould got control of the Nickel Plate, he could wreak havoc with the Central's balance sheet.

While the Nickel Plate negotiations dragged on, William Henry, in 1882, had taken over the Canada Southern, which he put together with the Michigan Central, and had purchased a handful of shortline railroads that moved him into the Illinois coalfields. He was dickering, that year, for control of the Pittsburgh and Lake Erie line. That October William Henry set out in a private train to survey his northwest empire and take a vacation from the cares of high office. Traveling in private cars were William Henry, son Willie K., son Frederick William, Uncle Jake (who was near eighty but still spry), and a half-dozen executives of the New York Central System.

At Michigan City, Indiana, reporters from the Chicago press boarded the train for a conference with the president of the powerful New York Central. They asked him if he was going to buy the Nickel Plate. William Henry chuckled. He had no use for it, he said. Certainly he had been approached to buy the road, but he did not see how he could find any freight or passenger business for it since it paralleled his own lines.

William Henry talked to the press about sleeping cars—comparing the virtues of the Pullman cars used on the western roads with the Wagner cars he favored. He discussed government rate regulation, which he detested, and labor unions, which he liked no more. He expressed contempt for antimonopoly politicians; that kind, he said, were the cheapest and most easily bought.

He talked about the Chicago Limited that the New York Central operated, and grimly explained that the only reason he kept it going was competition, of the Pennsylvania Railroad in passenger traffic.

"But don't you run it for the public benefit?" asked a reporter.

"The public be damned!" said William Henry Vanderbilt.

In later years he was to deny that he made that rash statement, and everyone else in the New York Central was to deny that he meant it, but it was a typical remark, and it represented exactly the kind of thinking that went on in William Henry Vanderbilt's head. He was not unique in his contempt for the public; he would have been unique had he adopted any other attitude in this era of monopoly. But William Henry, thin-skinned, was distressed by the public outcry that followed. He became moody, more snappish than ever with reporters, and less inclined to open his life to public inspection. The soirees at the mansion on Fifth Avenue became more formal and less frequent. William Henry began to retire within his shell.

17

THE TRIUMPH OF WILLIE K.

By 1883 the face of New York had undergone some remarkable changes. The trains of the elevated railway made the great curve on top of the trestle at 110th Street, then coursed down the length of Manhattan, belching around the snake curve at Coenties slip. The majestic towers of the Brooklyn Bridge loomed above Manhattan and citizens flocked to the East River on Sunday afternoons to watch the completion of the remarkable new bridge. Like the city's bridges, buildings were rising higher. The new passenger elevators made it easier for an office worker to reach a room on the tenth floor than it was to walk to a fourth-floor room.

The first really good public school system in New York City had been opened under Superintendent John Jasper. The children of the poor and middle classes had a better chance for self-improvement than ever before.

The city's port authorities had blown up most of the old obstructions to navigation in the rivers, such as the rocks at Hell Gate that had lent so much spice to the Commodore's steamboating days on Long Island Sound. But William Henry Vanderbilt was not interested in such improvements. He had never taken a fancy to steamboats, and after the Commodore's death the Vanderbilt shipping holdings dwindled steadily. Neither was he excited by such developments as the elevated street railway. At one time he could have taken that railroad over, but he did not.

The truth was that by 1883, William Henry Vanderbilt was tired of the business world and wanted to be out of it.

He now had two great interests in life: his trotting horses and his art collection. Until the Commodore died, many acquaintances thought that William Henry's interest in horses was professed only to impress the Commodore. But in 1877, after the Commodore's death, day after day William Henry could be seen driving out in his maroon rig, with a handsome trotter or a pair hitched to it.

He had inherited from the Commodore a fast horse called Small Hopes, after Frank Vanderbilt had taken her pick of the thoroughbreds, but he was never really aroused by his horses until one day when Robert Bonner, a well-known horseman, took Vanderbilt out for a wild ride behind his favorite trotter. Bonner handed William Henry the reins and Vanderbilt drove Peerless, Bonner's great mare, twice around the DuBois half-mile track in 2:23¼. It was nowhere near a record, but the feeling of power that went with the speed caught William Henry's imagination. He became a real trotting buff.

The natty Bonner and Frank Work, Vanderbilt's broker, had the fastest trotting horses in all New York. They assembled at various race courses on the north end of Manhattan, in the Bronx, and on Long Island with other horsemen, to race, bet, and argue over the merits of trotter and rig. DuBois's half-mile dirt track, not far from the old Macomb's Dam, on Jerome Avenue in the Bronx, was one of their favorite meeting grounds. In the old days, when the Commodore had begun his racing, it was easy enough to find places to race on the east side of Manhattan and at the north end of the island, but New York City had straggled up the island, sending the pleasure seekers farther afield into the meadows of the country.

Once his enthusiasm was up, William Henry bought a Hambletonian gray mare named Lady Mac to pair with Small Hopes, hitched to a stripped-down roadwagon. They were a fine pair, matching one another stride for stride, and they were clocked at a mile in 2:23½. They were fast enough to beat Bonner's horses but not speedy enough to whip the grinning Frank Work, who boasted that in the famous pair, whimsically named Edward and Dick Swiveller, he had the finest trotters in America. Work delighted in whizzing up Jerome Avenue at breakneck speed, frightening pedestrians out of the way of his rig with the clatter, and passing every team on the road, including Vanderbilt's.

Frank Work was riding for a fall, and Vanderbilt was determined to give it to him.

He bought Aldine, a chestnut trotting mare sired by Toronto out of Mother Hubbard—a famous pair—and a chestnut mare named Early Rose. These trotters could travel a mile in 2:16½, which was enough, Vanderbilt believed, to send Broker Work back to his Wall Street office.

For a few months Work shied away from the track on the days Vanderbilt raced his famous horses, but one day the broker hitched up Edward and Dick Swiveller, and issued his challenge. Vanderbilt was eager to race, and the two swift teams pranced to the starting place, their drivers nervous, dry-lipped, and brandishing their slender whips, while a crowd gathered to watch. They were well matched, and made a strong race, but in the end Frank Work's horses, or perhaps his greater driving experience, won the day.

This defeat made Vanderbilt more determined than ever to own the finest trotting team in America, so he made a public offer of $20,000 for any trotter that could do a mile in 2:20 or better. There was such a horse, or rather a mare, named Maud S. She belonged to a Captain Stone who lived in the blue grass country of Kentucky. Stone heard of the offer, and the price William Henry was willing to pay, and arranged for an official trial where observers could clock his mare. If she could do 2:20, Stone told his professional driver Bair, the driver could count on a tip of a thousand dollars.

Maud S. and the driver were both in fine form that day, and they circled the mile track at Lexington in 2:17½. When Vanderbilt heard the results, he wanted Maud S., and he got her, but not for $20,000. Captain Stone decided that Vanderbilt should also pay driver Bair's tip. William Henry grumbled, but he paid.

The promising mare was loaded into a boxcar in Lexington and shipped to New York, where Vanderbilt sent her immediately to the famous trainer Carl Burr on Long Island. Burr maintained a stable, practice track, and training establishment at Commack, a few miles east of Huntington in Suffolk County. Maud S. proved to be a great disappointment in the northern climate. She was slow, not nearly matching the 2:17½ she had clocked in Lexington, and finally, in the repeated efforts to push her, she went lame. At first Vanderbilt was inclined to blame Burr for the incident, but the trainer stoutly denied any responsibility; she had a weak leg when he had received her, Burr said.

Vanderbilt's wrath then descended on Captain Stone. The millionaire claimed the Kentuckian had cheated him, a charge which Stone denied, and Vanderbilt sent Maud S. back to Kentucky, where the lameness vanished. Vanderbilt then decided to keep his original bargain and Maud S. was brought north again.

After more training, Maud S. took the place of Early Rose in the team with Aldine. They raced at DuBois track, up and down the roads north of the city, and at Fleetwood Park outside the city. On June 14, 1883, at Fleetwood Park, the pair did a mile in 2:15½, setting a new world's record for trotters, and effectively settling the dispute with Frank Work, although Work never forgave Vanderbilt for eclipsing him.

When he was not with his trotters, on the course or in the stable, Vanderbilt sought relief from business pressures in his expensive art collection. He had begun collecting art when he lived in the house on Fortieth Street, but art became a passion with him after he moved into the mansion at 640 Fifth Avenue. William Henry searched for paintings in France, Italy, and England. On one trip he narrowly escaped death when the steamer on which he was traveling across Lake Como caught fire, but the incident prejudiced him neither against European travel nor against steamer trips, which he thoroughly enjoyed. A trip to Europe became at least an annual event.

The Impressionist school of painters had begun exhibiting in Paris in 1874 and after 1880 had aroused a storm in the art world. Paul Gauguin, Cézanne, and Van Gogh were all at work, but William Henry eschewed the work of the moderns; his interest ran to landscapes and animals pictures. As the interior of his mansion indicated, Vanderbilt had very little taste for art, and most of his taste was shockingly bad, a respect in which he differed very little from most American millionaires of his day.

On one occasion when William Henry was visiting Paris, a nobleman of the Bonaparte family wrote that he wanted to sell his houseful of art treasures. Vanderbilt and his art advisor drove out from Paris to see the collection. But after William Henry had examined the Louis XIV furniture, Madame Pompadour's dressing table, and Louis XVI's exquisite personal china service, Vanderbilt left without buying. There was no argument about price or the authenticity of the works of art. William Henry had a house full of furniture, but above all, he said, it would be nearly criminal to take these pieces from France, where they were appreciated for their workmanship and historical value and ship them to America, where his friends would neither know the history of the treasures nor care about them. William Henry's tastes were pragmatic, he wanted paintings to hang on the wall, not furniture, but at least he realized his limitations, and admitted them, which was far more than could be said for most of the new class of American millionaires.

Generally, when William Henry toured the galleries in Paris he refused to look at nude paintings, and certainly would not hang one in his collection.

At the Boucheron gallery he was intrigued by a painting of a yoke of oxen which were turning to leave a field after plowing. M. Boucheron began to tell him something about the artist, Constant Troyon, the great French animal painter of the nineteenth century. William Henry listened impatiently. He knew nothing about the artist, or the art, but he did know about the action of the oxen. He had seen them turning just like that thousands of times on the Staten Island farm. He wanted that painting.

William Henry tramped the streets of Paris, visiting galleries and the artists in their studios. He would wrap his boots in brown paper and carry them himself to the bootmaker on the Avenue de l'Opera. Then he would go off to visit Mlle. Rosa Bonheur, or

Jean Louis Ernest Meissonier, to talk about a painting for which he was prepared to pay $20,000.

He bought nearly $190,000 worth of paintings from Meissonier. The two became such good friends that the aging military artist agreed to do William Henry's portrait and Vanderbilt went day after day to sit for it. He ordered a dozen paintings from French artists. He particularly liked paintings in which farm animals dominated the scene; thus his interest in Mlle. Bonheur and in Troyon. But he also purchased from galleries and at sales Albert Aublet's "Duc de Guise," the "Good Fortune" by Charles Baugniet, the "Shephardess of Barbizon" by Millet, "Lunch Time" by Tissot, "Going to the Bath" by Bouguereau, "Ladies of the First Empire" by Boldini, "Mid-day" by Dupré.

They were fine paintings of the day, but in the Vanderbilt mansion they were displayed so closely together and arranged so hastily that viewers came away with an impression of clutter. Poor William Henry had neither the high taste nor delicacy to match his hunger for the arts.

Still the collection was William Henry's delight. By 1883 he had lost interest in the railroads. He had worked hard and long in his sixty-two years, and he was discouraged by poor health as well as by the financial mistake he had made the year before when he had paid so heavily to acquire control of the Nickel Plate road—just as it was sinking into bankruptcy.

William Henry thought it was time for his sons to take over.

The task fell to the two sons who had grown up in the railroads: Cornelius Vanderbilt II and Willie K. Both had joined the Central when their grandfather was still alive, and their careers, in the beginning, had received the Commodore's personal attention. The old Commodore, of course, fully expected that eventually his namesake Cornelius would head the family, and the railroads; he had given that understanding in his will, when he singled out Cornelius II as the recipient of money in his own right, and the lesser personal memorabilia. But the old man in his prime would also most certainly have disapproved of Cornelius II's way of life. Cornelius II was a Sunday school teacher. He also burned his lights late at night, studying the problems of the Episcopal foreign missions, not at the whist table, and he gave away much of his income for charitable works and served on the vestry of his church.

The Commodore might have disapproved of Willie K.'s life, too, but on entirely different grounds. Willie was preoccupied with the good life. He played polo instead of teaching Sunday school, he burned his lights late at night, but at dancing parties, he spent his income on the entertainment of his wealthy friends, and he served on the boards of numerous private clubs.

Still, the Commodore would have approved of the way his grandsons tackled their jobs, and the understanding they had acquired of railroad problems, for Cornelius and Willie K. met almost daily with William Henry in the offices at Grand Central Station, to resolve the complex problems of their multiple railroads.

Willie K.'s preoccupation with the social whirl of New York was largely his wife's doing, for, as noted, Alva, the queenly Alva, had set out to make herself chatelaine of New York society. In the few years since her marriage, starting without entree in polite circles, Alva had entertained Roosevelts and Goelets; even Ward McAllister, the transplanted Savannah snob, who organized New York society affairs for Mrs. Astor, was now at her feet. McAllister invited the Vanderbilts to his parties, and went to theirs, a sign that they had achieved a certain social prominence. But Mrs. Astor did not invite the Vanderbilts to her parties, and until she did, the Vanderbilt family could not take a place as equals in the high world of New York society, but must lurk about the edges. The Vanderbilts might hold the greatest fortune in the world, but to Mrs. Astor they did not yet exist.

Alva Vanderbilt, beneath her honeyed southern ways, had a mind as shrewd as any railroad manipulator. She had already made every suitable overture to Mrs. Astor. She had done everything possible except to wheedle or declare a state of siege. She would never plead, and siege demanded some planning.

The Astors were relatively immune to attack from any direction. They had their own multiple millions, so mere wealth could be of no possible use in opening the door. William Astor was not a speculator, and it was inconceivable that William K. Vanderbilt could do him any kind of favor, even indirectly. The Astors' hotels, buildings, houses, tenements, and corporations were all doing splendidly.

Alva toyed with the problem through the fall season and into the winter of 1883. Eventually she found the grand Mrs. Astor's Achilles' heel: her unmarried daughter Carrie.

Carrie Astor was a shy young maiden, just out of finishing school, with brown hair that reached past her shoulders. While she awaited a proper offer of marriage, she threw herself into social and charitable activities with a group of friends in the very highest junior circle of Society. With the enthusiasm of youth, the youngsters organized parties, danced half the night away, and rose the next morning to ride in Central Park and begin it all over again. They were a gay, handsome, extravagant set, and for Alva Vanderbilt, a thoroughly easy target.

Alva let it be known that she planned a ball for the night of March 26, 1883. Her mansion had a touch of the court of Versailles about it. In such surroundings it was only fitting that the ball should be a costume affair—and that idea met Alva's needs exactly.

For weeks beforehand, Society made its preparations. Wall Street brokers deserted their offices to stand in their underwear in the shops of their tailors and be fitted for handmade costumes. Ladies lay awake nights beneath their silken canopies, worrying whether the ruff collar of a Mary Stuart or the décolleté gown of a French marquise would best show off their jewels and their charms.

No proper Society ball ever employed paid entertainers in those days. An orchestra, usually two, would be hired to play discreetly in the background. The guests planned such entertainment as there would be. The special entertainment for Alva's ball would be a series of quadrilles. These quadrilles were much like the ones of George Washington's time, although now they were normally made up entirely of young ladies—who would drill for weeks until they achieved ballet precision.

Carrie Astor belonged to a quadrille of just this sort. Neither

Carrie nor any of her chums thought about invitations—they were absolutely top-drawer Society, and were automatically invited to all the best parties.

Fate must have been playing into Alva Vanderbilt's dainty hands, for not only was Carrie engrossed in a quadrille, but Mrs. Astor had, herself, undertaken its supervision, and was drilling the girls in the manner of a true martinet. Each of the eight was to be dressed as a star, two in yellow, two in blue, two in delicate purple, two in white. Each would wear a lighted star on her head. They would call themselves the Star Quadrille.

Mrs. Astor was planning her dress. As the leader of Society, she would, naturally, have to appear both regal and dignified. Carrie and her seven friends went to their dressmakers for special gowns, different in color but exactly alike in style.

Thus the days went by, but suddenly, uncomfortably close to the day of the ball, Mrs. Astor realized that neither she nor Carrie had received a formal invitation. She let the oversight be called to Alva Vanderbilt's attention.

There had been no mistake, Alva said. There could be no Star Quadrille at the Vanderbilt ball. Why, Carrie Astor was not even on the invitation list! How could she be? The Vanderbilts really did not know the Astors. (Here one can almost see Alva rummaging through the calling cards in the vestibule.) Mrs. Astor had never called at 660 Fifth Avenue.

Immediately the word got back to Mrs. Astor that she and her daughter would not be invited to the ball. This was a matter of unconcern to William Astor, who seemed to care more for Europe and yachting than for balls. But the snub represented an annoyance for Mrs. Astor, and absolute tragedy for poor Carrie, who had counted on dazzling Society at the ball.

Mrs. Astor was a good soldier. She was also a good general who knew when she had been outmaneuvered. Ward McAllister, whom Mrs. Astor had made New York's social arbitrator, had accepted the Vanderbilts, so Alva's challenge was truly dangerous. What was now a minor defeat might become a catastrophe unless Mrs. Astor warded it off.

Mrs. Astor took cardcase in hand, and drove up Fifth Avenue, to the replica of the Chateau de Blois at 660. There she sent a blue-liveried footman inside to deliver a calling card which, like all her calling cards, simply said: *Mrs. Astor.*

The small, engraved piece of pasteboard Mrs. Astor left at the Vanderbilts that day was as important to Alva as the key to a kingdom; it was figuratively a key to the social kingdom over which Mrs. Astor ruled with so much finesse and authority.

Alva wasted no time in sending invitations to the Mr. and Mrs. William Astor, and to Carrie. Her siege had carried the day.

After that Vanderbilt victory it might seem that anything would be anticlimatic, but the ball, on March 26, was the most splendid ever given in America. It was to begin at eleven-thirty, but by early evening the streets were lined with hundreds of common folk, and at ten-thirty the first guests arrived.

An hour later a steady stream of carriages began to pull up before the great doors, and knights, ladies, and characters from Mother Goose land stepped down between the great stone lions at the entrance, to be swallowed inside the mansion before the crowds had more than a glimpse of them.

Alva, her sister, Mrs. Yznaga, and Lady Mandeville stood in the reception line, along with Willie K. Vanderbilt. The host was dressed to represent a painting that hung in his father's gallery in the palace across the street—Albert Aublet's "Duc de Guise." He wore yellow silk tights, black trunks slashed with yellow, a yellow doublet, a black velvet cloak trimmed in gold, a medal hung on a black ribbon, a white wig, and black velvet shoes.

Lady Mandeville was dressed in black, after a Van Dyck painting. Alva was a Venetian princess, dressed in red and yellow, dragging a long blue train. Mrs. Astor was a Venetian princess, too, but she went Alva one better, decking herself in an invaluable collection of precious stones.

Carrie Astor and her seven friends were there, stars in their own heaven.

Willie K.'s sisters appeared; Eliza Webb was a hornet; Margaret Louisa Shepard was a marquise; Emily Sloane was Bopeep; Florence Adele Twombly was a modern beauty in a blue skirt quilted with diamonds. Cornelius Vanderbilt II was resplendent as Louis XVI. He wore breeches of fawn brocade, a waistcoat trimmed with silver lace, and carried a sword with a diamond-studded hilt. His wife came as an electric light. His three children (those who were old enough to stay up so late) came as a rose, Sinbad the sailor, and a diminutive French courtier.

The William Henry Vanderbilts attended, although William Henry was already suffering from the illness that would kill him, and was preparing for his retirement. Louisa Kissam Vanderbilt came as a duchess. William Henry came in formal evening clothes, as did Ulysses Simpson Grant.

After a reception, the dancing began in the two-story dining hall.

In the Hobby Horse quadrille the ladies wore red coats and white satin skirts; the gentlemen wore red coats and white satin knee breeches. Both ladies and gentlemen hobbled through the square dance inside artificial horses made of real horse hide, with real horse manes.

A decorator and florist, Charles Klunder, had been commissioned to make the house over for the occasion. He arranged the expensive vases and baskets and urns with the most unseasonable blossoms, thousands of roses filled the nooks and crannies of the mansion. The supper room on the second floor was encircled by palm trees festooned with orchids. The food was fit for a gourmet, the wine was champagne. The dancing continued, with interruption only for supper, until four o'clock in the morning, when the exhausted guests began trouping home, their powdered wigs askew, costly gowns rumpled, and the Vanderbilt servants began to clean up the debris.

The Vanderbilts were not given to public announcement of the cost of their entertainments, but the newspapers said the price of the party was more than $75,000—plus the costumes, and some of these had cost their wearers $1000. All New York agreed that the William K. Vanderbilt ball was the most magnificent entertainment that had ever been given on the western shore of the Atlantic. Henry Clews, the broker with a sense of history, compared the Vanderbilt ball favorably to the antics at Versailles and the entertainments of the Roman emperors.

That winter the Vanderbilts were invited to Mrs. Astor's traditional ball. From that date on, no Vanderbilt had any difficulty in social matters. Willie K. and Alva built a country mansion at Oakdale, Long Island, called Idle Hour. There they extended their entertainments; Willie K. ran a little steamer up and down the little river near the house. Alva entertained royally on the estate that had stables, greenhouses, cattle barns, and a private hunting preserve of nearly eight hundred acres. The Vanderbilts, and particularly the William Kissam Vanderbilts, were leaders of Society. While Mrs. Astor could not be replaced in her lifetime as the grand dame of Fifth Avenue, it was quite apparent that the next Astor would have to look to her laurels and to the Vanderbilts if she were not to be eclipsed; on the basis of performance, Alva was certainly the one to be watched.

18

THE RICHEST MAN IN THE WORLD

After 1880 the enemies of the New York Central Railroad ganged up to give William Henry trouble along the route of the parent Hudson line.

Frederick D. Tappen, president of the Gallatin National Bank, was one of the New Yorkers who had lived on St. John's Park, and he never forgave the Commodore for turning the tree-lined park into a freight yard, this making Tappen's house uninhabitable and—the greater blow—lowering the value of his real estate. George M. Pullman, the sleeping car manufacturer, was angry because the Vanderbilts, father and son, had steadfastly refused to use his Pullman cars, even after their Chicago Express had been telescoped by the Tarrytown Special near Spuyten Duyvil in 1882, and Senator Wagner had burned to death in one of his own sleepers. Pullman was annoyed further when William Henry took control of the Chicago and Northwestern Railway, and promptly replaced the Pullman cars with Wagners.

Pullman, Banker Tappen, and scores of other businessmen were willing, even eager, to do the Vanderbilts a bad turn, particularly if they hoped to profit in the doing. So in the eighties they formed a group to construct a rival railroad along the west bank of the Hudson, almost paralleling the Vanderbilt line. The road was called the New York, West Shore, and Buffalo Railroad. It would use Pullman cars exclusively, and, its backers hoped, the new road would run the New York Central ragged.

In the midst of this fight, William Henry decided to resign from active direction of the New York Central's affairs.

"I am the richest man in the world. I am worth one hundred ninety-four million dollars," William Henry boasted to a friend one day. Apparently he was. His only rival, England's Duke of Westminster held a fortune worth somewhere around $200,000,000 but it was almost all in land; Vanderbilt estimated that Westminster's holdings did not pay him 2 per cent a year.

With all that wealth, William Henry was still concerned lest his money be held—and lost—in one place. The Commodore, even in his old age, had used money to help him build. William Henry was more concerned about keeping and consolidating what he had than in making more money or in extending the railroad to the growing West. "I would not walk across the street to make a million dollars," he said.

He kept $70,000,000 in government bonds; his income was $10,350,000 per year, $28,000 per day, $1200 per hour, or $19.75 per minute. Even though he had sold much of the Central stock he had acquired other rail shares and his railroad stocks earned $7,394,000 a year; accordingly, he felt that he could retire safely from active management of the railroads, and he wanted relief from the daily chores of management.

In May 1883 William Henry did retire. He gave up every position in the railroads save that of director. James H. Rutter was elected president of the New York Central Railroad, and the younger Vanderbilts moved up a notch in their apprenticeships as railroad operators.

Chauncey Depew, Vanderbilt's right-hand man, had been a director of the New York Central since 1874; now he became vice-president, and the main contact between William Henry and the operating management. (In 1885, at Rutter's death, he became president and from 1899–1928 he was chairman of the board.)

William Henry exercised his new freedom in many ways. Often he went to the Windsor Turkish Baths on Forty-sixth Street. He had taken a fancy to Turkish baths some years before, apparently finding them to be good for his blood pressure and general sense of well-being. The baths relaxed him, much as did the ocean voyages of which he was so fond. He loved to take a trip to Europe on a liner, then turn straight around and come home aboard her, without getting off the ship.

William Henry also spent a great deal of time with his horses.

He drove his fine teams up and down the avenues, and on the race tracks in the Bronx. Maud S. was his favorite. She was the nation's favorite, too, so much so that even a cake was named for her. But after a time the constant demand that he race and show the great mare began to rub on William Henry's frayed nerves. A patent medicine manufacturer insulted Vanderbilt by offering $25,000 if he would change the mare's name to that of the man's nostrum. Vanderbilt would not.

William Henry drove Maud S. often, now always able to defeat Frank Work or any other trotting buff who thought he might race the world champion. Then a single incident on the track that year changed William Henry's entire attitude toward racing. He was driving Aldine and Early Rose one afternoon, traveling in reverse direction on the track. On the first turn he was sideswiped by a careless trainer coming the other way. Vanderbilt's maroon rig was demolished, and the millionaire was thrown to the ground, senseless. Luckily he was covered with sealskin robes against the chill of early spring, so he suffered no scrapes or broken bones. John Quinn, who operated a stable at 125th Street and Madison Avenue, picked Vanderbilt up and took him to the track clubhouse. When the shock wore off William Henry's enthusiasm for driving was lost, from then on he drove very seldom, and when he did he usually allowed his stablemaster to take the reins.

With his racing enthusiasm gone, William Henry decided to sell Maud S. to Robert Bonner for $40,000. Suddenly William Henry was an old man.

But old or not, he kept an interest in the activities of his railroads, and when Depew and the boys decided to move south that fall to compete with the Pennsylvania, William Henry had to be convinced first. He was convinced because the Central management had a strong case. Andrew Carnegie, John D. Rockefeller, and other big interests said they wanted such a road, so the Vanderbilts announced in 1883 they would build a new railroad to Pittsburgh. The Pennsylvania, certain that the Vanderbilts had special rate arrangements with the big Pennsylvania capitalists, resented the move and quietly bought up control of the struggling West Shore line, which had never really troubled the Vanderbilts, and began a major railroad war. In the rate cutting that followed, the New York Central's stock dropped nearly a third, to less than $100 a share.

That year and the next the Vanderbilt family fortune decreased sharply in book value, for not only did William Henry's stock income fall off more than $2,000,000, but both Cornelius and Willie K. lost heavily in unwise speculation in the stock market. William Henry sold some $20,000,000 in government bonds to bail the boys out.

But the Vanderbilts were not the only investors in trouble in 1884, and their trouble was relatively minor. Another panic had seized Wall Street. Former President Ulysses Simpson Grant had started an investment house in New York with a financier named Ward. One morning in 1884 Grant left the house he owned on the upper East Side of New York to drive to the office, confident that he was a wealthy man. When he arrived at the offices of Grant and Ward, his son told him to go home—the bank had failed and he had been wiped out.

Grant did go home, never again to return to Wall Street. Among his debts, Grant owed William Henry Vanderbilt $150,000. Vanderbilt offered to cancel the loan, in view of his high regard for the former President, but Grant refused the charity. He insisted on paying the debt, to William Henry's embarrassment, even though it meant that Grant had to sell personal treasures given him by royalty on his triumphal tour of Europe after he had retired from the presidency.

The next year, 1885, the railroad war that had begun in 1883 was ended through the good offices of J. Pierpont Morgan. Chauncey Depew, then president of the New York Central, met with President George Roberts of the Pennsylvania on Morgan's yacht the *Corsair*. The meeting was held on a hot July day, but Morgan's choice of the yacht for the meeting place was not made solely to escape the heat. Aboard the yacht neither telephone nor callers could interrupt a conference, and more important, his conferees, outraged though they might become, could not get away until they had reached some sort of compromise.

What they finally agreed to was this: the Pennsylvania Railroad would take over the South Pennsylvania that the Vanderbilts had built. The New York Central would take over the West Shore line. And the New York Central, for sacrificing its competitive position in Pennsylvania, would be repaid, in good securities, for all the money it had sunk into the effort to scuttle the Pennsylvania Railroad. The New York Central would also give up its holdings in other Pennsylvania roads.

It was a master stroke for Morgan, once again. He had shown himself the keenest student of railroads in the nation. He had converted a situation of ruinous competition—a fight that threatened both the well-being of the Pennsylvania and the New York Central—into a neat arrangement where the two roads agreed not to compete with one another except on the New York-to-Chicago run. He had opened an era of good feeling in American railroading in which the only sufferer was the American public, which lost the advantage of competitive rates and fares long before it had acquired the advantages of strict government regulation.

William Henry Vanderbilt was pleased with the settlement, since it enabled him to recoup the $5,000,000 he had put into the South Pennsylvania venture. Vanderbilt's fortune was again secure, and the railroad empire was even stronger than before.

In 1885 the Vanderbilt railroads covered a very large section of the United States. They ran from New York City up both sides of the Hudson River to Albany and Buffalo, and thence west to Chicago, with separate lines covering the territory both north and south of Detroit, coursing Michigan and Indiana, and from Chicago extended into the northwest to the Twin Cities of Minneapolis and St. Paul, and as far south as St. Louis.

William Henry, the lord of these roads, was now sixty-four years old. A few months before he had suffered a stroke that had cost him the sight of his right eye and a great deal of his vigor. He had begun building the great tomb ordered by the Commodore, choosing Richard Morris Hunt, the architect who built Willie K.'s house on Fifth Avenue, to design the tomb. Hunt created a Romanesque chapel patterned after one at Arles, France, which would be set solidly against the side of a hill in the midst of fourteen acres of land in the cemetery behind the Moravian Church on Staten Island. Stones from France, Italy, the Holy Land, and the United States were to be used in its construction and its cost was to exceed $500,000. William Henry himself would never have spent as much on the mausoleum because this second wealthy Vanderbilt did not have the same sense of dynasty that had dominated the Commodore's last fretful years. William Henry, a good and loving father, was more worried about the happiness of his children than about the future of the railroad empire.

Of all the children, George Washington Vanderbilt was the only one who still lived at home. George was just twenty-three in 1885, but his father was feeling very old, and believed it was time to place responsibility in the boy's hands. George did not show any particular interest in the railroads, so William Henry decided as a starter to turn all his Staten Island properties over to his fourth son. In the fall of 1885 he made several trips to Staten Island to arrange the details, and on December 7, 1885, William Henry signed the last paper, and the Staten Island holdings belonged to George. It was a proud fatherly gesture, for in fact and deed he was recognizing the boy's maturity.

The following day William Henry arose at 7:00 A.M., as usual. He had a busy day ahead. He was scheduled to confer with his sons and with Chauncey Depew over New York Central matters. He also intended to go to the studio of the sculptor J. Q. A. Ward, where he was sitting for a bronze bust.

William Henry's valet Louis laid out his linen and a dark suit, while William Henry prepared his toilet. By nine-thirty he had eaten breakfast and was meeting with Cornelius, Willie K., and E. V. W. Rossiter, who was treasurer of the New York Central and William Henry's private secretary.

There was some management difficulty to be ironed out, and at eleven o'clock Vanderbilt sent for Chauncey Depew, who was at the office in the Grand Central Station, located then, as now, on Forty-second Street. Depew had an engagement at the time, so it was settled that he would drop by the house at one o'clock for a talk. William Henry then put on his topcoat and walked the three blocks to Sculptor Ward's studio. The bust was coming along nicely; it had been requested by New York City's College of Physicians and Surgeons, and the college was paying for it. William Henry was sitting as a favor for the college wanted the bust to remind them of William Henry's generosity—he had just given a half-million dollars for a new building to house the school.

An hour later William Henry went back to his house for lunch. He ate with his son George and Hamilton McKown Twombly, one of his sons-in-law, whom he rather liked. He was much happier eating with members of his family than when he was forced to schedule business lunches.

One o'clock came, and with it a contretemps. Chauncey Depew was due for his appointment, but Robert Garrett, president of the Baltimore & Ohio Railroad came suddenly, unannounced. His impromptu visit indicated an urgency, for the Garretts and the Vanderbilts were not bosom friends. Quite the contrary, if one remembers that Garret's father had been president of the Baltimore & Ohio in the days a dozen years before when the Commodore had forced the B.&O. into the eastern railroad trust. The Commodore had referred to the elder Garrett as "the rotten apple in the barrel" of railroading. Thus when Garrett came without an appointment, both Depew and Vanderbilt knew that there was a significant reason. Both men were quite sure they knew the reason for Garrett's call: the Baltimore & Ohio wanted access to the Vanderbilt holdings on the west shore of the Hudson River so that Garrett's line could move freight and passengers into New York City. The B.&O. was in serious financial trouble; Garrett's control of the railroad his father had developed was threatened unless he could recoup with the additional revenues a New York harbor railhead would bring him.

Chauncey Depew agreeably gave up his time with William Henry and went back to the New York Central office, noting that he would be available when Vanderbilt wanted him. Vanderbilt and Garrett went upstairs to William Henry's study, really a small sitting room, to talk.

Vanderbilt sat in his favorite fringed easy chair, and Garrett sat in one across from him. It was chilly enough in the room for a fire in the grate. The men talked earnestly and quietly. Suddenly, at about 2:20 P.M., members of the household heard a cry from the Vanderbilt study. Rushing into the room, they found William Henry lying on the floor, his head on a cushion Garrett had brought to him, and Garrett dashing a glass of water in William Henry's purple face. William Henry's valet Louis and the other servants were sent into the street for help, and moments later came running back with a doctor who had been passing the house. The doctor put a mirror to William Henry's silent lips. It was too late. The breathing had stopped.

Mrs. Vanderbilt fell into a faint in her own room when a servant told her that her husband was dead. Daughter Emily Thorn Sloane was summoned from her house next door to try to help her mother, and to bring some order into the household until the sons arrived. Emissaries were sent to locate Cornelius, Frederick, and William Kissam, who could not be reached by telephone, because they had all left New York Central Station for the day, but Chauncey Depew was at the office, on hand, as usual, at a moment of Vanderbilt crisis. Depew hurried to the house to take charge.

Dr. James McLane, Vanderbilt's physician, arrived to find the police and coroner in the house arguing over the disposition of the body and the death certificate. Dr. McLane had feared for some time that such an accident would be the cause of William Henry's death, but since he was not on the scene at the time of death, the coroner argued that the attending physician, now long since gone on his own calls, must be found to sign the papers. Dr. McLane disputed the officials, and won his argument after he had given William Henry's medical history, and recalled an earlier stroke some years before when the Vanderbilts were living at Fortieth Street and Fifth Avenue. Finally, the authorities capitulated, the dreadful prospect of an autopsy was avoided, and it was agreed that William Henry's suspect arterial system had finally killed him: it was apoplexy, the cause of death of his mother Sophia.

Finally, the four Vanderbilt sons were found and told the shocking news; Cornelius was attending a board meeting of the American Bible Society downtown at Astor Place; the other three were on personal business that afternoon. By evening the family was assembled in the great house, and William Kissam and George Vanderbilt sat up through the night with the body of their father, following the old custom of maintaining a watch over the dead. The other members of the family clustered together in the house to share their grief.

The news of William Henry Vanderbilt's death spread rapidly through the city that day, bringing shock, despair, and fear. In the evening J. Pierpont Morgan, along with financiers Charles Lanier and Edward D. Adams, went to Chauncey Depew's house on Fifty-fourth Street. Through clouds of Morgan's cigar smoke, the three talked low but long, agreeing to pledge, among them, $15,000,000 to protect the stock market against a panic.

In the library of Jay Gould's house at Forty-seventh Street and Fifth Avenue, Cyrus W. Field, Russell Sage, and Morgan's personal representative met with the host, to pledge another hedging sum—with which to buy 250,000 shares of New York Central and affiliated companies, if such a move seemed necessary to prevent a break in the market.

At the Windsor Hotel—the afterhours headquarters of Wall Street—the single night telegraph operator was quickly replaced by half-a-dozen veterans, who worked steadily through the long night sending messages to the correspondents of the New York financial houses in America and abroad.

William Henry Vanderbilt, dead, was creating as great an anxiety in the financial world as had the Commodore in his rousing fights for the Harlem, the Hudson, and the Erie railroads.

That night J. Pierpont Morgan cabled his London office that Vanderbilt's stocks would not be dumped—would not be thrown indiscriminately on the market.

A commotion arose in the lobby of the Windsor when one scary broker offered Lake Shore Railroad stock at 87, a point below the closing quotation for the day. There were no takers, and in a few moments the price dropped to 85, but then the pledged houses began to buy, on orders from their employers. Lake Shore was stopped at 85, and before an hour passed it was back to 88.

There had been a fear, a hangover from the days of the great manipulators, that William Henry Vanderbilt's holdings had not really been secure. Had this been true, and had quantities of New York Central stock been thrown immediately onto the market to cover indiscreet speculations, the whole railroad system might have collapsed. That was the worry of the financial world.

By morning, when the market opened on Wall Street, all the financiers were aware of Vanderbilt's death, and yet everything was serene. William Henry had no margin accounts in the stock market. He *owned* all his stocks outright. Once again he held $70,000,000 in government bonds, plus $22,000,000 in railroad bonds, $3,200,000 in state and city bonds, and $2,000,000 in mortgages and other paper.

Although William Henry was not much more devoted in church-going than his father had been, he had served for years as a vestryman of St. Bartholomew's Episcopal Church at Fiftieth Street and Park Avenue. That was where the funeral would be held. On December ninth and tenth William Henry lay in state at the palace at 640 Fifth Avenue, while his sons took turns in guarding his body.

J. Pierpont Morgan called to pay his respects; so did Dr. Deems, of the Church of the Strangers; so did John D. Rockefeller and hundreds of others. The sculptor J. Q. A. Ward came to take a cast for a death mask of William Henry.

The following day, December 11, the funeral was held at St. Bartholomew's. Earlier, at nine-fifteen, a simple service was conducted at the house, which only the widow and the immediate family attended. Then Louisa Kissam Vanderbilt retired to her private mourning, for she did not feel strong enough to face the public ordeal and she did not accompany the body to the church.

So many men and women had wanted to attend the funeral that entrance was arranged by invitation only. A cordon of police surrounded the church, keeping strangers away. Lambert Wardell, the Commodore's old private secretary, and Superintendent Toucey of the New York Central knew just about everyone who had a right to be there, and they helped New York police detective Heidelberg and his crew keep order. When a man in a faded black silk hat and black gloves appeared in the line of railroad men, Toucey spotted him, and Heidelberg recognized him as a well-known pickpocket, but he slipped away before he could be captured.

The Reverend Dr. Samuel Cooke, rector of St. Bartholomew's, officiated at the short, simple service.

Then the cortege assembled for the trip to Staten Island. The long line of carriages drove to the midtown slip at Forty-second Street, where the ferry stood waiting. She was the *Southfield*, the same ferry that had carried the Commodore to Staten Island on his last trip, now used in the service of the West Shore line. Railroad passengers waiting on the other side of the bay were delayed an hour that day while the steamer carried William Henry to the island that had been his home for so many years.

At twelve-thirty the funeral ferry reached Clifton, Staten Island, and the mourners took the winding road that led up the hill to the Moravian Cemetery. At one-thirty they arrived in front of the unfinished mausoleum. At one-fifty the casket had been placed and the slab over the vault sealed. Ten minutes later there was only one man at the site, a Pinkerton detective, one of two men assigned to a twenty-four-hour watch to prevent molestation of the grave.

William Henry Vanderbilt, the farmer from Staten Island, was at rest near the father he could never understand.

19

ENTER THE YACHTSMAN

William Henry Vanderbilt and his place in the business affairs of his nation were so often misunderstood by the industrialists of his own day that it was easy for an old enemy like Jay Gould to sum up the second Vanderbilt as a man who preferred a sure thing to a chancy one—a man who was interested only in gilt-edged securities. Gould's curbstone reprise was misleading. William Henry was certainly not as venturesome as his father, but he was no weakling, and he *ran* his railroads. William Henry had divested himself of the trappings of control, to be sure, but no important decisions of management were taken without his approval. When Robert Garrett wanted concessions for the Baltimore & Ohio Railroad, he went straight to Vanderbilt, on the day of William Henry's death, not bothering with the formality of consulting Chauncey Depew or any of the officers of the New York Central. William Henry was *the* head man of the railroad system no matter what it said on the railroad's annual report to stockholders; his power awed employees and impressed hardfisted labor organizers. Following the abortive strike against the Vanderbilt lines in 1877 the labor leaders exhibited a healthy respect for the man who put them down without even interrupting his summer outing at Saratoga.

There was another reason for William Henry's strong position. The public always linked him with the Commodore, whose name had become synonymous with wealth, power, and strength of character. The Commodore had built, and William Henry Vanderbilt

had consolidated, a great railroad combination. William Henry
was a man to be respected—a symbol of authority.

The death of William Henry created a real, if not readily
apparent, crisis in the Vanderbilt railroad empire, because that
empire, like any other, could exist and prosper only if it was controlled by a strong man.

Why was a strong man especially needed at this time? The reason was that by 1885 these consolidations of industrial firms disturbed a great number of Americans whom they did not benefit.
There was a growing fear outside the business community that
America was moving straight toward monopoly control.

J. Pierpont Morgan, who managed the West Shore compromise
so skillfully, did not end his efforts with the Vanderbilt properties.
Morgan had completed the intricate details of the New York Central–Pennsylvania reshuffle only three days before William Henry's death. Afterward, Robert Garrett, whose compaign for a
railhead on New York harbor had come to a standstill, went to Morgan for help, and Morgan began the tedious work of reorganizing
the Baltimore & Ohio in a way to secure the entry. This involved
endless negotiation with other lines, and special agreements that
allowed the B.&O. to use tracks and depots of two different railroads on the New Jersey shore. Morgan and other bankers and
financiers were perfectly convinced of their own ability to solve
such problems if they were only let alone by the government and
allowed to work them out, but the public saw small benefit to itself from the sleight of hand being worked in bankers' board
rooms, and a growing segment of the public was shouting loudly
for drastic reforms.

William Henry had shown himself aware of the changing times;
he had yielded to the outcries against monopoly, as far as the yielding fitted his own plans, by selling a majority of his railroad stock
in 1879, but he had remained a monopolist for all that. His interests, and those of the New York Central, were the interests of
big business.

By 1885 big business, on the one hand, and small business, farmers, and working men, on the other, seemed to be moving toward
a head-on collision on two basic issues: the tariff and monopoly

control. William Henry had approved of Grover Cleveland when that Democratic President began his term in 1885, but that was before Cleveland declared his advocacy of a low tariff. The Vanderbilts, like most big businessmen, held low tariff responsible for the high surplus of funds held in the U. S. Treasury. Already the surplus represented more than 25 per cent of the nation's capital, and when the federal government had the money locked up, it was not available to industry.

But outside the business community, farmers, workers, the debt-ridden, and the small businessmen attributed the nation's troubles, and their own, to the excesses of the monopolies. Some turned to a movement begun by Henry George in New York City. George, whose particular targets were men like the Vanderbilts, held that under existing social conditions the rich would grow richer and the poor would grow poorer. In the late seventies he wrote a book—*Progress and Poverty*—which was more widely read in the East than anything since *Uncle Tom's Cabin*. George's remedy for the sorry economic plight of the working man was the single tax, in which the entire burden of taxation would be placed on land. The Vanderbilts grew uneasy in the knowledge that such radical thinking was attracting thousands of New Yorkers, and well they might grow worried, contemplating the thousands of miles of right of way owned by Vanderbilt railroads.

Elsewhere in the country the mood was the same—angry—but the remedies proposed were different. Congress and the state legislatures were being pressed to put an end to monopoly by legislation. And in the sluggishness of the two major political parties, a new political movement had arisen, starting with the beleaguered farmers of the South and West. That movement was Populism, and it represented, among other reforms, the demand for government ownership of the railroads, to bring lower rates, better service, and greater safety.

Nor was the working man idle. Labor was organizing on a national scale and agitating for a workday of eight hours, which had been achieved by federal employees in 1868. In 1884 the federation of organized trades and labor unions gave employers notice that they had but two years in which to put into effect the eight-hour day. The Knights of Labor—successor to the organization that tried to unionize the New York Central in the seventies without success, was growing in the eighties, even while the monopolies were growing.

By the time William Henry Vanderbilt's body lay in state in his Fifth Avenue palace, the leaders of the Knights of Labor were planning to consolidate their power in the one manner they understood—by a show of strength. In part, the labor leaders paid a tribute to William Henry Vanderbilt's strength—they chose the railroads of the West as their testing ground. Within a few months they would strike the Gould railroads, tying up six thousand miles of road in four states in a daring, but in the end unsuccessful, revolt against long working hours. Had the union leaders felt they could strike the eastern lines successfully, they would have tried again.

When William Henry died, his world was in turmoil. A strong man was needed at the helm of the New York Central to maintain the railroad's leadership—even to maintain the railroad system as it was.

Thus the manner in which William Henry Vanderbilt disposed of his vast holdings was supremely important to the future of the empire the Commodore had founded, but if the son had meant to honor his father's deathbed injunction to preserve the Vanderbilt empire, he either forgot or prepared to ignore the old man's wishes when he made his own disposition of the family property.

In his will William Henry left to his two oldest sons, Cornelius Vanderbilt II and William Kissam Vanderbilt, the bulk of the fortune. Control was split! Cornelius inherited $67,000,000 and William K. inherited $65,000,000. The division of power that the Commodore had feared most had come to pass. The other two sons, Frederick William and George Washington, received $10,000,-000 each, as did each of the four daughters of William Henry. His wife, Louisa Kissam Vanderbilt, would receive an income of $200,000 a year for the rest of her life, and could dispose of another $500,000 in her own will, although she could not touch it in life. She kept the palace at 640 Fifth Avenue. George Washington Vanderbilt was to have it later, and all its objects of art.

More than a million dollars went to charity: to Vanderbilt University, to the Domestic and Foreign Missionary Society of the Protestant Episcopal Church, to the Y.M.C.A. The old family church at New Dorp received $100,000, because it had more meaning for William Henry, who had lived nearby for thirty years, than it had for his father. Those Staten Island days might be all but forgotten by the Vanderbilts, but these multimillionaire children had been born and raised as farm youngsters on the not-too-prosperous acres their father had cultivated for thirty years.

All of the girls were given the houses in which they lived. The boys already owned their houses, with the exception of George Washington Vanderbilt. Fifth Avenue seemed almost to be a Vanderbilt lane. Frederick William lived at 459 Fifth Avenue, in the old house that William Henry had occupied before he moved into the great palace. George and his mother lived at 640 Fifth Avenue; Emily Thorn Sloane and her family, in the other half of the mansion with entrance at 642; Margaret Louisa Shepard, in that same building at 2 West Fifty-second; William Kissam, in his house at 660 Fifth Avenue; Eliza Webb and her husband, at 680; Florence Adele Twombly, at 684; and Cornelius Vanderbilt II, at 1 West Fifty-seventh Street, whose side entrance was on the avenue.

Inheritances of $10,000,000 meant that each of the Vanderbilt children was endowed with a sum that seemed to the average American to be almost infinite—as much as the total expenditure of the state government of New York—and this in a period in which President Cleveland vetoed a congressional bill which would have given $12 a month to every disabled Union veteran. If $10,-000,000 was converted to gold, it would take five hundred horses to pull it from Grand Central Terminal to Wall Street.

The ordinary mind, as broker Henry Clews put it, could not grasp the idea of such a fortune; only a shrewd contemporary observer would have noted that Frederick William, the third son, was treated in an unusual manner in the will, considering his interest in the railroads and his willingness to work his way up in the New York Central organization.

Frederick William was a strong-willed young man, handsome, although not quite in the Vanderbilt tradition, for he was smaller and slimmer than his brother Cornelius, whose resemblance to the young Commodore was remarkable. Frederick William sported a sandy handlebar mustache and kept his hair slicked down and parted in the middle, following the tonsorial style of the time. As a child he had assumed that he would spend his life in the service of the railroads, and had prepared himself more thoroughly for railroading than any of his brothers; he was the only one of the four brothers to receive a formal American education; he was graduated from Yale's Sheffield Scientific school in 1876 and then began his working career by shuttling through the operating departments of the New York Central. He was the first Vanderbilt to become a director of the Chicago and Northwestern Railroad, in 1881, thus announcing the family's addition of that line to the holdings. Frederick William's future seemed as well assured as those of Cornelius and Willie K., but he angered his father by falling in love with the wrong woman. She was Louise Anthony Torrance, the wife of a Wall Street broker, and she was a dozen years older than Frederick William. Equally scandalizing in a generation that abjured divorce, she was the wife of Frederick William's first cousin; her husband's father was Daniel Torrance who had married William Henry's sister, Sophia.

Louise Torrance came from a good family, but one of only moderate means, and neither the family nor young Torrance had the wealth to support her in a grand manner. She was considered one of the great beauties of New York, and she was badly spoiled.

When the romance began in 1875, Frederick William and Louise were believed to be indulging in a mild flirtation, but within a few months William Henry learned to his chagrin that the affair had gone much further than anyone suspected. He ordered his son to break off with Louise. Frederick William refused, and in 1877 Louise Torrance quietly divorced her husband in Rhode Island and resumed her maiden name.

On December 17, 1878, in a private parlor of the Windsor Hotel, Frederick William Vanderbilt married Louise Anthony. His father did not attend the ceremony—William Henry was not even informed of the marriage until the middle of February 1879. Then he grumbled that there was no sense in arguing with a headstrong son.

William Henry never really forgave Frederick William for the dual injury of ruining his own life and keeping the marriage from the family, but the depth of the hurt was kept secret for years. On the surface the Vanderbilts seemed to get on well enough; only in the disposition of his property did William Henry show his true feelings. He had better judgment than to try to cut his third son off as his father had cut off Cornelius Jeremiah. William Henry recalled the hurt the great will fight had brought him too clearly to sow the same seeds in his own will.

In leaving Frederick William only $10,000,000, and no real share of the Vanderbilt railways, he showed his doubts about his third son's judgment. He had, he thought, quite effectively removed one problem from the railroads.

The case of George Washington Vanderbilt was quite different. George was a young man when his father died. He had exhibited no interest in the railroads, nor did he enter the world of business. George was retiring, and mother-ridden. He was well read, intelligent, quiet, well behaved, and altogether a proper son, but one without much spark. The $10,000,000 he received was cushioned by the bequest of the family art treasures, and his father's pride and joy, the Vanderbilt palace.

The bulk of the Vanderbilt fortune went to the two sons whose good sense William Henry trusted, and they alone had free wheeling in the use of great sums of money, for as an additional safeguard, William Henry had made sure that none of this generation could waste the entire patrimony. Five million dollars of each child's share was to be held in trust, the income on that amount could be spent, and the principal willed as desired, but the trusts themselves could not be touched by that generation.

The division of power did not immediately have any apparent effect on the fortunes of the railroads. When William Henry retired from active management of the railroads in 1883, Cornelius and Willie K. assumed the chairmanships of the major roads. Cornelius became chairman of the board of the New York Central and the Michigan Central railroads. Willie K. was made chairman of the Lake Shore and president of the Nickel Plate. After a minimum of confusion, the two settled down in their posts, appearing both content and able. When their father died, they had two years of management experience behind them, and between them controlled enough stock in the railroads to discourage outsiders.

Yet more and more the management of the railroads was ceasing to be a family business. The new president of the New York Central, Chauncey Depew, was an old Vanderbilt man, but he was not a Vanderbilt; and there were now new names on the roster of the board of directors. Even if the most important of those new directors was J. Pierpont Morgan, a Vanderbilt banker, Morgan's interests were not identical with those of the Vanderbilts. Morgan's influence on the fortunes of the Vanderbilt lines was to be far greater than press or public suspected, for the two young railroad barons depended heavily on the banker for advice and support, nor was either of the younger men so single-minded about his job as William Henry or the Commodore.

Cornelius Vanderbilt spent a great deal of time on charities and church affairs. He showed no interest in horse racing or other rich men's sports except sleigh riding in Central Park in the winter; and being of a solemn turn of mind he cared little for the balls, excursions, and other usual entertainments of the wealthy.

His brother, Willie K., could not have been more different, for William Henry had scarcely been buried in the family vault on Staten Island before Willie found a new and glorious amusement, one which promised excitement and adventure—he built a yacht.

Willie's father had never liked yachting. By the time William Henry was wealthy enough to afford expensive hobbies he was too old and too ill to adjust to anything so strenuous. Nor had William Henry ever learned to spend money with the grace of the born-rich; he believed a yacht was more of a waste than a luxury.

Nevertheless, a handful of other New York millionaires had yachts, and they intrigued Willie K. In the spring of 1886 he decided to build an ocean-going steam yacht that could carry enough coal to speed across the Atlantic at twelve knots an hour. As with everything of Willie K.'s, the yacht was to be better than first class, and the largest private ship afloat.

Contracts were let to Harland and Hollingsworth of Wilmington, Delaware, that spring, and scarcely six months later the yacht was ready to be launched, a masterpiece of steel plates, 285 feet long, heralded as the most expensive private ship in the world. She had cost a half-million dollars.

On October 14, 1886, Willie K. boarded his private railroad car and set out for Wilmington. With him were his wife and brothers George and Frederick William, Alva's sister, Mrs. Yznaga, Chauncey Depew, and a number of friends. The party arrived just before noon at the shipyard, to join nearly five thousand people who had come to view the launching—most of them shipyard workers and their families. All the men employed by the shipbuilders were taking a half day off at full pay, at Willie K.'s, suggestion and expense, so most of them came out to line the shores of Christiana Creek and give Willie K. the audience he wanted.

A platform had been built near the bow for the launching ceremonies. Mrs. Yznaga, Alva's sister, had been chosen to do the honors and promptly at one-thirty she made her way to the platform followed by Willie K. and Alva, and George Washington and Frederick William. Mrs. Yznaga grasped a silver-headed hammer firmly in her hand. Over the starboard bow hung a bottle of American champagne. A bottle of French champagne had been hung there first, but Willie K. demanded a domestic vintage.

The yard superintendent shouted "Wedge up," and fifty workmen below began hammering the shoring blocks away from the sides of the steel ship. Ten minutes later the superintendent gave Mrs. Yznaga a little nod, and she swung the silver hammer against the bottle of champagne, just as the ship began sliding down the way. "I christen thee *Alva*," she cried, amid the tinkling of broken glass and the cheers of the crowd on Christiana Creek.

The *Alva* gathered speed as she slid down the ways into the water, righted herself, and moved rapidly across the creek. No one seemed surprised when the yacht then buried her stern ignobly in the mud on the other bank and stuck there, for this was a typical Harland and Hollingsworth launching. The superintendent of the shipyard assured everyone that the yacht would work free in a day or so; then the boilers and the other necessary machinery could be installed. After that, she would be furnished with the most expensive appointments ever seen on a yacht.

The Vanderbilt party boarded the special car and went back to New York, the others well pleased with the success of their day's outing, and Willie K. basking in the glory of his latest acquisition, quite uncaring about the expense of yachting, a sport far too rich for the blood of any save a Vanderbilt, an Astor, a Gould, or a king. Willie K. estimated that it would cost him $5000 a month to keep the *Alva* in commission. But he had never felt at home in the landlubber resort surroundings at Saratoga, where William Henry liked to amuse himself.

It took three and a half months to outfit the *Alva* to the satisfaction of Willie K. and his wife. The flesh-and-blood Alva thought rich furnishings were out of place; she wanted simplicity, even if she had to pay twice as much for it.

When finished from stem to stern, the *Alva* lived up to her advance billing completely. She was rigged as a three-masted topsail schooner with boilers and an engine capable of sustained cruising at, not twelve, but fifteen knots an hour, and a coal capacity of three hundred tons in her hold. Her coamings, stanchions, and rails were teak, so was the deck; and the three cabins on the main deck were framed and plated with steel, then paneled with teak outside. All the spars were made from the finest Oregon pine, her standing rigging was the finest American steel wire rope, her iron-work was the best American iron, her blocks were American white-wood, brass sheaved and finished. She was an American ship from trysail to keelson, and only a few necessary foreign items, such as the four-stranded Russian hemp of the running rigging came from any other land. No wonder Willie K. had insisted on American champagne!

Inside, the steel cabins were paneled in mahogany. The forward cabin held the chart room, galley, and reception room where Willie K. greeted and entertained his guests. From the reception room, passengers descended by a mahogany stairway to a large hall, which opened onto the main dining saloon and the owner's private quarters. These quarters consisted of nine rooms and a nursery, each furnished in a different variety of hardwood period pieces.

The dining saloon ran the full width of the ship—32 feet—and 18 feet fore and aft, with a full 9 feet of headroom. This cabin was paneled in a soft, light wood, and finished, as was all the rest of the woodwork in the yacht, in white enamel with gold trim. Across from the entrance to the dining saloon stood a wood-burning fireplace, while above, the room was lighted from a sky-light covered with clouded glass (which also slid back for ventilation) and by two chandeliers of brass and gilt and a half-dozen twin wall fixtures.

There was a piano in the dining saloon, across from the round mahogany table that would seat a dozen comfortably, and on the starboard side of the ship the entire length of the room was given to a cushioned settee.

From the dining saloon, a narrow passageway, open to the boiler room on one side, led to the ship's library. At one side of the aisle, directly over the boiler room, a cushioned settee was installed so that passengers could watch the machinery and the engine-room crew at work.

The library was on the starboard side of the ship, 16 feet by 18 feet, paneled in French walnut, with its own fireplace.

The library had its own skylight but no chandeliers. It was lighted by fixtures set flush in the ceiling and by wall brackets. Along the walls stood well-anchored, seagoing bookcases, fitted with brass rods in front of the books to keep them steady in heavy weather. The library table was round, made of French walnut and covered by a heavy fringed tablecloth on which stood a potted plant in a wicker and metal container. Above the mantelpiece of the library was a painting of the Commodore's old *North Star*, the first Vanderbilt family yacht.

On the port side, and behind the library, were seven small guest staterooms each about 7 by 10 feet, each with a narrow canopied bed, and every stateroom held the most modern of conveniences —a private bathroom—as did each of the rooms in the owner's quarters. The deck in every room occupied by the owner and his guests was strewn with expensive oriental throw rugs and runners.

The ship's officers had their own, smaller staterooms, private baths, and a messroom; the crew lived forward and aft in large, light, and airy bunkrooms, with communal bathing facilities, but plenty of lockers and closets.

Alva carried a crew of fifty-three, including Captain Henry Morrison, whom Willie K. had hired away from a steamship line. Morrison had a chief officer, a second mate, four quartermasters, two boatswains, a ship's carpenter, eighteen seamen, a chief engineer, first and second assistant engineers, six firemen, three coal passers, three oilers, a donkey engineman, an electrician, an ice machine engineer, a chief steward, three cooks, two mess boys, and a surgeon under his command.

On February 15, 1887, the yacht was put in commission. Willie K., Alva, daughter Consuelo, and sons Willie K. II and Harold went aboard for a cruise to the West Indies. So did the children's governess and Alva's personal maid. Besides the family, there were five of Willie K.'s friends on the trip to provide male companionship.

The first voyage was as pleasant as anticipated, but heroic too. The yacht arrived March 4 at Santiago de Cuba. Promptly the crew rescued part of the crew of a Spanish gunboat whose small boat had capsized. Although there were Spaniards all around, it was the *Alva's* small boat that made the rescue. A few days later the *Alva* moved north fifty miles to Guantanamo Bay, where an acquaintance maintained a shooting box. Willie K. went shooting and bagged a doe. They went to Nassau and Port-au-Prince, and then to Georgia.

Finally on the return trip to New York they ran into rough weather, the children became seasick, and Alva wanted to go home by rail rather than face the voyage around Cape Hatteras in the storm they knew was coming.

Vanderbilt ordered Captain Morrison to put into Port Royal, South Carolina, and there Alva, the three children, the maid and the governess departed. The owner, a few of his hardier guests, and the *Alva* then put out to sea.

On the first day out of Port Royal the weather was thick and the barometer was falling, but they sailed easily through the squalls, flying only the fore main and mizzen trysails and the fore-topsail in the easterly wind. But the next day the wind reached gale force, and just after darkness closed in, about five o'clock, the cringles, sheets, and overhauls of the trysails parted with sounds like pistol shots, and the sails flapped in the wind. The sails would have been torn to shreds had they not been new, but they stood the storm until the crew could get aloft to furl them, and the yacht made ready to navigate under steam alone. They passed Hatteras at about seven o'clock, but the next morning the wind veered to the northwest and became a true hurricane. They were caught in a cross sea, and every time a wave bore down on them, the spray made a clean breach over the yacht, mast high. The mahogany table in the dining saloon broke loose and crashed into the silver chest across the saloon. In the library the heavy French walnut table, which was weighted with six hundred pounds of lead, broke away, turned turtle, and split squarely in two.

It was a rough trip. Where a lesser man might have been trembling below decks, Willie K. braved the storm in oilskins and rubber boots, pleased that the *Alva* took weather so well.

In July of that year Willie K. and the family took a much longer cruise to Europe, then to Turkey, and to Egypt, entertaining a succession of guests, who included Willie's close friend Winfield Scott Hoyt, and Oliver Hazard Perry Belmont, one of the wealthiest and most likable bachelors in Society.

When they reached Athens, the crew went on strike for higher pay, so in a gesture reminiscent of his grandfather, Willie ordered the men off the ship and put the *Alva* out to sea with only four hands to help sail her.

In Egypt they chartered a river steamer for a trip up the Nile to the first cataract. The ladies wore long cotton traveling dresses, gauntlets, and were heavily wrapped in silken scarves to ward off the dust and sand. The gentlemen wore white duck, four-in-hand neckties, and sported the inevitable topis that served both to protect them from the African sun and to give them an air of authority. Daughter Consuelo, a budding teen-ager, wore high-button shoes, long stockings, calf-length dresses, pinafores, and her long black hair in ribbons and a bonnet. Ten-year-old Willie K. II dressed in short pants, heavy sweaters, and a deerstalker's cap. It was cold in the evenings—the temperature often dropped down around 35 degrees. There was some hardship: on January 14 the electric light machine broke down and they had to spend the night with only oil lamps and candles for illumination.

They spent one dreadful week in Alexandria harbor, all because a sharp-eyed Egyptian had sold Captain Morrison three hundred tons of inferior coal. It would not burn, so every pound of it had to be unloaded by hand, a tedious, dusty job that annoyed Alva so much she took the children ashore to stay at the Hotel Abbat until the ship was hosed down, the oriental rugs were cleaned, and the black dust was washed from the paneled walls and the beautiful white enamel woodwork.

Willie K. seemed strange and preoccupied throughout the long voyage, and often he went sight-seeing, calling, or on unnamed errands with his friend Hoyt, without Alva or the children. Alva then was thrown constantly in the company of O. H. P. Belmont, the most attractive bachelor of her set, and a man known widely for his handsome figure, charm, and gentle manners. And when the *Alva* nosed into the Hudson River channel at the end of the first week in April and tied up at the New York Central elevator dock it was apparent that all was not as it should be within the family of William Kissam Vanderbilt. Alva had been left too much alone.

20

ENTER THE DUCHESS

The America to which William Kissam Vanderbilt and his family returned in the spring of 1888 seemed unchanged, but even riding along the cobbled surfaces of New York's water front a sensitive observer might have noticed the difference. Certainly in the padded hallways of Willie K.'s clubs men of business were talking about something new.

The tariff, which had caused such ferment three years before, had become the most important political issue of the day. President Grover Cleveland, a kind of "liberal conservative," entered office in 1885 knowing next to nothing about the tax on foreign goods and its effect on the rise and fall of American manufactures. By the spring of 1888, when he was preparing to campaign for reelection, Cleveland knew a great deal about the tariff. He set himself against a high tariff policy, and so turned the big businessmen of both parties squarely against him. The trouble was that the issue seemed so simple. The Republicans favored a high tariff, as the one on textiles, to protect American manufacturers (and workers' jobs) from being undercut by the cheap labor of other countries. Some of the Democrats, led by the President, believed equally strongly in a low tariff, which they said would encourage foreign trade and create new markets for American manufacturers (and hence more jobs for Americans).

In this dispute there was no question where the sympathies of the railroad operators lay, even if they did not understand the causes. Many of the railroad owners were manufacturers. (The Vanderbilts, for example, still owned a large interest in the Wagner railroad car manufacturing company.) But even if they had not owned factories, the railroad kings knew where their interests lay—with the manufacturers, whose shipments of goods and materials made the profits of their railroads.

That year Chauncey Depew, chief operating executive of the New York Central, had a good chance to win the Republican nomination for the presidency. Had he been anything but a railroad man, Depew probably would have been nominated. But the heads of railroads were anathema to a nation which was surging with an antitrust and anti-big-business movement—Populism. Depew sensed this distrust and withdrew his name.

Among the Vanderbilts it was Cornelius who took his political responsibilities seriously, and actually worked for the Republican party. Willie K. was far more concerned with his responsibilities as a leader of American society.

Less and less of Willie K.'s time was spent on New York Central business, and more and more on the business of amusement. Alva told a friend that she could not think of anything more taxing than the job of being a leader of society. The problem was to do something new, something different, something that nobody had ever done before. Then, once it was accomplished, the problem was to start all over and do something different again.

In summer the members of New York society deserted their stuffy city to relax at Saratoga, Bar Harbor, Southampton, and, above all, at Newport, the famous old port of Rhode Island. At one time Newport had been an important city. Before the Revolution the docks were stacked with sugar and tobacco, cotton and rum; and fast, stinking slave ships skirted her shores and sometimes came close in to land human cargoes. The cotton, rum, and slave trades drew many southerners north, and when these gentlemen came to Newport, they found the summer climate a welcome change from the heat of Charleston and Mobile and Savannah. Gradually the wealthy merchants brought their families and began arriving early in June and staying until early autumn. By the late eighties, Newport was also beginning to attract the leaders of New

York society, who built magnificent houses along the shore, erected high stone fences, planted heavy hedges, and hired platoons of gardeners, maids, and footmen to care for their estates.

Vanderbilts had been going to Newport for a long time. Several of the Commodore's daughters had summered at Newport regularly, but the Vanderbilts had made no effort to dominate Newport society.

Between parties at 660 Fifth Avenue, country shooting week ends at Idle Hour, and cruises on the *Alva*, Willie K. and his wife found time to spend a month or so at Newport each season, where they first rented and later purchased a large summer house.

On August 21, 1889, Alva gave a unique ball in the new stable Willie K. had built at their Newport summer cottage, for which the walls were decorated with red peppers and pumpkins and squashes, while turnips and eggplants hung from the ceiling. A wiring system with a hundred electric lights had been led in especially for the occasion, a display that impressed Newport's cottagers with Alva's ingenuity, and set the other matrons to racking their brains for even more interesting ideas.

Most of the Vanderbilts lived in this same rich style, even Cornelius, who was more restrained than most of them, and Frederick William, who was half estranged both from his family and the social whirl.

George Washington Vanderbilt was the great exception. Newport bored George; so for that matter did most of the social affairs of Willie K. and his friends. George had summered at Bar Harbor since before his father died. Now, in 1889, he decided to go even further afield, and he bought five thousand acres of land near Asheville, North Carolina, and began to plan an American model of a medieval fief. In December of that year he brought architect Richard M. Hunt to Asheville to draw plans for a chateau, and he made arrangements for a spur rail line to be built from the Southern Railway yard at Asheville. He intended to build a giant private forest and hunting preserve, and a great house that would outdo anything in America.

George's use of the wealth would have puzzled and shocked the

Commodore, as would Willie K.'s parties and Cornelius's charities, but these were modern times, and ways had changed.

But if the attitudes of his grandchildren would have annoyed the Commodore, so would other changes, for old landmarks, including the house he had built less than half a century before, were disappearing in the expansion of business and industry.

Frank Vanderbilt, the old man's second wife, died in May 1885, leaving a million dollars of her own, but the house on Washington Place had been hers only for life. Actually she had not lived in the house for more than a few months after the Commodore's death; instead, she had turned it over to her brother Robert, who had lived there with his family until 1889, and then the Vanderbilts (to whom it reverted) sold the house for $210,000 to a furrier, who began to raze the old mansion so he could erect a factory on the site.

Even the Commodore's tomb had been replaced, as ordered. All the Vanderbilt caskets were moved into the new mausoleum a few months after William Henry's death, and the old tomb stood unattended, overgrown with vines and underbrush, while this new generation continued the merry pace. In February 1890, Willie K. and Alva were off for Europe again on the yacht, again with O. H. P. Belmont and Winfield Scott Hoyt aboard.

As on the yacht, so when they were at home, Willie K. alternated between paying great attention to Alva and ignoring her. He would go off for a trip of several days by himself. But in 1890 he commissioned the building of a palace of white marble on the cliffs at the end of Newport; it was to be the finest of all the summer cottages, a term the idle rich senselessly used to describe their expensive houses.

That same year Frederick William also rented a Newport cottage, and began to build a mansion which he called Rough Point, while his wife Louise entered the cycle of lavish entertainment. Frederick William bought a yacht, the $75,000 *Conqueror*, in England, Cornelius worked conscientiously at the railroad offices, and George Washington Vanderbilt buried himself in his plans to become the baron of North Carolina.

In February 1891, Willie K. went to Europe again, aboard the

Alva. But on this trip neither Alva nor O. H. P. Belmont was aboard. Alva remained at home with her children and gave parties to improve her social standing.

These were years of rivalry between the strong-minded Alva, mistress of 660 Fifth Avenue, and Alice Gwynne Vanderbilt, wife of Cornelius, who lived up the street a few blocks. There was no rivalry between their husbands, for while Cornelius and Willie K. were worlds apart in their ambitions, they were almost equally endowed with riches, and there was no jealousy between the men.

Alice Vanderbilt, however, could not help feeling that Alva Vanderbilt was stepping on her toes by parading herself in Society, for was not Alice the wife of the head of the Vanderbilt family? Alice was incapable of anything so crude as an open scandal, but she had a will and a way of her own.

In 1885, wanting a summer home for the family, Cornelius Vanderbilt II had purchased an estate at Newport between fashionable Bellevue Avenue and the cliffs. The estate consisted of eleven acres of land, a brick-and-frame house of three floors called The Breakers, a caretaker's lodge, and stables. Cornelius added a wing on the north end of the house, built greenhouses, more stables, and a children's playhouse called "the cottage." The family stayed at Newport during the hot summer months, the elder Vanderbilts entertaining and being entertained, and the seven children playing in their little house. The three girls took cooking lessons from the French chef at a miniature stove in the kitchen of the two-room playhouse. With their four brothers, they played "house" under the supervision of their governess, with a real walk-in fireplace, complete sets of cooking utensils, and monogrammed china. Each room was equipped with a button to summon the butler and another to summon the upstairs maid, both of whom were in charge of the tiny cottage.

The Breakers was not overly opulent as Newport cottages went, and, unfortunately, not fireproof. On November 25, 1892, the ivy-covered wooden house caught fire and burned to the ground. When it came to rebuilding, Richard Morris Hunt was called in to execute the plans. He must have sought the advice of Mrs. Vanderbilt, for the palace that emerged was so splendid as to be totally out of character for the simple tastes of Cornelius Vanderbilt II.

What a palace it was! Cornelius had one sensible masculine stipulation—that the new building be absolutely fireproof—so not a stick of wood was included in its basic construction. Since Mr. Hunt exhibited a predilection for the architecture of Renaissance Europe in all that he did for the very rich, the new Vanderbilt palace was to be modeled after a North Italian villa. Those villas were built as oblongs, rising several floors, around a central open courtyard. But one could not have an open courtyard in Newport, for despite the salubrious nature of the spring, summer, and fall seasons, the Rhode Island winter can be wicked, so Mr. Hunt and the Vanderbilts settled for an enclosed courtyard. The roof covered the entire house, but the interior room design was as in the original villas. The central court rose to the roof, rooms above the first floor opened off balconies that looked down on the great hall. And above, on the ceiling, Mr. Hunt ordered the painting of a blue, cloud-strewn sky.

The Breakers had one too many floors for architectural purity. The top floor was an afterthought—to house the army of servants the Vanderbilts needed to operate a household that ran to seventy rooms (thirty-three of them for the help). It took two years to assemble and construct the conglomeration of gingerbread, gilt, carved marble, carved Caen stone, brass, wrought iron and bronze that was planned so intricately, and it was a tribute both to Mr. Hunt and to the men he hired that it could be done in that short time.

The grandest single feature of the new Breakers was a magnificent circular staircase, with a fountain beneath. The music room and the morning room were designed by a French architect, built in France, torn apart, and sent to Newport to be installed by French workmen who were shipped along with the gilt, the draperies, the marble, and the self-reflecting mirrors. Fireplaces, columns, and tapestries were ripped out of the villas of impecunious European noblemen to grace this new-world villa. The billiard room was marble and alabaster from floor to ceiling, trimmed in mahogany, furnished as a man's retreat, including a polished English weighing chair that gave the weight of the sitter in stones. The bathrooms were immense, some with marble tubs, all with hot and cold running fresh water, *and* hot and cold running salt water. Like several other Vanderbilt homes, the borders of acorns and oak leaves and lions were repeated time and again. Lions, oak leaves, and acorns—these were the foundations of the Vanderbilt coat of arms, created by Alva Vanderbilt in the period in which she was entering Society. Alva said that great oaks from little acorns grow, so acorns and oaks surrounded columns, ceiling paintings, corner moldings, and every other suitable place in Vanderbilt mansions.

The over-all effect of The Breakers was paralyzing. The architects had planned a house that would be as ornate as any palace in Italy, and they succeeded. It was magnificent, no question of that, and it was to become the most important house in all Newport. The latter distinction, naturally enough, was what Alice Vanderbilt wanted. For she wanted to be Mrs. Vanderbilt, the *leader* of Society.

As it turned out, however, it had not really been necessary for the Cornelius Vanderbilts to spend $5,000,000 to win the title of biggest and best. Alva, the mistress of the Marble House, let her sister-in-law have the title by default.

In the early 1890s it had become most apparent that the William Kissam Vanderbilts were not getting along. When Willie K.'s first yacht sank in the Atlantic after a collision near Martha's Vineyard in 1892, Willie K. immediately built a larger one, but he did not name it the *Alva II*. It was called the *Valiant*. In 1893, when the Vanderbilts set out for a voyage to India in the new yacht, daughter Consuelo, now old enough to have a guest—and a beau— invited Winthrop Rutherford, a young attorney from a Society family, and once again O. H. P. Belmont was on the passenger list.

The cruise ended in a dispute at Bombay. Willie K. and Alva disembarked and both hurried back to Paris, where they stayed at the Hotel Bristol for a few days. Then Alva went on, alone, to London for a time. Brother Cornelius Vanderbilt traveled to

Europe to try to reconcile them, but in the fall of 1894 Alva went home alone and took her children to the house at Newport.

It was rumored that Willie K. was paying attention to a Parisian lady, and it was well known that Willie had a Continental attitude about marriage which he had acquired in his Geneva school days. When he returned to New York in December, there was no doubt about the rift in the family, for Willie stayed at the Metropolitan Club, going neither to his house nor to Newport.

A few months later, when Alva and the children had returned to New York City, Willie did go to Newport for a few days, but only to remove his personal belongings from Marble House.

In March 1895 the W. K. Vanderbilts were divorced in New York—where the only legal ground was adultery. Very few details were ever revealed, because Willie and Alva put a damper on publicity and most of the case was handled behind locked doors. Besides, the Vanderbilts had ranged so far afield in their search for pleasure, in seclusion aboard their ships for months on end, that no one could possibly keep track of all their activities or of their special friends.

It was revealed that Willie K. had taken the blame for the divorce. A Nellie Neustretter, of Eureka, Nevada, apparently a demimondaine who was living in Paris in the middle eighties, was named corespondent in Alva's suit. But, significantly, the time of the impropriety in question seemed to be *after* the argument at Bombay and the subsequent breakup of the Vanderbilt cruise.

In the settlement, Alva received an annual income of $100,000, the multimillion-dollar Marble House at Newport, custody of the three children and an unspecified amount of cash. She was offered the mansion at 660 Fifth Avenue, but found it far too expensive for her reduced circumstances.

She did retain the Vanderbilt name, but in the divorce, Alva lost her place in the running for Queen of Society. No Society woman had ever before been divorced; no matter how miserable or how mismated they might be, the men and women of the upper classes were expected to maintain the outward appearances of conjugal happiness. Alva broke the rule, and the immediate inclination of high society was to snub her.

The Vanderbilts did snub their former sister-in-law, but Alva had moved so widely and so long in the highest reaches of Society that she did not lose caste—as a lesser woman most certainly would have done.

Her membership in New York society survived even the most pointed slurs on her reputation. Everyone in Society had noted that in recent years O. H. P. Belmont always seemed to be on the periphery of the Vanderbilt entourage, whether aboard the yacht, at Newport, or on Fifth Avenue. Of course, Belmont was no hanger-on, he was a multimillionaire in his own right, the money having been earned in the family banking house. He had every right to own a cottage at Newport and to travel as he would, but he traveled too often with the Vanderbilts, and Willie spent too much time away from Alva's side for Belmont and Alva to escape the rumors.

The persistent rumor, after Alva's divorce from Willie K., was that she was planning to marry O. H. P. Belmont within the year. Alva denied the story indignantly, and squelched reporters when they came to ask again. She was careful to keep her name from being linked with Belmont's, although she continued to entertain lavishly and to be seen at the entertainments of others. And even as tongues wagged over the divorce in the spring of 1895, Alva Vanderbilt planned the greatest social coup of her life, a greater stroke even than her successful siege of the stronghold of Mrs. Astor.

On the long yacht trip to India Consuelo Vanderbilt had fallen in love with young Winthrop Rutherford. But Alva had other plans for Consuelo; ruthlessly she broke up the romance, bending the gentle, trusting, raven-haired Consuelo to her will.

Winthrop Rutherford was jettisoned and on the scene came Charles Richard John Spencer-Churchill, ninth Duke of Marlborough, twenty-four years old, slightly undersized and dissipated, but son of an old and honored English family.

Alva began her campaign without notice early in the 1895 summer season at Newport. Then, on August 28, she held a ball and supper for five hundred persons at Marble House. The excuse for the ball was that it was nineteen-year-old Consuelo's coming-out celebration, but the guest of honor at this celebration was the young duke.

Afterward, Newport's scribes said Alva's party was the most expensive social function ever held anywhere, outdoing even Alva's great costume ball in New York twelve years before. That was probably exaggeration—but at least the ball was the high spot of the 1895 season at Newport.

Alva transformed the first floor of Marble House into a floral garden. A bronze fountain in the great hall was made the center of an African water tableau and hyacinths mingled with lotus of the Nile around the pool. A few yards away a swarm of humming-birds was suspended so artfully amid real flowers that the birds looked quite alive. In another bower, pale hollyhocks stood high above the floor, surrounded by three-dimensional butterflies and bees.

On the ocean side of the house thirty-five small tables were placed to catch the summer breeze. The entire lawn was turned into a courtyard bounded by palms and tree ferns imported for the occasion.

Alva Vanderbilt and Consuelo received guests in the Pink Room, which was famous for its Nubian marble. Consuelo wore a gown of white satin trimmed with rich white lace which had belonged to her grandmother, Mrs. Smith, who had worn it at the finest balls in Mobile before the Civil War.

Mullally's Casino Orchestra and a Hungarian band entertained the guests. The favors, fans and pins, cost $5000; all of them had been made by hand in Paris. Scores of natives in far-off China had labored for weeks to make the white silk lanterns that hung all around the house and lawn.

Richard T. Wilson, Jr., an old friend, led the dancing with Consuelo. The senior Wilson had been born to wealth in Georgia; during the Civil War he had sold blankets to the Confederate Army and in 1864 had gone to England to sell cotton for the Confederacy. His family joined him there, after running the Union blockade. At the end of the war Wilson had come back to New York, where his knowledge of southern conditions and values stood him in good stead. In the poverty of the South Wilson had been able to make excellent investments, particularly in southern railroads. So, while former southern friends cut him dead on the street, Richard Wilson prospered in New York business, and made a successful entrance into Society. He and Mrs. Wilson embarked on a joint career as the most successful matchmakers in New York and Newport—until Alva Vanderbilt came on the scene.

Wilson's eldest daughter had married Odgen Goelet, whose family held more real estate than anyone else in New York except the Astors. The eldest son, Orme Wilson, married Carrie Astor. Wilson's second daughter married the Hon. Michael Henry Herbert, a rising star in the British diplomatic service. Dick Wilson was not yet married, nor was his sister Grace, who was in her middle twenties, and one of the prettiest young ladies in Newport society, considered a great catch by even such a royal judge as the Prince of Wales, who was to become Edward VII of England.

Grace had been engaged to Cecil Baring, the son of Lord Revelstoke of African fame, but that engagement had been broken off the previous year, and now she was back in Newport for the season, and this most brilliant affair of Alva Vanderbilt's.

The rumor was already out about Consuelo and the duke, and the assemblage waited expectantly for an announcement of the engagement that night. But there was no announcement. Consuelo, pale—and looking even more like a china doll than usual— was fighting a rear-guard action with her iron-willed mother. Like most girls, she wanted to marry for love. Like most dowagers, her mother was more interested in a good match.

The duke remained in Newport for two weeks more, entertained heavily by the Vanderbilts. Willie K. took him cruising on the *Valiant*. Even Frederick William and Louise Vanderbilt entertained him, although their relations with the rest of the clan were not too amiable. Stirred by the exciting thought that a Vanderbilt might marry a full-fledged duke, newspaper reporters pestered Alva day after day. On September 19 Alva said impatiently that there was no engagement, but the next day the reporters found the duke, without protection, at the Waldorf-Astoria hotel in New York, where he was stopping on the eve of a trip to

Niagara Falls. Naïvely he admitted the truth: Consuelo Vanderbilt would become his duchess.

Alva could no longer deny the report and Consuelo was not
available for comment, but the preparations for the wedding began
within a fortnight.

In London, the *Gentlewoman* took a maternal view of the
betrothal, and an approving view of Consuelo, but could not refrain from noting that two centuries before, when Jan van der
Bilt had been a lowly soldier in the Dutch army, John Churchill,
Earl of Marlborough, had been sent to London Tower for having
displeased William III. (The fact was that Jan Aertson van der
Bilt was already in America, had served out his time as an indentured servant, and had established an independent if lowly
farm.)

The *Gentlewoman* found Consuelo properly retiring and properly awed at the prospect of becoming the ninth Duchess of
Marlborough, princess of the Holy Roman Empire and princess of
Mindelheim. She detested knickerbockers and divided skirts, she
rode side-saddle as a lady should, and she was having her trousseau
made by Worth and two other Paris houses, quite properly. And
then there was the dowry—2,000,000 pounds, which at 3 per cent
would come to an income of 60,000 pounds a year. The *Gentlewoman* need say no more.

Actually the marriage settlement on the duke was not so great.
Willie K. had given him life interest in a trust fund of $2,500,000
in railroad stock, with a guaranteed 4 per cent yield every year,
plus an annual allowance of $100,000 for the couple.

The wicked claimed that Alva had bought the title—a spiteful
view. Willie K. was not stingy, Consuelo was his only daughter,
and she was certainly entitled to a proper dowry from a man who
had inherited $65,000,000 from his father.

On the wedding day, November 6, 1895, it was apparent that
Alva, the chief engineer of the wedding, had a vengeful soul as
well as a stout one. Except for the father of the bride and Consuelo's brothers, not another Vanderbilt was invited to the ceremony at St. Thomas's Episcopal Church.

The church was decorated fittingly for the wedding of a duke and an heiress. From the dome, 95 feet to the floor, the interior was festooned with flowers. Walter Damrosch led a sixty-man symphony orchestra which played selections from suitable classic music. Willie K. smiled and his handsome face crinkled pleasantly as he came up the aisle with his daughter. Willie K. II was dressed in top hat and morning coat, and Harold wore an Eton collar, proper for an eleven-year-old. The wedding proceeded with nary a hitch in plan, the contract was signed, and the duke and his new duchess went to Willie K.'s Idle Hour estate for their honeymoon.

Alva Vanderbilt felt she could now relax. She had brought the Vanderbilts into Society and she had taken the family into the upper reaches of the British nobility. William Waldorf Astor had moved family and fortune to England and bought a title, but Alva had accomplished the same feat without moving an inch. She had done something no other Vanderbilt could do, and again she had kept the Vanderbilts in the forefront of her world. She had led the family into its period of glory.

21

THE MAN WITH THE IRON WILL

An acquaintance once said of Cornelius Vanderbilt II that in all the years he had known this grandson of the old Commodore, Cornelius II had never been known to smile.

It was true that Cornelius was not given to levity. Despite the riches of the family he had known little of the leisure of wealth until he was forty years old. As a youngster Cornelius had taken a clerkship in New York's Shoe and Leather Bank, as ordered by his grandfather. The youth had transferred later to the railroad, first working as an accountant in the treasurer's office, moving up through the business department. Even as a young man he was solemn; his spare time was devoted to church affairs, not high jinks. Cornelius met his wife, the former Alice Claypool Gwynne of Cincinnati, in the Sunday school of St. Bartholomew's, where he was a regular teacher.

This Cornelius Vanderbilt was stern but charitable. Chauncey Depew claimed that Cornelius gave half his annual income to charity, and even if this statement represented the exaggeration of which Depew was capable, it could not be contested that Vanderbilt, in his high, round collar of almost clerical cut and his curly sideburns, was a charitable figure. Vanderbilt's three daughters adored him, and his four sons respected both the stern jaw and their father's good judgment. How could they do otherwise? This Cornelius Vanderbilt was as near an ascetic as the family ever produced. He neither drank nor smoked, he was mild of language and fair in all dealings with his family and fellow men.

It had been an evil blow to Cornelius in May of his forty-ninth year when William Henry Vanderbilt II, his first son, died suddenly of typhoid fever. The boy was just twenty-two years old, a student at Yale University, and the hope of his father as successor in the management of the railroads. Before young William Henry's death it was rumored around New York and Newport that the boy had very serious intentions toward Grace Wilson, who had come out two or three seasons before, and was considered to be one of the most eligible young women in Society.

A heartbroken Cornelius had built a million-dollar memorial to his son's memory—a dormitory at Yale—and then settled down to nurse his grief and bring his other boys to maturity.

During the summer of 1895 when Alva Vanderbilt had captured Newport's season by managing Consuelo's engagement to the Duke of Marlborough, the Cornelius Vanderbilts opened the doors of society for their daughter Gertrude, who had also come of proper age that year.

The Cornelius Vanderbilt party was not only to present Gertrude but also to open The Breakers to Newport society, and although it was a simple party, for the Vanderbilts, the magnificence of the surroundings made the word "simple" meaningless. Mrs. Vanderbilt decorated the halls with only a few bouquets of flowers; she made no effort to overwhelm her guests. (She didn't have to try. The house was enough.) Some five hundred roses were placed in bouquets, along with a few dozen rare potted plants brought over for the occasion from the greenhouse three blocks away, a minimal floral decoration that scarcely disturbed the majestic contours of the marble and alabaster walls. The favors for the gentlemen were gold and silver scarf pins and for the ladies there were French fans—all imported, of course. But long after the guests had forgotten the favors at this party, they remembered the attention that Neily Vanderbilt, then just twenty-two years old and a graduate of Yale, had paid to Grace Wilson, who was three years his senior. The elder Vanderbilts had also noticed this, and with more than a little alarm, for Neily—Cornelius

Vanderbilt III—was a headstrong young man in spite of a frail figure and chronic rheumatism that often sent him to bed for weeks at a time.

In September Neily suffered a rheumatic attack, ending what his father and mother hoped was only a summer romance with Grace Wilson. The Cornelius Vanderbilts packed their son off to the popular resort at Hot Springs, Virginia, for a rest, but also, it was suspected, to get him away from the young lady. The suspicion was confirmed when Mrs. Vanderbilt went to Mrs. Wilson's for tea and asked if Grace was going to Europe that year. When she learned that Grace had no European plans, Neily was sent abroad for the winter, and shortly afterward Chauncey Depew, the vizier of the Vanderbilt empire, wrote Richard T. Wilson that he would like to discuss the subject of Miss Wilson on behalf of Mr. Vanderbilt.

Wilson's sense of southern chivalry was outraged by the intervention of an outsider. He refused indignantly to talk about his daughter with any less a personage than Vanderbilt himself. Vanderbilt was not happy to do so, apparently because the subject was so delicate, and his well-mannered, Christian soul could not stand the thought of a stormy meeting.

But the two met. Vanderbilt told Wilson he would not countenance the wedding. Wilson told Vanderbilt he was not going to interfere. Thus they parted, enemies, and immediately Grace Wilson sailed for France with her sister, Mrs. Ogden Goelet. Within a few days Grace and Neily were holding hands on the Champs Elysees.

The Vanderbilt family did all possible to break up the romance. Whether Cornelius, Sr., really worried about the difference in ages, whether he felt the Wilsons unsuitable for alliance, or whether he had grave reservations about Grace Wilson's character and morals (as he indicated later)—all these points were made in argument to Neily. But the younger man set his own Vanderbilt jaw and steamed ahead. His uncle George wrote him a warning letter. His mother wrote such an intemperate letter that Neily burned it; but he showed George's letter to Grace's brother-in-law, Michael Herbert, the British diplomat. George had inferred that

Grace Wilson was no better than she ought to be. Why? No one ever knew, except that she had been "out" in Society a long time, she had been engaged at least once before, and she had been linked with Neily's elder brother. Herbert erupted in rage, and Neily's determination to marry Grace seemed to harden.

Neily traveled that season from Paris to Constantinople and to Cannes where the family troubles attracted international attention, to Cornelius Vanderbilt's dismay. In Cannes the Prince of Wales pumped Grace's sister about the match, and Neily was asked to appear after dinner one night for inspection by His Royal Highness. Neily and Grace, chaperoned by her married sisters, spent several weeks cruising on a yacht in the Mediterranean. Neily was totally, hopelessly in love. Grace, who seemed much calmer, told her sister Belle (Mrs. Goelet) that she intended to go through with the marriage because she felt that it would bring her ultimate happiness. That was hardly a protestation of undying love, but Grace *was* fond of Neily, and she was touched by his willingness to defy his family for love of her.

Distracted and upset, Cornelius Vanderbilt called on nearly every member of his family to help bring the boy around.

But the other Vanderbilts were occupied with their own affairs:

Willie K., having lost a wife and married off a daughter in 1895, had purchased a French chateau and was busying himself with the breeding of race horses.

Frederick William was willing to write what the Wilsons called "insulting letters" but he was busy building a new estate. At thirty-nine, Frederick William had found himself bored by the never-ending sameness of life at Newport, and while he had bought the summer cottage there called Rough Point in 1891, by the summer of 1895 he was tired of it. He wanted a house for the months of early spring and late fall, when the New York house seemed confining and most of Newport was as tightly shuttered as the rickety club bathhouses on the exclusive, rockstrewn patch of sand known as Bailey's Beach.

So Frederick William had bought the old Langdon place at Hyde Park that year, an estate that had once been part of John Jacob Astor's holdings. Frederick William hired the architectural firm of McKim, Mead, and White to renovate the old house, and, in the interim, to put up a place where he and Louise could stay. At the time Neily became so deeply involved with Grace Wilson, workmen were erecting a $50,000 temporary house for Frederick William called the Pavilion; it was a Greek revival cottage. Eventually this house would be used as a dormitory for male visitors, so it was planned to be informal and very masculine. Most of the first floor was given over to a single room, a combination hall, lounge, and dining room off which stood a butler's pantry and kitchen for the preparation of game dinners. A balcony around the central hall opened into small bedrooms and servants' quarters.

By the end of November, while Neily Vanderbilt was mooning over Grace Wilson's shoulder in Paris and Cannes, his uncle's new house on the Hudson was ready for a housewarming. Obviously Frederick William could do nothing about Neily.

But now the most logical person to try to talk some sense into Neily's head was his uncle George, because George was a bachelor himself and at thirty-three by far the closest of the senior Vanderbilts to Neily's own age.

Yet, except for more letters, George, too, was unavailable. In 1891 he had undertaken the building of his Carolina barony, and the job was so near completion by the fall of 1895 that he had no time to spare. The original 5000 acres had become nearly 100,000 acres, including the 80,000-acre Pisgah Forest. Richard Morris Hunt was building George the most pretentious house in the United States, after his favorite Chateau de Blois, a house with the largest roof of any in the country. It had forty bedrooms, a 75-foot-high Norman banquet hall with three fireplaces, and library space for 25,000 volumes.

George had wanted an estate that was *truly* unique, so he employed Frederick Law Olmsted, the little, lame man who was America's pioneer landscape architect, to treat with the problem of grounds and forests. Olmsted, in turn, recommended a young forester named Gifford Pinchot, who had studied in Germany and returned with some modern ideas about conservation. So Vanderbilt hired young Pinchot and gave him more money to work with than Congress gave the Secretary of Agriculture for scientific forestry in all the rest of the United States.

Biltmore was planned to be self-sufficient. It included a model farm for breeding fine cattle and hogs, an arboretum of trees from temperate zones that was the finest and most complete in the world, and a village of its own that included schools, shops, a water system, an infirmary, and a chapel with stained-glass windows. George had built it all from the ground up. When he began acquiring property the area was full of one-room cabins of the Appalachian mountaineers—and little else. The deed for one piece of land he bought specified one boundary as ending at a mudhole in the road.

By the late fall of 1895 George's estate had been made into a community. Labor was cheap: George hired men to work for 90 cents a day, and he could get mules thrown in for another 75 cents each. Pinchot had gone to the North Carolina woods in 1891 to take charge of the forestry project, thrilled by his work, but bemused at the contrast between wealth and poverty and the injustice of unearned power, a liberality of mind which caused him eventually to leave Vanderbilt for government, although Pinchot always professed admiration for George's combination of intellectuality and love of the outdoors.

When the estate was complete, George installed 750 employees to operate separate divisions of forestry, agriculture, and landscaping and by December 1895 the house and grounds were ready to show—the $5,000,000 house with its seventeen miles of macadam roads, private village, and thousands of acres of forest. On Christmas Eve the private cars of the Vanderbilts were brought onto sidings of the Southern Railroad near Asheville, and the family was taken by carriage to the chateau. Cornelius and Alice Vanderbilt came, with all the children except the recalcitrant Neily. Frederick William and his wife were there; so was Willie K. and Eliza and her husband William Seward Webb. It was an unusual Christmas reunion for the family, in the most opulent surroundings—marred only by the stubborn absence of Cornelius's eldest living son.

But Neily simply would not come home, even when he was threatened.

Cornelius Vanderbilt cabled his son that he would cut off the young man's remittances, leaving Neily dependent on his own resources, and while Neily did have a small trust fund, providing an income of some $6000 a year, it was not enough money to live like a Vanderbilt.

For a few weeks after Christmas the Vanderbilts were diverted from consideration of Neily's affairs by the final act of another family drama. On January 11, 1896, Alva Vanderbilt married Oliver Hazard Perry Belmont at her new house on Seventy-second Street in New York City. The couple had tried for weeks to find a minister to marry them, but since they were both divorced, no Episcopal minister would officiate. Finally they married in a civil ceremony conducted by New York Mayor W. L. Strong, attended by Alva's two sons and some of her relatives. No other Vanderbilts or Belmonts appeared.

The Vanderbilts ignored the wedding—and Alva. The family was shy of publicity, sickened of notoriety, and wanted to be left alone by the newspapers, but the society columnists could not keep from talking and speculating about the affairs of the nation's most prominent family, and particularly about the storybook romance between Neily Vanderbilt and Grace Wilson.

To stop the gossip, Cornelius Vanderbilt II set out for Europe, himself, in February 1896, to fetch his son home.

By this time, but for different reasons, the Wilsons were upset about the romance. They realized that the scandal was compromising their daughter's good name and while Neily *talked* about marriage, he had not offered to set a date. He and Grace were not even officially engaged. Grace's English brother-in-law told young Vanderbilt that something had to be done; either Neily must stop seeing Grace or he must make a commitment and Neily agreed, but he wanted Grace to go home first, and he would follow her to make one last appeal for family reconciliation to the marriage.

It did not work that way. In the spring, after Cornelius Vanderbilt's trip to Europe, Neily returned to take a job in the engineering department of the New York Central. It was rumored around New York that a stern Cornelius had told Neily that if he married Grace he would be disinherited. In exposing him, as well, to the New York Central, his father was showing him both the carrot and the whip.

When Grace Wilson returned to New York, some time after the Vanderbilts, father and son, she remained in seclusion for several weeks and did not even see Neily. Then on June 10 the newspapers announced the engagement of Cornelius Vanderbilt III and Grace Wilson.

The next day the papers carried an announcement of Gertrude Vanderbilt's engagement to Harry Payne Whitney, son of the former Secretary of the Navy, a story approved and released by the Vanderbilts—and a flat statement that Cornelius Vanderbilt disapproved completely of his son's plan to marry Grace Wilson.

When the Wilsons sent invitations, most of Society fled New York rather than be accused of taking one side or the other by appearing or failing to appear at the wedding, so the Wilsons decided on a family ceremony to be held in the rear drawing room of the Wilson house on Fifth Avenue.

On Sunday, June 14, Neily dined at the Wilson home and discussed plans for the wedding, then walked home through the rain to the lonely mansion. (His family had gone to Newport to escape publicity and the wedding.) On Monday evening Neily apparently had a change of heart, for at Newport his father received a telephone call from him, and set out for New York, and Neily's mother followed shortly afterward. On Tuesday Neily appeared at the New York Yacht Club, but on Tuesday afternoon Mrs. Vanderbilt announced the wedding had been indefinitely postponed because Neily had suffered an attack of rheumatism and was confined to bed.

On Wednesday the Wilsons announced that Neily was seriously ill, but the Vanderbilts said he was suffering a mild indisposition.

On Thursday, Grace's wedding day, Richard Wilson ordered the florist Hodgson to send the ten thousand roses and other floral decorations ordered for the wedding to various New York hospitals. That day Neily Vanderbilt was nowhere to be seen, apparently confined to bed. The senior Vanderbilts were seen placidly walking in Central Park, and Grace Wilson was left with a houseful of wedding presents, but no groom.

Cornelius Vanderbilt III, it seemed, could not stand up to the strong will of his father.

But that was not to be the end of the affair, for the newspapers continued to speculate on the fates of the two young lovers. Neily's position in Society was scarcely better than Grace's, and Grace had been compromised so completely as to become almost unmarriageable. Neily stayed at home, moody and pale. Servants in the Vanderbilt mansion at Fifty-seventh Street and Fifth Avenue reported that he and his father engaged in long and bitter arguments every day.

Nearly a month passed. Neily remained in New York while the remainder of the family went again to Newport. He was suffering, it was said, from a renewed attack of rheumatism. On July 13 his father boarded his private car at Wickford Junction, Rhode Island, bound for New York to pick up Neily and bring him to The Breakers. After he arrived in New York at eight o'clock on Tuesday morning, July 14, Vanderbilt breakfasted and went to his office on the ground floor of the mansion to take care of some business affairs. At noon his wife joined him there. A few moments later Dr. William Draper entered the room to discuss Neily's condition, but noticed that the elder Vanderbilt seemed pale and ill himself.

"You are not well," the doctor said to Vanderbilt.

"Oh, yes, I am all right," Vanderbilt replied.

"You look queer," the doctor said—and at that moment Cornelius Vanderbilt slumped over on the arm of his chair and collapsed.

Neily's illness was forgotten as they put Cornelius Vanderbilt to bed in a large room on the second floor and called Dr. James W. McLane, the family physician.

Soon there were five doctors in the house. They diagnosed the father's case as paralytic stroke, which affected the entire right side. His condition was so serious that the rest of the family was notified, and a city permit was secured to sprinkle a layer of tanbark on the streets around the house in order to deaden the noise of the wagons and horses' hoofs. There was no question of taking Cornelius Vanderbilt to a hospital. He could not be moved.

Some of the family began to arrive in New York that day. Harrison McK. Twombly came from his summer place at Orange, New Jersey.

That night Cornelius Vanderbilt slept five hours, and seemed better, but the next day he suffered a relapse. His daughter Gertrude and second son Alfred Gwynne Vanderbilt arrived from Newport. Neily stayed in bed with his rheumatism. Police began diverting traffic off Fifth Avenue. Coaches of the Fifth Avenue Coach Company, owned by one of the Vanderbilt daughters, were turned into Madison Avenue for two blocks. One wagon driver, who attempted to argue about his right to pass in front of the Vanderbilt home, was invited to accompany a policeman to the station house. He turned meekly off the avenue.

Grace Wilson sent Neily Vanderbilt a wire that day, asking about his father, but they had no other communication.

Two days later Cornelius Vanderbilt seemed much improved. His third son Reginald and younger daughter Gladys came up from Newport, and Vanderbilt spoke with the younger children for a few moments. He was still partly paralyzed, but he could speak and eat.

On the eighteenth Cornelius Vanderbilt was much better. He was hungry and said he wanted solid food, for the first time since the stroke. They had been cooling the room with ice and fans, but this day they felt it possible to move him to a room on the Fifty-eighth Street side of the house, overlooking the plaza. This was the cool side of the building. Vanderbilt had ignored this side of the house years before when the city had erected an undraped statue in the adjacent plaza. Earlier, Vanderbilt took exception to the statue. Now he was in no condition to worry.

That day the tanbark on Fifty-seventh Street was shoveled up and moved around to Fifty-eighth Street, since the tanbark supply of the Newark tanners was running low.

Chauncey Depew was in London, as was the Rev. David H. Greer, rector of St. Bartholomew's, which was now known as the

Vanderbilt church. Both men had offered to sail immediately for New York. Messages were sent to forestall them, but Depew had already sailed that very day on the *Lucania* from Liverpool.

On July 19 father Cornelius Vanderbilt's condition seemed enough improved that the household took on some semblance of normal activity. Neily was up and around, his rheumatism forgotten. Harry Payne Whitney called in the afternoon and took his fiancée Gertrude into Central Park for a walk. At the Protestant Episcopal Mission, established in Harlem by Vanderbilt for his railroad porters, the minister offered prayers of thanks.

On July 20 Alfred and Reginald Vanderbilt went back to Newport, carrying the news that their father would be well enough to travel to The Breakers in two weeks. And the next day the thinning cover of tanbark was allowed to scatter, for the first time since Cornelius Vanderbilt had been stricken. Heavy wagons and carriages began grumbling and clattering past the mansion as usual. Stonemasons who had been making some changes on the outside of the house were back at work after a week's silence.

A week later Frederick William's yacht *Conqueror* sailed up the Hudson to the New York freight dock, and Vanderbilt was taken aboard for the trip to Newport. There he was moved in an improvised ambulance with rubber tires to The Breakers and installed in a front room on the water side of the villa where no sound from Bellevue Avenue could disturb him. The heavy English bell on the great front door was muffled, and more tanbark was scattered along the gravel walks. Willie K. spent several days at Newport to be sure his brother was recuperating properly, then sailed on his yacht, the *Valiant*, for New York.

When the excitement died down, the rumors started. One story going about New York was that the stroke was a direct result of an argument between Vanderbilt and his eldest son, in which Neily had actually struck his father.

Whether or not the report of violence was true, the report of violent feeling certainly was correct. Neily Vanderbilt moved out of the family house into a small apartment.

A week after his father had been moved to Newport, Neily

Vanderbilt married Grace Wilson in an unannounced ceremony that was conducted in the Wilson drawing room. Not another Vanderbilt was there, and from the grand mansion on the cliff at Newport came a silence as cold as the deep sea below.

22

THE UNPLEASANTNESS

Cornelius Vanderbilt began the slow process of recovery from paralysis at Newport. He was only fifty-three, yet the illness had made him an old man and the family knew he would never be the same again. The illness brought a crisis in the affairs of the New York Central, since he was the active one in railroad management. But in the crisis, William Kissam Vanderbilt stepped in at Grand Central Station to assume a far more active role in the New York Central Railroad than ever before.

The Vanderbilt lines were feeling the panic that had begun three years before, in 1893, when stocks dropped as much as 50 per cent in value. Nearly six hundred banks failed in that depression and money was again in short supply throughout the country, as it had been after the panic of 1873.

William Jennings Bryan had won the 1896 Democratic party nomination for President on a platform—really a crusade—that demanded increased silver coinage. This increase in the amount of money in circulation would cause a mild inflation and promote recovery. William McKinley, the Republican nominee that year, stood solidly on the gold standard, so the issue in the election of 1896 was money: should it be cheap, and silver, or dear, and gold?

The Vanderbilts, of course, were opposed to cheap money, for cheap money could do nothing but lower the real values of the property they owned. The immensity of those holdings was best explained by a note about the ailing Cornelius Vanderbilt: he was a director of fifty different railroads. The Central, alone, had property worth nearly $175,000,000 with a capitalization of $100,000,000 and a bonded debt around $75,000,000. The nature of Vanderbilt control of the railroads had changed greatly since the days of the Commodore; the family had not owned a majority of stock in the Central since William Henry's day, and in 1896 the Central was owned by no less than thirteen thousand stockholders, many of them in England, but the control was still in friendly hands. J. Pierpont Morgan represented the English stockholders on the board, so for practical purposes, Morgan, the Vanderbilt banker, voted the English stock.

There were other advantages in having an important banker in the workings of the railroads. In the year of the panic the little independent fifty-two-mile New York and Northern Railroad met disaster and the property was put up for forced sale at the end of 1893. The sale was set for high noon on December 28 at the Yonkers railroad station, and on that day Morgan went to Yonkers with the Central's counsel, Judge Ashbel Green, to acquire the line. The banker sat in an office just off the waiting room, smoking cigars and acting as though he were waiting for an appointment with his barber, until the stroke of noon. When the bidding was opened, he offered a cool million dollars for the railroad on behalf of the Central. Within one minute the sale was completed, and Morgan sat down to write a check for $100,000 to bind the bargain. Another annoying, if small, competitor had been eliminated from the field.

Yet there was a considerable degree of railroad competition, largely between the New York Central, the Erie, and the Pennsylvania. In the spirit of competition, Central passenger agent George Daniels had coined the slogan "America's Greatest Railroad" for the Central, and by 1896 had begun to give free red cap service at the stations.

William Buchanan, the Central's superintendent of motive power, was told to make his railroad's service the fastest in the country. He put an Empire State Express on the day run to Buffalo that averaged 61.4 miles per hour. At the World's Columbian Exposition in Chicago in 1893 Central men had proudly unveiled the latest in railroading—their new engine No. 999, which boasted powerful driving wheels more than seven feet high. It was an age of speed and the Central intended to give the public speed.

Despite his foreign education and exclusive ways, William Kissam Vanderbilt ably assumed his brother's railroad duties. The opposite in nearly every way of his brother, William Kissam was not a detail man. Where Willie K. did shine was in selecting his subordinates, and in directing them in a kindly, unruffled manner. He was quite indifferent to what others thought of him and, like his grandfather, he kept his business to himself. It was not very long, consequently, before the New York newspapers began to draw an image of William Kissam Vanderbilt as a second Commodore.

He proposed to absorb the Boston and Albany Railroad. He exhibited greater interest than Cornelius had in the Union Pacific and the Chicago and Northwestern—whereupon Wall Street and the press prophesied that he would become head of a great transcontinental line that would run between Boston and San Francisco.

This was the atmosphere of success from which William Kissam's nephew Neily Vanderbilt had departed, perhaps forever, when he walked out of the chief engineer's office to marry Grace Wilson and begin an extended honeymoon.

Their first stop was Saratoga Springs, the Commodore's old watering place, and scene of his honeymoon with Frank.

From Saratoga, Neily sent wires to his brother Alfred to check on his father's condition. He received terse wires in return, which described his father's condition in cold medical terms. That was all.

But where the Vanderbilts were cold, strangers were more than kind to the celebrated young couple. At the United States Hotel at Saratoga, where they took a five-room cottage, secuded from the other guests, they were treated royally by the management. Young Vanderbilt's financial condition was no better than before, but Grace had a $25,000 annual income of her own, and her brother sent them a handsome check as a wedding present. They had enough money.

Late in August they sailed for Liverpool aboard the *Majestic*.

When the ship docked, the chairman of the White Star Line made personal arrangements to speed their trip to London. Then they went to Paris where they stayed at an inexpensive hotel near the Arc de Triomphe. Grace was amused by their surroundings; she had been accustomed to spending as much as her total personal income on her wardrobe each year, and here they were living on it.

Neily Vanderbilt was not amused. He was haunted by conscience, distressed by the estrangement with his father, tormented by rheumatism and pains around the heart. The tranquillity of their honeymoon was interrupted by the death of his grandmother, Louisa Kissam Vanderbilt. Worst of all, Neily learned of the death from Chauncey Depew, not from his own family. Neily cabled home but received a chilly reply from his father, who gave only the bare details.

There was no question about Neily's going home for his grandmother's funeral. He and Grace could not possibly arrive in time by steamer, nor was there anything else they could do except cable flowers.

Louisa's four sons attended the funeral, coming from locations which, alone, indicated the great changes time had worked in the family. Willie K. was in New York, working at Grand Central; Frederick William came to New York from his house at Hyde Park; George Washington brought a private train from his vast estate in the South; and Cornelius made his first major outing from The Breakers since his illness. They all met at St. Bartholomew's to take Louisa Kissam to her husband's side in the mausoleum on Staten Island.

The widow of William Henry left an estate of $1,100,000. Her husband had provided well for her widowhood in his own will eleven years before, but most of her income came from trust funds that now reverted to the residuary estate controlled by Cornelius and William Kissam.

Perhaps Neily Vanderbilt might have expected a share of his grandmother's estate in his reduced circumstances, but if his grandmother knew of Neily's situation, she did not recognize it in her will. William Henry Vanderbilt's widow left most of her

fortune to needy members of the Kissam family. She gave
$250,000 to St. Bartholomew's Church, and she gave her pew in
the church to her son George.

Under the terms of his father's will, George also was to have
the Vanderbilt mansion at 640 Fifth Avenue, after the death of
his mother. As a bachelor whose tastes ran to esoteric literature
(he spoke and read a half-dozen languages) and not to wine,
women, or song, George had no desire to enter the social whirl.

Since he planned to spend a minimum of time in New York, he
had no use for such a big house there. He cut the staff that had
manned 640 Fifth Avenue during the old days. He also closed the
family farm on Staten Island that William Henry had worked so
many years ago. The farm had been maintained all these years,
simply to supply flowers and produce for the big house at 640
Fifth Avenue. Each day for thirteen years a wagonload of milk,
eggs, butter, fresh fruits and vegetables, and flowers from the
greenhouses had been shipped across New York harbor and
carted to the service entrance. These changes were made to cut
waste, not in concern over expenditure, for none of the third
generation of Vanderbilts worried about how much money they
spent.

The biggest spender of all—William Kissam—had given away
some $10,000,000 to Alva and to Consuelo and her Duke; after
Alva's second marriage he continued annual allowances of $50,000
each for William K. II and Harold, his sons. He gave Consuelo
and the Duke $100,000 a year plus costly houses and presents. He
had built three houses that cost not less than $5,000,000 each, all
in the United States, and had spent uncounted millions for houses
and race horses in France. He had built the yacht *Alva* for
$500,000, and a second yacht, the *Valiant*, which was reported to
have cost a million dollars. Yet he had more money now than the
$65,000,000 his father had left him! It was not magic: the Van-
derbilt railroads and the Vanderbilt stocks and bonds earned
money faster than any human being could spend it. Taxes drained
practically nothing from a domestic fortune such as theirs. The
income tax, which had been first imposed during the Civil War,
had lapsed in 1872 and not been renewed. Besides, even when

that first income tax was in effect it excepted money earned on railroad stocks, and that was where the Commodore had kept his fortune.

In the last decade of the nineteenth century taxes were still not troublesome, although for the first time—each year since 1893— the federal government had shown a series of deficits. In 1894 Congress passed a new income tax, but the wealthy sighed with relief, for it was held unconstitutional by the U. S. Supreme Court. Still, anyone could see that changes in the tax laws were inevitable. Customs duties no longer supported the federal government, and state tax collectors were enforcing the laws more literally as their own deficits grew. William Kissam had been recently involved in a bitter tax wrangle with the town fathers at Islip, Long Island, over the property assessment on Idle Hour, his country estate. George Washington Vanderbilt had imported ten cases of books on forestry in 1896, and they had been held up in New York while the tax collectors decided how to treat them. The law said that books in the English language, less than twenty years old, were subject to import duty. The customs collector, Colonel J. Wilkinson, had examined the books and scratched his head for weeks, then finally levied duty on about twenty volumes, much to George's disgust.

The tax system still favored wealth, but the royal habits of the Vanderbilts and other wealthy families were under grim scrutiny by reformers; in 1896 the Vanderbilts led the 10 per cent of the population who controlled 90 per cent of the wealth of America.

The unfortunate Neily was the single Vanderbilt who had money problems. He squirmed in his dependence on his wife and on her father's fortune. During the fall of 1896 and the beginning of 1897 when they remained in Paris, he tried continually to make up with his family, but the only word from his father came through Dr. McLane, who told the son that he should not come home; his father would not see him.

Finally Neily could stand his dependence and ostracism no longer. New York was alive with stories that Grace had been forced to marry because she was with child. The newspapers printed allusions to the charges, and then ridiculed them; small wonder they persisted. Driven by conscience, by the need to prove Grace's innocence, and by the pangs of the hero worship he felt for his father, Neily insisted on going home, so they embarked in January 1897.

The couple moved in with the Wilsons at their Fifth Avenue house, and Neily decided to go back to school to earn a master's degree in mechanical engineering. Neily and Grace lived at the Wilson house, but Neily commuted three times a week to New Haven for classes during the spring and summer of 1897, while Grace joined her family at Newport.

In the fall of 1897 Neily Vanderbilt went to the New York Central to ask for a job. He appeared at the railroad employment office, not at the executive suite where he could have been gently turned away. President Chauncey Depew had little alternative but to hire him as an engineer in the motive power and rolling stock department. The pay was not munificent, but it gave Neily enough to restore his self-respect and to take a house on Thirty-sixth Street just off fashionable Fifth Avenue, where in the spring of 1898 Cornelius Vanderbilt IV was born. Six weeks later Grace took the baby off to Europe to escape the humdrum life of her husband, who kept his nose glued to books, either in a tiny office on the sixth floor of the Grand Central Terminal building or in the library at home.

No family argument preceded Grace's departure; she and Neily seemed happy enough, but it was apparent that the vivacious, party-loving Grace and her scholarly husband had very little in common, and this separation confirmed the Vanderbilt family's opinion that Neily had wrecked his life in the horrible mistake of marrying the wrong woman.

Grace danced across Europe with her princes and counts and dukes that summer, and Neily stayed home and made a name for himself as one of two Vanderbilts active in the railroad. He surveyed the mechanical operations of the Lake Shore Railroad, and reported directly to the office of the president of the system. He designed a new locomotive, which was adopted by the Central, and by the non-Vanderbilt Baltimore & Ohio and Missouri Pacific railroads. In railroading he was regarded as an up-

and-coming engineer. His immediate superior, Superintendent Buchanan, liked his work and said so. But at the ownership level of the New York Central Neily Vanderbilt's best efforts were greeted by cold silence.

The silence itself was flagellation to Neily Vanderbilt. His marriage was not bringing him the companionship he had expected. He had gone to work because he needed money, but he applied for a job on the New York Central staff in hope of reconciliation with his father. Hard as Neily worked, it seemed, the only notice came from outside—particularly from the press, which found the story of the Vanderbilt breach of unending interest to readers.

Anyone named Vanderbilt found it difficult to keep his name out of the newspapers because the public delighted in reading of the parties and peccadilloes of the very rich. If the average American could not mingle with European royalty or drink champagne every night, at least he could read about those who did, and the Vanderbilts, Neily's uncles and brothers and cousins, led the life of high society. Always, it seemed, one or the other of them was doing something that brought his name before the public.

Frederick William alternated between his New York town house, Newport, and the $600,000 mansion he was building high above the Hudson at Hyde Park, with an occasional cruise on his current yacht. (He seemed to change ships every year or two.)

George Washington Vanderbilt, having put the finishing touches on his Biltmore estate and having enjoyed life there for a few years, became bored by the routine of a country lord and went to India to shoot tigers. He returned to Paris in the spring of 1898 to marry tall, dignified Edith Stuyvesant Dresser, a socialite who had a sizable fortune of her own.

Neily's father Cornelius lived quietly in New York and at Newport, seldom going out since the stroke had left him a semi-invalid. Alfred Gwynne Vanderbilt, Neily's closest brother in age, was in his junior year at Yale, and William K. II, Neily's cousin, was studying at Harvard.

Although Willie K. II had been given the $50,000 allowance

by his father's divorce settlement, in his early years at college he received only $1500 a year over his actual expenses, and lived in much the same manner as other students. He was democratic, others said, and very well liked. That was understandable, for Willie K. II was a handsome dark-haired young man, who had a ready smile, a vast amount of erudition, and a flair for sports. Even during the summers of his prep school years at St. Mark's School in Massachusetts, Willie had shown himself to be an excellent sailor. As a college student he raced his own yacht, with a great deal of verve and some competitive success.

Something changed in Willie K. II in 1898, however. He became a man of the world, applied for and received an increase in his allowance, took private rooms and established the richest apartment ever seen around the Harvard Yard. He tore out walls and put in green Japanese cloth. He added fireplaces, and large exposed oak beams to one room that was paneled after the style of a feudal castle.

Apparently the cause of this splurge of worldliness was love. Willie K. II was courting Virginia Graham Fair, daughter of a western Senator who had made millions in the Comstock lode. "Birdie" Fair, as she was known, was a lively, athletic brunette, if not a great beauty or a great belle. She had come to New York after her father's death to live with her sister, Mrs. Hermann Oelrichs, whose mansion was at 1 East Fifty-seventh Street—just across from that of the ailing Cornelius Vanderbilt II. "Birdie" was several years older than Willie K. II, but Alva Vanderbilt Belmont and Tessie Oelrichs were great friends. They favored a marriage between Birdie and the sturdy young Willie II—it was quite unlike the attitude of Neily's family. William Kissam Vanderbilt also turned a genial eye on the romance.

The engagement was announced just after Christmas that year, and it was expected to be a long one. Six months was considered a proper time for a society girl to wait between betrothal and wedding, but the family wanted Willie K. II to finish college before getting married.

His father gave a ball for the happy pair on January 27, 1899, at 660 Fifth Avenue. Three hundred and fifty came, the same old crowd of Society folk: along came Sloanes, Webbs, Twomblys, Shepards, Burdens, Harrimans, Goelets, Mrs. Astor, and Mrs. Stuyvesant Fish. Most came in the new automobiles, which bumped up the avenue like huge beetles.

There were Panhards, whose engines were hidden under metal bonnets, ancestors of the modern hood; two-seater Renaults with horns that twisted like snail shells and were operated by huge rubber bulbs; tall, snub-nosed Daimlers with chain drives and fold-back carriage tops, whose carbon lanterns peered ahead like eyes; and Mercedes, with bugle horns and naked rubber-tired wheels, the front pair larger than the rear.

The motorists looked like later-day aviators, in heavy leather coats with black fur collars, the men with close-fitting caps, the ladies in taller driving hats with scarves wrapped round to keep them on; both sexes were protected by big round goggles that gave them an inhuman, froggish look.

With so many guests in the house, there was no room even in the servants' quarters for the visiting chauffeurs, who gathered out on the sidewalk in the cold January wind to drink coffee and eat sandwiches provided by church temperance society vans, which brought the cold men a little cheer and made certain they did not look for stronger refreshment.

Willie and his fiancée were toasted at party after party. In the impatience of young lovers, they decided not to wait longer. With parental blessing they were married in a Catholic ceremony, in deference to the bride, at Mrs. Oelrichs's house on April 4, 1899. Neily Vanderbilt was there. So was his father, but they did not speak, and old Cornelius was helped in and out of the mansion by his two younger sons Alfred and Reginald, who handled him —quite rightly—as tenderly as one of the precious Meissen china figures that filled the cabinets at The Breakers.

After the wedding, Willie and Birdie set off for their honeymoon, which they intended to spend at Idle Hour in the same suite of rooms used by Consuelo and the Duke of Marlborough when they had begun married life at William Kissam's Long Island estate.

A week later, long after the newlyweds had retired for the

night, a Pinkerton detective who had been assigned to keep interlopers away discovered a fire in the cellar of the Queen Anne-
style mansion. Observing protocol, he called the superintendent
of the estate, who roused Willie and his bride. Birdie remembered
the half-dozen household servants on the third floor; she sent the
superintendent to get them out before it was too late.

There was little time to waste, for the fire burned quickly in
the frame building. The first small blaze was discovered at four
o'clock in the morning, but in half an hour it had coursed through
the first floor and was leaping the stairs.

Neither Willie nor his wife had time to dress properly. Willie
had thrown on slacks and an old sweater. Birdie rescued a shirt
and her underclothes, but no blouse. But she found a fur-trimmed
opera cloak and a soft black hat in which to go outside. In a plain
wooden chair that Willie brought her, Birdie sat a safe distance
from the fire with a quilt over her feet, and watched the mansion
burn.

The servants dragged out a small steam engine to pump water,
but they had no hose. Willie went to the nearby railroad station to
call for help on the telephone, but the phones were dead—all the
operators had gone to bed. Finally someone roused the Sayville
fire department, and soon firemen were running onto the scene,
dragging hose behind them as they came. Their hose, unfortunately, would not fit the coupling on the steam engine, and when
it was adapted, the hose squirted water everywhere but from the
nozzle; it was rotten and full of holes.

At six-thirty in the morning seven gaunt chimneys blackened
the April sky, standing above a pile of brick and rubble that had
been William Kissam Vanderbilt's pride. Willie and Birdie Vanderbilt walked shakily to the lodge at the west gate of the estate,
where the servants made them some breakfast. Then they climbed
on the seven-thirty train for New York, bound for the Waldorf-
Astoria Hotel, to inform Willie's father, rest, and buy new ward-
robes. Two hours later they arrived at the Waldorf looking like a
pair of ragamuffins. Telephone operators had awakened by then
and were on the job, so the pair were met with motherly sympathy
by both Mrs. Oelrichs and Alva Belmont.

William Kissam Vanderbilt accepted the loss with his usual equanimity, and put an architect to work on plans to rebuild— rather, to build a bigger house. The young couple resumed their interrupted honeymoon.

That fall Willie and Birdie went to Paris, and stopped at the exclusive Elysée Palace. Willie bought an open 6-hp Panhard et Levasseur automobile whose seat was fully five feet off the ground; it had one head lamp and a horn on the steering wheel. They decided to begin with a motor trip to Nice and on November 1, 1899, they set out on their adventure, the back loaded with extra Michelin tires, circulating pumps, *brûleurs, tubes de platinum,* and all the other necessities for the motorist of 1899. Birdie was almost invisible in a heavy double-breasted fur motoring coat, a lap robe hitched up snug, and a rakish velvet hat pulled low over her forehead, surrounded by bags, extra wraps, hot-water cans, and a small lunch basket. Willie wore an overcoat with a rolling black silk lapel, a sport jacket, a white shirt with high collar, a bow tie, and a black derby hat. The mechanic rode on a little hard seat in back with the *brûleurs* and *tubes de platinum.*

They departed at 11 A.M. and drove to Villeneuve, to Melun, through the green-black forest of Fontainebleau and past the cross erected in memory of a disastrous robbery of the Lyons mail coach years before.

At Fontainebleau the mechanic tried a little robbery of his own. He announced, quite suddenly, that he wanted $100 a month and expenses, or he would not go a step further. Quite obviously this poor mechanic did not know the Vanderbilt tradition; he was hustled aboard a train and sent back to Paris without further conversation. Willie and Birdie drove to the Hotel de l'Aigle Noire for lunch, then left the automobile in the care of the concierge and returned to Paris by train to find another mechanic. They had traveled 60 kilometers by car in two hours and twenty minutes, at an average of 15 miles an hour.

Two days later the Vanderbilts were in Fontainebleau again, this time with a mechanic whose only apparent fault was his insistence on having his picture taken in the automobile at every opportunity. They traveled over hills to Sens, over rolling land to

Auxerre, where they stopped at the Hôtel de la Fontaine (dirty rooms and poor eating); 116 kilometers in four hours and twenty minutes.

They set out the next morning at eight o'clock, to get out of their musty rooms and into the fresh country air. Luckily they were too late for the procession of French farm carts, for the drivers, who rose with the sun, slept their way to the fields, their horses plodding down either side of the road that took their fancy.

The trio stopped for lunch on the bridge that crosses the Arroux River. In the afternoon they reached the village of Cluny, where they asked a small boy if any gasoline was available in the town. The boy jumped on the step of the machine, and with what seemed to be the entire population of the village trailing behind, conducted them to La Grande Place, where the hotel was situated.

Willie and Birdie left the mechanic to fill the tank and went inside for dinner. Willie asked if the proprietor had a private room where he could serve them, since Birdie was tired after the long, jouncing ride, and did not wish to enter a public dining room.

"You can have what you want, Mr. Vanderbilt," said the proprietor.

Willie started. How could a village innkeeper in the heartland of France know who he was?

He was about to ask, when the man moved off to find a menu for Mme. Vanderbilt.

"How is Mr. Hoyt?" the man asked, as he handed over the menu.

Willie thought for a moment that he was losing his mind, but the *hôtelier* identified himself as a former cook on William Kissam Vanderbilt's yacht, the *Alva*, and an old acquaintance of both Willie and his father's traveling companion, Winfield Scott Hoyt.

After dinner that night they debated the next move. The road to Mâcon, the next large town, was both mountainous and lonely. Rich American motorists were a novelty, but unloved by the peasants, who were not fond of the racket and dust of automobiles, and resented the high death toll the new autos caused among their fowl and farm animals. Since Birdie was aboard, Willie decided the wisest course was to take the train to Lyons, so they did, and the mechanic brought the automobile along the next day.

The trip proceeded smoothly enough as far as Marseilles, where they stopped at the Hôtel de Louvre et de la Paix. Birdie stepped down and entered the hotel, and Willie began collecting the baggage, when suddenly the mechanic infuriated the crowd of townspeople who had gathered around the machine by shaking the dust from the lap robes in their faces. The crowd began to snarl, and to close around the machine. Willie was ready for violence, but several gendarmes arrived on the scene, and scattered the mob.

From Marseilles they drove to Toulon, then to Saint-Maxime, where they were detoured from the main road and lost their way. Finally, they reached Fréjus, and began the ascent of the rugged mountain called Esterel, along a wild, steep road. At the summit they breathed a sigh of relief, but the worst was yet to come. On the descent Willie burned out both sets of brakes and the right front tire went flat.

Out came the Michelin tires, the circulating pump, and a *brûleur* to heat the patch. In half an hour they were on their way again, and three hours later, after lunch at Cannes, they arrived safely at the Hôtel Grande Bretagne in Nice. The trip had taken eight days of travel time, and thirty-nine hours and six minutes of driving time.

In Nice Birdie occupied herself with the sun and visits to her friends while Willie went out almost daily to risk life and limb in his motorcar.

On a trip to Pau with a companion, he killed two dogs which had attacked the automobile's tires. A mob started after them, crying for revenge, but the Panhard outran the villagers, with Vanderbilt at the wheel, coaxing every bit of power out of the machine. That same day he ran into a hay wagon, damaging the wagon but leaving the Panhard unscarred.

Willie drove Birdie to Toulouse one day but they ran into rain and decided to leave the car with the mechanic and take the train as far as Pau. The train stopped for lunch en route, and Birdie dawdled over her food, even after the guard had announced departure. With husbandly courtesy, Willie sauntered out of the restaurant with her, only to see the train moving out of the depot with all their luggage on board. He rushed to the platform and jumped on the last car, put his head through the window, and hung on outside while he shouted to the people inside the last compartment to pull the alarm signal. Those inside jumped up shouting directions to him and to each other, and all began trying to pull the alarm at once. Willie heaved a sigh of relief—until he felt the train gathering speed. He jumped off, and luckily landed on soft ground without injury.

They waited six hours for a train so they could catch up with their baggage at the next stop.

A few days later, François, the mechanic, broke the drive chain on one axle, and somehow the lamp burner got out of kilter. Willie took the machine into the shop, where he learned that François had used ordinary carbide to refill the lamp instead of the Bleriot carbide that was needed. Willie was to be greatly congratulated, the Bleriot people said, smiling, because fortunately the machine had not blown up.

When the motor trip was ended, Willie jotted down a few notes to guide other travelers, advising them about maps ("*les Cartes Taride*, available at any librarian's"), routes ("keep as much as possible to the national highways, *les Routes des Departements* being usually in bad repair"), and starting point (Fontainebleau, not Paris, because it always seemed impossible to get away from Paris on time, and Fontainebleau had an excellent hotel).

Later, he published these notes, as part of a privately printed book titled *Log of My Motor*, and added some other "little tricks in the game" which he had discovered:

First: Take as little luggage as possible.

Second: Overhaul all extra parts, tools, and tire supplies yourself before leaving Paris, and see that all are intact.

Third: Eat no solid food at the luncheon hour, as the vibration of the car prevents digestion.

Fourth: Remember that all hotel-keepers are ready to "do"
the motorist, and fix a price for rooms before retiring.

Obviously touring in those days was not a set routine of arrival
and departure, guided tour to museum and instruction on the direction of the *lavabos* at all stopping places. Only the rich could
afford to travel, and they had to be prepared to undergo inconvenience and sometimes hardship. Travel really was a young man's
affair, even to the civilized spas of Europe. The danger and inconvenience were more than doubled in such out-of-the-way
places as the Orient, and for that reason, when Willie's cousin
Alfred Gwynne Vanderbilt announced his intention of traveling
around the world in 1899, his trip was the talk of New York and
Newport society.

Alfred was a tall young man, just a year younger than Willie,
but a serious youth. At twenty-one he had studied at St. Paul's
School and later at Groton, and had been graduated from Yale in
the spring of 1899. After graduation he planned the world trip.
Late in July, Alfred and three friends borrowed Cornelius Vanderbilt's private railroad car (No. 403) for the first leg of their
journey to Vancouver, British Columbia. Car 403 had four staterooms, all finished in mahogany. Each stateroom was equipped
with a washstand, a bureau, and a wardrobe. The car had a dining
compartment, a library, an observation room at the end, and a
main saloon upholstered in rich blue velvet. It carried a piano
and a harp, a pantry, a kitchen, a wine cellar, and a private bar.

No one saw the boys off at the train, except a half-dozen rail-
road men in gold lace and a Pinkerton who kept away the press.
Four servants and their baggage went on ahead, to meet them at
Vancouver. A few days later they all sailed on the *Empress of
India* for the Far East.

Alfred had reached China on September 12, 1899, when his
father died suddenly in bed in his Fifth Avenue house, early on
the morning that was to have been devoted to an important meeting of the New York Central board of directors. Chauncey Depew
had arrived early that morning from Newport to attend the board
meeting and called for Vanderbilt. When he learned the news, he

called the coronor and rushed to the house to take charge of arrangements.

William Kissam came to the house and took over for the family. He called the others together, including Neily, who was visiting at Newport. Reginald, the third son, a sophomore at Yale that year, was staying at The Breakers and he came in to the city. The one conspicuous absence at the sober family gathering was that of Grace Wilson Vanderbilt, Neily's wife. She pleaded illness and remained at the house the young Vanderbilts had rented in Newport. (The birth of her second child was expected momentarily.)

Few people in New York realized just how well loved Cornelius Vanderbilt had been, or how deeply his charities had penetrated beneath the skin of his city. Shortly after his death wires and messages of condolence began to arrive at the house by the hundreds. The St. Nicholas Society, the Y.M.C.A., the Episcopal missionary society—all sent special greetings from their governing bodies. So did the Newport Casino, and scores of other organizations in which Cornelius Vanderbilt had been active. He was a director of a dozen important charities and he not only gave his name to these institutions but, until his illness, had been active in their affairs.

They took him to St. Bartholomew's Church on Park Avenue for the funeral. J. Pierpont Morgan was a pallbearer. The funeral cortege drove to the Staten Island ferry, in the Vanderbilt tradition, and the second Cornelius was buried in the family mausoleum. The most impressive monument to his memory was the stream of personal and written condolences that continued to pour in for months. This Cornelius Vanderbilt was beloved to many other Americans; he was a man whose charities had extended far beyond the knowledge of any of the other Vanderbilts.

Yet with all his Christian charity the father had refused to see the son who had angered him. Neily's pale face reflected the emotions that tore him as he joined the funeral ceremonies. Others, outside the family, could not help regarding Neily speculatively. The interesting—and important—question about Neily Vanderbilt was, What had his father left him in his will?

V

THE FRAGMENTATION

23

THE SCHISM DEEPENS

The cachet of the head of the Vanderbilt family for two generations had been the gold medal Congress had bestowed on the
Commodore for his gift of the S.S. *Vanderbilt* during the Civil
War. That medal had been passed down to William Henry with
the fortune. He had willed the medal to Cornelius II, while splitting the vast residual estate between his two eldest sons. The disposition of Cornelius II's half of the fortune would now indicate
what road the Vanderbilts intended to follow: the Commodore's
way would have been to restore the bulk of the fortune to one
set of hands, and that would have meant making William Kissam
Vanderbilt head of the family. William Henry's way would have
been to put the fortune in the hands of the sons who showed interest in the railroads, and that would have placed the bulk of
Cornelius II's share in the hands of Cornelius III, who was the
only son old enough to have actually begun a railroad career.

What course had Cornelius II decided on?

Before the will could be read the family had to await the return
of Alfred Gwynne Vanderbilt from the Far East.

In the interim, William Kissam took over the management of
his brother's affairs. Neily Vanderbilt, pale but outwardly impas-
sive, kept to his office in Grand Central Terminal, with week ends
in Newport, where a daughter, Grace, was born on September 25,
1899. Alfred Gwynne caught the first ship home from China. The

widow repaired to The Breakers to await Alfred's return and to supervise the younger children.

The will must wait, but the affairs of the New York Central could not wait so long. The Central had adopted a system of paying quarterly dividends—then 1 per cent—and the board of directors had to act. The meeting that had been called for the day Cornelius II had died was rescheduled, and William Rockefeller, brother of the petroleum millionaire, was elected to replace Cornelius on the board.

This action raised a murmur of speculation in financial circles because, for the first time, outsiders on the board of the railroad represented business interests that in the aggregate were more powerful than the Vanderbilts, and William Rockefeller was one of the largest stockholders in the New York, New Haven and Hartford Railroad. What did that mean to the Central? What did the failure of the board to elect Cornelius Vanderbilt III mean?

Only the publication of the will of Cornelius Vanderbilt would tell.

On October 14, Alfred Gwynne returned, first to Newport, aboard the private car of President Charles Clark of the New Haven line, accompanied by eight trunks and a valet. Two days later he was in New York, closeted for three hours with William K. in the latter's office at Grand Central Terminal, while Neily worked quietly at his desk in the office of the chief engineer a few yards away.

But nothing was revealed to the public that day, or any day until the will was read in the library of The Breakers at Newport, in an atmosphere of tension as heavy as that at the reading of the Commodore's last will. The estate was not so large as that left by the Commodore, for in only two generations the family holdings had been eroded by bequests to no less than nineteen descendants, as well as several major grants to charities, and innumerable annuities, trusts, and minor inheritances for distant relatives and faithful employees.

Yet, like William Kissam's half of the fortune, Cornelius II's wealth had increased even as he spent and gave away his money and now was valued at $72,500,000.

The widow received the house on Fifty-seventh Street, The Breakers, and a trust fund of $7,000,000. Four of the five living children shared a $20,000,000 trust fund and $5,000,000 outright. Daughter Gertrude also received a million dollars in her own name.

But Alfred, not Neily or Uncle William K., received the Commodore's gold medal, the designation as head of the Cornelius Vanderbilt line, and the residuary estate of $42,575,000. Neily was cut off with a million-dollar trust fund and a half-million dollars in cash.

The date of the will was June 18, 1896, the day on which Neily had first planned to marry Grace Wilson against his father's wishes.

It was apparent that Neily's momentary change of mind, three nights before the day set for his wedding, had interrupted his father in the work of rewriting his will, and while the older man had joined his son in New York that next day, he had adopted an attitude of wait-and-see and approved the drastic changes. When Neily, after all the arguments, had changed his mind again and defied his father's wishes, Cornelius II had let the will remain in force.

Cornelius II's intent to cut off his eldest son was quite plain. The will provided that if Alfred died, the residuary estate would go to brother Reginald. If Reggie died, the estate was to be shared among the girls. Neily, tight-lipped, consulted his lawyers, Messrs. Carter and Ledyard. Like his great-uncle, Cornelius Jeremiah, Cornelius Vanderbilt III was not willing to accept the judgment of his father.

Within a few days the family interlocutor, Chauncey Depew, announced that out of the goodness of his heart Alfred Gwynne Vanderbilt was giving up an additional $6,000,000 of the estate to his elder brother, to make Neily's share as large as those of his other brother and sisters. At the words "goodness of his heart," Neily snorted. There had been an agreement with Alfred, he told the newspapers, that he would get $10,000,000 from the estate.

Would he sue, the newspapermen asked?

Neily Vanderbilt, at home, thought that over for a moment, looking first at the ceiling and then at his parlor floor, one slim foot cocked on the seat of a red plush chair, his hands in his pockets, and only his hollow cheeks and red-rimmed, sunken eyes betraying the emotions that had ravaged him in the last few days.

Finally, he scratched his head, and answered.

"Per . . . haps," he drawled.

Neily did not try to break the will, but from that day the relations of Cornelius Vanderbilt III and his immediate family were never the same.

The following summer—1900—while twenty-three-year-old Alfred was traveling in Europe, cementing his engagement to the heiress Elsie French, and while cousin Willie K. Vanderbilt II was charging up and down the hills of Newport in his motorcar, frightening horses and annoying the constabulary, Neily Vanderbilt labored over his drawing board in the office of the New York Central. He had an idea for a type of locomotive firebox, containing a cylindrical boiler, which would cut costs and increase locomotive efficiency and power. Neily's superiors in the chief engineer's office encouraged him. They told the Baldwin Locomotive Works about the plan, and Superintendent Vauclain was interested. Baldwin then built a model, tested it on a locomotive July 26, and Superintendent Vauclain announced that it was a success.

Neily also showed some interest in politics that year—Republican politics, of course. He had met Senator Edward O. Wolcott of Colorado while traveling abroad, and in an idle conversation, thousands of miles from home, had said he would like to attend the New York state convention, not as a spectator, but as a participant. The Coloradoan had informed Senator Thomas C. Platt, the Republican boss of New York, and Platt had passed the word along to Smith Pine, leader of New York's Twenty-fourth District. Smith Pine took over from there. When the Republican convention met on September 3, 1900, at Saratoga, Neily Vanderbilt was an elected delegate.

Neily was standing on the steps of the convention hall, talking to Postmaster Cornelius Van Cott, when some reporters in search of a story walked up to ask Mr. Vanderbilt what he thought about the fight between "Mousy" Platt and Governor Theodore Roosevelt, whom Platt had virtually railroaded, it was said, into the vice-presidential nomination to get him out of the governor's chair.

As Neily pondered the question beneath his wide-brimmed straw hat, Postmaster Van Cott grinned at the reporters slyly and straightened them out in a hurry on Mr. Vanderbilt's position in politics.

"Ask him about railroads, boys," said Mr. Van Cott. "That's something he is posted on."

New York's Republican politicos were interested in Neily—no politician could help being interested in that magic name VANDERBILT—but they had not won their political spurs without becoming hardheaded and, besides, Chauncey Depew was a power in Republican circles. How did this Vanderbilt stand with him? Young Vanderbilt was informed that if he was interested in a high elective office, he would have to be prepared to donate heavily, and commensurately, for the chance at jobs from state legislator to U. S. Senator. That was the answer: Chauncey Depew was neutral.

Neily made no bid for a political job. He did not distinguish himself on the convention floor, but this was his first convention, and he was not expected to make speeches or take over the New York City delegation, either. He did show enough interest and make enough of an impression that he was enrolled as a political speaker for the forthcoming campaign.

After the convention Neily went to Newport to join his wife and children, for while they were "poor relations," as Grace put it, they still belonged to the same society in which all Vanderbilts moved; and a summer without Newport for Grace Wilson Vanderbilt was like a dinner party without a viscount. Neily's first political speech was scheduled for October 2, before a meeting of the Austro-Hungarian Republican League of New York, a meeting which had drawn an unusually large attendance in its promise that a real, live Vanderbilt was to be the speaker of the evening.

The meeting was scheduled to begin at eight o'clock, but by that hour no Vanderbilt had put in an appearance at the hall. The chairman called the meeting to order, and the officers began to delay the proceedings with as much business as they could muster on short notice. At nine o'clock Vanderbilt was still missing, but at least the crowd was informed that he had been seen in front of his house on Fifth Avenue, and could presumably be expected to arrive at any moment.

Ten o'clock came, but no Vanderbilt. The crowd was irritated and restless by that hour, and the chairman had difficulty in keeping order. Finally, at eleven o'clock a messenger arrived with a telegram from Cornelius Vanderbilt III. He had missed his train at Newport, and must be excused from making the speech, he said.

There was no return engagement, nor any more political activity for this Vanderbilt in the campaign. Neily, the introspective, frail engineer, was not cut out to be a politician. If he had not decided so, the Republican organization decided it for him.

Neily was prepared to devote his life to railroading, however, and had given every indication of following that course, when his brother Alfred decided to enter the company that fall, following their father's steps into the office of the treasurer. On the day Alfred moved into his clerk's desk, Neily moved his simple belongings out of his place in the chief engineer's office, convinced that the handwriting was on the wall, and that the railroad empire was not big enough for both of them.

The treasurer of the New York Central, E. V. W. Rossiter, let it be known that Alfred Vanderbilt would be expected to work from nine to five, with an hour out for lunch. It was too much to expect that a young man who belonged to the exclusive Coaching Club and enjoyed polo and riding as much as Alfred did would stick to clerking, or that such a lean idol of New York society would find it easy to adjust to the workaday world. The world of the very rich was isolated from the rest of America and as the Vanderbilts gradually relinquished the operational control of their railroads, their avenues of exchange between these worlds grew fewer and narrower.

Willie K. Vanderbilt II, for example, when arrested for speeding in Milton, Massachusetts, that summer, had sent his lawyer back from Newport to plead the case and pay the $15 fine. Willie K. was busy. He had a new 70-foot yacht to sail.

Neily Vanderbilt had fallen afoul of the law when he failed to acknowledge a summons to appear for New York City jury duty. After several months of bickering, an outraged judge had fined young Vanderbilt, *in absentia*, $100, and had delivered a lecture from the bench on the failure of the wealthy to meet their obligations to society.

Neily regarded the matter as a tempest in a teapot. But the year was 1900. It was a new century, and the current of Progressivism was sweeping through the air. The Vanderbilts were no longer a law unto themselves.

In 1897 the New York State inheritance tax laws had been strengthened. The cost of government was rising; the services demanded of government multiplied, year after year, and all government, city, state, and federal, sought new ways to raise money to fill the emptying treasuries. When Cornelius Vanderbilt II died, the lawyers estimated that inheritance taxes would take $1,500,000 of the estate. That amount was paid, as due, but the state was still not satisfied. New York Controller Coler wanted an additional share of the $5,000,000 trust fund left by William Henry to Cornelius, and passed along by him, untouched, and in trust, to his children. The Vanderbilt lawyers held that the fund was not taxable. The state argued that the money was no longer part of William Henry's original estate, as claimed, but was something new. In 1900 New York Surrogate Fitzgerald decided that the Vanderbilts must pay. The amount of tax claimed was around $50,000, enough, certainly, to warrant a fight, but far more important, from the Vanderbilt point of view, was the principle involved.

Nor was the state the only tax agent threatening the Vanderbilts and other millionaires. Alfred had just passed his majority when his father died, so the bulk of the estate had been left to him in trust, but the federal government still demanded an inheritance tax of $541,000. The lawyers said no taxes were due on the part in trust and paid only $311,000, and that under protest.

In 1901 Alfred Gwynne Vanderbilt was assessed on $5,000,000 worth of personal property in New York. Not only were rates going up, but the government was increasing the values it placed on the property of the wealthy. The Vanderbilts were not alone, even if this was small consolation. The heirs of Collis P. Huntington, of the Central Pacific, Southern Pacific, and Chesapeake &

Ohio railroads, were assessed on a valuation of $3,200,000 that year.

The wealthy could see the nets of government closing in on inherited wealth, and under the generalship of William Kissam, the Vanderbilts began to fight the government claims.

Since management of his own vast fortune and the administration of the fortune of Alfred took much of his time, William K. Vanderbilt found less energy, or inclination, to concern himself with railroading. In 1901 when President S. R. Calloway resigned from the Central, William H. Newman became president of the parent line. The Central embarked on an extensive program of modernization under the new board of directors, reducing grades, rebuilding tracks, straightening curves. A new station was planned for Grand Central, with all trains to run underground almost to the northern end of Manhattan Island. But all this was accomplished by professional management, with only a casual glance from William K. and the other Vanderbilt directors. They were sitting atop the railroads now, no longer in them. The only Vanderbilt engaged in operations of the transportation industry was Neily, who had opened an office near Wall Street as a consulting engineer, and had joined forces with August Belmont to form the Interborough Rapid Transit Company, and build a subway system for New York City, a plan in which the Commodore had once been interested.

The other Vanderbilts were abroad a good deal. William K. established his house and stable at Chaumont, France. Alfred married Elsie French in the spring of 1901, and began to concentrate his interest in his farm outside Newport. The chunky Reginald was establishing a name as a scapegrace at Yale. Uncle Frederick William moved between Newport, his $600,000 mansion at Hyde Park on the Hudson, and his current yacht. Uncle George traveled from the estate in North Carolina to his Bar Harbor mansion, where he dined Van Rensselaers, Webbs, Auchinclosses, and the Swedish and Danish ministers. Cousin Willie K. spent some time at his father's house in France, bought a villa at Newport, where he was fined for speeding again along Ridge Road, and where he saved the life of Foxhall Keene by using his head in a canoeing accident off Bailey's Beach—the canoe tipped over in deep water well outside the lifeline stretched in front of the beach. Keene suffered a cramp in trying to swim back, and Willie K. rescued him and towed Keene to shore and safety.

Yet the most noteworthy of all Vanderbilts in this period was not truly a Vanderbilt at all, but the wife of one: Grace Wilson. In 1901, with enough millions to make the kind of splash she wanted, Grace Wilson set out to conquer Mrs. Astor—to rule the New York society whose doors Alva Vanderbilt had opened. With her husband Cornelius dead, Alice Gwynne Vanderbilt was the family matriarch, and Grace's only serious rival for the queen's crown, but Alice-of-The Breakers was no match for her daughter-in-law, who had breathed the perfume of European royalty almost from the day she was born. Besides, Alice Vanderbilt operated at a serious disadvantage; she was still in mourning in 1901, as her daughter-in-law began the campaign to conquer.

Neily Vanderbilt cordially detested the trappings of society, but was persuaded to buy a Newport villa on the cliffs not far from The Breakers. Grace named it Beaulieu, then set out to show all the people of any note that her summer home was important as well as beautiful. She kept seventeen vehicles, thirty horses, fifteen stable boys, a coachman, a French chef, an English butler, maids, nursemaids, footmen, and an English governess named Miss Coxhead who raised the children while Grace Vanderbilt gave parties and went calling.

In New York, Grace Vanderbilt entertained as much as she did at Newport, but entertainment alone was not enough to gain her the tiara she sought. Any number of matrons could boast the presence of dukes, earls, senators, cabinet ministers, and even Presidents of the United States at their tables. To become the leader of New York society, Grace would have to do something no one else could do. In the winter of 1902, at the height of the opera season, Grace made her move. She showed herself to be the darling of royalty—real royalty.

In February, Prince Henry of Prussia, Kaiser Wilhelm's brother, visited the United States. At the opera, with the instinct of a homing pigeon, he headed straight for Grace Wilson Vanderbilt's box.

After he had left, Mrs. Vanderbilt let it be known that she, among all the matrons of New York society, would be the one whom German royalty had decided to honor by allowing her to give a dinner for the prince. The society columnists talked of her coup for days.

It was a victory as carefully planned as the Commodore's invasion of Nicaragua. First, she had written a letter to the German ambassador, recalling that she had been kindly treated by the German Imperial family in Potsdam some years before. As the guest of her sister, Mrs. Goelet, she had met the Kaiser and his brother. What could she now do in return?

What, indeed? That was not for a mere ambassador to say, so he cabled the contents of Grace Vanderbilt's letter to Berlin. Kaiser Wilhelm never stood on ceremony, so he sent Grace Vanderbilt an Imperial cablegram ordering her to ask brother Henry to dinner, since it was the Imperial wish that the prince dine with a *representative* American family.

Before His Highness arrived, before Mrs. Astor or any of Grace's unfriendly relatives by marriage could move, Grace Wilson Vanderbilt was already worrying over guest lists and menus. J. Pierpont Morgan had the prince to lunch, and snubbed society men who had been snubbing him for years; Mrs. Ogden Mills had the prince to breakfast; but Grace Vanderbilt had the prince to dinner! It was the only full-fledged society dinner he attended in America.

Mrs. Astor retreated to Europe before the onslaught and Grace Vanderbilt moved ahead in the society sweepstakes.

In her quest of the crown, Grace's parties became more grand, and, of course, more expensive. She spent $5000 to bring the cast of *Wild Rose*, a Broadway musical, to entertain her guests at Beaulieu, and built a theater in which to house the performance. The newspapers devoted a column and a half to President Teddy Roosevelt's trip to New England, and a half a page to the Vanderbilt party at Newport, columns of words of praise for the daring young hostess who was setting Society on its ear.

Neily Vanderbilt's answer to all this activity was to closet himself in his study, to rearrange his wife's guest lists so that he sat next to debutantes instead of the dowagers she foisted upon him, and to join the New York National Guard.

He went to meetings of the Twelfth Regiment at the armory, and rode up Fifth Avenue in the big parades on a prancing charger while his children sat in the windows of their house at 677 Fifth Avenue, restrained by their governess, and admired their handsome military father in his blue and scarlet cape.

Then Lieutenant Vanderbilt went on maneuvers with the National Guard, and put a serious crimp in his wife's social plans for weeks by catching typhoid fever. He nearly died when the typhoid became peritonitis. The other Vanderbilts were notified. Alice-of-The Breakers was in Europe and she did not interrupt her trip. Alfred, the titular head of the family, was in New York, staying at the Knickerbocker Club, and he indicated that he was ready to rush to his brother's bedside just as soon as he was sure Cornelius Vanderbilt III was dying. Of all the male Vanderbilts, only Uncle Willie K. called at the house, although Reginald called on his brother in a formal sense, stopping by the house to leave a card.

And when the dowager Mrs. Vanderbilt finally returned from Europe, after Neily was out of danger, she did not pause to visit her emaciated son but drove directly to her own house on Fifty-seventh Street. Reporters asked her what chance their might be for a reconciliation of the families. Mrs. Vanderbilt indicated there was none.

The enmity between the Vanderbilts had come into full flower, pulling the family apart, and eroding the family's position in the New York Central as effectively as a series of funerals.

24

TRAGEDY ON THE HIGH SEAS

The Vanderbilt family developed no tradition whatsoever to guide the younger sons; since the Vanderbilts were not needy, the secondary heirs did not strike off abroad as did the younger sons of their peers, the nobility of England but without parental guidance or purposeful existence, these young Vanderbilts were left to shift for themselves.

Frederick William Vanderbilt and George Washington Vanderbilt were not involved in management of the railroads, nor were they directed by their father to any other profession or business. Frederick William was to succeed as a capitalist in his own right, as we shall see, but he did so through native shrewdness and by learning the vagaries of the stock market for himself. George Washington renounced the social and business worlds almost completely, as we have seen, and devoted himself to gentlemanly farming, study of languages, including Indian dialects, and big game hunting. George amused himself by translating contemporary works into Ancient Greek, which, while a pleasant and erudite occupation, scarcely advanced the sum of useful human knowledge. He did establish one of the first nurseries and private forests in America, and his foresters taught the American government the sound conservation practices they had learned from the Germans. George was, as Gifford Pinchot put it, a millionaire with a sense of responsibility. But he came by this himself, not through training.

In 1902, when the chubby Reginald Claypoole Vanderbilt

reached his majority, his mother was discharged as guardian of the share of the Cornelius Vanderbilt II fortune that had been left this third son.

It was not remarkable to see this third son's tastes turn to wine, girls, horses, and fast motorcars. Reginald might resemble the Gwynnes of his mother's side more in looks than he did the Vanderbilts, but his tastes descended straight from the Commodore— except the wine. The last was Reginald's own contribution.

He was supposed to be graduated from Yale in the spring of 1902, but with eleven other young men Reggie was denied his diploma, for the twelve had failed the law examination of Professor Henry Wade Rogers, former president of Northwestern University and later dean of the law school. After the turn of the century he was the scourge of the Yale campus. Professor Rogers set high standards. If the young men did not conform, he did not care who they were—they would not get their sheepskins.

It was a disappointment, but failure did not induce Reggie to return to college to make up the deficiency and the following autumn all twelve of the offenders were granted their diplomas, without comment.

That year Reggie became engaged to Cathleen Neilson, a twenty-year-old heiress and one of the most beautiful girls in Newport society, whose golden brown hair, soft eyes, and clear skin had bewitched most of society's eligible bachelors and when he was not squiring Cathleen to Bailey's Beach or the Spouting Rock Club, sailing, or dancing, Reggie might be found in New York enjoying some of the brighter spots of the city's night life.

One place of excitement in New York was Richard Canfield's brownstone house at 5 East Forty-fourth Street, a few steps off Fifth Avenue. There, behind intricate wall panelings inlaid with mother-of-pearl, Mr. Canfield kept roulette wheels and other gambling equipment. When Mr. Canfield was reasonably sure that the police and their informers were looking the other way, he opened the house to men and women who sought refined excitement. Alfred sometimes went there. So did Reggie. When Canfield's was raided by a reforming district attorney, the officers found $300,000 worth of Reggie's I.O.U.s in the Canfield safe. While Reggie's fortune amounted to approximately $7,000,000, nothing like that amount was readily available to him, even after he became twenty-one, for most of his money was held in trust, from which he drew the income. Finally, to Canfield's disgust, Reggie's attorneys settled the debt for $130,000. But at least young Vanderbilt had the good grace to refuse to testify in court against Canfield (as did nearly all the gambler's wealthy clients).

In Reggie's case, the refusal involved both courage and resourcefulness. The district attorney, William Travers Jerome, was doing his best to put Richard Canfield behind bars, and he knew that the testimony of a Vanderbilt would stimulate the press and sway a jury, so for months Jerome's detectives lay in wait for Reginald Vanderbilt whenever it was reported that he might be in the city but Reginald stayed in Rhode Island where he made his home at Sandy Point Farm, Portsmouth, not far from Newport. In 1903 he and Cathleen were married, and in 1904 Cathleen gave birth to a baby girl who was named for her mother.

Even as late as this, District Attorney Jerome's men continued to set traps for Reggie, at his mother's house, at all his clubs, and at the house of his father-in-law at 100 Fifth Avenue. But tracking a rich young man who is insulated from the ordinary world and catching him were two different things, as the district attorney's men discovered.

Like his brother Alfred, Reggie loved thoroughbred horses. He traveled widely to enter his harness racers in fashionable shows. In the spring of 1904 he set out for Philadelphia, stopping quietly in New York to visit his wife's parents. District Attorney Jerome's men heard of his appearance in the city and rushed to the scene to capture this elusive young man. They waited for days. Finally, the butler came outside the house, walked straight to the horse-drawn coupé behind which two of the D.A.s men were standing in their bowler hats trying their best to look like honest loiterers.

"You might as well go," the butler said, grinning. "He was here, but he's gone."

The detectives looked at the sky and tried to pretend they did not know what the butler was talking about, but the newspapers got wind of the story, and soon the police were joined in their ambush by a handful of reporters who gleefully reported the course of events.

Meanwhile, however, Reggie Vanderbilt and his wife *had* flown the coop and had motored to Philadelphia for the horse show, stopping at the Bellevue Stratford Hotel.

The show was a miserable failure from Reggie's point of view. Main Line society was conservative to the core. The dowagers were scandalized by Reggie's game of hide-and-seek with the police, so the young Vanderbilts were not invited to a single reception or ball during this gay season and even the judges discriminated against Reggie on the tanbark. He drove his own horse—Dr. Selworth— in the harness class. It was common knowledge around the ring that the $8000 Dr. Selworth was the best horse of its class in the show, yet Reggie won only the orange ribbon of third prize. The insult was repeated when he drove Fad and Fancy, his prize blacks into the ring and put them through their paces. His prize was another orange ribbon.

Even fate was against him. On the morning of June 6, having shipped the horses down to the Wilmington show, Reggie and Cathleen stepped into their motorcar and directed the chauffeur to drive to Delaware in time for the first event. On a lonely country road in Chester County the motorcar broke down. They shoved the auto into a field and left it in the care of a sympathetic farmer, who was not, however, so sympathetic that he offered to drive them. So they walked, the chauffeur in his tight boots and heavy uniform, Reggie in his straw hat and flannels, and Cathleen in her heavy, long motoring dress. For miles they walked, feet blistering and perspiration running down their faces, stopping from time to time to let Cathleen catch her breath. The hour for the show arrived and passed, and still they walked, breathless and angry. Finally they reached a station of a branch railroad line and returned to Philadelphia by train, the horse show over, the car in the far reaches of Chester County.

"Automobiles?" growled Reginald, with the greatest dignity he could muster, when they met the press. "I'm through with them forever."

So Reggie and Cathleen went home to Sandy Point by train,

not through New York, where District Attorney Jerome's detectives lay in wait, but by way of Detroit, Montreal, and Boston. It was weeks before the district attorney discovered what had happened, and by that time Reggie had lost his momentary distaste for the unreliable motorcar and was whizzing up the roads of Newport once again.

In Newport automobiling, Reggie joined his brother Alfred, who had a great deal of interest in auto racing, and his cousin Willie K. II, who had been totally captivated by the sport and was to become the leading automobile enthusiast in America.

Alfred, as the chosen "head of the family" was the Vanderbilt who was expected to assume control of the railroad empire eventually, but it was Willie K. II, not Alfred, who showed interest in railroads. Alfred had a desk at Grand Central but he was never there. Willie's was the only interest shown by a Vanderbilt in railroad work, outside that of Cornelius Vanderbilt III, who had come as close to disinheritance as any Vanderbilt. Willie K. II went into his father's office in Grand Central and he worked up to become a vice-president of the New York Central. His railroad career did not interfere with yachting and motoring, however; almost every year after his marriage he sailed to Europe and spent happy days motoring through France, Italy, and Switzerland.

Motoring, Willie decided, was the one true adventure. In March 1902 he nearly froze to death in a snowstorm when he and his friend David Bishop were caught in the mountains near the village of Luc-en-Diois. That same year he was thrown out of his Renault racing car when traveling 60 miles an hour. He feared he had lost his taste for fast driving—but the next week he won third place in the *Circuit des Ardennes* race, and set a new record for the longest run in automobiling history—571¼ miles in 13 hours' running time.

The next year Willie K. was arrested while speeding along the Côte d'Azur countryside in his 60-hp Mors racer. The gendarmes took him to jail in Monte Carlo, threw him into a dungeon, and left him with a candle stuck in a beer bottle. The charge was driving without lights. He persuaded a gendarme to feel the car headlamps; they were hot, but the policeman shrugged his shoulders and left Willie to his fate. There had been a complaint.

Finally, Willie persuaded the police to call their chief (who was an old friend) and he was freed thereafter within minutes.

In 1903 Willie entered the grueling Paris–Madrid race, which began at Madrid on May 24. Vanderbilt started in sixtieth place but was immediately disqualified for having approached on the wrong side of the timer and bowled over nearly a hundred men and women sitting on boxes and barrels at the beginning of the race, without, however, injuring anyone. He was allowed to start again, as No. 64.

Maurice Renault, of the motorcar company family, started just behind Vanderbilt. Not long afterward Renault was killed, as was his mechanic, when the dust from a car ahead blinded him and the car ran headlong into a tree.

Lorraine Barrow, a friend of Vanderbilt's, was killed between Versailles and Paris when he swerved to avoid a dog in the road, and split his car in two against another tree.

The race was finally stopped on the second round, at Bordeaux, after fifteen people had been killed, but Vanderbilt had been knocked out of the race at Chartres, having started sixty-fourth again from Paris on the return trip. His time showed he was well up among the front-runners, and he had passed several cars—when the bottom fell out of his 60-hp Mors racer, a twin of the car that eventually won the race.

By this time, having suffered through nearly a decade of the motorcar fad, French peasants were thoroughly annoyed by the automobilists who came racing through their country lanes, wrecking property, and speeding on without stopping. The motorists, of course, were afraid to stop, for a number of them had been badly mauled by villagers when they had tried to make reparation for damage done.

On a trip from Avignon to Hyéres, with Birdie, accompanied by Leon Graves and James Arden Harriman in another car, Willie came as close to losing his life as he had ever come.

Willie and Birdie whizzed around a corner to find a cart pulled across the road, being unloaded in the field on the side. Willie slowed down almost to stopping as they crawled past, but the owner of the cart suddenly raised his whip and tried to strike Willie in the face. Willie and Birdie ducked and the lash went over their heads. Willie stopped the car. The men around the cart picked up rocks while the cart owner waved his whip and urged the men on. They began, ominously, to advance on the Vanderbilt car. Willie pulled the revolver he always wore stuck in his belt when motoring and fired a shot over their heads. The men stopped, then began, without saying a word, to advance again. Willie shouted in French that the next time he would not shoot over their heads.

Then they heard the hum of Graves's motorcar coming around the bend. The leader of the band smiled evilly, and turned with his whip, ready to lash at the heads of the next drivers. The others made their rocks ready. Willie warned them that if they slashed the whip or threw one rock, he would shoot. His stern tone and his revolver cowed the peasants, and with lordly aplomb, Vanderbilt and his party drove on.

A few days later, when Willie passed through Villefranche, a man with a stick tried to hit him on the head. Willie drew his gun, but unfortunately the man was a plain-clothes policeman, who promptly arrested Willie for threatening an officer and clapped him into jail. He was condemned to two days' imprisonment, but finally, after telegraphing Paris for legal help and diplomatic support, he was let off with a lecture and a fine.

On March 17, at Melun, when Willie turned a corner in the road he came upon a two-wheeled cart standing in the middle of the road, next to a three-story house. Inside the cart was a ladder which leaned against the house, and on the ladder stood a man, painting. Willie put on his brakes, but he sideswiped the cart before he could stop and knocked off two of its wheels. The ladder came crashing to the ground, leaving the painter hanging onto the roof and screaming. Willie looked back. A crowd was beginning to collect. He drove on.

But if touring was a thrilling and dangerous game, it could not compare with auto racing for sport and danger. From European racing, Willie turned to competition in the new sport in America. He won the American Automobile Association cup in 1904 and set a record: a mile in 39 seconds at Ormond Beach, Florida. That year, at Palm Beach, he gave newspapermen an exhibition of gymnastic skill and trick bicycle riding in front of the Hotel Poinciana. He vaulted over the handlebars of his bicycle, rode backward, bucked the bicycle up onto its hind wheel, and jumped with it. He stood on one pedal, and he stood on the saddle, white flannels shimmering against his legs, small dark mustache standing starkly against tanned skin. He was a handsome devil, twenty-six years old, athletic and strong—every inch a sportsman.

But not all Americans looked with approbation on the sportsmanship of the Vanderbilts, or on their fondness for motoring.

The problem with motorcars was that they were foreign (most of them) and that they represented great riches. Willie decided to woo the public by encouraging American manufacture and motoring: he offered a cup and a $20,000 prize for road racing on a course he selected on Long Island. He chose Long Island because of the terrain, for one reason, but because he had bought an estate there, on Lake Success, for another. The course ran from his estate out east of Mineola and back again. It was dangerous and fast, and from start to finish the race was a thrill each year, although the French usually seemed to win it. The 30-mile course was run ten times, over the dirt road whose thin film of oil made the driving both fast and treacherous. Thousands lined the raceway each year, sometimes as many as ten thousand at the hairpin turn at the end of the course, and other thousands rode by train to Mineola, then tramped the three miles to the grandstand at the start and finish line, where the drivers lined up with their cars, pulled on their gauntlets, adjusted their goggles, and sped off.

By 1906 Willie K. saw enough enthusiasm for automobiling to plan a special motoring road. He formed a corporation called the Long Island Motor Parkway, Inc. William Gibbs McAdoo invested in it as did August Belmont and Harry Payne Whitney. The plan called for a special toll road that would run from Lake Ronkonkoma (in the middle of Long Island) to Horace Harding Boulevard in New York's metropolitan area.

Willie liked Long Island. At Deepdale, his Lake Success home, he opened a chicken farm, and kept a game preserve for his hunting friends. He spent a good deal of his time riding around the area, especially around Lake Success, which he was trying very hard to acquire for himself, although the people of North Hempstead owned three rights of way to the lake.

Willie built a house on Fifth Avenue, too, next to his father's mansion, and like his father, Willie and Birdie moved back and forth from Europe to Newport, to Long Island, to New York. They had three children: Muriel, Consuelo, and William Kissam Vanderbilt III, and while Willie was a good father, and sometimes even worked at railroading, still he found plenty of time for motoring at home and abroad, and for yachting aboard his *Tarantula*.

This period was the heyday of the millionaires, who were then virtually free from any kind of interference—although not for long. Willie's father, William Kissam, had married again, eight years after his divorce from Alva; his second wife was Anne Harriman Sands Rutherford, and, after his marriage, William K. spent most of his time at his stately horse farm in Normandy, enjoying life after a hectic career in society and the business world. New York Central stock was doing well: in 1906 the directors raised the dividend to 6 per cent. And if death taxes and inheritance taxes were becoming harsher, still there was no income tax to harass the millionaire. The Vanderbilt money, when properly invested, continued to earn faster than the Vanderbilts could spend.

So Willie K. built his highway, motored on his yacht and sailed his boats, and raced his motorcars around the Deepdale estate with skill and daring. One day he was out driving along Lake Success when an axle gave way and the car careened along the bank, throwing Willie into the lake. Birdie was frightened when she heard of the experience, but Willie K. just laughed. He thought it was a huge joke.

Cousin Alfred, nearly as smitten as Willie with motorcars for a time, rode in the Vanderbilt cup race in 1905, in his own 90-hp Fiat. Yet Alfred was not so skillful a driver as his cousin, and he knew it, so he put himself in the mechanic's seat and hired a professional racing driver named Sartori to handle the car. They did not finish. The car broke down before the end of the race.

But Alfred often drove around Newport, and sometimes drove

from Newport to New York. American farmers were not so different from their French brethren, he found, for at Newport both he and Reginald were harassed by rock-throwers who lay in wait for them along the roads that led to Alfred's Oakland farm and Reggie's Sandy Point.

Alfred was by far the most handsome of this fourth generation of wealthy Vanderbilts. Reggie had a round, homely face; Cornelius III's face was saved from weakness only by the heavy black beard and mustache that he kept sharply trimmed; and that resulted in a look of great severity, one that matched his growingly misanthropic disposition. Of the other branch of the family, Harold was a good-looking young man with clear eyes, a ready smile, and that Vanderbilt eagle's look about him; Willie K. was dapper, a man of the world. But of them all, Alfred was the ideal American millionaire. He stood just over 5 feet 8 inches in height, average for his day; he was slender, although not skinny as was his brother Neily, and Alfred's regular features were of the type later to be characterized as "matinee idol."

Like Willie K., Alfred was a sportsman. His taste ran more to horses than to sailing, and motorcars were scarcely more than a passing fancy for him, as it turned out. He built the largest exercise ring in America for his farm and began to raise racing horses and exhibition horses. He was active in the American Forestry Association, the American Jersey Cattle Association, the Irish Terrier Club of America, and the New York Historical Society, and belonged to every distinguished social club in which he had the slightest interest. His interests were wide and they included nearly every gentlemanly pursuit. They did not include railroading.

When he was twenty-eight years old, in 1905, the courts finally settled the inheritance tax question that had been raised by the federal government after the death of Alfred's father. The $311,000 that William K. had paid the government on Alfred's behalf was supposed to be returned if and when Congress got around to making an appropriation, for the law governing the inheritance tax had been repealed, and since under that law the tax would not have been due for two more years, now it would not be due at all.

The next year the taxes on the trust funds left by Cornelius II

were settled, as well, for a total of $66,000 and the problems of
millionaires seemed less pressing. Even in the depression of 1907,
when Central stock fell to 91½—a low point it had not reached
since 1885, the Vanderbilt fortunes were only mildly, or momentarily, affected.

Yet not all the Vanderbilts fared so well. George Washington
Vanderbilt, Alfred's uncle, had invested his money very heavily
in land and buildings. George's foresters sold quantities of young
stock to nurseries all over the United States, but that only began
to meet the expenses of operating a barony, which had its own
tiny village to support, too. By 1903 George had tired of the estate
and leased 125,000 acres to a group of North Carolina rich men
who planned to use it for a private hunting preserve for ten years.
George retained only a thousand acres around Biltmore itself. He
grew tired of the mansion on Fifth Avenue, so in 1904 he leased
the house to millionaire Henry Frick, while that steel magnate's
own house at Seventy-first Street was being built.

The highest living Vanderbilts of all were Cornelius Vanderbilt
III and his family, largely because Grace Wilson Vanderbilt had
set herself an expensive assignment in keeping ahead of Society.

Neily, who liked yachts anyhow, was persuaded to buy one of
the most luxurious afloat, although he could ill afford it and it
made a steady drain on his capital—at $7,000,000, slender capital
as Vanderbilt fortunes went. He named the yacht the *North Star*,
in honor of his great-grandfather. She was 233 feet long and 30
feet wide, and it cost several thousand dollars a month just to
keep her in the water. On board, Vanderbilt played Commodore
—ascending the gangplank ahead of his wife, according to marine
protocol, and always wearing the blue jacket and white trousers of
his yachting suit. His two children had special yachting outfits,
complete to English sailor hats labeled S.Y. (Steam Yacht) *North
Star*.

Grace Wilson had some ideas of her own that fitted well with
Neily's yacht and yachting. She knew everyone who was anyone
among the crowned heads of Europe, and she announced that
she and Neily could sell enough of his engineering inventions to
pay for the cost of yachting.

This idea was typical of Grace Wilson's approach to business matters. Neily was an inventor, and she knew he fussed around with fireboxes, dynamos, and other strange things about which she knew absolutely nothing, but if he could invent them, they must be useful to other people, too, and she would sell them to the Kaiser and other acquaintances.

And on that basis (Neily, of course, yielding to this strange reasoning because he really liked to play Commodore) the "poor" Vanderbilts went abroad to sell Neily's inventions, Grace being quite convinced that Neily was just as great an inventor as Thomas Alva Edison.

That first year they went to Naples, where they visited Britain's King Edward VII aboard his yacht in the bay. The children saw for the first time a king, who impressed them because his pants were creased on the sides, not down the center of the knees as were their father's and those of all ordinary men. They cruised along the German coast, gave a party with fireworks for Kaiser Wilhelm on the Fourth of July, and Wilhelm saved little Neil from falling overboard. They visited Russia and Czar Nicholas II —and Neily, who had the same kind of beard, was mistaken for the Czar by Russian peasants on the outskirts of St. Petersburg. Grace was all smiles to royalty and all haughtiness to everyone else.

Neily went home at the end of the yachting season, but Grace and the two children stayed on in Paris, with an occasional trip to Bad Nauheim or Bad Homburg to sweat in hot tubs, take the waters and relax. Relaxation for Grace, in those days, consisted largely of giving small parties (twenty or thirty people) rather than large ones (two hundred or three hundred guests). Her idea of heaven was to give parties in New York during opera season, to give parties in Newport during the summer, to give parties on the yacht, to give parties in Paris, and Rome, and Berlin, Cannes, and Geneva, London, and any other place she happened to light for even a day or two. It was exhausting work that might have felled one not born to the spirit royal, and twice a year even Grace felt it was necessary to take a rest, which she did at Hot Springs, Va., lying in bed late, soaking in the springs, and readying herself again to enter the lists and do battle to retain her crown.

When he got away from Grace, and out on the high seas among cronies of his own, Neily drank heavily. By this time, a decade after his marriage, Neily had begun to realize that the marriage was very definitely a mistake. He had nothing in common with his wife except the children, and in truth, he was a better engineer than a father, although he played with his son's electric train and sometimes took the boy riding in Central Park in the mornings.

The old breach in the Vanderbilt family was not yet healed. Neily and Alfred nodded but did not speak when they met at the New York Yacht Club or on Fifth Avenue. Neily and his mother did not get along well either, particularly since Alice-of-The Breakers had never recognized Grace, had not spoken to her for eleven years, and practically never spoke about her.

But finally, Gladys Vanderbilt, Neily's sister, became engaged to Count Laszlo Széchényi, a Hungarian nobleman who maintained a palace on Andrassy Utcza in Budapest. Gladys wrote Grace about it, swearing her to secrecy—and naturally, Grace, whose life revolved around European royalty, revealed the secret to everyone in New York who counted.

Gladys was too happy to care. She insisted that her mother invite the Neily Vanderbilts to The Breakers for an engagement party. Grace, of course, refused to attend, but Neily went—and at the end of the party he invited his mother to Beaulieu for lunch the next day, and his mother, after setting her lips, said, "All right, if Grace will not come to me, I shall go to her." Grace may not have liked it, but there was nothing she could do except be cold, which she was. Grace did not arise when her mother-in-law came into the room, or in any other way bestir herself. The dislike the two women felt for one another was never to be overcome, but at least they began speaking, exchanging invitations, and writing notes to one another. It was a great relief to the rest of Society, whose members often felt as though they were walking on eggs in their efforts to keep out of the fray between the Vanderbilts, and it had taken a minute knowledge of the *Social Register* for others to know which members of the extensive clan were involved, and on which side.

It was too much to expect that the scars of bitterness that separated Neily and his brother Alfred would be erased, and they were not. Both might have attended the fashionable St. Paul's School, both might be Yale men, and blood brothers, but the matter of their father's money had intervened, and money, to the Vanderbilts, was always more important than blood.

By this time, with William Kissam Vanderbilt living semi-retired in France, only one of the Vanderbilts was actively engaged in increasing the family fortune. The sole fortune maker was Frederick William Vanderbilt, who displayed a financial genius that would have done the old Commodore proud in his finest days. To be sure, there were a number of Vanderbilts on the board of the New York Central and allied roads: William K. was a director, George was a director, William K., Jr., was a vice-president and director, and Harold Stirling Vanderbilt, Willie K.'s young brother, was a fledgling director. Frederick William was not only director of the New York Central but a director of forty-three other railroads and scores of other corporations as well. He kept more than a million dollars in a checking account, and had increased his original ten-million-dollar inheritance by three or four times.

One reason for his affluence was that Frederick William Vanderbilt spent relatively little money. His tastes were simple—compared to other Vanderbilt tastes. The house at Hyde Park had cost only $600,000, not millions, as had other Vanderbilt mansions. He had houses at Newport and Bar Harbor, and a Japanese fishing camp in the Adirondacks, on Upper St. Regis Lake, complete with Japanese buildings, art, and gardens; he kept a house in Florida for some time, and he changed yachts as some other men change automobiles, but seldom at a loss. For a Vanderbilt of the third generation of wealth, Frederick William was a frugal man.

Like his nephew Neily, Frederick William was an introvert, who often slipped out a side door of the mansion when his wife was entertaining, having first instructed the butler just how much champagne and liquor was to be made available. He would wander on the grounds for hours, alone, then come silently into the house and retire to his room; not sullen, just uninterested in the social whirl that so intrigued his wife.

These particular Vanderbilts did not move much in Grace's circle of society. Grace never forgave anyone anything, and she did not forgive Frederick William for the letters he had written his nephew in the Vanderbilt war to prevent the ill-matched union. She liked Frederick William's wife, whom she called Aunt Lulu—perhaps because Louise had suffered much the same snubbing treatment accorded to Grace Wilson by the Vanderbilt clan. But Grace's likes and dislikes, or those of anyone in Society, at least in this country, were not a matter of much concern to the Frederick William Vanderbilts, as long as they maintained their friends abroad.

They took three of those friends—the Duke and Duchess of Manchester, and Lord Arthur George Keith-Falconer, the son of the Earl of Kintore—on a Caribbean cruise in January 1914. Off the coast of Colombia, at the end of the first month, Frederick thought it would be a good idea for the captain of his *Warrior* to take the ship close in shore so the royal British guests could get a good look at the tall Sierra Nevada de Santa Marta, whose snow-capped peaks jutted above the land 16,000 feet in the air, almost rising straight out of the sea itself.

Alas, the *Warrior* ran aground on Cape Aquatia, a huge submerged ledge of rock that lies off the coast. Normally such gentle grounding would not have caused the passengers and crew more than minor inconvenience, but soon after she hit, the wind increased, and she was driven heavily onto the cape, wedged tight, and the waves began to batter her.

The *Warrior's* operator ranged the dial, seeking assistance from ships offshore. A United Fruit Company's ship, the *Frutera*, came to the rescue within a few hours. One after another, the *Frutera* launched lifeboats, but as each swung out, it was swamped, or crushed against the side of the ship, or overturned the moment it struck the water and smashed against the hull. Men were thrown into the sea, time after time, and it was only by the most dramatic acts of bravery that the rescuers themselves were saved.

In a few hours more, the wind had reached gale proportions. The captain of the *Frutera* was afraid that the *Warrior* was breaking up on the rocks, but he also feared that he was about to run aground and lose his own ship.

Finally, all eight of the *Frutera's* lifeboats had been launched in the rescue attempt, and every one of them had been smashed to pieces before the eyes of the shivering passengers and crew of the *Warrior,* who stood lashed to the rail of their struggling ship.

The *Warrior* party was losing heart when suddenly the radio operator heard that the *Frutera* had made radio contact with her sister ship, the *Almirante.*

"*Almirante,*" the *Frutera* wirelessed. "All our boats are gone. Party on Vanderbilt yacht lost unless you come quick!"

The other ship was about forty miles away. By the time she arrived, the wind had died and the seas were no longer rushing from peaks to gulfs. The *Almirante* lowered two boats as she came, and within a few moments the passengers of the *Warrior* were taken off while the crew of the *Frutera* stood at their rail and cheered.

The captain of the Vanderbilt yacht elected to stay aboard and try to salvage the ship; in the lessening wind, he thought he had a chance. The crew elected to remain with him, and stay they did, despite the pleas of the rescuers.

The Vanderbilts and their guests each managed to salvage a suitcase full of belongings. That was all, for the moment. But once the storm was over, the *Warrior* rested easy on her rocky bed, and it was no great task, a few days later, to tow her free at high water, and into port for repairs. The damage was quickly repaired.

The yachting party remained aboard the United Fruit ship. The duchess inclined to hysteria, but Mrs. Vanderbilt—Aunt Lulu—was chipper, and unconcerned, although she was more than seventy years old. The *Warrior* was insured for $250,000; that covered the cost of all the repairs, handily, and later Frederick William sold the yacht to Harry Payne Whitney at a profit despite the accident. He was a canny man, unlike others of his generation and the next.

Not two months after the yacht trip, Frederick William helped bury his brother George, who had died March 6, 1914, at the early age of fifty-two of a heart ailment, following an appendectomy in Washington, D.C.

After he tired of the responsibility and loneliness of Biltmore, George had moved to 1612 K Street in Washington, a house that had formerly belonged to Matthew Quay, the old Senator and Republican boss of Pennsylvania. George's death came as a great shock to everyone, including his three doctors, for he had been recovering remarkably well from the operation. On the afternoon of March 6 he had chatted with his wife and daughter and eaten lunch, cheerfully. Late in the afternoon he fell unconscious quite suddenly, and within an hour he was dead.

Reckless newspaper estimates put George's estate at "over $50,000,000," but when the lawyers untangled his affairs, they found a different story. George had been as unlucky in investment as Frederick William was lucky. His net disposable estate, besides the real estate, was only $900,000. He held only $11,000 in stocks and bonds. He had a $5,000,000 trust fund, left to him by his father, and he left that, in turn to his daughter Cornelia. The widow received the house on K Street, Biltmore, and the Bar Harbor summer cottage.

When they buried him in the family vault at New Dorp, George was by far the poorest of the Vanderbilts to be interred there, the poorest since old Cornelius, the Commodore's father.

Within three months, George's widow had sold off 86,700 acres of Pisgah Forest for a half-million dollars in cash. The purchaser was the U. S. Forestry Commission, and the government's purpose was to make a national game preserve. Little by little, the widow continued to dispose of the property, to turn expensive real estate into income-producing bonds.

Not all the real estate was hers, however. By a quirk of fate, Cornelius Vanderbilt III received the William Henry Vanderbilt mansion at 640 Fifth Avenue. Old William Henry had left the house to George, with the provision that if he died without male children the house would revert to the eldest of Cornelius's boys, who would be, William Henry presumed, head of the family. Now the house went to Cornelius III, to the delight of Grace, who needed a bigger mansion than her house at 677 Fifth Avenue to accomodate her growing entertainments.

But Grace took one look at the old, ornate house and sent for the decorators. George had not been interested in the mansion, so it had remained as it was built just a little over thirty years before, but so much had time and taste changed that the house seemed dark, old-fashioned, and, to Grace, thoroughly scrubby. It would take a year or two and a great deal of money to fit the house to her needs.

Cornelius III started to draw the plans for remodeling, but turned them over to an architect that summer of 1914 and set out on the *North Star* to cruise European waters. When war broke, Grace was in Paris, Cornelius was on the yacht off Le Havre, and the children and their governess were in St. Moritz, Switzerland, keeping busy and out of the way of both mother and father.

The declaration of war raised a panic among Americans in Switzerland. Some of them rode for days and nights in cattle trains to get back to Paris. Rail communications, telephone, and telegraph from Paris to Geneva were discontinued. Vanderbilt rushed to the American embassy in London and was issued a passport, then went to France to pick up a money belt full of gold, letters of credit, an auto and a government supply of gasoline, and set off for Switzerland. He called on American consuls at Zurich, Lucerne, Berne, and St. Moritz, gave them letters of credit and the gold to bolster the credit of the American community, which had no idea what would happen next. Then he picked up the children and took them back to Paris.

Ambassador Herrick paid tribute to Vanderbilt's daring and useful action. The simple announcement that a Vanderbilt was going to Switzerland, he said, had caused the rate of exchange for the dollar to jump 10 per cent.

Cornelius Vanderbilt was not the only member of the family to take an active interest in the European war.

William Kissam Vanderbilt and his wife, who had been living quietly in their Normandy chateau, came to the aid of the French Red Cross and the American hospital at Neuilly. Gladys Vanderbilt, now the Countess Széchényi, who was on the German side of the lines in Budapest, turned her mansion on Andrassy Utcza into an orphanage. She housed three hundred of the children of men who had been killed at the front, fighting against the French, the British, and the Italians. Willie K. II offered his yacht to the American government for patrol, Frederick William did the same, and Cornelius immediately gave the *North Star* to the British for use as a hospital ship—glad, in a way, for legitimate reason to end a draining expense without losing prestige, and Alfred Gwynne Vanderbilt helped the British Red Cross. He had been spending almost as much time in England as in America since 1908, when Elsie French Vanderbilt had divorced him. The charge had been adultery—specifically, misconduct aboard his private railroad car, the *Wayfarer*, with Agnes O'Brien Ruiz, the wife of the Cuban attaché in Washington. On the basis of the evidence, much of it supplied by Howard Kempster, a former valet of Vanderbilt's, the divorce was granted, and Elsie French Vanderbilt took 10 million dollars of Alfred's money, custody of their son, William Henry Vanderbilt III, and the name Mrs. French Vanderbilt. Not long afterward, Mrs. Ruiz, divorced by her husband, committed suicide in a London hotel. Alfred later married Mrs. Margaret Emerson McKim, heiress to the Bromo Seltzer fortune, whose husband, a doctor, had once threatened to sue Alfred for alienation of affections, but the matter was settled out of court.

Before the First World War broke out, Alfred had built the Vanderbilt Hotel on Park Avenue, south of Grand Central Station, where he made his home when he was in New York. Two sons had been born to Alfred and his second wife: Alfred Gwynne Vanderbilt II in 1912, and George Washington Vanderbilt III, in the year the war began.

When war came Alfred began to feel restless. He had spent so much time in England that he felt somehow unpatriotic in not being involved, although his country was not yet concerned, or even sure where American loyalties lay. Alfred wanted somehow to get into the fight. He intended to offer a fleet of wagons to the British Red Cross.

Besides, the board of directors of the International Horse Show Association was scheduled to meet in London in May, and Alfred, as one of the directors, wanted to be on hand. He had been conferring with officers of the National Horse Show Association in New York, and they had agreed that it would be safe, despite the war, to resume American participation in the international show, although the 1914 show had been canceled in the initial excitement and anxiety of the first few weeks of war.

On the afternoon of April 30, 1915, Alfred met for the last time with the National Horse Show Association directors, then he returned to his apartment in the Vanderbilt Hotel, and after dinner, went to the Empire Theatre with his wife and another couple to see A Celebrated Case, a popular Broadway show starring Florence Reed.

The next day he boarded the Cunard liner Lusitania to sail for England.

The liner's departure was set for ten o'clock on the morning of May first, but at that hour passengers were still boarding the ship. The customs and immigration processes seemed interminable, and that day they were delayed much longer than usual, for scores of extra officials of the line, government officers, and detectives were on hand to inspect the passengers and their baggage with an unusual amount of care. The extra activity puzzled some of the passengers, but not those who had read the New York morning newspapers, and especially the shipping pages, where that morning—and adjacent to the Cunard sailing schedule —had appeared the following advertisement:

NOTICE

Travellers intending to embark on the Atlantic voyage are reminded that a state of war exists between Germany and her allies; and Great Britain and her allies; that the zone of war includes the waters adjacent to the British Isles; that, in accordance with formal notice given by the Imperial German Government, vessels flying the flag of Great Britain, or any of her allies, are liable to destruction in those waters and that travellers sailing in the war zone on ships of Great Britain or her allies do so at their own risk.

Imperial German Embassy
Washington, D.C., April 22, 1915

Some passengers, frightened by this notice and by German claims that Britain was using her passenger ships to carry munitions, had canceled passage. Fear of sabotage—that was the reason government and Cunard officials were so concerned and delayed the sailing schedule to check passengers and crew with extra care. Reporters, far more of them than were sent to cover a run-of-the-mill sailing, boarded the *Lusitania* in search of a story, buttonholing passengers and recording their opinions.

Alfred Gwynne Vanderbilt, of course, was one of the most newsworthy passengers to be consulted, when they found him on the promenade deck, dressed in a charcoal gray suit, polka dot bow tie, and tweed cap, with a pink carnation in his buttonhole.

"Ridiculous!" Vanderbilt replied, after his attention was called to the German advertisement. "The Germans would not dare make an attempt to sink the *Lusitania*."

And if they did?

"Why should we be afraid of German submarines?" he asked. "We can outdistance any submarine afloat."

Most Americans agreed with Vanderbilt, for it was unthinkable that any belligerent would fire on an unarmed passenger ship; war had never been waged against civilians, and the rules of conduct of war at sea specifically forbade firing on noncombatants. Even when a ship was to be captured and sunk by a submarine or surface raider, she was always warned, and the crew was given time to escape in lifeboats before firing began, and if the worst came, the *Lusitania* was still six knots faster than any submarine afloat.

Alfred received a telegram aboard ship warning that the liner was definitely on the German target list, but he jeered at the message.

Just after noon the gangplanks were pulled ashore, the smokestacks began to spew forth thick black smoke, and the screws began to turn. The *Lusitania* was sailing.

For six days the voyage was uneventful, then on Friday, May 7, at 2:30 P.M., off the Irish coast, a German submarine sighted the *Lusitania*, rammed two torpedoes into her, and sank her. The loss was 1198 lives, although in the beginning reports coming back to New York said that everyone had been saved—then that nearly all had been saved. There was no word about the fate of Alfred Gwynne Vanderbilt.

The family cabled the New York Central representatives in London, who did everything possible, but they could not produce any news of Alfred Gwynne Vanderbilt.

Then the story of the sinking began to trickle out as survivors returned to America; one survivor remembered that Vanderbilt had been on deck when the torpedoes struck, and had put on a life jacket as directed. Then he had seen women and children without jackets, frightened in the confusion. The heavy list of the ship to port made it impossible for the crew to lower starboard lifeboats, and many passengers were near panic.

Vanderbilt had taken off his life jacket and given it to a woman passenger, then went to find another jacket for himself.

Another passenger recalled seeing Vanderbilt send his valet, Ronald Denyer, out to round up all the children he could find, with instructions to load them into the boats, and then Vanderbilt had disappeared to do the same.

Another passenger recalled seeing Vanderbilt locking hands with four other men, and singing, as the ship began to go down, and still another said he saw Vanderbilt struggling in the water, after the ship went down, with his life jacket fastened improperly. He swam to him, he said, but could not fix it. Then Vanderbilt disappeared.

No matter what the stories, and they were legion, the fact was that Alfred Vanderbilt did not return from the sailing of the *Lusitania*, nor did his valet, Ronald Denyer. Alfred's relatives, except the Cornelius Vanderbilts III, came to offer the widow sympathy. Even Cornelius Vanderbilt III and his wife attended the memorial services for Alfred, held at their mother's house on Fifty-seventh Street. After all, Alfred had waited in New York when Cornelius was apparently dying with typhoid, prepared to attend the wake. Cornelius could do no less.

25

THE GENERAL AND THE GENTLEMAN

Alfred Gwynne Vanderbilt left a fortune of $26,375,000. When added to the amounts he had given away—$6,000,000 to Cornelius III to avoid a family fight and $10,000,000 to his first wife in the divorce—the total estate nearly equaled the $42,500,000 Alfred had been willed by his father. But in 1915, when income taxes and death duties were very small, the character of the Vanderbilt wealth still changed. Alfred's death left a number of comfortable fortunes—but no large one, for the loss by attrition was great; the portion of the Commodore's wealth remaining in the hands of this branch of the family was less than a quarter of the original fortune.

The second Mrs. Alfred Vanderbilt received $8,000,000. Brother Reginald inherited $500,000. Alfred's first son, William Henry Vanderbilt III, received a $5,000,000 trust fund, a fund that had come down intact from the first William Henry Vanderbilt. William Henry III also inherited Oakland Farm, the historic bust and family portrait of the Commodore, and the gold medal that proclaimed him head of the family. The remainder of the money and property went to Alfred Gwynne Vanderbilt II and George Washington Vanderbilt III, Alfred's sons by the second marriage. They were designated as residuary legatees.

Alfred's death created an ironic situation in the Vanderbilt family, which emphasized the fragmentation of the great fortune the Commodore had left less than forty years before. A fourteen-year-old boy was declared "head of the family," although two mature uncles survived, as did two great-uncles—either of whom could have bought and sold all the rest of the family. Great-uncle William Kissam Vanderbilt still retained, intact, the entire half of the original fortune he had inherited from William Henry Vanderbilt. Great-uncle Frederick William had built his inheritance of $10,000,000 into a fortune almost as large as William Kissam's. What Alfred left his family—less than $26,500,000—showed what havoc fecundity can work when it is not accompanied by commensurate effort on the part of the children to use their money constructively. One more generation of gentlemanliness would threaten to wipe out at least one portion of the Commodore's legacy as a factor in American affairs.

It was remarkable how quickly the money disappeared, but it was equally remarkable how much the fortunes of the railroad had changed after the Vanderbilts ceased to regard it as their personal possession.

By 1914 the New York Central Railroad comprised 14,000 miles of track. The Central served eight states, which held 40 per cent of the population of the United States and produced 65 per cent of the nation's manufactured goods. It served twenty-two of the fifty biggest cities, and it employed seventy-five thousand people. The railroad paid $12,000,000 in dividends to stockholders, and since the turn of the century the Central's gross business had doubled.

The depression of 1914 hit all the nation's railroads—hard. The New York Central dropped $18,000,000 in revenue that year, but by stopping improvements and laying off men, the management cut expenses by $15,500,000. Still, a $2,500,000 operating loss could not be countenanced, and the members of the board met to consider the future.

Their solution to the cost problem was consolidation. The vast network of connecting and related lines was merged in the New York Central System. A group of minority stockholders of the valuable Lake Shore Railroad fought the change. They lost the fight, but did emerge with five shares in the new system for each share of Lake Shore stock surrendered. New York Central share-holders received one for one.

This merger had more than one consequence. It solidified the position of the parent railroad, but it lessened Vanderbilt influence on the larger board, and strengthened the influence of the Rocke-fellers and the Morgan banking interests. Vanderbilt family members were still directors of scores of railroads, but the Vanderbilts no longer controlled the roads. A few years later the Nickel Plate Railroad was sold. William Kissam Vanderbilt was blamed for this sale and for letting the bankers take control, but these were new times, and no Vanderbilt in the twentieth century had shown himself willing to dedicate his life to the railroads.

Cornelius Vanderbilt III, who had once given evidence of be-coming a real railroader, occupied himself with his New York subway system, the National Guard, and civic affairs. A jittery local government had asked him in 1915 to head a committee of a thousand to draw plans for the defense of New York. He had served, with Bernard Baruch, Cleveland H. Dodge, and William N. Dykman to assist him. It was not Vanderbilt's first civic job; on the return of Theodore Roosevelt from his long African safari Cor-nelius had led the welcoming committee. He had also headed the committee in 1914 that planned the three hundredth celebration of the founding of New York as a port of commerce.

In 1916 the New York National Guard was called up and sent to the Mexican border to help stop the border raids of Pancho Villa, the Mexican bandit and revolutionary. Lt. Col. Cornelius Vanderbilt III accepted reduction in rank to major, as required by the federal authorities of National Guard officers, and moved out with his troops; although he was an engineering officer by specialty, he had moved patiently through the ranks of the New York Guard to become inspector general. After months in the field he returned at the end of 1916 to march with the troops up Fifth Avenue in a victory celebration, although the victory they had won was slight indeed. But a few months later, when the United States declared war on Germany, the National Guard was called to active duty again, and this time the soldiering was serious. Vanderbilt was sent to Camp Wadsworth, at Spartanburg, South

Carolina, commissioned a colonel and made commander of the 102d U. S. Engineers, later to become acting chief of staff of the Twenty-seventh Division (the Empire Division) of the New York National Guard.

While her colonel was chasing bandits on the Mexican border and preparing to go to war, Grace put the finishing touches on the mansion at 640 Fifth Avenue, and continued her round of entertainments, wherever she happened to be. Even before the war, she had looked upon herself as the reigning queen of Society, the unofficial entertainer of visiting royalty. The war made little difference in her life; she employed her own army of footmen, who dressed in the maroon knee pants and tail coats of the Vanderbilt livery, maids who wore black dresses and white aprons, and a butler who could be distinguished from the guests only by his black waistcoat. Scores of other servants stoked furnaces, repaired wiring, cleaned the thirty-three bathrooms, and maintained the furnishings. Like a sergeant major, Grace Wilson Vanderbilt periodically inspected her domain, rubbing spotless white gloves over lintels and picture frames and woe to the maids when she did: a trace of dust set off a wave of terror.

Grace controlled almost what she would, except her husband and her nineteen-year-old son, Cornelius Vanderbilt IV, known as Neil within the family.

Neil, this fourth Cornelius Vanderbilt, admired the spare, distinguished figure of his father and itched desperately to get into the war himself, while his autocratic mother opposed the boy with every fiber of her being. But in 1917 Neil Vanderbilt fought his mother's objections. He was a strange, lanky youth, who had been educated by an English nanny and a succession of private tutors, and afterward pushed into and pulled out of private schools in America, England, and Switzerland. He had even attended a royal school for a time, with the children of the Russian czar in St. Petersburg. He spoke with an English accent and he knew Teddy Roosevelt well enough to eat lunch at the White House and later to seek the former President's advice and counsel on joining the Army. (T.R., of course, backed him wholeheartedly.) Grace Wilson Vanderbilt could think of a thousand good reasons for her son to stay home at her side, but he insisted on going to war and he did. He enlisted as a private.

In the Army poor Neil was not even given the protection of anonymity. He was sent to Spartanburg where his father was stationed, as a private in his father's division, and there he tried but really never had a chance to overcome the differences between himself and his fellows. The stigma of his name followed him wherever he went. They made him a driver, and then a dispatch carrier, and designated him as one—of very few enlisted men—to go overseas with a group of officers from the division.

With both her men in South Carolina, Grace Vanderbilt decided they deserved a visit from her, so she petitioned William Gibbs McAdoo, director-general of the railroads, which had been seized by the federal government for the duration, for a private car to take her South. She could not conceive of traveling by rail with the commoners. The unsympathetic McAdoo turned her down—so she did not make the trip. But McAdoo was not bad-tempered, nor was it discrimination against the mistress of Society; he also turned down the request of James B. Duke, the head of the American Tobacco Company, when that millionaire made a similar request. Private high life, McAdoo thought, did not serve the public's interests in the war.

Nearly all the Vanderbilts served in World War I. Frederick William, who was far too old to fight, bought $300,000 in bonds in one day, and gave $100,000 to the Red Cross another day. William Kissam Vanderbilt, who remained in France and financed the Lafayette Escadrille, and won the rosette of the Legion of Honor for it, bought $500,000 in American bonds. He also ordered that much of his Long Island estate be dug up to plant potatoes, since planting potatoes was the patriotic thing to do. Willie K. II turned his yacht into a coastal patrol vessel, served as a lieutenant commander in the Naval Reserve and captain of his own ship, and then went ashore to become president of the New York Central System when President Alfred H. Smith was drafted by McAdoo to supervise all the eastern American railroads. (Another Navy officer took over Willie's yacht, and lost her in an accident off the New York coast.)

Colonel Cornelius Vanderbilt not only joined the Army, he also bought $100,000 in Liberty bonds and if the first gesture let him escape his wife's parties, and the second helped preserve his slender capital from her spending—he was still a talented soldier and a patriot whose financial contribution was valued. All bond buyers were appreciated.

The pressure to finance the war was on everyone, shoeshine boy and millionaire. J. P. Morgan, Jr., one of the greatest securities salesmen of all, walked into the Liberty Loan exhibit in New York one day to examine the captured German Fokker brought back to promote the sale of Liberty bonds, and was promptly cornered by an eight-year-old boy who had been pressed into service for the day as a salesman. The boy demanded that the banker buy a bond.

"I am a bond salesman, too," Morgan said.

The boy looked at him suspiciously.

Morgan could not stand that look of distrust. Under the following eyes of the junior salesman, the banker slunk to the counter and subscribed for another bond to clear his record.

The bond salesmen were everywhere, it seemed. At the Astor Theater, one May evening in 1918, the United States Navy octette from the Brooklyn Navy Yard sang a few stirring songs during an intermission rally, then Earle Foxe, a movie star, called for subscriptions to the Liberty Loan.

At his call, almost as if responding to a cue, a private in the Army stood up and offered his wide-brimmed campaign hat to anyone who would subscribe for a $5000 bond.

Immediately a civilian in the audience accepted the soldier's offer. The soldier handed over his big hat and the civilian had the hat in hand when someone shouted that the poor doughboy would probably be arrested by the military police for appearing on the street out of uniform. The civilian returned the hat, and the audience applauded both gestures.

In such atmosphere of patriotism and good will, the bond pledges came quickly—$92,000 worth of them. The doughboy of the hat incident himself pledged to buy a thousand-dollar bond—

and the hall was ringing with cheers as a salesman edged his way through the seats to secure the particulars. A reporter, who smelled a story, looked over the soldier's shoulder as he wrote:

Cornelius Vanderbilt, Jr.
Special Dispatch Driver, 27th Division, U.S.A.
American Expeditionary Force
Home: 640 Fifth Avenue, N.Y.

A few days later, the Cornelius Vanderbilts, father and son, sailed for France. Private Vanderbilt carried dispatches to and from posts that were under heavy fire until he was gassed near the front lines. But his father, the colonel, had hardly reached the shores of France when he was commissioned a brigadier general —and then, to his disgust, sent home to train troops. The decision dismayed General Vanderbilt, but he was too good a soldier to protest, nor was he alone. That same day Brigadier General Douglas MacArthur was ordered home from France, too, MacArthur to command Camp Meade in Maryland, Brigadier General Vanderbilt to take command of troops training at Camp Lewis, near Tacoma, Washington.

After her husband returned to the United States, Grace Wilson Vanderbilt decided to go along to Lewis, bringing their debutante daughter Grace. This meant leaving New York in the middle of the social season, but she felt Grace's debutante year had already been ruined by the dreadful war and, besides, it was one thing for her husband to be a colonel of engineers in a division of a great military establishment as he had been at Spartanburg, and quite another when he was a general, and commander of a military camp. The ladies leased a big summer house close to Camp Lewis and settled in, but it was not long before Grace began to fret. Tacoma, Washington, was not Fifth Avenue, or Newport, no matter how charitable might be one's view. The provincials welcomed her with open arms, but she found it hard to return the compliment.

One night Grace and her daughter went to the theater in Tacoma, escorted by one of the General's aides because the general was occupied with military duties. When they returned, they found an anonymous threat scribbled on a sign and stuck to a post with a sickle: BEWARE. When they reached the house and tried to call the General to report the threat, they found the telephone wires had been cut. Grace had had enough! The war was over then anyhow. Grace went home to Fifth Avenue to entertain her dukes and duchesses, ambassadors and heiresses, delighted to be back to what she called a "well-rounded" life, and the General breathed a sigh of relief, for Grace's social demands on him had been heavy.

Just after the turn of the year 1919 when there was really nothing left to do, and the War Department was eager to disband its reserves and return to a peacetime routine, General Vanderbilt resigned from the Army to return to his private business affairs. Grace was no respecter of money, and if the grandiose schedule of entertainments was to be maintained, the general would find it helpful to resupply the family coffers. Grace had inherited $3,000,-000 on the death of her father, but she never slowed her spending, and now the tax system in America had undergone some drastic alterations which were enough to give a millionaire, especially a minor one, cause for worry.

The once-discarded income tax had been revived. While treasury officials were talking about an income tax of one per cent, with enough deductions and exemptions to keep all but the most wealthy free of tax, this approach to taxation threatened inherited wealth. So did the vastly increased death duties that were levied in early postwar days, although at the rate Grace was going with her parties, it is doubtful whether the General could concern himself with such hypothetical problems as inheritances.

But William Kissam Vanderbilt, the richest member of the family, was seriously concerned, and although he spent most of his time in Europe, he was the first Vanderbilt to counter the moves of the tax authorities with a rebuttal of his own. In 1919 William Kissam gave $15,000,000 to his daughter Consuelo, the Duchess of Marlborough. As a gift it was tax free, but if he had left her the same amount in his will, it would have been subject to death taxes. Later, it is reported, he gave a house and a million dollars to one grandson, the Marquis of Blandford (and a priceless pearl necklace to Blandford's bride) and another million dollars to another grandson, Lord Ivor Spencer-Churchill, all for much the same reason: taxes.

One kind of money problem or another dogged the Vanderbilts in this period—the problems varying with the size of the various Vanderbilt fortunes. George's estate was so meager that the executors had to scale down all the bequests he had made in his will—there was not enough money to fulfill them as written. Yet unfeeling New York City tax commissioners tried to assess William Kissam $5,000,000 because he was George's executor, and George had owned the house at 640 Fifth Avenue. The case was thrown out of court because William K. was not a resident of New York City, but of Oakdale, Long Island, and France, but it showed how searching had become the tax gatherer's inquiries into the affairs of the rich.

The New York State Controller's office tried to collect $80,000 in extra tax against Alfred Gwynne Vanderbilt's estate. In a prenuptial agreement, Alfred had promised to leave $2,000,000 to his second wife, Margaret McKim, in his will. The surrogate held that this was a debt, not an inheritance. The state said it was a bequest, and took the question to the higher courts.

But Reggie, the hard-driving, hard-drinking Reggie, and Frederick William Vanderbilt, the country squire, were in the worst tax trouble of all the Vanderbilts. They were accused by the federal government of falsifying their income-tax returns in 1915, with intent to do the government out of them, and they were, because the rich regarded income taxes as a dreadful imposition.

Tax troubles, however, were only part of Reggie's problems in these postwar years. In 1912 he had deserted Cathleen and their daughter for no reason that anyone could imagine except that they did not conform to his requirements for the wife and daughter of a high-stepping millionaire. He deserted them in a particularly muddy fashion, too, one typical of his unique way of doing things. They all went to Paris and he simply returned without them—neglecting to leave a note of explanation or any money.

When Cathleen protested to the Vanderbilt agent in Paris, the agent cabled home, and finally, reluctantly, Reggie arranged passage for Cathleen, daughter Cathleen, who was fifteen, and young Cathleen's governess. But when the ladies left their ship at the pier in New York City they were indignant because there was no one to meet them. Again, Reggie had forgotten to leave word. After that, he made no further pretense of keeping up appearances, but set off on a life of the high, wide, and handsome.

Either Reggie or his chauffeur incurred a series of automobile accidents, all involving pedestrians. One man was killed by Reggie's car, and on another occasion a small boy was badly injured when Reggie's limousine ran him down on a New York street. Reggie's record was akin to that of Toad, of Toad Hall, in *The Wind and the Willows*, for like Toad, Reggie was full of flaming enthusiasm and indomitable wilfulness, both behind the wheel and before the cocktail bar.

In 1919 Cathleen Vanderbilt finally sued Reginald for divorce, charging desertion. Nothing could have been further from his mind than to contest the suit and the divorce was granted without argument. But as for settlement, that was something else again. Reginald had always spent money the way he thought a Vanderbilt should, so what capital he had left was only the trust fund so sensibly established by his father. He had received $500,000 in the will of brother Alfred, but had gone through all that in four years, with nothing to show for it. He had $6,500,000 in trust in his name, which gave him an income of more than $250,000 a year, but he was continually pressed for funds, a kind of poverty-stricken playboy between quarter payments.

For several years a dumfounded federal government had been investigating those 1915 income-tax returns of Reginald and his uncle Frederick, and in 1920 the government finally filed suits against both of them.

Frederick William, the Treasury charged, had filed a return in 1915 showing a gross income of $2,196,000 and allowable deductions of $161,000 for a net income of $2,035,000. But he had taken additional deductions of more than a million dollars. The government charged that he owed a tax of $88,000 more than he had paid, plus a penalty of $4000. (Penalties, like taxes, were light in those days.)

Reginald, the government said, had shown a gross income of $217,000 in 1915, but no taxable income *at all*, after he completed the deductions to which he thought he was entitled. The government said Reginald's gross income that year was $650,000 (for they included the bequest from Alfred as income), and his net income was $440,000. So Reginald owed $30,000 in taxes for 1915, the government said, plus a penalty for cheating. Small as the sums were, those cases, which went to court, showed how the wind blew: the heyday of the millionaire was drawing to an end. The tax rates were still low, but after all, the government had just begun taxing incomes, and to the Treasury's credit it must be said that each year the government thought of some new device for obtaining money. General Cornelius Vanderbilt, for example, had been taxed just before the war on the *North Star* because she was a foreign-built yacht, and though he had fought the case through the courts before paying, in the end he lost—and paid. Taxes on houses, estates, and other real estate climbed year after year, and after the war they began to rise so high it was hard for a lesser millionaire to keep a yacht.

Yet through it all, Reggie kept on spending all his income every year and Grace Wilson Vanderbilt forged ahead, dragging New York and Newport society behind her. In 1919, while the General made a military tour of the old European battlefields on behalf of the War Department, Grace entertained the Queen of the Belgians at home. The Belgian monarchs had come to America to express their gratitude for help during the war. King Albert visited West Point, gave a hurried lunch for a number of businessmen, and rushed off from the table to accept a Doctor of Laws degree at Columbia University. Elizabeth, his queen, spent the same afternoon at Mrs. Vanderbilt's, at tea.

A hundred and twenty-five guests were invited to 640 Fifth Avenue, all of them from the absolute peak of Society. Grace ordered the footmen to roll the red carpet down the stairs on the avenue, something she always did for visiting royalty, rain or shine (if it rained too hard, she got a new red carpet for the next time). Then Grace stood at the top of the carpeted steps, paused when her guest of honor's limousine stopped outside the door, and started down the stairs at the moment the other queen started up, beaming a smile of sorority. Grace was, as usual, dressed to the nines, in a shimmering hostess gown, a dog collar of pearls high around her neck, and a large diamond suspended on a rope of pearls, dangling carelessly across her bosom; her trade-mark, a bandeau of the same material as her dress, which in later years gave her a slightly rakish air, was wrapped tightly around her head at the forehead.

Her guest of honor, the European queen, was dressed far more simply, in stylish turban, fur wrap, and black afternoon dress. A single strand of pearls encircled that queen's throat.

Grace had planned a tea with music, but before the guests could assemble to hear the strains of Mendelssohn and Bach they must first meet the other queen, and she them. Grace took Elizabeth into the reception room, and there stood by to present each and every guest to Her Majesty. Alice-of-The Breakers came to her daughter-in-law's latest triumph. Birdie Vanderbilt, wife of Willie K. II, was there. So were a dozen other Vanderbilt women, sisters in the clan, or wives, or cousins. When the introductions had been made, they all adjourned to drink tea and hear the music, until the royal guest found it necessary to leave. Privately, Grace must have found the Queen of the Belgians rather like weak tea, but Elizabeth *was* a queen, and Grace felt that as one queen to another it was up to her to do the honors for America.

At Newport that summer Grace gave a fabulous party for the Duke and Duchess of Roxburghe. It was the same as always, only the decorations and a few of the faces were different. The parties and the people bored the General to sleepiness, and he took to eating on a tray at Beaulieu or when in New York in his explosive-proof study and laboratory upstairs at 640 Fifth Avenue. But Grace really had begun to believe she was the queen of an American nobility.

Not so the rest of the Vanderbilts who had already begun to drift off along their own paths, and did not recognize the sovereign. Frederick William gave up his house on Fifth Avenue, and bought a much smaller town house uptown. He spent the bulk of his time outside New York, and very little of that in the fashionable resorts of the day. He lived simply at Hyde Park much of the time, for he loved the grounds and the view of the sleepy Hudson far below. In the clement months the big house was kept open, but even that held only a single dining room, where Frederick William and his Louise ate at a small round table in one end of the room when the state dining table was not in use to seat thirty or forty guests. In the winter months Frederick and Louise often came up to Hyde Park for the sleighing and stayed in the small Greek Pavilion he had first built when the big house was under construction. Louise entertained Consuelo and her duke, Mrs. Potter Palmer, wife of the Chicago real-estate magnate, Mrs. Ellen Yznaga, grandmother of the Duke of Manchester, and their neighbors the Franklin D. Roosevelts.

(Franklin and Eleanor Roosevelt were visiting in Newport that summer of 1919 when Grace was feasting the Duke of Roxburghe, but FDR was only Assistant Secretary of the Navy then, and scarcely worth Grace Vanderbilt's attention.)

Willie K. Vanderbilt II retired from the operating staff of the New York Central System when the war ended and President Alfred H. Smith returned, and although he remained a director of the railroads, he adapted to the life of a gentleman. Automobiles had lost their fascination for him; he returned to an earlier love: yachting.

This Vanderbilt was by far the most restless of all the fourth generation. He could never seem to find his métier. He switched from one expensive hobby to another, making each hobby a full-time occupation until he tired of it and went on to the next. First, as a boy, it was yachts, and then, as a young man, it was motorcars. For a few years, after the turn of the twentieth century, the New York Central was his hobby, and he studied the railroad's operations with the air of an enthusiast working with a scale-model railroad. Now he was back to yachting again; later he would turn to airplanes. Altogether, as his friends and family could see, Willie K. II's life was not a happy one. An acquaintance, considering Willie's plight and character, noted this Vanderbilt's restlessness, yet was puzzled, for how could a man be unhappy when he had "all the money in the world?"

But Willie was not alone in his unhappiness. The biographer of John D. Rockefeller, Jr., expressed the problem one way when he said Rockefeller had overcome the "handicap of great wealth." Willie's father put it another way, never having made that huge leap:

"If a man makes money, no matter how much, he finds a certain happiness in its possession, for in the desire to increase his business, he has a constant use for it. But the man who inherits has none of this. The first satisfaction, and the greatest, that of building the foundation of a fortune, is denied him. He must labor, if he does labor, simply to add to an over-sufficiency."

William Kissam Vanderbilt I's lament was a summation of his own life. He had labored, for a time, before he had tired of working with no goal in mind. By April 1920 this grandson of the Commodore had retired almost completely from America and American affairs, and thenceforth devoted his time and efforts to the breeding and racing of his own horses in France, until he suffered a heart attack one day at the Auteuil race track, lingered in the hospital for a time, then died July 22, 1920, aged seventy-one, an intelligent, disillusioned, gentle man, the first gentleman among the Vanderbilts.

The elder William Kissam Vanderbilt's estate had begun with $65,000,000 inherited from his father. He had made vast gifts to his children, the last of them a few months before his death—when he disposed of more than $17,000,000. Yet he left $54,500,000 when he died.

William Kissam Vanderbilt provided for his second wife, her children by a previous marriage, Vanderbilt University (which was a recipient of gifts from nearly every Vanderbilt), and a number of charities. Consuelo, the duchess, received the income on a $2,500,000 trust, and another $1,600,000 in cash. His younger son, Harold, received the estate Idle Hour. Then Harold and Willie K. II shared almost equally in the remainder. The inheritance tax of nearly $2,000,000 was paid, the highest tax collected to that date in Suffolk County, New York. Still, when all was completed, Willie K. II and Harold Stirling Vanderbilt each received more than $21,000,000 to take with them on their separate ways. Obviously William Kissam Vanderbilt had added considerably, over his years, to the "over-sufficiency" he had inherited; yet when he died the splitting of his fortune reduced each child's share to only respectable proportions. And all he, like the others, left was money. He gave his children nothing else to cling to.

26

THE LAST TRIUMVIRATE

In the Frivolous Twenties it became an annual custom for American newspapers to rank the great fortunes of the world. After the death of William Kissam Vanderbilt I and the division of his fortune, not one descendant of the old Commodore was listed among the top ten millionaires.

Henry Ford led the list in 1923 with a fortune estimated at a half-billion dollars, followed by John D. Rockefeller and the Duke of Westminster. Forty years before, William Henry Vanderbilt had sneered because Westminster's wealth was all in land, and thus not readily negotiable. In the twenties, Westminster's fortune continued to exist relatively intact, but what had been the greatest fortune in the world in 1885 had been cut into no less than nineteen different parts, not counting minor bequests and settlements on wives who divorced Vanderbilt men, and the Commodore's original fortune—really immeasurable—had been cut into thirty-two different parts.

In that same year, 1923, only three members of the Vanderbilt family belonged to the select list of seventy-four Americans whose income was more than a million dollars: Frederick William, who had pyramided his original $10,000,000 inheritance; Willie K. II, and Harold Stirling, the sons and major heirs of William Kissam. All other Vanderbilts fell well below the second rank.

The poorest living Vanderbilt of all—at least in terms of money he could reach—was Reginald. Reggie had inherited nearly

$7,000,000, but adventures at Canfield's gambling casino, ladies of the evening, show horses, and high life cost dear, so it was fortunate for him that in 1920 when Cathleen's divorce became final he did not have to support her in the grand manner, since she was an heiress in her own right. That left Reggie free, both legally and financially.

Three years later Reggie married seventeen-year-old Gloria Morgan, the daughter of a well-born diplomat, after a whirlwind courtship which so reduced Gloria's resistance to disease that on their wedding night she came down with diphtheria.

Gloria was an attractive girl. Alice-of-The Breakers was very fond of her, and one day, when Gloria and Reggie came to dine with her at the Ambassador Hotel, Alice showed how fond.

"Where are Gloria's pearls?" Alice asked her son, when the three were sitting down.

Reggie flushed, and then told his mother that he did not have the money to buy Gloria the kind of pearls she ought to have.

"That won't do," said Alice-of-The Breakers. "All Vanderbilt women have pearls." Whereupon she ordered a pair of scissors, unwound the $200,000 string she was wearing around her neck, snipped off a third of them, and handed them to Gloria.

Reggie and his wife enjoyed two short years of the wild happiness of the twenties, racing from horse show to speakeasy to European spa. Gloria took time out only to have a baby—whom they christened Gloria, too. Then they were off again on the whirlwind.

In the summer of 1925, after Reggie had suffered a series of collapses, Gloria persuaded him to take the cure at Vichy, and he temporarily traded his highball glass for the medicinal cup, complaining all the while that the mineral water was not fit to wash in, let alone drink. The doctors warned Gloria that her husband would have to go home, take life easy, and stop drinking hard liquor forever if he hoped to survive. Reggie promised dutifully, he and Gloria sailed for home at Sandy Point Farm— but he broke his promise the moment they arrived at Newport, even though it was the middle of the afternoon. Instead of accompanying Gloria to The Breakers, where they had been invited to dine with his mother, Reggie repaired to the Reading Room, Newport's most exclusive club. He went, ostensibly, to discuss the coming horse show with the secretary of the local association. But he did not arrive at The Breakers until 8:00 P.M., ruddy with an alcoholic glow.

Two weeks later Gloria accompanied her tempestuous mother to New York on the first leg of a planned trip to South America. On that night, September 4, 1925, Reggie suffered two internal hemorrhages. His mother came to the bedside from The Breakers, but Gloria could not reach Sandy Point Farm until five o'clock in the morning. Reggie died three minutes before she reached the house.

When Reggie's estate was settled, and debts (such as a $14,000 butcher's bill) had been paid, there was nothing left except the $5,000,000 trust fund established by his father. That fund was earmarked for Reggie's two daughters. Reggie's first wife, Cathleen, had money of her own, but Gloria Morgan Vanderbilt was forced to live on an allowance from the inheritance of her daughter, little Gloria. Within a few years the older Gloria's pleasant circumstances had become desperate, by Vanderbilt standards. Gloria and her daughter were caught in a crossfire of emotions and court cases which involved Mother Morgan, the lawyers, and Gertrude Vanderbilt Whitney; and little Gloria grew up in an atmosphere of bickering that delighted the Sunday supplements well into the 1940s, but completely soured the entire Vanderbilt family on newspapers and publicity. Little Gloria was married three times, once to Leopold Stokowski, who had been the conductor of the Philadelphia Symphony and other orchestras.

The social position of the Vanderbilts in the twenties was still staunchly maintained by Grace, and less willingly by the General, who had his own reasons for hating newspapers and publicity. His son, Cornelius Vanderbilt IV, decided at the end of World War I that he would become a journalist, despite deep family distaste and previous advice from old J. Pierpont Morgan that he could think of no worse fate: a journalist either ended up a drunkard or remained a journalist, and the old banker would not decide which was worse. Neil set out to establish a chain of tabloid newspapers in California. The chain foundered, leaving Neil entangled in debt, from which his father partially extricated him. Then Neil had other big plans. He would put a railroad through the Florida Everglades, he announced in 1924. He would build a commercial air base at Atlanta to connect the West, the South, and the Caribbean, he announced in 1925. But in the end, Neil achieved fame, and family displeasure, by following his first love, journalism. Banker Morgan, who would have been scandalized, had died in 1913. Grace and the General bore up under the horror of it as well as they could, but his grandmother, Alice-of-The Breakers, refused to allow Neil's filthy news sheets in the house. Neil compounded his crimes against Society. He wrote a number of books, including one called *Farewell to Fifth Avenue*, which was an intimate memoir of family life, and which enraged all the Vanderbilts. He went to work for William Randolph Hearst's New York *Mirror*, the most scandalous paper in New York, and then he roamed the world, interviewing crowned heads, dictators, and other dignitaries to whom the Vanderbilt name meant much, cozening forth a wealth of detail of the lives of the great for biographers, but annoying their sycophants and his peers by his brazenness.

Neil's father, the General, became the acknowledged head of the family with the death of Reginald Vanderbilt, despite the accolade Alfred had tried to bestow on his eldest son, William Henry III. The General had made the arrangements for Reggie's burial at New Dorp, and he had walked behind the coffin, escorting the bereaved widow, with all the others in train behind him.

But the General spent very little time at home now. He was almost completely estranged from his wife and if they did not divorce, it was only because neither believed in divorce. He spent his time attending to duties as commodore of the New York Yacht Club, and as director of a number of railroads, all outside the New York Central System—until 1921, when the federal Interstate Commerce Commission ordered a drastic change in the structure of American railroading.

Since the days of Teddy Roosevelt, the federal government had given more or less serious attention (often less) to trusts, the

great combinations of financial interests so common in the days
of the Commodore and the first William Henry Vanderbilt. At
the end of 1921 the commission outlawed interlocking directo-
rates. A man could serve on the board of one railroad, and perhaps
on the boards of all its subsidiaries, but if the railroad claimed to
be in competition with another road, the same man could not sit
on the boards of the competing roads.

The I.C.C. ruling affected all the Vanderbilts who were active
in railroads. Harold Vanderbilt was told that he could be a director
of the Central and subsidiaries, but not of the Delaware and
Lackawanna line, which was in competition with the Central.

The same rules applied to George F. Baker, William Rockefeller, and Chauncey Depew, all of the Central board, and to
W. Averell Harriman, of the Union Pacific, Illinois Central, and
Baltimore & Ohio. The General was given his choice between his
place on the board of the Illinois Central or the Missouri Pacific,
and he resigned from the latter.

His cousin Willie K. II was even more deeply involved in
railroads financially, but only financially. Willie held twenty di-
rectorships in the Central system and two in the Chicago and
Northwestern system. But Willie was no longer working in railroad management. It was yachting again that attracted him, as
noted, but a new kind of yachting, with a purpose of sorts. Willie
was captain of his own steam yacht, and used her to collect fish
of all kinds, other marine life, tropical animals, and curios from
the islands of the southern seas, all to be placed in the private
museum he was building at Centerport, Long Island.

By 1918 Willie had passed his examinations for a master's
certificate, and it was not long before his certificate was endorsed
for all oceans and unlimited tonnage, which meant he could take
the *Mauretania* to Europe if her owners wanted him to. Since
Willie's *Tarantula* had been sunk on naval duty during the war
Willie bought the *Genesee*, an auxiliary schooner 110 feet long,
and sailed off on a cruise to the West Indies in the year peace
returned to the world, but not, unfortunately, to Willie's household. Willie's private war was eight years old—he and Birdie had

not lived together since 1910, and the only reason they were not divorced was that Birdie was a Catholic.

So his yacht now served Willie in two ways: it gave him something to do with himself during the long hours of the long days, and it provided him a home where he would not be embarrassed by encountering Birdie or her friends.

Willie's headquarters now became a small house he had built at Centerport, really as a hideaway, which he called Eagle's Nest. He divested himself of his other property on Long Island and began to build up his Centerport estate. The Vanderbilt highway, which ran down the center of Long Island, was given to the people of New York, and much of it was pressed into service as a public highway. Deepdale, Willie's house on Lake Success, had never given him full satisfaction, for he could not have the privacy he wanted—he could never buy up all the rights of access to Lake Success and interlopers kept wandering into the area to disturb him. But in Centerport, well out past the limit beyond which no man in his right mind would live and commute to New York for daily work, Willie found a spot that suited him completely. His estate, which he expanded several times, occupied a narrow spit of land that jutted out into a protected bay, with deep water all around. That meant he could steam right up to his front yard, figuratively speaking, and by controlling the spit, he could have the privacy he wanted, too. It was ideal, so he began planning what would become the most charming and comfortable of all the Vanderbilt houses. Willie's house was to be built in the Moorish style, pink stucco with red tile roofs, somewhat reminiscent of the Alhambra, but with a clock tower, a bridge before the entrance, and a huge, spiked portcullis suspended above, which gave visitors a momentary chill as they passed beneath it into the safety of the courtyard within the gates. The house was to be built around that courtyard, a marvelous house, with flagstone floors and walls of paneling made of rare woods from many lands, heavy oriental rugs on the floors, and oriental artwork scattered throughout. It was luxurious, but there was every difference between this house and all the other Vanderbilt mansions. This villa was built to be lived in. It had no marble columns, no alabaster cornices, no air of overpowering wealth. Each room was comfortable and pleasant, and built for use, not to impress Society. Willie lived in a sunny room that overlooked the bay, and his yacht when she was in the harbor. The room was decorated in French furniture of the Napoleonic period, and the foot of the bed bore the royal initial N within a wreath—Napoleon Bonaparte's own crest. If some visitors were cynical about the authenticity of the bed (Which one of Napoleon's beds? one cynic scoffed), it made no difference to Willie, for to him it was Napoleon's bed, and that was all that mattered.

But in these years just at the end of the war, Willie still lived in the little house at Eagle's Nest and sailed his yachts. On a trip to England in the fall of 1921 Willie saw the former French sloop of war *Ara* in mothballs in Camper and Nicholson's shipyard in Southampton. She was a three-decked motor yacht with a 10,000 mile-cruising range, 213 feet long at the water line, and 32 feet wide at the beam. She was just what Willie wanted for his fish and wildlife collecting, so he bought her.

Then Willie began ranging farther into the oceans, on longer trips. In August 1924 he sailed from Newport on a 13,000-mile trip to North Africa, stopped off for a bit of hunting in Scotland, and came home by way of Miami. Two years later Willie added a professional touch to his collecting: he employed William E. Belanske, an artist and naturalist from the American Museum of Natural History, to help establish his private museum. He hired a professional fisherman to direct the collecting and save his guests the work if they didn't feel like fishing while yachting.

A small party, including Mr. and Mrs. Barclay H. Warburton, Jr., sailed with Vanderbilt on January 20, 1926, from Tebo's Basin in Brooklyn, bound for Jacksonville and the sunny Caribbean. That night a bugle blew to announce the first dinner of the cruise. After dinner, the group adjourned to the saloon where they listened to records played on Willie K.'s new Brunswick Panatrope. It was a marvelous beginning but, alas, the trip ended in confusion. When they were but two days out, Mrs. Warburton's grandfather died and she had to be put ashore. Willie and the others sailed on to Florida, then took the train back to New York to

wait while Mrs. Warburton performed her family duties, for she
was the belle of the cruise and they would not go on without her.
The cruise finally got under way again on February 10.

It was dull enough for the most part. Off Jamaica the starboard
engine broke down, and they went into Colón for repairs. They
traveled through the Panama Canal, and set course for their destination—the Galápagos Islands, in the South Pacific off the coast
of Ecuador.

In the beginning the passenger list was divided in two parts:
those who ate and those who did not. But as the trip wore on, the
division changed to fishermen and lounge lizards. Mr. Barclay Warburton spent a great deal of his time fishing. Mrs. Warburton spent
much of her time with Willie K.

Barclay Warburton and professional fisherman Thompson
hooked a great number of fish—bonito, tuna, mackerel, and others,
but sharks took more than half the fish before they could get them
into the boats. Mrs. Warburton was definitely not interested in
fish; she spent her time with Willie.

They passed the equator, and reached Galápagos, where they
had come for turtles. Mrs. Warburton thought the turtles were
big and ungainly, but she did love turtle soup. They collected
penguins, which they kept in a cage on deck to Rosamond
Warburton's delight, and tried to introduce flightless cormorants
into the same cage which saddened her. But the cormorants attacked the penguins, and the crew had to haul out the ship's fire
hose to save Rosamond's pets, then knock the cormorants on the
head to get them out of the cage.

They caught a mother seal and her baby. Willie and Rosamond
collected iguanas on the rocks, which Rosamond held gingerly by
their tails at arm's length while she wrinkled her nose in distaste.
Willie wore a candy-striped bathing suit top and plaid Bermuda
shorts. Rosamond wore men's shirts, canvas shorts, and kept her
shapely legs bare. She was slim, and bright-eyed, and always gay
when with her host.

Of course, life at sea, à la Vanderbilt, was not entirely roughing
it, except when the Swedish quartermaster mutinied and tried to
throw the *Ara's* officers overboard. But they took the quartermaster

off the ship, had him thrown in jail to await the next boat for Sweden, whenever that might be—a day or a year, and sailed on.

The guests ate and drank well, champagne and still wines, naturally, at every meal but breakfast. Warburton fished industriously almost every day. He caught grouper, pompano, snappers, and barracuda for the table. Willie and Rosamond swam inside the anti-shark net the crew threw over the side for them. In the evenings all gathered in the music room, a cabin 30 feet wide, 17 feet long, furnished in the early American style (with a Steinway grand piano), to play and sing. Then some adjourned to the card-room behind the dining saloon for bridge, but seldom Willie and Mrs. Warburton.

In the beginning it was Mrs. Warburton and Mr. Vanderbilt, but at the end it was "Willie" and "Rose," and none of the others mattered.

The cruise ended on April 9. Willie K. had collected hundreds of specimens for his museum, many of them unidentified fish which would be sent first to the Smithsonian Institution or the American Museum for study: a strange eel, a six-inch shark, odd remóras, transparent hatchet fish, sea devils, surgeonfish, throat-whiskers, deep-sea squids and sharp-nosed puffers. Warburton had caught hundreds of fish to eat and stuff and boast about, but Rose had caught the biggest one of all—Willie.

Some years before, Birdie Vanderbilt inquired in Rome whether or not her marriage could be annulled by the Vatican, but no one seemed to be able to tell her.

The Pope was busy with Vanderbilts that year—1926. Consuelo, the Duchess of Marlborough, had led a wretched life in England almost from the beginning. She and the Duke—"Sunny" she called him—had separated in 1907, lived together again after 1919 for a little while, then parted forever. Consuelo wanted to try to patch up their marriage, but the Duke would not come home, for he had other romantic interests.

Since Consuelo had married into the Catholic church, only the church could dissolve the marriage by annulment in a church court, a long and tedious process. Consuelo finally was freed late in 1926, on Alva's testimony that she had done everything but

horsewhip Consuelo to force her into the marriage with the Duke
—which all Society already knew. Then, both the Duke and Consuelo remarried more happily; the Duke had profited financially,
the Vanderbilts had profited socially, and only poor Consuelo had
lost—her beauty and her youth sacrificed in a marriage of convenience.

One Vanderbilt petition apparently was quite enough for a year
or two as far as the courts of the Vatican were concerned. Birdie
applied, and inquired, and waited, but nothing happened, and no
definite word was ever heard from the church at Rome in time to
be of use. For Willie and Rosamond, having found love, could not
wait long to join together. In the summer of 1927 both Birdie
and Rosamond Warburton divorced their husbands. In September, Willie K. married Rosamond in a quiet civil ceremony in Paris.

At Centerport, Willie completed his masterpiece of a house,
where they spent part of each summer, joined by Rosamond's son
and daughter, and by his two daughters and son William Kissam
Vanderbilt III from time to time. He built a round swimming
pool outdoors, maintained acres of grass and shrubbery, and a nine-
hole golf course, whose greens were named for Willie K.'s succes-
sive yachts. Rose had her own bedroom a few yards away from
Willie's Napoleonic room. And Rose's mother, who stayed with
them, had a room of her own on the ground floor. The children
were housed in a separate wing, with maid and governess to look
after their needs.

The music room of Eagle's Nest was the principal family room
—it held a $150,000 pipe organ equipped with a player-piano at-
tachment and hundreds of rolls of music since Willie was the only
one who could play. Separate from the house, Willie maintained
his museum, where he mounted all the rays, whales, sharks, saw-
fish, and other creatures that crawled or flew that Warburton had
so kindly helped him collect.

In 1928 Willie K. and Rosamond took *Ara* on a trip around the
world. To the chagrin of the Hawaiian Chamber of Commerce,
they found Honolulu disappointing and Waikiki beach "disillu-
sioning." At Truk they were permitted by the smiling Japanese to
land only at the trading wharf on the island of Dublon, since no

Americans were welcome in this important though concealed naval base.

In the China Sea they dredged for marine specimens; in India they had their pictures taken aboard elephants, and visited the Maharajah of Jaipur, one of the richest men in the world. They went to Port Said, where Willie hired a troupe of belly dancers to come aboard and entertain; they stopped in France long enough for Willie to play roulette at Monte Carlo. Then they sailed home.

In 1931 Willie built his dream yacht, the *Alva*. Because they had suffered a water shortage during the round-the-world trip on the *Ara*, Willie felt he needed a ship capable of spending more time at sea. The *Alva* was bigger and better in every way than the *Ara*. It had three cabins, four lifeboats and a launch, a gymnasium with two stationary bicycles, an electric horse, a rowing machine and a punching bag, and it carried a $57,000 seaplane. The living room on the ship had fifteen feet of clear headroom, and the eight staterooms, each with bath, had nine-foot ceilings.

Restlessly, always collecting for his museum, Willie K. sailed again around the world, but this time by a different route, to see new places and new people. He saw George Vanderbilt (the son of Alfred Gwynne, and Willie K.'s nephew) aboard his yacht *White Shadow* at Panama. He saw the authors Charles Nordhoff and Norman Hall in Tahiti, who arranged a fishing trip for him. They held costume balls aboard the ship, and Willie played the accordion—badly.

Eventually, however, Willie found each trip less exciting than the one before; finally it was almost painful for him to take the *Alva* to sea, and she spent much of her time in port. Were he twenty years younger—Willie told his cousin Neil, in tones that hinted at the empires he might create, the forces he might command, but . . . he was not twenty years younger. So he would continue to sail the seven seas, collect his fish, and gain what pleasure he could in the age of the vanishing millionaire. His world was crumbling, and he knew it.

Willie K. did not succumb completely to the temptations of pleasure in his later years. At sea he maintained a rigorous daily schedule. He plotted the courses himself and stood regular watch on the bridge. He left orders to be called at the slightest sign of deviation from normal, and he settled, personally, all the problems that arose aboard his ship. Aboard her he kept in touch with his New York office, and gave orders for trading in the market. During the depression years of the 1930s, even as income taxes began to rise toward the 90 per cent bracket, Willie K.'s personal fortune increased.

From time to time Willie's son and namesake joined the family on cruises, but the younger man spent most of his time on adventures of his own. In Paris, in 1927, William Kissam Vanderbilt III introduced the Treasure Hunt that had captivated New York society and had been popularized in England by the Prince of Wales. Willie was captured by the gendarmes one night as he climbed the Eiffel Tower in search of "treasure" clues. He interrupted a showing of *Ben Hur* at the Madeleine cinema on the same search, and finally ended up with his group at the Boeuf Sur la Toite night club behind the Hotel Crillon. The younger Willie was entering adulthood in the same light-hearted spirit as his father. This third William Kissam Vanderbilt also had the family passion for speed, and by 1933 he had owned a number of fast automobiles. In November of that year young Willie was slightly cut in the face when a bird struck the windshield of his car while he was racing down a Florida road. But the next day he started north, speeding in the sedan, with his English chauffeur in the back seat, and his cousin Erskine Gwynne in the seat beside him.

Outside Ridgeland, South Carolina, about 25 miles north of Savannah, Georgia, a fruit truck driven by a New Jersey produce dealer had stalled on the edge of the road. It was a straight, safe stretch of pavement, and the truck driver went unhurriedly about his work while his wife sat in the cab and waited.

Young Willie approached the truck at 75 miles an hour, sideswiped it, spewing oranges and grapefruit into the road; his car careened 150 yards, then landed on its back in the ditch. The chauffeur was seriously injured. Erskine Gwynne was hardly scratched. But Young Willie, who had been thrown from the car, died on the way to the hospital.

The death of his son was a blow to Willie K., for he was fifty-five years old, and his own death would mean the end of his branch of the family line. Slowly, surely, as he saw, both the family and the fortune were being reduced and would pass away.

Alice-of-The Breakers died in 1934, the year after Willie K.'s son; she was eighty-nine years old. She left her property to her three children, Gertrude Whitney, Gladys Széchényi, and the General —a sign that the family breach had been healed forever, now that all the damage was irrevocable and it was too late to save that branch's interests in the railroads. But in six years the depression had reduced Alice Vanderbilt's fortune (which had been invested in gilt-edged properties that suddenly seemed to have lost their gilt) by more than a million dollars. The three children inherited less than seven million dollars among them. Such attrition was not unusual for the times: the millionaire railroader George F. Baker had died in 1931, leaving an estate of $77,000,000. In three years of probate the estate had decreased in value by $23,000,000— and taxes took $25,000,000 of the rest.

In this period, Harold Vanderbilt was for a time the largest individual holder of New York Central Railroad stock—but what a change from the days of the Commodore! Harold's 157,000 shares of New York Central were still second to the 249,000 shares held by the Oregon Short Line Railroad, and stock ownership in the road was spread so widely that no individual could hope to gain actual majority control by his own holdings.

Harold's principal interests, besides the railroad, in which he had come up through the legal branch, were sailing and bridge. He was truly a great sailor. He had been active in the defense of The America's Cup, yachting's most famous trophy, since the early 1930s. Other Vanderbilts had been so engaged since the days of the first William K. Vanderbilt, so his connection with yachting was not unique.

In 1893 William Kissam Vanderbilt and Frederick William had joined with a syndicate to finance an entry that lost out in the trials for the right to defend the cup; but in 1896 William Kissam's *Defender* won the trials, and defeated Britain's *Valkyrie III*. In 1903 Cornelius Vanderbilt III had been a member of the syndicate which put up the *Reliance,* to beat Sir Thomas Lipton's *Shamrock III.*

But that was financing cup defenders, not sailing them. In 1934 Harold Vanderbilt had captained the winning *Rainbow,* which defeated Britain's *Endeavour.* And Harold, as an expert on bridge, helped frame the rules that govern contract bridge. He invented one bidding system which was called the Vanderbilt Club—although he always preferred to call it the Club Convention, without reference to his name.

Harold lived a quieter life than his brother Willie. He did not marry until he was forty-nine years old, although he shared his father's masculine good looks and there was no question about his rank among eligible American millionaires.

Among all the Vanderbilts, surprisingly, by far the most wealthy in the 1930s was Frederick William, the oldest member of the family, the only living grandson of the Commodore. He had increased the $10,000,000 left to him in 1885 by eight times, almost entirely by shrewd investment in the stock market; he endured the crash of 1929 with scarcely a flicker, and watched his wealth increase in the years when other Americans were selling apples on the streets, when even the fortune of Alice-of-The Breakers was sliding downhill.

By 1938 Frederick William was eighty-two, and he had been a member of the New York Central board of directors for sixty-one years!

In the 1930s the Central fell on evil days, like most of the nation's railroads, and nearly all business for that matter. In 1938, the year Frederick William Vanderbilt died, the Central lost more than $20,000,000. Jesse Jones, chairman of the federal Reconstruction Finance Corporation, attributed the disaster to "too much banker management" of the Central. Something *was* definitely wrong in management, for despite the gloomy picture shown by the Central, the trend of the American economy that year was up, not down. At this time, Frederick William Vanderbilt's personal holdings—which included millions in stocks but only a few thousand shares of New York Central stock—increased four million dollars between the day of his death and the settlement of the estate fifteen months later.

The total of Frederick William's estate came to $76,000,000, after taxes. More than seven million dollars was divided among Yale University, Vanderbilt University, the Salvation Army, and the New York Association for Improving the Condition of the Poor. The bulk of the estate was put into a trust fund divided into a hundred shares, with a quarter of this left to his wife's niece, Mrs. James Van Alen, and the remainder widely distributed among lesser relations of hers, friends, and servants.

As the real head of the family, the General buried his uncle in the family mausoleum. One of the less wealthy Vanderbilts, he had evidently hoped for an important share of this last great portion of the family fortune, but after the reading of the will, General Cornelius Vanderbilt came home tight-lipped and angry. Frederick William carried a scar from the wound caused by family opposition to his marriage, he never forgot, or forgave, his father for shunting him aside in distributing the control of the railroads, and he had small use for Grace Wilson Vanderbilt or for the General, who had ignored Frederick William's advice, too, when he married her. There was only one way Frederick William could show his true feelings toward the family—in his will, and he did. No Vanderbilt was left a single dollar.

27

TRIUMPH OF DEATH AND TAXES

After Frederick William died, only two members of the Vanderbilt family remained on the board of directors of the New York Central Railroad—both of them William Kissam Vanderbilt's sons.

As for the rest of the Vanderbilts, they had retired to smaller arenas, where their diminished fortunes served them best—all save General Cornelius Vanderbilt and Grace, who continued to entertain and be entertained as though money existed only for that purpose. The General was more cautious than his wife. Much as he loved yachting, he put up his 30-knot *Winchester* for months at a time because he could not afford the $7000 a month it cost to operate her. After World War II began in Europe, he sold the *Winchester* to the Canadian government to use as an escort vessel. The gift was in character—the general was always an Anglophile—but war also relieved him of the expense of maintaining the yacht—once again, at a time when his expenses were growing burdensome.

Taxes, by 1940, had become an important factor in the life of the Vanderbilts, not just income taxes but property taxes as well. The General paid $67,000 a year in real-estate tax for the privilege of maintaining the mansion at 640 Fifth Avenue, and another quarter of a million dollars a year to run the house, pay the servants, and maintain Grace's Newport mansion and the entertainments.

There was enough money to last his lifetime, but as for his children, the future was doubtful. Yet there was nothing to be done, either about the drain on wealth or about Grace's determination to maintain her hold on a vanishing "Society."

The General, until he cut down on his personal spending, had belonged to more clubs than any other man in New York. But he had cut down. Grace had not. They had entertained nearly every American notable and nearly every notable in the world who came to America, from General Pershing to Prince Svasti of Siam. But, still, Grace Wilson Vanderbilt never had enough of it. She continued, year after year, to do the same things she always had done, in the same lavish way—hiring butlers, footmen, armies of gardeners, cooks, maids, chauffeurs, and maintenance men, buying royal red carpets, spending a fortune on her wardrobe which was acquired in Europe for the most part, and buying enough produce, fine foods, and meats each year to support a good-sized supermarket.

Grace Wilson Vanderbilt's parties were the most lavish in New York, and wherever she went she was always the most expensively dressed woman in the crowd—perhaps not the prettiest or even the most chic, but the most heavily decked in jewels—and the most arbitrary woman in all America. Her social secretary came into her bedroom each morning to discuss the events of the day and of future days and evenings; Grace lay in bed and read the mail that was important enough for her eyes, and dictated or directed answers with a haughty gesture. She never saw anyone who did not have a pedigree as long as that of a champion poodle. And the General, retired within his bombproof study upstairs (for he sometimes had explosions with his experiments), sat, careworn, listless, gaunt, measuring the inroads of his wife's entertainments on their diminishing capital. He drank, but as he contemplated the money going down the drain, it was small wonder.

His son, Cornelius Vanderbilt IV, commuted between New York and Europe, interviewing crowned heads and dignitaries, or Hollywood actresses, annoying the remains of Society with his exposés of the life of the very rich, working in behalf of Franklin Delano Roosevelt (to the disgust of nearly all his class), and marrying, and divorcing, many wives. He established residence in Nevada, traveled abroad constantly, and never seemed able to sit still for a moment.

His cousins Alfred Gwynne Vanderbilt, Jr., and George Washington Vanderbilt III, who represented the fifth generation of Vanderbilt wealth, settled down to more nearly normal American lives. Both were wealthy young men. The sale of the Vanderbilt Hotel alone gave them $3,000,000 apiece and from their father and their mother they inherited nearly $10,000,000 each. Yet neither showed a taste for the world of big business or for their Aunt Grace's "society." Alfred devoted his efforts to the turf, following in the footsteps of his father, and in his twenties he became president of both Belmont and Pimlico race tracks and owner of a successful racing stable. (His greatest horse was Native Dancer.) Young George devoted himself more to casual sportsmanship: big game hunting and voyages to the South Pacific in his yachts.

William Henry Vanderbilt III, their half brother, entered public life at an early age, but not in the usual Vanderbilt manner. After beginning a career in banking, this William Henry went into Republican politics. He had the handsome Vanderbilt look about him, and the Vanderbilt air of well-being and success. At twenty-nine he was made president pro tem of the Rhode Island state senate. In 1938 he was elected governor of Rhode Island. This Vanderbilt was a conservative governor, and, like all Vanderbilts, unaccustomed to the compromises necessary in everyday politics.

Nor was he prepared for the political infighting he encountered as governor, nor experienced enough to defeat his enemies within the party.

When his term as governor was ended, he retired, embittered, from Republican politics—so angry that eventually he sold Oakland Farm, which he had inherited from his father Alfred, and moved to Massachusetts.

Willie K. Vanderbilt continued his rounds of fauna collecting and travel. When he was nearly sixty he bought a Sikorsky S-43 amphibian airplane, and began seeking adventure by air. He took the wheel of the plane from time to time, but always under the eye of a professional pilot, for he felt he was too old to learn this new skill of the twentieth century.

The amphibian was kept either on a six-acre island Willie had developed on the edge of Miami Beach or at the Centerport estate. In Florida, where the *Alva* was also based, he maintained a large, sumptuous house, with a full staff of servants, an African gray parrot which loved to escape from its cage and roost in the palm trees, and a dachshund, Poopie, which really belonged to his wife Rosamond's daughter.

Each day the menu was typed in French, after the chef had conferred with Rose, who selected the meals for the family. It might be chicken livers and toast, which was Rosie's favorite meal, steak, or red snapper. Whatever the food, it was served in proper style, be it breakfast, lunch, dinner, or high tea. At night Rosie always drank a split or even a pint of champagne. A footman placed two splits of wine in an ice bucket beside the bed before she retired.

The family routine was generally the same, with climatic variations, whether the Willie Vanderbilts were in Florida, aboard the yacht, in their town house on Park Avenue, where Willie had moved after his first marriage collapsed, or at Centerport. In later years, Willie opened the Centerport museum and park to the public several days a week.

In the winter of 1937 Willie and his wife, with two guests and a crew of two, began a flight around South America in the amphibian. In a Panama hat with upturned brim and a Bond Street suit, Willie set out, looking only a generation older, grayer, and more tired than the Willie Vanderbilt who had driven breakneck through southern France, and had sailed his own ship around the world.

But flying, unless one is the pilot, is a dull pastime, and this was a dull trip. They completed the journey in three weeks, through the help of Pan American World Airways, which lent its facilities at all its ports of call; but absolutely nothing exciting happened. Willie K. was getting tired, and feeling as if the world had passed him by.

In New York his father's house, where Alva had scored the triumph over Mrs. Astor, had been torn down to be replaced by a commercial building. His uncle Cornelius II's house, between Fifty-seventh and Fifty-eighth streets had been torn down, too. The gates of that house had been re-erected in Central Park, before the conservatory garden. The statue of the Commodore, which had graced the New York Central freight station at St. John's Park for so many years, had been removed when the station was abandoned, and the bronze, seventeen feet and four tons of it, had been placed on the south side of Grand Central Terminal, looking down on the automobile ramp that ran around the building.

The house of his Uncle Fred at Hyde Park, too large and too expensive for private use in this new era was given to the U. S. Park Service, which agreed to maintain the property as an example of American wealth in a departed age. The Greek revival house—the smaller one on the estate which Frederick William had preferred—became the office of the National Park Service rangers who administered the estate as a national historic site.

Thirteen years after his death, Frederick William Vanderbilt's taxes had not finally been settled, so complicated were his affairs, when war came at the end of 1941. The Vanderbilts went to war —not Willie K., who was too old, or the General, who was too feeble, but young men of the fifth generation: Alfred, Jr., George, and William Henry III to the Navy; Neil to the Army.

The General could not serve. His health had deteriorated in the last years before the war. In 1942 he appeared gray-faced, hollow-cheeked, with the mark of death upon him. In March of that year he died aboard his yacht in Florida. He had suffered a cerebral hemorrhage several days before, and Grace had been notified. But instead of taking an airplane, which she distrusted, she had gone south by train, to arrive too late.

The General's estate, less than four million dollars, was left to his children and his widow. The house at 640 Fifth Avenue had already been sold to the William Waldorf Astor estate with the provision that the family could live there until a year after the General died—a sale that had ended the drain of real-estate taxes on the General and had also brought in $1,500,000 in needed cash. At the General's death, his daughter inherited nearly a million dollars from the estate, but not his son Neil. The General noted that he had advanced Neil more than $900,000 to settle the debts of the abortive newspaper venture, that amount was to be deducted from Neil's share of the estate, and as it worked out, Neil was to receive nothing under his father's will.

Grace Vanderbilt had taken the two Mountbatten daughters, cousins of the British royal family, to live with her in New York during the war, thus showing her kind heart (toward royalty) and her loneliness. Finally, after the General's death, even with the girls to look after, the fifty-eight-room house at 640 Fifth Avenue became too large and too empty. She decided to move, even before she had to move, and bought a more manageable twenty-eight-room house far uptown at Eighty-sixth Street, out of the business district which had grown around the house at Fifty-first Street. Still, she lived on Fifth Avenue. Grace Vanderbilt, termed by her son the "Queen of the Golden Age," could not live anywhere else. For her the world began and ended on Fifth Avenue, where still she maintained her *salon*, in a world where the word was scarcely remembered.

Willie K., who was better able financially to carry on the social tradition of the Vanderbilts, had no such inclination. He kept to his Florida, Long Island, and New York residences. He had even deserted Newport years before, for the obligations of Society bored him.

In January 1944 Willie K. died at his home on Park Avenue, leaving an estate of $36,000,000, increased over his inheritance by his own good investment. After a few minor provisions, he left his estate to his wife, with the exception of Eagle's Nest and the museum, which he wanted made into a park, and he set aside a $2,000,000 trust fund for its upkeep.

In Willie K.'s generation the demands of federal and state government had increased sharply, with crushing effects on inherited wealth. When Frederick William Vanderbilt had died in 1938 the state of New York had taken $11,000,000 and the federal government $30,000,000 of his $77,000,000, but when Willie K. died only six years later, the government took $30,000,000 of his $36,000,000, effectively wiping out the fortune as a factor in either American business or in American society.

The small remainder left to his widow would again be fragmented when she died and it was divided among the children until finally it vanished altogether.

"Shirtsleeves to shirtsleeves in three generations," said one of Willie's Long Island neighbors, when apprised of the fate of Willie's wealth. He was nearly right in the case of the Vanderbilts; only the Commodore had negated this truism, by leaving his wealth in the hands of a single member of the family. But as for the rest—it was downhill, and fast going all the way.

There was only one Vanderbilt left on the board of directors of the New York Central Railroad at the end of World War II— Harold, the sole male survivor of the fourth generation of Vanderbilts. In 1947, however, the board nominated William Henry Vanderbilt III of the fifth generation, more as a courtesy than anything else. He had served ably in the war on the staff of Admiral Chester Nimitz, and had left the Navy with the rank of captain—a real distinction for a man who had not graduated from Annapolis. At the same time, President William White of the Central announced that seats on the board would be offered to Robert R. Young, chairman of the board of the Chesapeake and Ohio Railroad, and Robert J. Bowman, president of C. and O., since that line had just purchased 400,000 shares of New York Central stock and had thus become the largest single stockholder in the Central.

The Central truly had fallen on evil days. Some stockholders blamed banker management for the dirty cars, poor service, and unfavorable balance sheet, and when they spoke of bankers these days they were speaking of the Vanderbilts, too. William Henry Vanderbilt III had begun his career with a New York bank, then had taken a job with the Boston banking firm of Lee, Higginson and Co. Harold had served for many years on the board of the First National City Bank of New York. Commodore Vanderbilt had said at the beginning of his New York Central career that he knew nothing about railroads, and regarded them only from the point of view of investment. But having made the investment, the Commodore learned railroading and put his abilities behind his investment. No other Vanderbilt ever took the same interest in building the property. By the fourth and fifth generations the Vanderbilts were accustomed to wealth and unaccustomed to hard work and uncertainty. Neither Harold Vanderbilt nor any of those who came after him could remember the old Commodore (whom they had never seen) nor had they ever known a day when they were not members of the privileged class of Society.

That Society, as such, had passed out of existence with the Second World War, and its remaining members had scattered. Wealth, not family and deportment, was the criterion of the new social grouping that took its place. Newport was no longer *the* spa of the very rich. Even New York City had lost its eminence as the center of the nation's wealth. There were more millionaires in Texas, Oklahoma, California, and Florida than in New York. In past years the Ogden Armours and the Marshall Fields and the Potter Palmers had felt it necessary to journey east for at least the Newport season to mingle with their peers. The new millionaires did not think so. There was as much swank in a suit from Nieman Marcus in Dallas as in one from Bond Street, and quite probably the former cost more. The climate of southern California was to be preferred to that of New York. San Francisco had its own opera, and the California and Florida bathing beaches were far superior to the rocky shore of Bailey's. Mexico, Puerto Rico, Hawaii, Bermuda, the Bahamas were all to be preferred to New York in the winter.

Besides, the structure of Society had been changed by the federal tax laws. High income no longer was desirable; the only road to wealth was to make a capital gain, taxable at 25 per cent instead of the 90 per cent rate that would be applied to a million dollars made in one year.

Almost anything within reason could be charged against income as an expense, but even with that prop no one could afford to maintain forty or fifty servants as had the first William Henry Vanderbilt, and even Grace Vanderbilt in her prime.

The Mrs. Vanderbilt had to recognize the truths of American postwar life, and cut her expenditures. When she moved to her smaller house at 1048 Fifth Avenue, Grace Vanderbilt pared her staff. She had to eliminate some servants, for she had gone through her own fortune and most of the General's by 1945. She kept her English butler, and a smaller army of maids and footmen and still maintained her position as the leading party giver in New York. But it cost dearly. Living on this smaller scale, with prices rising in inflation, she spent $250,000 a year to run her households. In one year in her heyday she had entertained thirty-seven thousand people. Even on a smaller postwar scale, her guests numbered into the thousands.

The great brownstone house at 640 Fifth Avenue, for sixty years the symbol of American wealth, was vacated in the fall of 1945. Grace gave the great green malachite urn to the Metropolitan Museum of Art. The General had spent $250,000 on modernizing the house in 1914, but now the fixtures and rooms sold for a fraction of their cost. After she moved uptown, Grace Wilson Vanderbilt lived alone, growing into a crotchety old woman. She was a monomaniac to the last, a woman who determined in her youth that she would become the queen of American Society, and who had let nothing stand in her way. She had outlasted all her kings and queens in Europe, her husband, and all her friends in America. She was a relic of what seemed to modern Americans to be an ancient and almost unrecognizable era, a *grande dame* who had outlived her time.

In 1953, when Grace Wilson finally died at the age of eighty-three, Mrs. Franklin Delano Roosevelt came to the funeral, although Grace had told Roosevelt to his face during the depression years that she did not like him. There were a few other mourners whose names stirred memories, but they were pitifully few; Vincent Astor came, as did Mr. and Mrs. John Jacob Astor, and Robert Goelet; her son, Cornelius Vanderbilt IV, was the only male member of the Vanderbilt family in the funeral cortege—so far had the branches of the Vanderbilts drifted apart.

After Grace was buried, the family learned that this Mrs. Vanderbilt had been spending *capital* at the rate of $125,000 a year, almost each year since her husband's death. This Vanderbilt fortune was reduced to less than two million dollars, to be shared between son Neil and daughter Grace. Her death marked the end of a chapter of the Vanderbilt story.

28

THE END OF THE LINE

In 1947 President William White of the New York Central Railroad had tried to placate Texas-born Robert R. Young of the Chesapeake & Ohio with a seat on the board of the Central, but his conciliation did not work. The slight, white-haired Young was out for blood. For ten years he had been trying to gain control of the Alleghany Corporation, a railroad holding company set up by old J. Pierpont Morgan in the days of railroad trusts, only to be balked time and again, by the bankers of the Morgan company.

But as the years rolled by, Young gained important support from a new group of men in his home state of Texas. Clint Murchison of Dallas and Sid Richardson of adjoining Fort Worth had made millions of dollars in oil. They were aggressive men, both of them, who were eager to expand their holdings both north and east. Murchison, in particular, was spreading his investments; he built a skyscraper in Denver, with an eye to making the Rocky Mountain city the new petroleum center of the United States; he and his sons bought the New York publishing house of Henry Holt and Co. and the outdoor magazine *Field and Stream;* and both Murchison and Richardson joined Robert Young in his struggle with the New York bankers. Backed with these hundreds of millions of dollars, Young gained control of the Alleghany Corporation, and extended his railroad interests immeasurably. Then he set out to take over the New York Central Railroad.

In the change in structure of American railroads, it was no longer feasible to attempt to gain control of a railroad empire by buying all or almost all the stock, the way Commodore Vanderbilt had bought first the Harlem, then the Hudson, and at last the tiny New York Central line which gave him a route to the west. By 1954, when Young was ready to make his move, the Central had 6,447,400 shares outstanding, in the hands of more than forty thousand different stockholders, and the railroad property was valued at more than 2 ½ billion dollars. It was too vast and valuable a property for the Commodore's style of control to be achieved in a new century. But in 1954 the Central was in trouble again. In the first four months of 1953 the railroad's books showed profits of more than $10,000,000. In the first four months of 1954 profits were shown as over $29,000. Young charged manipulation of the figures in 1953 to show big gains, of course, but his major complaint was with the operation of the railroads, which he called fusty and old-fashioned. He had selected an aggressive and relatively young man to head his operation of the railroad, if he won. This man was Alfred E. Perlman, from the Denver and Rio Grande Western Railroad, who had helped turn a rundown little western railroad into a snappy, satisfactory, and profitable line.

The battle began in early spring when Young began to bombard the Central's board with charges of mismanagement. The board, and President White, answered back with countercharges that Young was a financial manipulator, only interested in a quick deal and a quick profit.

Further, they said, Young did not know how to run a railroad, and misled the public in his charges against the Central management.

Each side spent a million dollars in pamphleteering, fact-finding, and advertising to put its side of the story across to the stockholding public, to persuade stockholders to vote for one of the two slates of directors in the coming annual meeting of the railroad. The side that could convince the most stockholders (really the holders of the most stock since each share had a vote) would win control of the railroad. While not all the forty thousand stockholders could possibly be expected to attend the annual meeting of the railroad, they could all vote by proxy—in other words, they could designate either Young or White to cast their vote, knowing full well that they were thus siding with one or the other.

Harold Vanderbilt was in the forefront of this battle for control, on the side of William White and the status quo. He had served on the Central board and had been intimately connected with the railroad management for more than forty years. Young's indictment of the board and the railroad management was obviously an indictment of him, too, for President William White had been his personal choice as chief executive officer of the railroad. Harold fought back, and increased his personal holdings of New York Central stock.

He was joined in the fight by other board members, among them Alexander C. Nagle, president of the First National City Bank of New York, George Whitney, chairman of the board of the J. P. Morgan Co., James A. Farley, chairman of the board of the Coca-Cola Export Corporation.

The charges and countercharges continued for eighteen weeks, and they would have continued longer had the officers and board of the Central had their way, for up to the last day before the annual meeting the railroad's lawyers had tried to persuade a New York court to delay the meeting. The court refused.

On the afternoon of May 25, 1954, President White of the Central rode up to Albany, where the meeting was to be held, traveling in his private railroad car to be sure that all arrangements were made. He returned to New York that evening, after dropping by Albany's Ten Eyck Hotel where his forces had taken three floors to house men and women who would count the proxies sent to White. Close by, the Young forces had taken two floors in the DeWitt Clinton Hotel for the same purpose.

Both sides announced supreme confidence of victory for the next day. It still looked all right, President White said as he boarded the train for New York. The challengers would win by 800,000 votes, Financier Young reported, smiling.

That night the National Guard held a drill session in the old brick armory of the Tenth Regiment on Washington Avenue, Albany, but immediately after it ended, workers swarmed through

the drill shed, putting up portable theater seats, decorating the
hall with the blue and yellow colors of the Empire State, and
unrolling the 40-foot gold-and-red banner that said "New York
Central Railroad." Some twenty-five hundred of the forty thousand shareholders were expected to arrive in the morning for the
meeting.

As was customary, a special train in two sections left Grand
Central Station at eight o'clock on the morning of May 26, bound
for Albany. President White was aboard. So was Challenger
Young.

The train arrived at the Albany station, and the passengers,
most of them in a festive mood, climbed into a special fleet of
motor buses for the ride to the armory, which was some dozen
blocks from the center of the town. President White called the
meeting to order. Robert Young took a seat in the front row of
the audience, surrounded by admirers and supporters.

By twelve-thirty President White was ready to ask for nomina-
tions for slates of officers. The Central slate of fifteen board
members was nominated. Robert Young grabbed a microphone
and nominated his own slate, emphasizing the fact that one
nominee, Clint Murchison, owned 400,000 shares of Central stock,
and another, Sid Richardson, owned another 400,000 shares.
Young himself owned 100,000 shares. Another important shareholder, a Young nominee for one of the board positions, was
Lila Acheson Wallace, co-owner and co-editor of the *Reader's
Digest.*

Then the voting began; at one forty-five the railroad served a box
lunch to the hungry travelers; and late in the afternoon, the voting
completed, the stockholders began the return journey to New
York.

But while the election was held that day, the results were not
known on the twenty-sixth or even on the twenty-seventh of the
month. The results were not known for nearly two weeks, for
three college law professors had been chosen to certify the vote
and it took them that long to check each ballot, throw out the
improper ones, and adjust the count.

In the end, Robert Young and his powerful allies polled

3,407,512 votes to the White group's 2,340,239, or a plurality of just over a million votes. A new group of millionaires now controlled the New York Central Railroad, and a new board of directors moved into the office building, taking control of a railroad that the Vanderbilts had built, but so far had the Vanderbilts grown from their railroad that few Americans appreciated the underlying drama of the election and the change.

The few hundred miles of track that the Commodore had bought in the beginning—strictly as an investment and a hedge against the chance that his Atlantic steamship operations might be interrupted—this railroad had become a line 10,000 miles long, serving eleven of the most populous and wealthiest states in the Union. But the tragedy was that no Vanderbilt was now connected with the New York Central. The Vanderbilts had come to the end of the line.

29

THE SUMMING UP

Commodore Vanderbilt had earned an enormous fortune, starting with a harbor scow, creating a steamboat line, extending that into an ocean-going steamship line, and finally consolidating his holdings into the control of a tight railroad which gave him the greatest collection of wealth in all America. Yet three quarters of a century after the Commodore died, his fortune was scattered to the four winds and the Vanderbilts had lost all touch with the railroad. Was it inevitable that the fortune be dissipated, and is this then the pattern of American wealth? Is the American tradition of wealth, as Willie K. II's Long Island contemporary put it—"shirtsleeves to shirtsleeves in three generations?"

The story of the Vanderbilts indicates that this is so when a family becomes interested in wealth for its own sake, when the family has no tradition and the members ignore the source of the wealth, and fall out among themselves. There, in a nutshell, is the story of the Vanderbilts.

The Commodore was uncouth, profane, the son of a man who in Europe would have been called a peasant, but the Commodore set out, in the remarkable freedom and opportunity of a new nation that had no traditions of wealth, to make something of himself. Without education, without money, without anything save a hundred-dollar boat, boundless energy to work day and night, and absolute determination to become rich, the Commodore forged ahead. In the Staten Island periauger trade he learned the importance of hard work. In the New Brunswick steamboat war he learned the importance of playing his cards close to his chest. In the steamboating years on the Hudson River and on Long Island Sound he learned the place of money and the importance of finding capable men to manage the instruments he created. In the struggle for the California trade, he learned that money alone was not enough; one needed shrewdness, skill, and vision—all of which he exhibited in finding the Nicaraguan route, capitalizing on it, protecting it, and discarding it before the California trade faded.

Yet all these were preliminary lessons, for it was in Wall Street and in the development of the railroads that the Commodore learned the great truth by which he lived thereafter: power is the goal, and wealth is important only because it is a key to power. In the last ten years of his life that was Vanderbilt's creed, and also the source of his greatest worry—how to pass the power on?

Barring a system of communication with the "other world" of spiritualism, in which Vanderbilt believed, there is no way for a man to direct the course of his family after death. Vanderbilt tried, year after year, to establish contact with the "world beyond," but in the end he gave it up and turned wholly to the solace of organized religion—acceptance of the hereafter without haunts.

Since he could not take his wealth along, or control it by extrasensory perception, he took the next best course he knew—he left almost all his acquisitions to his son William Henry and made William Henry promise that he would carry out the terms of the will faithfully. He hoped, of course, that William Henry would follow the same course when the time came for the son to dispose of his holdings, but William Henry had his own ideas, he was the product of his environment, and the son his father had made him.

William Henry did not share his father's philosophy, no wonder, for this eldest son scarcely knew his father. He had aroused the Commodore's anger when he failed in his first job as a ship chandler's clerk, because he had no interest in the sea. William Henry had only begun to redeem himself in his father's eyes, as a rising clerk in the banking house of Daniel Drew, when the son's health broke down under the strain and long hours of work.

The Commodore had reluctantly given William Henry the money
to buy a small farm on Staten Island, but he had also rejected
William Henry as a successor and ignored the young man for
twenty years, the years in which the youth became a man, and
then a middle-aged man, settled in his own approach to life.
Those twenty years on the land gave William Henry the philosophy of a conservator, not an adventurer.

In place of the vision of the Commodore, William Henry had
a native shrewdness, as was apparent in the story about the loads
of manure he took from his father's stable, but if to be shrewd
was what passed in the business community for intelligence, still
it was not the same. William Henry suddenly realized, after his
father was dead, that he was the richest man in the world, and
the idea frightened him, because it would take so little change in
business conditions to make him only the second richest man
in the world, or the third. Then he sold off more than half his
holdings, trading railroad stocks for good, hard cash—which was
about as bad a bargain as he could have made, in the long run.

The Commodore knew what he had when he finished devel-
oping this railroad which drained the richest area of the United
States, and he knew how easy it would be for someone else to
take it away unless he guarded it, because he had taken away
other men's kingdoms himself. But William Henry seemed singularly blind to the importance of *operating control*, and it was easy
enough for a shrewd banker like J. Pierpont Morgan to point out
how the spreading of stock need not lose William Henry financial
control—if the stock was spread far and wide enough. By selling
much of his stock in England, where the interest in American
railroads was only monetary, William Henry thought he was quite
safe from his enemies—and so he was, during his generation.

But aside from differences in the times in which the Commodore and his eldest son lived, the Commodore was responsible
in quite another way for the dissipation of the fortune. He never
seemed to realize that if William Henry was to know how to
dispose of the vast estate, in his own right, the son needed a
positive philosophy and basic goals. The Commodore had his
philosophy, and if it was a dog-eat-dog philosophy, why, that was

the kind of world he lived in, and no one without that strength could have become the richest man in the country. The Commodore worked at his business, but he did not pass this philosophy of work along to William Henry, whose times it did not fit exactly, anyhow, nor did he impress upon his son the responsibilities of dynasty. Unfortunately William Henry was not by nature a builder or a visionary. He had no desire to follow his father's path—to extend the railroad system across the continent as he might have done. He had no goal, except to keep what he had and make his children happy.

Having no dynastic urge himself, William Henry could hardly pass along such a goal, and that was where the line broke, never really to be mended. William Henry was a passive father; he did not direct his boys in the course of their education, he established no traditions that remained within the family.

It is tempting to believe that William Henry Vanderbilt sold off half his stock in the New York Central because he was worried about the effects of monopoly, in the loud public outcry of the eighties against monopolies. Such a face has sometimes been given to his startling decision to dispose of a fortune in Central stock. But William Henry never gave a damn for public opinion, really, except that it annoyed him to be attacked in the newspapers—and he did not consider this public opinion at all but the opinions of the newspaper proprietors. As for legislators, William Henry was used to buying and selling them, as was the old Commodore, and he would not have changed his way of doing business in fear of them.

No, William Henry sold off his birthright because he did not comprehend a basic economic truth in the capitalistic society in which he lived: that wealth is simply the product of men's work, luck, brains, and character, that money is nothing but a medium of exchange, and that control of a producing, successful enterprise by men who will work to further it is everything.

The Commodore had brought his grandsons into the railroads at the bottom and made them work their way up, not because he was cruel, but because he wanted them to understand this truth—but the Commodore was scarcely in his grave before William

Henry released his sons from service and gave them important positions in the railroads.

So while Cornelius Vanderbilt II and William Kissam Vanderbilt began their lives in a tradition of service, they were released from the bondage before the tradition had taken hold—and since they had never grasped it, how could they pass it along to their sons? And when William Henry died, the boys relaxed even more, Willie taking to his yacht and Cornelius to his charities. The course was ever downward.

That was the Vanderbilt way for three generations, but the dissolution of the empire did not occur until the fourth generation, and even then it might have been saved. As noted, when Cornelius Vanderbilt II fell ill, and William Kissam stepped in to assume control of the New York Central, there was a chance to strengthen the family holdings and maintain control of the railroads. Had William Kissam tried to convince Cornelius II of this, and had Cornelius been convinced, then and there the brothers could have combined their stakes in the railroads in a form of trust, keeping control of the Central within the family, even without an actual majority of stock.

Is that hindsight? Other millionaires, the Du Ponts, Fords, and Rockefellers, followed the path of dynasty and their empires and fortunes survived.

The Du Pont family, in particular, has many similarities to the Vanderbilt family; both are large families, and both have been full of strong and stormy characters. Yet the Du Ponts had traditions, and so the wealth and industrial power survived—how, we shall now see.

At the turn of the nineteenth century, a little young Frenchman named Éleuthère Irénée du Pont de Nemours settled on the banks of the Brandywine in Delaware, and opened a dangerous enterprise in which he was certain either to make a lot of money or get blown to kingdom come—and probably both: he became a manufacturer of gunpowder. In those days of coarse black powder, the ingredients were liable to explosion without warning; a spark from a mule's hoof, or a nail in a man's shoe, or even "spontaneous combustion" could blow the makers and the powder sheds to blazes, and did with some regularity.

Éleuthère was killed in an explosion, as he had long expected, but before he died he had brought other members of his family to the Brandywine to go into the business, and he had children of his own, who never considered any other way of making a living. The children grew up in the powder business, starting with the making of the powder, and moving along to executive positions when their elders thought they were ready for them.

There was a tradition in the Du Pont family: they were powder makers and proud of it, and in later years, when Du Ponts went to Massachusetts Institute of Technology and other fine schools, and when they acquired the best in culture that a large fortune could buy, the Du Pont children still grew up in the tradition. They did not simply *own* the powder mills, they worked in them, and any Du Pont who did not conform found himself eventually cast out of the family business, with other Du Ponts coming in to take his place.

No one removed the boulders from the road the Du Ponts traveled, nor was the fortune immediately and always secure. At several points it seemed likely that the Du Pont family would sell out to other interests, but always a Du Pont came forward to save the company, as did Thomas Coleman Du Pont in 1902, eventually to reorganize the company, and to swallow sixty-five rival powder firms and capture a virtual monopoly of American powder making.

The Du Ponts never worried about charges of monopoly, either. Let the government prove its case was the Du Pont attitude, and when the government did prove its case, as it did in the powder trust prosecution of 1912, and more recently in the ruling that Du Pont must cease to control the giant General Motors Corporation, government action did not stop the Du Ponts. They simply conformed, changed their way of doing business, and went on. When their monopoly of the powder business got them into trouble, they expanded to paints, cellulose, dyes, and rayon. And when other troubles appeared on the horizon, they moved into synthetic textiles and plastics. Even the changes in the tax laws did not destroy the Du Pont holdings, for the Du Ponts have never tried to see how much money they could spend, or to treat the fortune as a pie, to be cut up and eaten with the will and speed of hungry children.

It was the same with the Fords. Old Henry Ford established the wealth, and at one time he was the richest man in America, just as the Commodore had been in his day. Henry brought his son Edsel into the business, and now, in Henry Ford II and his brothers, the family tradition is carried on. The Fords were not just rich men's sons; they were and are members of a family of motorcar manufacturers, they have a purpose in life, which is to make cars, not just to keep control of corporation stock or to enjoy their personal fortunes. Further, as evidenced by the billion-dollar Ford Foundation, the Fords have a sound sense of public purpose, and if it might be said that their foundation was a direct result of the peculiarities in the federal tax laws, the fact remains that the Fords both benefit humanity and work at their trade.

The Rockefeller family, which one might say "invented" the idea of the family foundation for public service, is the finest example of dynasty among all the American families which achieved great wealth. Old John D. Rockefeller, starting out in Ohio, scraped and scratched his fortune from the ground, after oil was discovered at Titusville, Pennsylvania, in 1859. John D. and his brother William established the Standard Oil Company, and John D., too, became for a time the richest man in the United States.

The Rockefellers established trusts, which were broken up by the courts, but whenever the government took one action to curb their expansion, the Rockefellers took another, to enable their empire to survive. In the Rockefellers, more notable perhaps than in any of the other millionaire families, there has always been a strong sense of purpose. The first John D. Rockefeller was an ardent member of the Baptist church, and if his religion was strict, at least it gave him a sense of responsibility that was passed down to his son and his grandchildren. Old John D. Rockefeller gave away millions of his $900,000,000. He was often called "eccentric," for he rode the streetcars, took long walks through the streets, played golf in public, and attended public meetings and public barbecues—where he enjoyed himself.

He retired from business in 1897, but John D. Jr., carried on, holding the family properties tightly together. Then shortly after the turn of the twentieth century, the Rockefellers found a new tradition, a visionary plan for public service, and in 1913 the Rockefeller Foundation was born, "to promote the well-being of mankind throughout the world," not just to give money to worthy causes, but to lead the way in eradicating "individual or social ill-being and misery." John D. Rockefeller had what his biographer Allan Nevins calls an "instinct for the future," and not only did he carry this instinct all his life, he transmitted it to his children, and they to theirs, and the dynasty and the fortune survived and prospered.

Now in the fourth generation, the Rockefellers are a tightly knit family. Instead of building half-a-dozen multimillion-dollar estates scattered around the country, and competing one against the other in showiness, the Rockefellers live quietly if richly. Their fortune is a family fortune—no one talks about the individual holdings of David, or Nelson, or Laurence, or Winthrop, or John D. Rockefeller III, or their children: each is a member of the Rockefeller *family*.

In no way has this strong family binding kept the younger Rockefellers from exhibiting their individualities, however. Nelson Rockefeller made himself known in public service, holding positions in the Democratic administration of President Franklin Roosevelt and the Republican administration of Dwight D. Eisenhower before he was elected governor of New York. John III became chairman of the board of the Rockefeller Foundation; Laurance turned to medical charity and conservation; Winthrop became chairman of the board of Colonial Williamsburg, Inc., and a trustee of the National Urban League, an organization dedicated to racial equality; David took over the Rockefeller Institute for Medical Research and chairmanship of the executive committee of International House of New York, an organization that maintains a living place for foreign students.

These are not just lists of charities—each Rockefeller became active in these jobs, and began to work at them, as hard as other men work at their jobs for pay.

And their incentive? John D. Rockefeller, Jr., summed it up, when he said, "I was brought up to believe that worthy accomplishment is its own reward." The Rockefellers, once the fortune was established, found new goals. The Rockefellers have established a dynasty.

There have been other American business dynasties, of course. John Jacob Astor who was the first man to be famous as the "richest man," died and left $20,000,000 in 1848. His son, William Backhouse Astor managed the fortune, which had been placed in New York real estate. And, naturally, when New York grew, the Astor fortune grew as well. But in the nineteenth century the Astors became so completely involved in the pretense of Society that William Waldorf Astor traded American citizenship for a British title. In 1890 he moved to England, to become first Baron Astor and then Viscount Astor; he took with him both the illustrious name and the major share of the fortune, and on these American shores the name of Astor has languished since (although an Astor company bought the mansion of William Henry Vanderbilt when it was finally sold). One reason, of course, is that the Astors, like the Vanderbilts, ceased their constructive activity in the business world. The Astors became real-estate operators, after old John Jacob, the trader. The Vanderbilts became bankers and gentlemen spenders. Both families, unlike the other wealthy families mentioned, became famous in America for their displays of conspicuous wealth. Late in the eighties, if a citizen wanted to object about a high price, he often said, "Who do you think I am, John Jacob Astor?" A decade later the tune was the same, but the refrain slightly different—"Who do you think I am, a Vanderbilt?"

Like old John D. Rockefeller, the Commodore had an instinct for the future; the trouble for the Vanderbilts began in the days of William Henry, for neither he nor any of his descendants accepted the philosophy that the fortune existed for constructive use, not for personal spending, and that money meant power, not simply privilege.

There was, too, another reason for the decline of the Vanderbilt fortune: a new philosophy of government dedicated to the elimination of vast fortunes through heavy taxation. But the government's decision to tax great wealth greatly could be circumvented—as the stories of the Du Ponts, Fords, and Rockefellers show. The manner of the holding of the wealth had to change, to be sure. The corporation and the foundation replaced the partnership and the individual enterprise, but dynasty could be maintained, where a family had a mind to maintain it—if the family made its decision in time.

In the case of the Vanderbilts, the last chance came with William Kissam Vanderbilt, and when he abdicated his responsibility after the death of Cornelius Vanderbilt II, and removed himself to France, leaving the railroad in the hands of banker J. Pierpont Morgan and professional managers, the die was cast. There was no more chance to save the vehicle that had brought the family to power.

William Kissam's brother, Frederick William Vanderbilt, was an anomaly within the family—a pure capitalist, what the Europeans call a banker. While he ran a fortune of $10,000,000 up to one of $80,000,000, he did this completely by investment. If he had left children, he would have left them nothing but stocks and money, and these are not enough.

Willie K. Vanderbilt II, Alfred Gwynne, and Harold Vanderbilt had neither the personal fortunes, nor the tradition to guide them back to the Commodore's path. It was too late by the time they appeared.

It was too late also for Cornelius Vanderbilt III, but for a different reason. His fate might have been linked with that of William Kissam. Had this Cornelius, the General, not defied his father to marry the wrong woman, and had he gone into the railroads, as he did go, but without the animus of the family against him, it might have been that he could have persuaded father and uncle to combine forces and save the railroads. But he did none of these things, and his life was ruined the moment he married Grace Wilson against his parents' wishes—not just because he defied them but because he chose the most restless moth ever to circle the flame of Society.

Harold Vanderbilt made a desperate attempt to stem the flood tide that was sweeping the Central out of Vanderbilt hands in the 1940s and the 1950s, but he did not have a real chance to win. His hope of success lay in his ability to persuade the bankers of the New York Central Board by argument and reason—the weapons of a lawyer and a banker.

In the end, Harold was overwhelmed by the juggernaut of economic power—committed wealth, with men of purpose behind it. Clint Murchison and Sid Richardson, two of the new class of American millionaires, committed themselves to the New York Central and to Robert Young. They invested millions of dollars, and they would have invested more if they had found it necessary to achieve control—just as the old Commodore had kept buying and buying Harlem, putting up his steamship fortune to back something he believed in.

That was the difference between the Commodore, the energetic visionary creator, and all the rest of the Vanderbilts. The others allowed themselves to be persuaded that control could be achieved and retained by manipulation, without backing it by money and hard work. The theory held true only as long as no one else wanted to exert himself enough to take control away.

On May 26, 1954, the day the Vanderbilts lost the New York Central Railroad, if the family had been watching, they could have seen in Robert Young's victory over Harold Vanderbilt an illustration of the great truth the Commodore knew and practiced, but never put into words so his descendants could understand:

Lawyers and bankers might rule for a time, but finally, power goes to the man who can combine wealth, high purpose, and his own abilities.

BIBLIOGRAPHY

Albion, R. G. and Pope, J. B. *The Rise of New York Port (1815–60)*. 1939.

Andrews, Wayne. *The Vanderbilt Legend*. 1941.

Bailey, J. I. *The City of Brooklyn*. 1840.

Barron, C. W. *They Told Barron*. 1930.

—. *More They Told Barron*. 1931.

Bayles, Richard M. *History of Richmond County*. 1887.

Beach, M. Y. *Wealth and Biography of the Wealthy Citizens of the City of New York*. 1846.

Beebe, Lucius. *Mansions on Rails*. 1959.

Benedict, W. H. *New Brunswick in History*. 1925.

Booth, Mary L. *History of the City of New York*. 1859.

Breakers, The (pamphlet), prepared by Holbert T. Smales, printed at Newport, R.I., by Remington Ward. 1952.

Butler, Frederick. *Memoirs of the Marquis de Lafayette*. 1825.

Catalogue of the Sale of "Idle Hour," American Art Association.

Child, L. Maria. *Letters from New York*. 1843.

Choules, John Overton. *The Cruise of the Steam Yacht North Star*. 1854.

City of New Brunswick, The. Published by the New Brunswick Times. 1909.

Clews, Henry. *Fifty Years in Wall Street*. 1908.

Clute, J. J. *Annals of Staten Island*. 1877.

Corey, Lewis. *The House of Morgan*. 1930.

Croffut, W. A. *The Vanderbilts*. 1886.

Crowninshield, Frank. "House of Vanderbilt," *Vogue*, November 15, 1941.

Curry, Daniel. *New York: a Historical Sketch of the Rise and Progress of the Metropolitan City of America*. 1853.

Curtiss, John S. "Sloops of the Hudson, 1800–1850," *Proceedings of the New York State Historical Association*. 1933.

Davis, Stephen. *Notes of a Tour in America*. 1832.

Depew, Chauncey M. *My Memories of Eighty Years*. 1922.

—. *A Retrospect of Twenty-five Years with the New York Central Railroad and Its Allied Lines*. 1892.

Devoe, T. F. *The Market Book*. 1862.

Duer, William Alexander. *New York As It Was*. 1848.

Fiske, Stephen. *Off-hand Portraits of Prominent New Yorkers*. 1884.

Floyd-Jones, Thomas. *Backward Glances; Reminiscences of an Old New Yorker*. 1914.

Flynn, John T. *Men of Wealth*. 1941.

Fuller, R. H. *Jubilee Jim; The Life of Colonel James Fisk, Jr.* 1928.

Gilder, Rodman. *The Battery*. 1936.

Glardon, August. *Les Vanderbilts et Leur Fortune*. 1889.

Guernsey, R. S. *New York City and Vicinity during the War of 1812–1815*. 1889.

Hagedorn's Semi Weekly Staten Islander.

Hampton, Vernon B. *Staten Island's Claim to Fame*. 1925.

Harlow, Alvin F. *The Road of the Century; The Story of the New York Central*. 1947.

Hart, Smith. *The New Yorkers*. 1938.

Haswell, Charles H. *Reminiscences of an Octogenarian of the City of New York (1816–60)*. 1896.

Heyl, Erik. *Early American Steamers*. 1953.

Historic Morristown, New Jersey. Published by the Town of Morristown. Undated.

History of Commerce of New York. American Publishing and Engineering Co. 1891.

Hone, Philip. *The Diary of Philip Hone, 1828–1851*. 1889.

Hubbard, N. T. *The Autobiography of N. T. Hubbard.* 1875.

Hungerford, Edward. *Men and Iron, the History of the New York Central.* 1938.

Hunt's Merchant's Magazine and Commercial Review.

Iconography of Manhattan Island, The.

In Memoriam Cornelius Vanderbilt. Vanderbilt University. 1877.

Inventory of the County Archives of New York City. Historical Records Section, WPA, New York. 1942.

James, Henry. *The American Scene.* 1907.

Jamison, James Carson. *With Walker in Nicaragua.* 1909.

Jones, Willoughby. *The Life of James Fisk, Jr.* 1934.

Josephson, Matthew. *The Robber Barons.* 1934.

—. *The Politicos.* 1938.

Kolff, Cornelius G. *A Short History of Staten Island.* 1926.

—. *Stories by a Staten Island Real Estate Broker.* 1927.

Lane, Wheaton J. *Commodore Vanderbilt.* 1942.

Lang, C. W. and Davis, W. T. *Staten Island and Its People: A History, 1609–1929.* 1930.

Life of Colonel James Fisk, Jr. 1872.

Lloyd, J. T. *Reminiscences of the Two Vanderbilts.* 1887.

Log of the Alva. Privately printed. 1891.

Lundberg, Ferdinand. *Imperial Hearst, a Social Biography.* 1936.

Lynch, Denis T. *"Boss" Tweed.* 1927.

McAdam, Roger Williams. *Salts of the Sound.* 1939.

McAlpine, R. W. *The Life and Times of Colonel James Fisk, Jr.* 1872.

McElroy, Robert. *Grover Cleveland, the Man and the Statesman.* 1923.

Marshall, David. *Grand Central.* 1946.

Marvin, Winthrop L. *The American Merchant Marine (1620–1902).* 1902.

Memorial History of the City of New York. 1892–93.

Memorial of the Golden Wedding of Cornelius and Sophia Vanderbilt. Privately printed, New York. 1864.

Metzman, Gustav. *Commodore Vanderbilt (1794–1877), Forefather of the New York Central.* Published by The

Newcomen Society of England, American Branch, New York. 1946.

Minnigerode, Meade. *Certain Rich Men*. 1927.

Morris, Charles. *The Life of Queen Victoria*. 1901.

Morris, Ira K. *Morris's Memorial History of Staten Island*. 1898.

Morrison, John H. *The History of American Steam Navigation*. 1903.

Myers, Gustavus. *History of the Great American Fortunes*. 1936.

Nevins, Allan. *John D. Rockefeller*. 1940.

—and Thomas, Milton Halsey (eds.). *The Diary of George Templeton Strong, 1835–1875*. 1952.

New York Historical Society Quarterly Bulletin. October, 1945.

Northrop, H. D. *The Life and Achievements of Jay Gould*. 1892.

Parton, James. *Famous Americans of Recent Times*. 1884.

Pinchot, Gifford. *Breaking New Ground*. 1947.

Preble, George Henry. *A Chronological History of the Origin and Development of Steam Navigation*. 1883.

Private Collection of William Henry Vanderbilt, The. 1884.

Public Papers of Daniel D. Tompkins, Governor of New York 1807–1817. Vol III. Published by the State of New York. 1898–1902.

Riesenberg, Felix. *Clipper Ships*. 1932.

Ritz, Marie Louise. *César Ritz, Host to the World*. 1938.

Root, Anna H. V. *Hand and Vanderbilt, a Sketch of Grandmother Vanderbilt's Early Days, Written by her Granddaughter, Anna H. V. Root*. Unpublished, in possession of New York Historical Society.

Rowland, Eron. *Varina Howell, Wife of Jefferson Davis*. 1931.

Sachs, Emanie. *The Terrible Siren, Victoria Woodhull*. 1928.

Schurz, Carl. *Reminiscences*. 1907–8.

Scroggs, W. Oscar. *Filibusters and Financiers*. 1916.

Seward, William. *Autobiography of William Seward from 1801–34*. 1891.

Ships and Shipping of Old New York. By the Bank of Manhattan. 1915.

Smith, Arthur D. H. *Commodore Vanderbilt, An Epic of American Achievement*. 1927.

Smith, Matthew H. *Twenty Years Among the Bulls and Bears of Wall Street*. 1870.

—. *Sunshine and Shadow in New York*. 1868.

Steinmeyer, Henry G. *Staten Island, 1524–1898*. 1950.

Stevens, W. O. *Discovering Long Island*. 1939.

Stiles, Henry R. *History of the City of Brooklyn*. 1867.

Strahan, Edward (pseudonym). *Mr. Vanderbilt's House and Collection*. 1884.

Trollope, Mrs. Frances. *The Domestic Manners of the Americans*. 1832.

Vanderbilt, Cornelius IV. *Personal Experiences of a Cub Reporter*. 1922. *Farewell to Fifth Avenue*. 1935.

Vanderbilt, Gertrude Lefferts. *The Social History of Flatbush*. 1881.

Vanderbilt, Harold. *Enterprise, The Story of the Defense of the America's Cup in 1930*. 1931.

—. *On the Wind's Highway; Ranger, Rainbow, and Racing*. 1939.

Vanderbilt Papers. The New York Public Library.

Vanderbilt-Vanderbilt University Correspondence. New York Public Library.

Vanderbilt vs. The Management. Chicago, Rock Island and Pacific Railway, Chicago. 1884.

Vanderbilt, W. K. II. *Log of My Motor (1899–1908)*. Privately printed. 1908.

—. *A Trip through Italy, Sicily, Tunisia, Algeria and Southern France*. Privately printed. 1918.

—. *Across the Atlantic with Ara*. Privately printed. 1924.

—. *To Galápagos on the Ara*. Privately printed. 1927.

—. *15,000 Mile Cruise with Ara*. Privately printed. 1928.

—. *Taking One's Own Ship around the World*. Privately printed. 1929.

—. *West Made East with the Loss of a Day*. Privately printed. 1933.

—. *Flying Lanes*. Privately printed. 1937.

—. *Across the Atlantic with Ara, Summer of 1924*. 1925.

Van Pelt, John V. *A Monograph of the W. K. Vanderbilt House*. 1925.

Veblen, Thorstein. *The Theory of the Leisure Class.* 1918.

Walker, William. *The War in Nicaragua.* 1860.

Warshow, Robert I. *Jay Gould, the Story of a Fortune.* 1928.

Watson, John F. *Historic Tales of Olden Time.* 1832.

Weed, Harriet A. (ed.). *Life of Thurlow Weed, including His Autobiography and a Memoir.* 1883–84.

Wharton, Edith. *The Age of Innocence.* 1920.

White, Bouck. *The Book of Daniel Drew.* 1910.

White, Trumbull. *The Wizard of Wall Street and His Wealth, or the Life and Deeds of Jay Gould.* 1893.

Willis, N. P. *Hurry-graphs, or Sketches of Scenery, Celebrities and Society.* 1851.

Wilson, James Grant (ed.). *Memorial History of the City of New York.* 1893.

Winkler, John. *Morgan the Magnificent.* 1930.

Women's Auxiliary to the American Scenic and Historic Preservation Society. *A Historic Sketch of Certain Defenses of New York City during the War of 1812–1815.*

Yellen, Samuel. *American Labor Struggles.* 1936.

The following magazines, newspapers, and encyclopedias were also consulted: *American Magazine, The Arts, Collier's, Dictionary of American Biography, Harper's Weekly, McClure's, Magazine of Western History, Munsey's,* New York *Daily Graphic, The New Yorker,* New York *Gazette-Post Boy,* New York *Herald,* New York *Mercury, New York Packet,* The New York *Times,* New York *Tribune,* New York *World, Peerson's Magazine, The Saturday Evening Post, Theater Magazine, Weyman's Gazette.*

INDEX

Jan Aertsen van der Bilt
(?-1705)

Aris van der Bilt
(1653-1715)

Jacob Van Der Bilt I
(1692-1760)

Jacob Van Der Bilt II
(1723-66)

Cornelius Van Derbilt
(1764-1832)
  m. Phebe Hand
    (1767-1854)

Mary

Jacob (1789-1805)

Charlotte
  m. Capt. John De Forest

Cornelius Vanderbilt
(1794-1877)
  m. Sophia Johnson
    (1797-1868)
  m. Frank Crawford

Phebe (1798-?)

Jane

Elinor

Jacob Hand (1807-188-)

Phebe (1810-?)

Phebe Jane
  m. J. M. Cross

Ethelinda
  m. Daniel B. Allen

William Henry Vanderbilt I
(1821-85)
  m. Maria Louise Kissam

Emily
  m. William K. Thorn

Cornelius Jeremiah Vanderbilt
(1815-82)
  m. Ellen Williams

Eliza
  m. George A. Osgood

Sophia Johnson
  m. Daniel Torrance

Mary Alicia
  m. Nicholas LaBau

Catherine Juliet
  m. Smith Barker
  m. Gustave Lafitte

Mary Louise
  m. Horace F. Clark
  m. Robert Niven

Frances

George Washington Vanderbilt
(died in infancy)

George Washington Vanderbilt
(1841-66)